MW00876842

Silver Snippets

CARLENE POFF BAKER

WESTBOW
PRESS®
A DIVISION OF THOMAS NELSON
& ZONDERVAN

WestBow Press books may be ordered through booksellers or by contacting:

WestBow Press
A Division of Thomas Nelson & Zondervan
1663 Liberty Drive
Bloomington, IN 47403
www.westbowpress.com
1 (866) 928-1240

Scripture taken from the King James Version of the Bible.

ISBN: 978-1-9736-7164-0 (sc)
ISBN: 978-1-9736-7163-3 (hc)
ISBN: 978-1-9736-7165-7 (e)

Library of Congress Control Number: 2019911354

Print information available on the last page.

WestBow Press rev. date: 08/19/2019

Foreword

Having lived more than seven decades, and filled the many roles I have taken on, I have seen God's handiwork manifested in my experiences as well as in the lives of others. I became a child of God in my youth, and during that time in my childhood home, and years following, as a student, career person, wife and homemaker, mother, grandmother and, currently, great-grandmother, as well as in church service capacities, I have been aware of the Lord's presence all around me, which I welcomed. This book is composed of scenarios of my experience and happenings in the lives of others, where I recognized God at work. Because of my "silver" finds that are of such value in my Christian walk, I reasoned that perhaps others, who need inspiration, encouragement, aspiration, or challenge, might find a scenario in this book with which they could identify, and, the result being that they would draw closer to God, trust Him more, and gain strength for whatever they might meet.

God bless all who read my book!

Carlene Poff Baker

We have begun a new year. Let's ponder these two words: *new year*. The word *new* means untried, unspotted, unused, unfamiliar, untouched. And the word *year* is a span of 365 days or twelve months in a specific period, as in a decade, century, era, or millennium. The seconds and minutes *tick, tick, tick* without pause, with exactly the same number of ticks per day.

Therefore, having been blessedly allowed to continue living, we realize we cannot go back and redo anything in our past year. Nor do we have the ability to forecast how much of this new year we can claim as ours.

Thus, we make our entrance with three basic tools. They are all two-letter words, but they are enormously powerful. The words are *be, do,* and *go*. The energy for accomplishing with these tools comes with two powerful words of action: *trust God*. He alone knows what this new year's calendar entails.

Time is precious, not because of itself but for the opportunities for service to God and to our fellow humans as well as for future improvement in ourselves. We may well consider that what we call time is in fact motion, advancement, and progress toward something. We are in reality approaching a commencement rather than an ending, the greater usefulness for which we are preparing during this period we measure by the calendar.

You and I have the year ahead curtained off from our view. We can be sure that there will be blessings, delights, wonderful events, and to the contrary, disappointments, losses, reversals, and perhaps illnesses and even the death of someone we love. But we know the Sovereign God, in whom we trust, knows every detail of each day of our lives, and He has promised that He will never leave us or forsake us. What peace we can avail ourselves of when we stay close to Him!

I love Psalm 34:8, which says, "O taste and see that the Lord is good; blessed is the man that trusts in Him."

So, as we *be, do,* and *go*, each tick of the clock, day by day of this new year laid out before us, we will be richly blessed!

Trust in the Lord with all thine heart; and lean not unto thine own understanding. In all thy ways acknowledge Him, and He shall direct thy paths. (Proverbs 3:5-6 KJV)

January 2   Out of the Mouth of Babes

Children sometimes teach adults. Bible stories read to them affect their lives and they tell others about them.

There is a story of a little girl riding on a bus near the window. A man sat beside her. She looked at him and said, "My Father owns all that land out there. And those hills. Those are his cows out there in the field, too." As she told of these things, she pointed to them.

Apparently, the man decided she had a vivid imagination, but he said, "Your Dad must be a very rich man to own all that. What's his name?"

"Oh! His name is God."

Out of the mouth of babes and sucklings hast thou ordained strength because of thine enemies, that thou mightiest still the enemy and the avenger. (Psalm 8:2 KJV)

January 3   Conquering Obstacles

There is abundant evidence that God never intended man to have an easy time. The world is so structured that most of his time is spent in conquering obstacles. All progress is made by overcoming difficulties. Man's way is like that of the rower on the river: The current sweeps him down. Yet, that opposing current makes it possible for him to move up the stream. Man seems to be forever in conflict with nature, but by conquering it, it becomes a ladder on which he climbs.

History reveals the fact that there is a vital relationship between hardship and strength. The most massive corals are found not in still water, but on the ocean side, where the rocks are pounded into sand by combating waves.

In human life the same rule holds. For the building of character, conflict is better than peace, and work is better than ease. Many a person leaves half his soul in his easy chair.

Poverty is regarded by many as an obstacle to success, but the majority of successful men owe their prosperity to early poverty, which compelled them to work when other companions played and kept them working in spite of injustice because they needed the wages to provide the necessities of life. Thus, they learned the principles and attained the habits that brought success.

Sorrow is a great educator. In its depths we are prepared for the heights of life. Paul prayed that his "thorn in flesh" might be removed, but later he gloried in it because of the moral effect it wrought on him.

And lest I should be exalted above measure through the abundance of the revelations, there was given to me a thorn in the flesh, the messenger of Satan to buffet me, lest I should be exalted above measure. For this thing I besought the Lord thrice, that it might depart from me. And He said unto me, My grace is sufficient for thee; for my strength is made perfect in weakness. Most gladly therefore will I rather glory in my infirmities, that the power of Christ may rest upon me. Therefore, I take pleasure in infirmities, in reproaches, in necessities, in persecutions, in distresses for Christ's sake: for when I am weak, then am I strong. (2 Corinthians 12:7-10 KJV)

January 4   Get Up and Go

During the rendition of an opera several years ago, in one of the acts, a singer slipped on the way down a slope and broke his ankle. He got up and continued with his song so acceptably that no one in the audience knew of his plight. After his song finished, he hobbled off the stage, saying with a smile to a fellow tenor, "The show must go on!"

Joshua had a similar experience. Moses had died. Joshua had been named by God as his successor. Moses had gotten the children of Israel to the brink of crossing over the Jordan River into the land of promise God had given them. Now, God wanted Joshua to take charge as leader. It was a huge job, and apparently Joshua was fearful and lacked courage. God knew how he felt so He told Joshua He would be with him as He had been with Moses.

In the book of Joshua we read what God told Joshua.

> Moses, my servant, is dead; now therefore arise, go over this Jordan, thou, and all this people, unto the land which I do give to them, even to the children of Israel. There shall not any man be able to stand before thee all the days of thy life: as I was with Moses, so I will be with thee: I will not fail thee, nor forsake thee. Be strong and of a good courage: for unto this people shalt thou divide for an inheritance the land, which I sware unto their fathers to give them. (Joshua 1:2, 5-6 KJV)

Like Joshua and these other people, each of us is in the same predicament. The work of the Lord is ours to do. Each has a task. Each has a gift to be used. Nobody can do the other's job. So, let us too be up and doing!

January 5   From an Old Book

The late Dr. George Washington Carver, noted educator and philosopher, was called on one occasion to testify before a Senate Committee concerning his laboratory work with the peanut.

When he was asked how he had learned about the intricacies of the peanut, Dr. Carver replied that he had studied an old Book. When asked the name of the book, he said it was the Bible.

Somewhat puzzled about the answer, he was asked further. "What does the Bible say about peanuts?"

"Nothing, Sir," replied the educator, "but it tells about God who made the peanut. I asked Him to show me what to do with the peanut, and He did."

And God said, Let the earth bring forth grass, the herb yielding seed, and the fruit tree yielding fruit after his kind, whose seed is in itself, upon the earth: and it was so. And the earth brought forth grass, and herb yielding seed after his kind, and the tree yielding fruit, whose seed was in itself, after his kind: and God saw that it was good. (Genesis 1:11-12 KJV)

January 6   A Whale of a Blessing

In trying to escape spiritual responsibility, Jonah was swallowed by a whale. To be swallowed by a whale is bad indeed, but this experience can also be used for good.

Jonah's lot was really a blessing in disguise. He wasn't worth his salt until the whale came along, and many times it is so with us. We drift around without purpose until the whale of adversity, gulps us down. This can be our end, or it can be the beginning of a useful life. It all depends on how we take it.

Instead of wasting his time in gloom and despair, Jonah held inventory and took action. He did not minimize his plight, but recognized it for what it was and turned to God. After he prayed, he was ready to proceed.

Whales are very valuable, and so can be the whales in our life. They can be steppingstones to something better, or they can be the cliffs of destruction. Many men did not begin their success until a whale came into their lives.

Almost everyone has some whale in his or her life. What you make of it depends on you. The turning point for Jonah came when he prayed in the belly of the whale. Finding ourselves in a similar plight, we need to follow his example.

And said, I cried by reason of mine affliction unto the Lord, and He heard me; out of the belly of hell cried I, and thou heardest my voice. For thou hadst cast me into the deep, in the midst of the seas; and the floods compassed me about: all thy billows and thy waves passed over me. Then I said, I am cast out of thy sight; yet I will look again toward thy holy temple. The waters compassed me about, even to the soul: the depth closed me round about, the weeds were wrapped about my head. I went down to the bottoms of the mountains; the earth with her bars was about me forever: yet hast thou brought up my life from corruption, O Lord my God. When my soul fainted within me I remembered the Lord: and prayer came in unto thee, into thine holy temple. ... And the Lord spoke unto the fish, and it vomited out Jonah upon the dry land. (Jonah 2:2-8, 10 KJV)

January 7 — Empathy Better Than Sympathy

Everyone knows the meaning of sympathy and exercises it to the fullest from time to time. This is fine, but the word "empathy" takes up where sympathy leaves off. In sympathizing, we look down and pity, but in empathizing we come alongside and share.

A little girl was sent by her mother one day to buy a loaf of bread at a grocery store at the end of the block. After she had been gone much longer than was necessary to run this errand, her mother became alarmed over her extended absence. Finally, however, Susie returned with the loaf of broad, looking sad.

"Susie," her mother said, "What kept you so long?"

"Well, Mother," Susie answered, "on the way to the store I saw Betty, and she told me she had left her doll outside last night and this morning she found it all chewed up and broken, probably by some dog."

"Oh, I see," Mother replied. "Did you stay that long because you were helping Betty fix her doll?"

"No, Mother, that's not what kept me so long," explained Susie. "I was helping her cry."

The empathy that goes with the sympathetic tear can be a powerful factor in dealing with our fellowman toward the healing of hurts

The great need of us today is sympathy, to be sure, but even greater is the need for empathy.

Often you and I have no solution for a friend's problem, but just sitting or walking alongside that person is a welcomed comfort. Sometimes not even a word need be spoken.

We find God's Word speaks of this kind of caring. It not only helps ease the pain of the hurting one, but it makes the one observing aware he or she may need that empathy some time.

Rejoice with them that do rejoice, and weep with them that weep. (Romans 12:15 KJV)

And whether one member suffer, all the members suffer with it; or one member be honored, all the members rejoice with it. (1 Corinthians 12:26 KJV)

January 8   Etched Visage

The mother of a young boy told him one day the legend of the Great Stone Face of their valley. Someday, she said, there would arise a man born in the neighborhood whose face would resemble that of the great stone face which looked out from the side of the distant mountain.

Her son looked at that distant face every day of his life. He longed for the time when he should see in the flesh a face as kind and as wise. He found himself studying faces of men he met in the village, wondering if one of them could be the one. Each time he was disappointed.

No matter how many disappointments he had, he held his faith, went about his daily duties with calm cheerfulness, played the part of a helpful neighbor, and won the affection and respect of all.

One evening near the end of his life, as he was speaking to a group of neighbors, and his face was lighted by the setting sun, someone pointed to him and exclaimed, "Look! The speaker resembles the Great Stone Face!"

The others agreed with him. He had looked so faithfully at the Great Stone Face that, without his realizing it, he had taken on the likeness of that face in his own face.

And that's the way it is with the Christian, when he or she looks at Jesus often. That person will naturally take on the attributes of Jesus, maybe not in physical appearance, but in loving like Jesus does, being kind like Jesus is, being forgiving as He, and hating the things that He hates.

The more time we spend with Him in His Word and talking to Him daily, we will become more like Him. The apostles of Jesus had spent so much time with Him when He was with them on earth those three years of His ministry that they took on His likeness. So much so that others noticed, even the enemies of the Christians.

Now when they saw the boldness of Peter and John, and perceived that they were unlearned and ignorant men, they marveled; and they took knowledge of them, that they had been with Jesus. (Acts 4:13 KJV)

January 9   Glowing in the Darkness

It is not in the brightness of the sunshine hours, but in the dusk of evening, that flowers are the most beautiful. It is then that flowers are judged by their own brightness. In contrast with the surrounding gloom, the most colorful flowers stand out like bright and shining lights. The lengthening shadows bring out their true beauty.

Is it not true, too, of human character? It is not in the sunshine of success, but in the darkness of disappointment and despair that the true worth of a man is brought out. That person's personality still shines brightly in the dark moments of human experience, who in the face of adversity becomes more noble, more kind, more courageous, and more compassionate.

The Apostle Paul knew much about adversities, but he learned how to glory in them. Just look how his service continued to bloom all down the ages, even now through his letters. Remember Job met with horrible calamities, and through it all he said of the Lord, "Though He slay me, yet will I trust Him."

If I must needs glory, I will glory of the things which concern my infirmities. The God and Father of our Lord Jesus Christ, which is blessed forevermore, knoweth that I lie not. (2 Corinthians 11:30-31 KJV)

And not only so, but we glory in tribulations also: knowing that tribulation worketh patience; and patience, experience; and experience, hope. And hope maketh not ashamed; because the love of God is shed abroad in our hearts by the Holy Ghost which is given unto us. (Romans 5:3-5 KJV)

January 10   Love in Every Direction

I heard a pastor speak once, whose subject was on the love of God. He told the story he had heard about Charles Spurgeon. While riding in the country, Dr. Spurgeon saw on top of a barn a weather vane, and on its arrow were inscribed these words: GOD IS LOVE.

He turned in at the gate and asked the farmer, "What do you mean by that? Do you think God's love is changeable; that it veers about as that arrow turns in the winds?"

"Oh, no," cried the farmer, "I mean whichever way the wind blows, God is still Love."

Beloved, let us love one another: for love is of God; and every one that loveth is born of God, and knoweth God. He that loveth not knoweth not God; for God is love. In this was manifested the love of God toward us, because that God sent His only Begotten Son into the world, that we might live through Him. Herein is love, not that we loved God, but that He loved us, and sent His Son to be the propitiation for our sins. (1 John 4:7-10 KJV)

January 11   Hush and Listen

One day, after I had become a widow, I was afraid and beaten down. I bowed my face to the ground, and I was enveloped in darkness. In my perplexity, I cried aloud, "Lord, I am in a corner, and I cannot move out of it."

Suddenly from out the storm a still small voice came, saying "Be still." And then I grew quiet and listened. Suddenly I realized that a little bird had been singing all the while, sitting on a limb of the the tree my husband had planted long ago. In my despair, I had not heard it.

Then, I felt a calm. God used a bird's voice to quieten me. I was able then to come out of my corner.

Be still, and know that I am God: I will be exalted among the heathen, I will be exalted in the earth. (Psalm 46:10 KJV)

They reel to and fro, and stagger like a drunken man, and are at their wit's end. Then they cry unto the Lord in their trouble, and He bringeth them out of their distresses. He maketh the storm a calm, so that the waves thereof are still. Then are they glad because they be quiet; so He bringth them unto their desired haven. Oh that men would praise the Lord for His goodness, and for His wonderful works to the children of men! (Psalm 107:27-31 KJV)

January 12   Color the Drab

We may as well be honest with each other and agree that we sometimes come to drab patches in life. An unexpected loneliness crops up from nowhere, a yearning for spending time again with a long-ago friend, or there is a strange emptiness that crops up inside. Suddenly you feel so alone even in a crowd. And those of the crowd can't satisfy your pining.

Then it is that we need more than ever something within us, for when there are few riches to be gathered along the road, it is good to have some already in our minds and hearts to bring to surface. Happy are we if there is a gladness springing up inside us, a song singing in our thoughts when no lark sings in the sky, a portrait gallery of memories to look on when the way is across a countryside with few striking features, a close friendship for the lonely miles with One who is nearer than hands and feet.

David must have felt a deep loneliness even when surrounded by others, but he had within him that that would satisfy his need. He said the Lord gives songs in the night. And Solomon must have felt himself without friends at times, when he penned that there is One who sticks closer than a brother, that One being the Lord.

> Yet the Lord will command His lovingkindness in the daytime, and in the night His song shall be with me, and my prayer unto the God of my life. (Psalm 42:8 KJV)

January 13   Faithful Engineer

A man was being whirled through space in the parlor car of a passenger train during the era when railroad travel was popular. The interior was brilliantly lighted. Outside all was black. His fear of the train wrecking kept him on edge.

Across the aisle a child was climbing up on her mother's lap, and the mother, with the light in her eyes which only mother-love can inspire, was patting her curly head. They apparently were not afraid. Seeing their calmness, he realized they felt safe because they had faith in the engineer. have faith in the engineer.

The man, watching them, began to feel more and more at ease. I too have faith in the engineer, he mused. Otherwise, he would not be in charge of this train with its several hundred human lives. He knows his engine, knows the roadway, is aware of all things that could happen, and is alert to avoid them. So, knowing his trust was on the engineer, the man could focus on thinking of happy expectations at his destination.

The man who has unerring faith is not likely to go wrong. He is going to steer his ship through waters of misfortune, perhaps even adversity, with a serenity born of the consciousness that nothing can harm him. Even though adversities may come to him from all sides, yet placing his faith in the Great Engineer of his life, he could achieve come what may.

We who were on the train in the night have faith in our Engineer, and we will arrive at our destinations safely. Our Great Engineer is the Lord Jesus Christ, and our ultimate destiny is heaven where we will spend eternity with Him.

He that believeth on Him is not condemned: but he that believeth not is condemned already, because he hath not believed in the name of the only Begotten Son of God. (John 3:18 KJV)

But without faith it is impossible to please Him: for he that cometh to God must believe that He is, and that He is a rewarder of them that diligently seek Him. (Hebrews 11:6 KJV)

January 14   Genuinely Thankful

We are to be thankful in everything, if not for everything. There are things for which we just cannot find a reason to be thankful, but if we look deep enough, we may see something in everything that is just cause for thanksgiving. We at least can thank God that the wrong things are not the permanent things, that we have the glorious task of helping to destroy them; that here is our opportunity of rendering service to a needy world: a purpose and a reason for living.

We are not thankful for sickness or suffering, for poverty, ignorance, or crime, but we are thankful for the forces that are surely conquering them; for medical science that is grappling with disease; for institutions of mercy and healing; for the havens of refuge for the helpless, and for the ever-increasing army of noble souls who are giving their time and energy to bringing about a better social order.

Truly there is much in the world for which—and to which—we can be thankful.

Enter into His gates with thanksgiving, and into His courts with praise: be thankful unto Him, and bless His name. (Psalm 100:4 KJV)

Praise ye the Lord. O give thanks unto the Lord; for He is good: for His mercy endureth forever. (Psalm 106:1 KJV)

Some of my friends really enjoy taking cruises. I have never been on one and have no desire to. All my cruise-taking friends were never afraid. I once read a story about a cruise, when there was a terrible storm on the ocean. The ship rocked from side to side. Passengers had to keep to their cabins to be safe. The pilot was strapped in his position, but it looked as if the ship would wreck.

One daring passenger decided to find out whether there was any hope of saving the ship. He crawled on his hands and knees to the stairway. He made his way up and across the wave-lashed deck to the ladder to the pilot's quarters. Up he went until he could see the pilot, who by that time was maneuvering the ship away from threatened destruction against rocks.

The pilot looked at him and smiled, but said not a word. The passenger, sighed with relief, and returned to the others, who were almost hopeless, and said: "All is well. The pilot looked at me, and he smiled."

In like manner, Jesus is the Pilot of our ship during whatever storm we find ourselves in. We can look to Him in trust, and for sure He gives us His smile that all is well.

> Behold, God is my salvation; I will trust, and not be afraid: for the Lord Jehovah is my strength and my song; He also is become my salvation. (Isaiah 12:2 KJV)

There is a difference between worry and concern. Each of us has concerns about various things we encounter for ourselves and for others. But we are not to worry over them.

If we worry, we don't trust. If we trust, we don't worry.

Why do we worry? Some are anxious about their health. Others are depressed about business. Others fret over domestic problems. Still others worry over possible misfortunes of tomorrow.

Worrying just can't alter circumstances. Worry accomplishes nothing. The person who is anxious about her health usually worries herself into sickness. A mother's fretting over domestic problems intensifies them. Worrying about one's business makes him less able to focus on turning the problem around.

Most worry is due to fear about tomorrow. But we may not see tomorrow, and if we do, it may be a different tomorrow than we anticipated. The things we dread are usually worse than the things that actually occur. We cannot see around the bend in the road, and we don't need to see that far. Worry doesn't empty tomorrow of its grief, but it does empty today of its joy.

Jesus told us not to worry. He also said not to wonder about tomorrow. Then the trouble of today will be the joy of tomorrow. That is the way to escape worry.

The Lord is my Shepherd: I shall not want. (Psalm 23:1 KJV)

Wherefore, if God so clothe the grass of the field, which today is, and tomorrow is cast into the oven, shall He not much more clothe you, O ye of little faith? Therefore take no thought, saying, What shall we eat? or, What shall we drink? or, Wherewithal shall we be clothed? ... For your Heavenly Father knoweth that ye have need of all these things. But seek ye first the kingdom of God, and His righteousness; and all these things shall be added unto you. Take therefore no thought for morrow: for the morrow shall take thought for the things of itself. ... (Matthew 6:30-34 KJV)

January 17   **Fill Your Role**

Once an orchestra was having rehearsal with a vast array of performers. The man who played the piccolo, far away up in a corner, said within himself, "In all this noise, it matters not what I do. He stopped playing. Suddenly the great conductor stopped, flung up his hands, and all was still, and then he shouted, "Where is the piccolo?"

Every one of us has a part to play in the symphony of life. There is the family circle, the church, the neighborhood, the business involvement. How often we feel like that piccolo player, thinking that our small efforts energies are of no avail, and that they can do well without our services. So, we cease to play our part. Yet there is One, our symphony conductor: Jesus Christ.

Our appointed tasks may seem of little value in the great symphony of life. Yet all the music of God's universe is made richer and sweeter because of the harmony supplied by individuals, each one seemingly unimportant by himself, yet highly worthy in ensemble with fellowmen.

Let's assume our roles and give our best for the glory of our Great Conductor, Jesus Christ.

> But now God hath set the members every one of them in the body, as it hath pleased Him. And if they were all one member, where were the body? But now are they many members, yet but one body. And the eye cannot say unto the hand, I have no need of thee: nor again the head to the feet, I have no need of you. Nay, much more those members of the body, which seem to be more feeble, are necessary: and those members of the body, which we think to be less honorable, upon these we bestow more abundant honor; and our uncomely parts have more abundant comeliness. For our comely parts have no need: but God hath tempered the body together, having given more abundant honor to that part which lacked. (1 Corinthians 12:18-24 KJV)

January 18   ## Lift Up Your Eyes

We lift our eyes unto the hills; it is good for the soul. They are so steadfast and sure. Clouds can cover the peaks, and the lightning can flash, but after the storm the mountains, washed by the rains, glisten in the sun.

Year after year, century after century, they stand unmoved and unmovable. They stand unchanged in a changing world. Little men come on the scene for a brief while, and pass on, but the mountains abide. The enduring, the unafraid hills, how calm they are!

I will lift up my eyes unto the hills and refuse to become frightened at the little doings of little men. From whence comes my strength? Not from the hills, but from the God of the hills. They in their bigness – their stability, their God-ness – we look upon them, and peace and calmness come into our soul.

David penned Psalm 121, and he knew full well what it meant by the words. Often, he was afraid and needed the Lord's help. He addresses the psalm *to you* meaning others who also need God's help. Also, notice that he uses the personal pronouns *I* and *my* there as well.

I will lift up mine eyes unto the hills, from whence cometh my help. My help cometh from the Lord, which made heaven and earth. He will not suffer thy foot to be moved: He that keepeth thee will not slumber. Behold, He that keepeth Israel shall neither slumber nor sleep. The Lord is thy keeper: the Lord is thy shade upon thy right hand. The sun shall not smite thee by day, nor the moon by night. The Lord shall preserve thee from all evil: He shall preserve thy soul. The Lord shall preserve thy going out and thy coming in from this time forth, and even for evermore. (Psalm 121 KJV)

January 19   Young Lad Startles Professor

One Sunday morning an instructor in a theological school was sharing a seat with a small boy on a shuttle train. The boy was holding a Sunday School lesson leaflet, reading it diligently.

"Do you go to Sunday school, my boy?" asked the man in a friendly way.

"Yes, sir," answered the boy.

"Then, maybe you can answer a question about God?" continued the man.

"I'll try," the boy replied.

"Can you tell me where God is?"

"Oh, sure. He's everywhere. There's no place where He's not."

"What do you mean?

"Well, it's like this. At school, when the teacher calls the roll, and my name is called, I answer 'Here.' So no matter where the roll is called on this earth, when God's name is called, He says 'Here.'"

The man had no other question for the boy.

Whither shall I go from thy Spirit? or whither shall I flee from thy presence? If I ascend up into heaven, thou art there: if I make my bed in hell, behold thou art there. If I take the wings of the morning, and dwell in the uttermost parts of the sea; even there shall thy hand lead me, and thy right hand shall hold me. If I say, Surely the darkness shall cover me; even the night shall be light about me. Yea, the darkness hideth not from thee; but the night shineth as the day: the darkness and the light are both alike to thee. For thou hast possessed my reins: thou hast covered me in my mother's womb. I will praise thee; for I am fearfully and wonderfully made: marvelous are thy works; and that my soul knoweth right well. (Psalm 139:7-14 KJV)

January 20   Somebody Needs Your Friendship

One thing about which many persons are careless is the preservation of friendship through the years. The tragic loneliness of souls in the later years of life should warn us not to neglect this rich source of happiness. Friendship thrives on such homely, simple, and accessible qualities that we wonder why any of us should let it die. A bit of unselfish and unfailing consideration, an unending delight in the daily activities of one another, a contact that a letter can sustain and enrich – why do we fail in such simple ventures? Old friends will enrich the years of old age as nothing else will.

It is selfish, though, to think of our own gain alone. To be an honored friend requires character that will enrich another and add happiness to that one's life.

A friend loveth at all times, and a brother is born for adversity. (Proverbs 17:17 KJV)

January 21   How Rich Are You?

You are richer today than you were yesterday, if you have laughed often, given something, forgiven even more, made a new friend, or made steppingstones of stumbling blocks in your path.

You are richer today than you were yesterday if you have thought more in terms of *thyself* than *myself*, or if you have managed to be cheerful even if you were weary.

You are richer tonight than you were this morning if you have taken time to trace the handiwork of God in the commonplace things of life, or if you have learned to count out things that really don't count, or if you have been a little blinder to the faults of friend or foe.

You are richer if a little child has smiled at you, and a stray dog has licked your hand, or if you have looked for the best in others and have given others the best in you.

Withhold not good from them to whom it is due, when it is in the power of thine hand to do it. (Proverbs 3:27 KJV)

Put on therefore, as the elect of God, holy and beloved, bowels of mercies, kindness, humbleness of mind, meekness, longsuffering; forbearing one another and forgiving one another, if any man have a quarrel against any: even as Christ forgave you, so also do ye. And above all these things put on charity, which is the bond of perfectness. (Colossians 3:12-14 KJV)

January 22   Kindness Displayed

It seems many *traditional* kindnesses have ceased to exist now. People appear to be more selfish in many areas. So, when I do see acts of kindness it does me good. Such kind persons seem to be saying, "We're all in this together."

Just to mention a few examples I've noticed: when someone learns of another's need, be it financial, relationship, health, loneliness, somebody steps up to the plate to help, maybe no more than just *to be there* alongside. It is not always a family member, and can be even a stranger, and often the one helping does it anonymously.

I see other courtesies. For instance, in Nashville, TN numbers of people take public transportation on buses. Once recently an unexpected downpour came about and as I was driving by one bus stop, I saw only one person with an umbrella. Then I noticed her waving for others to join her under that little umbrella. About five heads were covered but the rest of their bodies were getting soaked. They were laughing and having a good time.

Since I have recently begun to need to use a walker to walk, I have been overwhelmed with how folks (many of them strangers) have rendered unasked-for courtesies. After having driven to my work site, I am stiff when walking to the building, and limp along. Not long ago, as I made my way to the building, I heard someone yell from across the parking lot, "Ma'am, wait, and I will open the door for you!" He was a young man, a total stranger. I allowed him to do so, and it looked like it made his day. I realized people who do those things enjoy doing it.

One other example I know about is that of an elderly widow who felt the need to be on hand at critical care units at the hospital, just sitting in the waiting room, available for someone who might need to talk or cry or rave over someone they love who is ill. She takes her knitting stuff and does handwork, just spending her time in readiness. She seems to know what to do when she sees a need.

And they spake unto him, saying, If thou be kind to this people, and please them, and speak good words to them, they will be thy servants forever. (2 Chronicles 10:7 KJV)

And be ye kind one to another, tenderhearted … (Ephesians 4:32 KJV)

Back in high school days, in the 1950's, we had assembly programs every Tuesday. Sometimes they were rather boring, but everybody had to attend. Also, to the contrary, now and then one would *stick* for the rest of our lives. Such were like the story about how a wounded soldier in the Civil War was so impressed. He shared the story of a Civil War soldier, who wrote:

"Badly wounded from a ball that had shattered my leg," said a private of the Army of the Potomac, "I lay on the ground not far from Cemetery Ridge, and, as General Robert E. Lee ordered his retreat (after the third day at Gettysburg) he and his officers rode near me. As he came along, I recognized him and, though faint from exposure and loss of blood, I raised up my hands, looked Lee in the face and shouted as loud as I could, 'Hurrah for the Union!'

"The General heard me, looked, and stopped his horse, dismounted and came to me. I confess I first thought he meant to kill me. But as he came up he looked down at me with such a sad expression on his face that all fear left me, and I wondered what he was about. He extended his hand to me and, grasping mine firmly, and looking into my eyes, said 'My son, I hope you will soon get well.'"

"If I live a thousand years I will never forget that expression on General Lee's face. Here he was, defeated, retiring from a field that cost him and his cause almost their last hope, and yet he stopped to say words like those to a wounded soldier of the opposition, who had taunted him as he passed by. As soon as the General left me, I cried myself to sleep there upon the bloody ground."

If thine enemy be hungry, give him bread to eat; and if he be thirsty, give him water to drink. (Proverbs 25:21 KJV)

But I say unto you, Love your enemies, bless them that curse you, do good to them that hate you, and pray for them which despitefully use you, and persecute you. (Matthew 5:44 KJV)

Persevere, Persevere, Persevere!

A young man who worked with Thomas Edison became thoroughly discouraged because they had tried an experiment about a thousand times without success. One day he asked Edison "How can you bear working so long without results?"

"Results?" exclaimed Edison. "Why, man, I've a lot of results! I know a thousand things that will not work at all!"

In failure Edison learned what not to do. That was the secret of his matchless success. He used his failures as stepping-stones to reach higher attainments. Failure, if accepted rightly, is an important part of our education. Experience may be a costly teacher, but if we profit by her teachings, the results will make the expenditure seem insignificant.

> The steps of a good man are ordered by the Lord: and He delighteth in his way. Though he fall, he shall not be utterly cast down: for the Lord upholdeth him with His hand. (Psalm 37:23-24 KJV)

> For a just man falleth seven times, and riseth up again … (Proverbs 24:16 KJV)

Content Under My Piece of Sky

Did you ever think that wherever you are, it is your assigned place under the sky? God knew when each of us would be born, and He knew where we would live, our dwellings, our address. Above us, at any place, would be our sky—God's canopy over our abode. Some folks have more spacious sky canopies, and some perhaps, like one in prison with one window in his cell, would have a little piece. However big our piece of sky, God knows where we are and can satisfy our every longing, make us content with where we are.

I especially thought of this when I went out on the deck and saw just little pieces of sky, but it was azure blue and white clouds decorated it. An airplane passed under it. I suddenly felt such peace, just knowing above my piece of sky, God was aware of me and all my circumstances. Peace and contentment overwhelmed me!

Not that I speak in respect of want: for I have learned, in whatsoever state I am, therewith to be content. (Philippians 4:11 KJV)

Let your conversation be without covetousness; and be content with such things as ye have: for He hath said, I will never leave thee, nor forsake thee. (Hebrews 13:5 KJV)

January 26   Human Hands

Sometimes I take for granted two special pieces of my anatomy that serve me aptly: my two hands. They begin being used in infancy, the first being to take hold of mother's finger. All of one's life, they serve. One uses his hands to feed himself, bathe, dress, do various childhood chores, and then just think of school days, where hands handle pencils, paper, books. At recess hands are used for any type of game or sport. In business years, I don't know of a single type of career where the hands are not needed. As a married person, ah, the many tasks in caring for the home. When one becomes a parent, at times it seems a person needs at least two pair of hands. God gave us these wonderful servants for our use and His delight. Let us pause and praise Him for our hands!

And the Lord said unto him, What is that in thine hand? … (Exodus 4:2 KJV)

Whatsoever thy hand findeth to do, do it with thy might; for there is no work, nor device, nor knowledge, nor wisdom, in the grave, whither thou goest. (Ecclesiastes 9:10 KJV)

And that ye study to be quiet, and to do your own business, and to work with your own hands, as we commanded you. (1Thessalonians 4:11 KJV)

A surgeon, whom everybody loved, was asked, "How does it feel to have the power of life and death in your hands as you operate?"

"I never do feel that way," he replied, and continued: "When I was a young, cocksure surgeon, I was proud of my ability and my record. Then one day I had to make a hairbreadth decision. I wasn't correct!

"For some time I would not operate. As I sat, depressed, thinking of my failure, it suddenly came to me, in all humility, that God had given me these hands, had given me these brains—not to be wasted. I prayed to Him then to let me have another chance.

"I still do. I pray each time I take scalpel in hand. 'Guide my hands, O Lord, and give me of Your knowledge.'

"You see, God is the Surgeon; I am only His servant."

God gives each of His children specific talents and skills to be used to earn a living, support the family, give to His church and missions, and He nudges each in the direction in which He wants that person to perform. The surgeon is an example. He felt called to be such a person and he developed and honed the skills through education and experience to achieve in that career. In all areas of employment people fail and sometimes get depressed when they fail, but God says "Get up and continue your work. Do not feel abandoned by me. Remember to trust me. I will guide you in all your endeavors."

Trust in the Lord with all thine heart; and lean not unto thine own understanding. In all thy ways acknowledge Him, and He shall direct thy paths. (Proverbs 3:5-6 KJV)

I can do all things through Christ which strengtheneth me. (Philippians 4:13 KJV)

A farmer, returning from the field one day, found that his old horse had fallen into an abandoned well. The hole was deep, and the horse had long outlived his usefulness.

The farmer could not devise an easy way to get the horse out of the well, and he knew that if he did succeed in rescuing him, he would never again be of any good. And the well was of no use. In fact, he had threatened to fill it in. So, what should he do?

The easiest way out was to fill the well and bury Old Jim. He would be dead in a little while anyway, he thought. It was a heartless thing to do, he knew, but he decided to proceed. He, and stepped back far enough from the hole so that he could not see the old horse struggle. Then he began to shovel in dirt as fast as he could, hoping that Old Jim would not suffer long. But Old Jim had a different plan. As the dirt began to descend on his back, he braced himself as best he could. Soon the dirt settled around him, but he kept treading it down under his feet. His owner worked feverishly, and the well began gradually to fill. Old Jim kept on top of the dirt and rose high and higher. Just as the farmer felt certain that the old horse had been covered with dirt and suffocated, Old Jim jumped out and staggered off toward the green pasture.

Many of us humans make troubles for ourselves, when a little foundation of common sense would enable us to jump out of the hole. It is possible either to be buried by our troubles, or to use them as did Old Horse Jim—to lift ourselves up.

Though I walk in the midst of trouble, thou wilt revive me: thou shalt stretch forth thine hand against the wrath of mine enemies, and thy right hand shall save me. (Psalm 138:7 KJV)

We are troubled on every side, yet not distressed; we are perplexed, but not in despair; persecuted, but not forsaken; cast down, but not destroyed. (2 Corinthians 4:8-9 KJV)

After a person becomes a Christian, the Holy Spirit comes to live within that one. The person then has two natures—the inner man and the outer (fleshly, carnal) man. He will keep the outer man until death, after which he will be resurrected with a new body to match the inner man.

The inner man follows the leadership of the Holy Spirit, while the outer man continues to sin. That sin causes the inner man discomfort so much he cannot be satisfied until he goes to Jesus and asks for forgiveness, which Jesus readily promises to give.

The inner man will show himself, because his heart has been changed to want to love and to serve God. There is a constant battle between the inner man and the outer man. However, the Lord gives strength and discernment to His child so he can triumph over the carnal nature.

> But God be thanked, that ye were the servants of sin, but ye have obeyed from the heart that form of doctrine which was delivered you. Being then made free from sin, ye became the servants of righteousness. (Romans 6:17-18 KJV)

> But ye are not in the flesh, but in the Spirit, if so be that the Spirit of God dwell in you. Now if any man have not the Spirit of Christ, he is none of his. And if Christ be in you, the body is dead because of sin; but the Spirit is life because of righteousness. ... The Spirit itself beareth witness with our spirit, that we are the children of God. (Romans 8:9-10, 16 KJV)

January 30   The Grand Artist

There is a place in Arkansas where some of the most famous potteries in the world are located. Tourists from all over the country go to see the potters at work, molding rainbow-colored vases, jars, and other beautiful wares.

One day a woman visited one of these potteries and paused to talk with one of the workmen. With his hands colored from the clay he had been molding into a finished vessel, he almost reverently took up a big vase and held it in the sunlight. It was like the golden pink of the sunset behind the green hills.

When she asked the potter how they ever got all those beautiful colors on a vase, he replied: "Why, we don't put the colors there – the colors are already in the clay. All we have to do is bring them out. You know, this is all the handiwork of the Master Potter. He just uses my hands to turn the wheel and mold the shapes of the vessels, but He put all that gorgeous coloring in the clay Himself, when He created the world."

> And God said, Let the waters under the heaven be gathered together unto one place, and let the dry land appear: and it was so. And God called the dry land Earth; and the gathering together of the waters called He Seas: and God saw that it was good. (Genesis 1:9-10 KJV)

> He hath made every thing beautiful in his time: also He hath set the world in their heart, so that no man can find out the work that God maketh from the beginning to the end. (Ecclesiastes 3:11 KJV)

January 31   Vision vs. Walls

A tribe of Indians had no contact with the outside world. The old chief, before he died, wished to choose the young man who would be chief after him. He called together the young braves of the tribe and said, "See yonder peak? You will climb that mountain and each one bring back something to show how far he has climbed."

By and by one young brave came back. "O Chief," he said. "I have traveled to where the fields end, and I have brought back a grain of wheat."

The chief said to him, "Go shoot the arrow, and wrestle with the wild ox, and strengthen thyself."

Another young brave returned. "O Chief, I have traveled beyond the fields of grain, and I have brought back this last branch of the last tree."

The chief replied to this one as he had to the first.

Then another returned. "O Chief, I have traveled past the cultivated fields, through the trees, and came to a place where there was no living thing, and it was cold, and I was afraid. I have brought this stone."

He received the same reply the old chief had given the others.

So, during the long day the young men kept coming back, some with one thing and some another, until it grew dark. The last man burst into the circle by the fire. His face was shining as he said, "O Chief, I have traveled beyond the fields and the trees until I came to the snow, and I struggled through the snow to the mountain peak. I have brought back nothing, but I have seen the Sea!"

The old chief said, "My people, this is the young man who will be chief when I am gone. He is worthy to lead you. He has seen a vision."

The one with no vision has erected walls all around. He cannot see beyond the present. He feels caged. But God wants that one to look beyond what he can see, because those things are temporary. He wants him to look beyond what he can see to the myriads of opportunities and blessings awaiting to be achieved.

> Where there is no vision, the people perish: but he that keepeth the law, happy is he. (Proverbs 29:18 KJV)

> For since the beginning of the world men have not heard, nor perceived by the ear, neither hath the eye seen, O God, beside thee, what He hath prepared for him that waiteth for him. (Isaiah 64:4 KJV)

> While we look not at the things which are seen, but at the things which are not seen: for the things which are seen are temporal; but the things which are not seen are eternal. (2 Corinthians 4:18 KJV)

 February 1   ## Speak with Clean Tongue

In an order issued by General George Washington in New York in July, 1776, appeared the following precept, which is rarely practiced in the present day:

"The General is sorry to be informed that the foolish and wicked practice of profane cursing and swearing, a vice heretofore little known in an American army, is growing into fashion. He hopes the officers will, by example as well as by influence, endeavor to check it, and that both they and the men will reflect that we can have little hope of the blessings of Heaven on our army if we insult it by our impiety and folly. Added to this is a vice so mean and low, without any temptation, that every man of sense and character detests and despises it!"

When General George Washington became America's First President, he continued to show his disdain for profane language, such as risqué stories. On one occasion, after he and Mrs. Washington had served a festive banquet at their home, their guests being other statesmen and their wives, the men and women segregated—the men going into a particular parlor and the ladies into another, where the two groups could speak more informally.

As the men took their places in their sitting room, one of the statesmen remarked, "Now that there are no ladies present, I want to tell you fellows a little off-color story I heard recently."

Suddenly, George Washington interrupted him. "You are correct that there are no ladies present, but there are gentlemen present."

Let no corrupt communication proceed out of your mouth, but that which is good to the use of edifying, that it may minister grace unto the hearers. (Ephesians 4:29 KJV)

Neither filthiness, nor foolish talking, nor jesting, which are not convenient: but rather giving of thanks. (Ephesians 5:4 KJV)

But now ye also put off all these; anger, wrath, malice, blasphemy, filthy communication out of your mouth. (Colossians 3:8 KJV)

February 2   **Bend, but Don't Break**

Did you ever watch the limbs of a tree bend before a March wind? At the first violent blast, the limb leans over, letting the onslaught of air stream harmlessly pass. When the gale has subsided, the limb whips resiliently back into position.

Many people have the quality of reacting similarly to the winds of life. When misfortunate hits them, they bend before it, not permitting it to break them. When it is past, they spring up again, ready for more.

During a lifetime, we are all bound to encounter a certain degree of misfortune. That is the way life is. Some encounter it to a greater extent than others, but we all experience it.

As someone has so aptly put it: "It is not so much the misfortune itself that counts, but the way you meet it."

It is God that girdeth me with strength, and maketh my way perfect. He maketh my feet like hinds' feet, and setteth me upon my high places. (Psalm 18:32-33 KJV)

And not only so, but we glory in tribulations also: knowing that tribulations worketh patience; and patience, experience; and experience, hope: and hope maketh not ashamed; because the love of God is shed abroad in our hearts by the Holy Ghost which is given unto us. (Romans 5:3-5 KJV)

February 3   Conclusion of the Whole Matter

So striking was Daniel Webster's personality, it was said that when he walked through the streets, strangers paused to look at him, and his mere visage seized and dominated before he spoke at all. His rugged features often expressed the most genial kindness and sympathetic tenderness. But when he wished to control, to conquer, to overcome, the stern intensity of the look from deep-set eyes, under craggy brows, was irresistible.

When Webster was Secretary of State in President Filmore's Cabinet, he gave a dinner one evening at the Astor House to a few of his New York friends. There were about twenty at the table. Mr. Webster seemed wearied, and speaking but little, if at all, plunged into a darksome sort of reverie.

This at length became so apparent that one of his warm friends endeavored to get him into conversation. He spoke to Mr. Webster, but the dark Secretary of State merely raised his head and answered simply, then became silent again.

Once more the man summoned courage and said to him, "Mr. Secretary, I want you to tell me what was the most important thought that ever occupied your mind." Here was a knotty, multifaceted query for Webster, and so thought everyone at the table.

Mr. Webster slowly passed his hand over his forehead and looked up over the table. In clear, resonant tones he answered, "The most important thought that ever occupied my mind was of my individual responsibility to God."

Let us hear the conclusion of the whole matter: Fear God and keep His commandments: for this is the whole duty of man. For God shall bring every work into judgment, with every secret thing, whether it be good, or whether it be evil. (Ecclesiastes 12:13-14 KJV)

February 4 **Put a Spring in Somebody's Step**

In the lobby of a large city office building, several people walked out, while the first person, an elderly, frail little man, held the heavy door open for them. Not one of the first seven so much as glanced at their benefactor. The eighth person was different.

He was one of the busiest men in town. Of all the people hurrying out of the building, he probably had the most reason to dash through the door—but he didn't. As people passed through the door, only one young man smiled at him, and even shook his hand.

"Thank you, my friend," he smiled at the older man. "Keep this up and they'll be putting you on the building payroll." He patted the man on the shoulder, and strode off down the street. The older man, surprised, went on his way, smiling, and with a spring in his step.

When someone is complimented genuinely for a courtesy or kindness, he not only gets the spring in his step, but he wants to go right out and help someone else. And the one expressing words of appreciation to others finds his own life richer and happier as well.

Withhold not good from them to whom it is due, when it is in the power of thine hand to do it. (Proverbs 3:27 KJV)

The Lord God hath given me the tongue of the learned, that I should know how to speak a word in season to him that is weary. … (Isaiah 50:4 KJV)

February 5   Grand Benefactor

A wise king of an ancient land announced he would set aside a day to do honor to the greatest of his subjects. On the designated day, people from all walks of life streamed into the city and gathered outside the palace.

Amid the cheers of his subjects, the king made his way to the center of the assembly where a throne had been erected for him, and instructed the various groups of citizens to present their candidates.

First to come before the king was a man of great wealth, owner of vast lands and great industries. "He is also a man of philanthropies," said his followers. "He gives much of his wealth to the poor."

Next was a man of the law, well known for his knowledge of legal matters. "He is a great judge, famous for his wise decisions and deep sense of justice."

A doctor, much sought after for his powers in the medical field, was next. Following him was a great statesman who had brought honor to himself and his country. One after another was paraded before the king and lauded for his accomplishments.

Finally, a hunched-over aged woman was led to the front. From her dim eyes shone the light of knowledge, understanding, and love.

"Who is this?" demanded the king. "What has she done to achieve greatness?"

"You have seen and heard all the others," was the reply. "This, O King, is their teacher."

Amid the applause of the throng, the king descended from his throne to proclaim her the greatest of them all.

And thou shalt teach them diligently unto thy children, and shalt talk of them when thou sittest in thine house, and when thou walkest by the way, and when thou liest down, and when thou risest up. (Deuteronomy 6:7 KJV)

February 6   ## Cattle on Hills or Cars on Highways

Roy H. Stetler, a successful publisher of Harrisburg, Pennsylvania, bought a new car. This is what he said editorially concerning it:

"When our new car was delivered, I could not resist taking a little spin along the river. I found myself thinking about the affair. So, as is my habit in matters of this sort, I started to talk to God about the new car. Don't know why, but I had never before discussed our other new cars with God. As I recall, I was led to say something like this: 'God, we are grateful to You for this new car. Because you made it possible for us to have it, we should like to dedicate it to You. First, we want You to go with us, for we feel we are likely to drive better if we know You are one of our riders. Then, we don't want to drive anywhere that would be objectionable to You. We want to go where You direct, and in no direction where You would have to leave us to ourselves.'

"Does such a prayer sound silly? It occurs to me that if more cars were thus dedicated, there might be fewer accidents. If the 'cattle upon a thousand hills' are His, I am sure automobiles on thousands of highways are His, too."

For every beast of the forest is mine, and the cattle upon a thousand hills. I know all the fowls of the mountains: and the wild beasts of the field are mine. If I were hungry, I would not tell thee: for the world is mine, and the fulness thereof. (Psalm 50:10-12 KJV)

For by Him were all things created, that are in heaven, and that are in earth, visible and invisible, whether they be thrones, or dominions, or principalities, or powers: all things were created by Him and for Him. And He is before all things, and by Him all things consist. (Colossians 1:16-17 KJV)

February 7 — Indian Version of Psalm 23

The translation of portions of the Bible into Indian dialect has been the interesting task of missionaries, and such translations often result in all-embracing versions. An outstanding example is the Twenty-third Psalm, which was translated into Indian dialect, as follows:

The Great Father above is a Shepherd Chief. I am His, and with Him I want nothing. He throws out to me a rope, and the name of the rope is Love. And He draws me, and He draws me to where the grass is green and the water is not dangerous, and I eat and lie down satisfied.

Sometimes my heart is very weak and falls down, but He lifts it up and draws me into a good road. His name is Wonderful. Sometime – it may be very soon, it may be longer, or it may be a long time – He will draw me into a place between the mountains. It is dark there, but I will not draw back. I will be afraid not, for it is there between these mountains that the Shepherd Chief will meet me, and the hunger I have felt in my heart through this life will be satisfied.

Sometimes He makes the Love rope into a whip, but afterwards He gives me a staff to lean on. He spreads a table before me with all kinds of food. He puts His hands on my head, and all the *tired* is gone. My cup He fills till it runs over.

What I tell you is true. I lie not. These roads that are away ahead will stay with me through life, and afterwards I will go to live in the *Big Tepee* with the Shepherd Chief forever.

Read all of Psalm 23 and John 10:14-18.

He shall feed His flock like a shepherd: He shall gather the lambs with His arm, and carry them in His bosom, and shall gently lead those that are with young. (Isaiah 40:11 KJV)

From the hills of Lebanon, the water flows down in a stream and empties in the Jordan River. It is a river below sea level. Two lakes are in this river's course. The first is lovely Sea of Galilee. Artists and poets have vied with each other in portraying its beauty. It is a Living Sea. Therein fish thrive and vegetation grows on its shores.

Southward the Jordan flows into another lake. It is the Dead Sea. It has the saltiest water in the world. There is no life in its depths. Vegetation cannot grow along its shores. It is impossible for a man to sink in it.

It is the Dead Sea. Galilee is a Living Sea. One river feeds both. What makes the difference? Just this: the river flows through Galilee; it empties into the Dead Sea. One lake gives of its waters, the other only receives. The slight saltiness that is in all water has for ages poured into the Dead Sea. Evaporation has left behind the salt.

Human beings are somewhat like these two bodies of water. There is a certain woman who has been denied many of the blessings of life. Does she repine and mope? Not for an instant. She is interested in an institution that brings health and happiness to crippled children. Her face is radiant. She is a Sea of Galilee.

Then there is the man who was born with a silver spoon in his mouth. For sixty years he has been receiving things. Everything that has come to him he has kept. He is now an old salt, crusted with selfishness. His friends endure him, while others avoid him. He is a Dead Sea.

The philosophy of the Dead Sea is, "The doctrine of service is all bunk. What I get is mine to keep. I can live without birds and fish and people."

Galilee has a different voice: "I pass on what comes to me; that keeps me fresh and pure. Little children love me, and come here to play. Birds come to drink and bathe their plumage. I am a place of pilgrimage for those who love and serve."

Cast thy bread upon the waters: for thou shalt find it after many days. Give a portion to seven, and also to eight; for thou knowest not what evil shall be upon the earth. (Ecclesiastes 11:1-2 KJV)

Give, and it shall be given unto you; good measure, pressed down, and shaken together, and running over, shall men give into your bosom. For with the same measure that ye mete withal it shall be measured to you again. (Luke 6:38 KJV)

February 9   ## Resplendent Inheritance

Just out of high school, I became employed by a law firm where I worked for nine years. My title was legal stenographer. Estate planning was one of the many services of the firm, and the writing of a Last Will and Testament was part of the proceedings. It set forth what each heir of the one making the Will would receive upon that one's death. I remember typing up many of those documents. After the decease of the benefactor, the law firm usually followed up with probating the estate. I was always impressed when seeing a person signing his or her Last Will and Testament.

In reminds me of the marvelous inheritance our Heavenly Father has planned for His children. When you and I were born again by receiving Jesus, God's Son, as our Savior, we became His children. He owns everything in this universe. Jesus, His Son, inherits everything that belongs to the Father. How marvelous! But, even more wonderful for you and me as believers, we will inherit everything that Jesus does! It is all so awesome and incomprehensible that God so loves us, and that Jesus wants to share everything He inherits with us! We will be privileged to enjoy our inheritance eternally!

The Spirit itself beareth witness with our spirit, that we are the children of God: and if children, then heirs; heirs of God, and joint-heirs with Christ; if so be that we suffer with Him, that we may be also glorified together. (Romans 8:16-17 KJV)

Blessed be the God and Father of our Lord Jesus Christ, which according to His abundant mercy hath begotten us again unto a lively hope by the resurrection of Jesus Christ from the dead, to an inheritance incorruptible, and undefiled, and that fadeth not away, reserved in heaven for you, who are kept by the power of God through faith unto salvation ready to be revealed in the last time. (1 Peter 1:3-5 KJV)

February 10   For God's Glory and Mankind's Delight

God designed everything in creation for the delight of his masterpiece, the human being. He gave him eyes to behold the beauties and He gave him ears to hear the sounds from every direction. Taste buds in his mouth were fitted to taste the sweets and the sours and all between. And He gave him the ability to feel with his hands the various textures and temperatures. His nose learns the odors and fragrances of every unique thing. Best of all, He gave man a voice, each man with his own resonance, to praise God and give Him all His worthy glory, for so having created him and bedecked him with all the wonderful delights.

After God created all things on the earth, He last of all made man and made him in God's image and gave him a living soul. Then He presented that man with all He had created and gave it to him to have dominion over.

> And God said, Let us make man in our image, after our likeness: and let them have dominion over the fish of the sea, and over the fowl of the air, and over the cattle, and over all the earth, and over every creeping thing that creepeth upon the earth. So God created man in His own image, in the image of God created He him, male and female created He them. And God blessed them, and God said unto them, Be fruitful, and multiply, and replenish the earth, and subdue it: and have dominion over the fish of the sea, and over the fowl of the air, and over every living thing that moveth upon the earth. ... And God saw everything that He had made, and, behold, it was very good. ... (Genesis 1:26-28, 31 KJV)

O the depth of the riches both of the wisdom and knowledge of God! How unsearchable are His judgments, and His ways past finding out! ... For of Him, and through Him, and to Him, are all things: to whom be glory forever. Amen. (Romans 11:33, 36 KJV)

February 11 — Word Power

Soft words sung in a lullaby will put a baby to sleep. Vigorous words will stir a mob to violence. Eloquent words will send armies marching into the face of battle. Encouraging words will fan to flame the genius of a Rembrandt or a Beethoven. Powerful words will shape the public mind as the sculptor molds his clay. Words are a dynamic influence.

Words are the swords we use in our exertion for success and happiness. How others react toward us depends, in a large measure, upon the words we speak to them. Life is a grand whispering corridor that ricochets back reverberations of the words we send out. Our words are undying, too. They go marching through the years in the lives of all those with whom we come in contact. Ah, how powerful are our words!

> A soft answer turneth away wrath: but grievous words stir up anger. (Proverbs 15:1 KJV).

> A man hath joy by the answer of his mouth; and a word spoken in due season, how good it is! (Proverbs 15:23 KJV).

> A word fitly spoken is like apples of gold in pictures of silver. (Proverbs 25:11 KJV)

February 12 — Stay In Tune

I heard a radio announcer tell this tale one night, as I listened to my radio. It was rather an interesting letter that a radio broadcaster received some time ago. It was from a sheepherder on a lonely ranch in the Far West. The letter ran, in part:

"Will you please strike 'A' on your broadcast? I'm far away from a piano, and the only comfort I have is my old fiddle. It's all out of tune. Will you strike 'A' so that I can get it in tune again?"

The radio man granted the simple but unusual request, and some days later received a letter of appreciation from the man, saying, "Now I'm in tune again."

And we are reminded that there may be some lives that need tuning, that need to hear the clear pitch of "A." One does not have to be on a lonely ranch in an isolated place in order to be out of tune. And to be in a position to sound the chord for those who have lost it and are groping for it, is a grand privilege. It is a blessed service in a discordant world.

> We then that are strong ought to bear the infirmities of the weak, and not to please ourselves. Let every one of us please his neighbor for his good to edification. (Romans 15:1-2 KJV)

February 13   Putting Legs to Prayers

The pastor of a little church in a rural community met with severe affliction one day. His wife and two children fell ill, and his modest wages not being sufficient for his needs, he was greatly distressed.

The leaders of the church decided they would meet at the pastor's home and hold a prayer service. While one of them was engaged in fervent verbal petition, punctuated with "Amen" from some of the others, a knock was heard at the door. Finally, when the door was opened, a cheerful, ruddy-faced farmer lad stood there.

"What do you want?" asked one of the church leaders.

"I've got Pop's prayers," answered the youth, grinning good-naturedly.

"This is no time or place for flippancy, young man," admonished the elder. "What do you mean?"

"Well, you see," explained the boy, somewhat abashed, "Pop heard as how the preacher's been havin' a spell of bad luck, what with sickness

in the family an' one thing an' another, an' that you folks was all prayin'
for him tonight, so Pop sent me over here with his prayers.

"His prayers?" repeated the puzzled elder.

"Yep, I've got 'em – Pop's prayers – out here in the wagon, an' if a
couple of you men'll help me, we'll get 'em in here."

In a few minutes it was discovered that Pop's prayers consisted of a
load of potatoes, flour, bacon, corn meal, turnips, apples, warm blankets,
and a lot of delicacies for the sick ones.

> If a brother or sister be naked, and destitute of daily food, and
> one of you say unto them, Depart in peace, be warmed and
> filled; notwithstanding ye give them not those things which are
> needful to the body; what doth it profit? (James 2:15-16 KJV)

> But whoso hath this world's good, and seeth his brother have
> need, and shutteth up his bowels of compassion from him,
> how dwelleth the love of God in him? My little children, let us
> not love in word, neither in tongue; but in deed and in truth.
> (1 John 3:17-18 KJV)

February 14   A Soul Takes Flight

When a life-long friend died, the friend who was left shared this about
him: He and I were in classes together from the second grade through
high school, and we became close friends, writes Leo Bennett. He often
told me of his hope that someday he could be an airplane pilot; and
when we both graduated from high school, he wrote in my yearbook,
reminding me of his life ambition to be a pilot. "Remember," he wrote,
"that if I crash, I will still be flying through some other unknown sky."

After Pearl Harbor, volunteering for the Air Corps, he ultimately
took hold of his dreams, and could call them reality. He became a pilot
of a Flying Fortress. Although he had no enthusiasm about participating
in warfare, he patriotically performed his duty while looking forward to
a lifetime of flying in peaceful years.

But in the autumn of 1944 his plane was shot down, and he crashed on some isolated Pacific outpost. When his surviving buddies examined the charred ruins of his plane, they could find among the cold ashes no trace of the pilot. And I believe I know why. When the crash came, he kept on flying "through some other unknown sky."

As I write these words, Easter is coming again to the world. Outside my window bulbs are shooting forth tender green feelers into the invigorating spring air; birds are caroling merrily in the trees, on which green buds are bursting. After a winter of death, all nature is coming alive again, testifying to the truth of Easter. All about me I can behold resurrection, and I believe there will be resurrection for my lamented classmate and me.

I have no doubt about resurrection. I shall keep my windows of faith clean, knowing that immortality is God's plan – and His plans are immutable.

Though in this life I may ultimately crash, because my faith is in the Resurrected One, Jesus Christ, I shall "still be flying through some other unknown sky!"

> Jesus said unto her, I am the resurrection, and the life: he that believeth in Me, though he were dead, yet shall he live: and whosoever liveth and believeth in Me shall never die. Believeth thou this? (John 11:25-26 KJV)

> For the Lord Himself shall descend from heaven with a shout, with the voice of the archangel, and with the trump of God: and the dead in Christ shall rise first: then we which are alive and remain shall be caught up together with them in the clouds, to meet the Lord in the air: and so shall we ever be with the Lord. (1 Thessalonians 4:16-17 KJV)

February 15   Chief Role of a Dad

"By profession I am a soldier and take pride in that fact; but I am prouder, infinitely prouder, to be a father. A soldier destroys in order to build; a father only builds, never destroys. The one has the potentialities of death; the other embodies creation and life, and while the hordes of death are mighty, the battalions of life are mightier still. It is my hope that my son, when I am gone, will remember me, not from the battle, but in the home, repeating with him our simple daily prayer, "Our Father, who art in heaven."

- Douglas MacArthur

And thou shalt love the Lord thy God with all thine heart, and with all thy soul, and with all thy might. And these words, which I command thee this day, shall be in thine heart: And thou shalt teach them diligently unto thy children, and shalt talk of them when thou sittest in thine house, and when thou walkest by the way, and when thou liest down, and when thou risest up. (Deuteronomy 6:5-7 KJV)

And, ye fathers, provoke not your children to wrath: but bring them up in the nurture and admonition of the Lord. (Ephesians 6:4 KJV)

February 16   Mother's Role Never Ends

When I began dating at about age eighteen, when I came home at night afterward, no matter how quiet I was, my mother would be awake, and she would ask from her bedroom, "Carlene, is that you?" When I answered yes, then she would settle down and go to sleep. As my other sisters began to date, they said she always asked the same of the, "Is that you?" calling that one's name. Years later, I found the little story below, and I cut it out because it sounded like my mother. You may identify with it as well.

There was something I did not know about mothers until the first time I came home after everyone else had gone to bed. I opened and closed the door very softly, took off my shoes, and crept stealthily up the stairs. I did not get very far until mother asked, "Jimmy, is that you?"

There were times in the years that followed when I wished mother would realize that I was no longer a child, and stop listening for my late returning footsteps. Comparing experiences with companions, however, proved that all mothers were alike, though we could not understand the love which condemned them to a ceaseless vigil for their own, and denied them complete rest until everyone was safely home for the night. At last I gave up trying to conceal my tardy arrival, and expected her sleepy inquiry, "Jimmy, is that you?"

Like most young people, I discovered that the freedom born of breaking home ties was not as glittering as anticipated. Out in the world of strangers, no one lost any sleep about the hour you kept. It just didn't seem right climbing to your lonely room without someone from the darkness demanding, "Jimmy, is that you?"

When all of life is over, and I enter my final home, heaven's welcome will be complete if mother's voice calls, "Jimmy, is that you?"

My son, hear the instruction of thy father, and forsake not the law of thy mother: for they shall be an ornament of grace unto thy head, and chains about thy neck. (Proverbs 1:8-9 KJV)

Her children arise up, and call her blessed; her husband also, and he praiseth her. (Proverbs 31:28 KJV)

February 17   ## So Rich am I Mentally!

I have a *mental treasury* of golden memories: water tumbling merrily over rocks, pine trees silhouetted against a star-strewn sky, mountaintops covered with snow, quiet talks by an open fire, the old swimming hole, baby smiles, flowers at dusk in an old-fashioned garden, the vastness of the open plains, a cathedral on a hill.

I have a *mental paint box* containing all the radiant colors of the autumn woods, the sparkling silver of moonbeams on rippling water, the flaming red of sunsets, the colored candles of rainbows reaching into the sky.

I have a *mental safety deposit box* full of the wisdom of the masters, the gold of friendship, the love of children, the devotion of a dog.

I have a *mental music box* on which I can hear again the immortal symphonies, the lullabies of childhood, a singing bird at break of day, the patter of raindrops on the roof, the music of the wind in the trees, and a boy down the street whistling.

I have a *mental bank book* with kind deeds, a clear conscience, a pure heart, brave living, and especially a faith in the Giver of all these my many riches, the God of Heaven.

Yes, I am mentally rich!

Thus saith the Lord, Let not the wise man glory in his wisdom, neither let the mighty man glory in his might, let not the rich man glory in his riches: but let him that glorieth glory in this, that he understandeth and knoweth Me, that I am the Lord which exercise lovingkindness, judgment, and righteousness, in the earth: for in these things I delight, saith the Lord. (Jeremiah 9:23-24 KJV)

Finally, brethren, whatsoever things are true, whatsoever things are honest, whatsoever things are just, whatsoever things are pure, whatsoever things are lovely, whatsoever things are of good report; if there be any virtue, and if there be any praise, think on these things. (Philippians 4:8 KJV)

February 18   Want to Delight God? Thank Him!

There is a story told of one of the wagon trains on the Oregon Trail in pioneer days. The expedition had reached the dry country. Water and grass had been scarce for several days. Some of the wagons had broken down, with consequent delays amid the stifling heat. A general feeling of fretfulness had succeeded the early optimism and cheer. So, it was decided that, at the next night's stop, a meeting would be held to consider all their troubles.

When the travelers had gathered around the camp fire, one of them arose and said, "Before we do anything else, I think we should first thank God that we have come this far with no loss of life, with no serious trouble with the Indians, and that we have enough strength left to finish out our journey."

This was done, and then there was silence. No one had any complaints to make. Each was thinking of the larger troubles they had been spared. Looked at in such a light, it seemed they really were fortunate.

Americans are fortunate in having the spirit of thankfulness wrought into a national heritage, to be commemorated each year. Yes, there are adversities and misfortunes, but when we stop and think of how many tragedies we have been spared and have come this far in such favorable condition, it causes us to sigh, be quiet, and lift our eyes and hearts heavenward for God's wonderful providence all along the way

> Giving thanks always for all things unto God and the Father in the name of our Lord Jesus Christ. (Ephesians 5:20 KJV)

> In every thing give thanks: for this is the will of God in Christ Jesus concerning you. (1 Thessalonians 5:18 KJV)

February 19 — Be Still and Listen

A man lost his wristwatch somewhere in the house. He and his wife looked everywhere for it and never found it. His little eight-year-old son saw his frustration and began looking for the watch too.

After hours of searching, he finally decided what he needed to do to find it, and, sure enough, it worked. When he handed the watch to his delighted dad, his dad asked him, "How did you find it, son? We had already given up ever finding it."

"Well," the boy explained, "I just laid down on the floor and got real quiet and listened for the ticking of the watch. And when I heard it, I went to where the sound came from."

Doesn't that remind us of God's words in Psalm 46:10, "Be still and know that I am God?" In another place we read of God's still small voice in I Kings 19:11-12. We have to be still, get off to a quiet place, away from the din and clamor of all the sounds of activity, and just listen to hear God speak.

And He said, Go forth, and stand upon the mount before the Lord. And, behold, the Lord passed by, and a great and strong wind rent the mountains, and brake in pieces the rocks before the Lord; but the Lord was not in the wind: and after the wind an earthquake; but the Lord was not in the earthquake: and after the earthquake a fire; but the Lord was not in the fire: and after the fire a still small voice. (1 Kings 19:11-12 KJV)

Be still, and know that I am God: I will be exalted among the heathen, I will be exalted in the earth. (Psalm 46:10 KJV)

February 20   Reach for the Next Rung

Men who have made the greatest contribution to the world have been those who went a little beyond their contemporaries in loyalty and devotion to things of worth. The very names of Abraham, Columbus, Florence Nightingale and Pasteur suggest personalities that went beyond their generation in their chosen field.

Back in the Fifteenth Century, a man whose name is worldwide because he dared to sail further than the expected, brought the world a great truth. At a moment when the sky was dark, the ship springing a leak, the food supply running low, and the magnetic needle showing a variation that frightened the crew, he cried, "Sail on, and on!"

The life of Columbus is the story of every man who has set out to rise. In going beyond the expected in one's desire and willingness to help others, one marks himself as a man who can be depended upon. Longfellow observed:

> The heights of great men, reached and kept,
> Were not attained by sudden flight;
> But they, while their companions slept,
> Were toiling upward in the night.

It is in the rugged crises of conflict that the true man is shown. When we go past selfishness in our loyalty and devotion to the things of worth, we put our contemporaries and our posterity under obligation to do the same.

> Know ye not that they which run in a race run all, but one receiveth the prize? So run, that ye may obtain. (1 Corinthians 9:24 KJV)

> ... Let us lay aside every weight, and the sin which doth so easily beset us, and let us run with patience the race that is set before us, looking unto Jesus the author and finisher of our faith; who for the joy that was set before Him endured the cross, despising the shame, and is set down at the right hand of the throne of God. (Hebrews 12:1-2 KJV)

February 21 Compassion vs. Grudge

William McKinley ranks among the most respected Presidents of the United States. During one of his congressional campaigns he was persistently followed by a reporter from an opposition newspaper, who seized every possible opportunity to misrepresent views, and to hold him up to ridicule. Mr. McKinley took this onslaught of unfair criticism with fortitude, and even remarked that he admired the young reporter's persistence.

Finally, however, Mr. McKinley's admiration turned to pity. The reporter was clad in a thin, much-worn coat, and the weather was extremely cold. It was evident that the young man's devotion to duty was causing him great discomfort, and one night the affair came to an interesting climax. Mr. McKinley was riding in a closed carriage, while the reporter sat shivering on the driver's seat outside. The statesman endured the chattering as long as he could; then he stopped the carriage and said, "Young man, come here; put on this coat, and ride inside with me."

"But, Mr. McKinley," the young man stammered, "don't you know who I am? I've been ripping you to pieces during this campaign, and I don't intend to stop."

"Yes, I know who you are," replied the statesman, "but put on this coat, and get inside where it's warm."

A little man would have said under the same circumstances, "You fool, just stay out there until you freeze. Good enough for you!" But Mr. McKinley was a big man – too big to hold a grudge. Big men will not lower themselves to the little man's level. They pay no attention to petty critics. That, too, has helped to make them big.

> Rejoice not when thine enemy falleth, and let not thine heart be glad when he stumbleth. (Proverbs 24:17 KJV)

> But I say unto you, Love your enemies, bless them that curse you, do good to them that hate you, and pray for them which despitefully use you, and persecute you. (Matthew 5:44 KJV)

> Let all bitterness, and wrath, and anger, and clamor, and evil speaking, be put away from you, with all malice: and be ye kind one to another, tenderhearted, forgiving one another, even as God for Christ's sake hath forgiven you. (Ephesians 4:31-32 KJV)

February 22   ## Talking About the Weather

People have been talking about weather signs for centuries. Jesus mentioned it when He was talking to His enemies. He said they could discern weather but not discern other eternally important signs.

Jesus did not say there was anything wrong with weather signs. Over time the following signs have been set up and adhered to by mankind:

- When the sunset sky is red, you may expect clear weather on the morrow.
- Watch the smoke from your campfire or chimney. If it rises high, it means clear weather. It also shows wind direction.
- A heavy dew at night is seldom followed by rain the next day. Think of it this way: wet feet, dry head.

- ✦ Spiders are good weather prophets. If they make new webs, the weather will continue fine. If they continue during a shower, the weather will soon clear.
- ✦ If the sky is red at sunrise, you may expect several hard, tempestuous showers.
- ✦ If there is a ring around the moon, don't count on continued fair weather. Rain is likely in a day or two.
- ✦ When the leaves of the white poplar show their silver lining, look out for rain.

A brilliant atmosphere so clear it seems to bring faraway objects quite near betokens wet weather. The saying is—the farther the sight the nearer the rain.

While the earth remaineth, seedtime and harvest, and cold and heat, and summer and winter, and day and night shall not cease. (Genesis 8:22 KJV)

Then the Lord answered Job out of the whirlwind and said . . . Where wast thou when I laid the foundations of the earth? . . . Hast thou entered into the treasures of the snow? or hast thou seen the treasures of the hail, . . . Who hath divided a watercourse for the overflowing of waters, or a way for the lightning of thunder; to cause it to rain on the earth, where no man is; on the wilderness, wherein there is no man; . . . who hath begotten the drops of dew? (Job 38:1, 4, 22-23, 25-26, 28 KJV)

February 23　　　　　　　　　　　　　　　Into My Garden

Your smiles blow into my heart, dear friend,
And neighbors across the way;
Then blow and blossom in buds of love,
A blessing to life all day.

Your life is a garden of love, dear friend,
And planted with kindly deeds,
So ever over the fence will blow
Into my garden your seeds.

Let your light so shine before men, that they may see your good works, and glorify your Father which is in heaven. (Matthew 5:16 KJV).

February 24   Just Say It

Some joy comes your friend's way. You rejoice with her. But she will never know it unless you *say it.*

An honor comes to your friend. He wins in the game of life, and you are glad – *say it.*

Your friend succeeds in some task which he has undertaken. You feel a grateful pride that he has done it – *say it.*

Distress comes to your friend. She may have lost her property. Some of her loved ones may have gone wrong. Disease may have laid its hand on her, taking away the glow of health. You would share the distress with her – *say it.*

Old age, or perhaps a breakdown in the human body, may shut in your friend so that he can no longer fare forth among his fellows. Perhaps the end draws near. In your heart you wish him bon voyage as he nears his sunset gate. A word of kindly sympathy would brighten the way – *say it.*

The messenger of death may have knocked at his door and borne away into the unseen world some loved one. A word of sympathy would help to lighten the load – *say it.*

A personal word, a telephone call, a postcard, a letter, and only a few minutes of time! Your own life may be better because of it, but your friend may go to the end of the journey and never know. You may add to the joy; you may lighten the load; you may brighten the way if you only take time to *say it.*

Withhold not good from them to whom it is due, when it is in the power of thine hand to do it. (Proverbs 3:27 KJV)

Let us therefore follow after the things which make for peace, and things wherewith one may edify another. (Romans 14:19 KJV)

As we have therefore opportunity, let us do good unto all men, especially unto them who are of the household of faith. (Galatians 6:10 KJV)

Wherefore comfort yourselves together, and edify one another, even as also ye do. (1 Thessalonians 5:11 KJV)

February 25   Send Forth Your Perfumed Blossom

A young woman who was a great lover of flowers had set out a rare vine at the base of a stone wall. It grew vigorously, but she could find no blooms on it. Day after day she cultivated it and watered it, and tried in every way to coax it into bloom.

One morning, as she stood disappointedly before it, her invalid neighbor, sitting in her wheel chair, called over and said, "You can't imagine how much I have been enjoying the blooms on that vine you planted!"

The young woman looked, and on the other side of the wall was a mass of blooms. The vine had crept through the crevices and flowered luxuriantly on the other side.

For none of us liveth to himself, and no man dieth to himself. (Romans 14:7 KJV)

Let every one of us please his neighbor for his good to edification. (Romans 15:2 KJV)

An unknown chaplain is credited with being the author of this letter, addressed to a young man about to enter the arena of life:

I am giving you the ball, Son, and naming you the quarterback for your team in the game of life. I am your coach, so I'll give it to you straight.

There is only one schedule to play. It lasts all your life, but consists of only one game. It is a long game with no time out and no substitutions. You play it all your life.

You'll have a great backfield. You're calling the signals, but the three other fellows in the backfield with you have great reputations. They are named Faith, Hope, and Charity.

You'll work behind a truly powerful line. End to end, it consists of Honesty, Loyalty, Courage, Devotion-to-Duty, Self-Respect, Cleanliness, and Discipline.

The goalposts are the Gates of Heaven.

God is the referee and sole official. He makes all the rules, and there is no appeal from them.

There is only one Game Manual, and it consists of Sixty-six books. The name of the Manual is The Holy Bible. Read it and practice it to the best of your ability.

There is also an important ground rule. It is, "As you would that men should do to you, do even so to them."

Here is the ball. It is your immortal soul! Now, Son, get in there and let's see what you can do with it!

Brethren, I count not myself to have apprehended: but this one thing I do, forgetting those things which are behind, and reaching forth unto those things which are before, I press toward the mark for the prize of the high calling of God in Christ Jesus. (Philippians 3:13-14 KJV)

At the time of the *great crash*, a business man sent word to his minister that he had lost everything. The minister went to see his friend, and the following conversation took place:

"I am very sorry to hear of the death of your wife," said the minister.

"My dear sir," replied the business man, "You have been misinformed. My wife is very well and has been my help and stay in this disaster. I have never fully realized before her devoted love."

"Oh," said the minister, "I may have been misinformed, but I do regret the disloyalty of your sons since you lost everything."

"What?" exclaimed the business man. "You are surely mistaken again. Each one of my four sons has come home and offered to place every penny he has to my disposal. I never knew how loyal they were to me until now."

"That may be true," said the clergyman, "but I knew you would find out that your real friends were very few when they learned you had lost your money."

"What do you mean?" retorted the business man. "I never knew I had so many unselfish friends until this, my day of great trouble!"

"Then," demanded the minister, "what do you mean by saying that you have lost everything? You have lost a few thousand dollars, it is true, but see what you have found: your wife and sons, and their unstinted loyalty, your many friends with their unselfish fidelity. What do you mean, sir, by saying you have lost everything?"

Blessed is everyone who feareth the Lord; that walketh in His ways. For thou shalt eat the labor of thine hands: happy shall thou be, and it shall be well with thee. Thy wife shall be as a fruitful vine by the sides of thine house: thy children like olive plants round about thy table. Behold, that thus shall the man be blessed that feareth the Lord. (Psalm 128:1-4 KJV)

Blessed be the God and Father of our Lord Jesus Christ, which according to His abundant mercy hath begotten us again unto a lively hope by the resurrection of Jesus Christ from the dead, to an inheritance incorruptible, and undefiled, and that fadeth not away, reserved in heaven for you, who are kept by the power of God through faith unto salvation ready to be revealed in the last time. (1 Peter 1:3-5 KJV)

February 28   Intertwining

Although the limbs of the trees in the Redwood Forest stretch tall toward the sky, their roots do not go downward all that deep. However, the amazing thing about those trees is the roots of one tree intertwines with roots of its neighboring trees to help each other to grow. Should one tree lack a bit of moisture, those alongside with moisture to spare contribute to that one's need.

Also, among the redwoods, the intermingling of these singular and corporate roots bar any entrance for parasites to attach and live off the labor of these hardworking trees.

With such intertwining, each one does its part to promote the beauty and splendor of the forest.

In parallel, that is the way it should be with God's children, especially church members. When one needs a lift or encouragement, fellow Christians should avail themselves to help to bring that one up to fulfill his purpose in the Lord's service. Then they can rejoice together as they see the glory and splendor of the flourishing of the Lord's Kingdom work.

We then that are strong ought to bear the infirmities of the weak, and not to please ourselves. (Romans 15:1 KJV)

Brethren, if a man be overtaken in a fault, ye which are spiritual, restore such an one in the spirit of meekness; considering thyself, lest thou also be tempted. (Galatians 6:1 KJV)

The house lights are dimmed; the curtain goes up; the spotlight swings to the stage wing and focuses on a man with a violin tucked under his arm. He comes upstage, center, and stops. There's an expectant hush in the great music hall. He lifts the violin to opposition, but as the bow contacts the strings the hush is broken by the loud snap of a broken string.

The audience instinctively offers a mild exclamation of surprise and concern. As the bow is again lifted to the strings, another snaps! This time the audience murmurs restlessly.

A third time the bow comes down on the remaining strings, and suddenly the third string snaps. This is too much! The hall hums with disgusted exclamations.

The man stands awkwardly, awaiting a silence that is slow in coming, but at last the disturbed audience settles back in displeased tolerance of this musical travesty.

But wait! The performer strikes a new pose. The violin with its three broken strings dangling, is lifted into position. The bow flashes across the one remaining string like a rainbow trout in the sunlight. The man's nimble fingers race the entire length of the string as it vibrates such melody that it electrifies the throng. The audience is caught up in the ecstasy of this musical rapture, and responds as one person to its persuasion of mingled emotions of smiles and tears.

When the man has finished, the applause, like the roar of ocean waves on the rocks, is thunderous. The violin that had been reduced to a one-string fiddle has been salvaged by a great violinist. The artist had shown that it is not what we have, but what we are, that determines success or failure. A fitting word for this man's pursuit to the finish is integrity. Someone defined integrity as "the real person you are in the dark with no one else around."

Let integrity and uprightness preserve me; for I wait on thee. (Psalm 25:21 KJV)

And as for me, thou upholdest me in mine integrity, and settest me before thy face forever. (Psalm 41:12 KJV)

Serve God or Be a Dead Relic

The great violinist, Nicolo Paganini, willed his marvelous violin to his native city of Genoa, but on the condition that it must never be played upon.

The condition was unfortunate, for it is one peculiarity of wood that as long as it is used and handled, it wears but slightly, but as soon as it is discarded, it begins to decay.

The lovely-toned violin has become worm-eaten in its beautiful case, and it is valueless, except, except as a relic.

The moldering instrument is a reminder of the truth that life withdrawn from all service to others becomes useless.

> For other foundation can no man lay than that is laid, which is Jesus Christ. Now if any man builds upon this foundation gold, silver, precious stones, wood, hay, stubble; every man's work shall be made manifest: for the day shall declare it, because it shall be revealed by fire; and the fire shall try every man's work of what sort it is. If any man's work abide which he hath built thereupon, he shall receive a reward. If any man's work shall be burned, he shall suffer loss: but he himself shall be saved; yet so as by fire. (1 Corinthians 3:11-15 KJV)

Never a Right Time to Do a Wrong Thing

An old Indian once bought some things from a white man who kept a store. When he got back to his wigwam and opened the bundles, he found some money inside one of them.

"Great luck!" thought the old Indian to himself. "I will keep this money. It will buy many more things."

He went to bed, but he could not sleep. All night he was thinking of the money. Over and over again he thought, "I will keep it. I will keep it for my own." But something within him seemed to say, "No, you must not keep it, that would not be right."

Early the next morning he went back to the white man's store. "Here is money," he said; "I found it in one of the bundles with the things I bought from you yesterday."

"Why didn't you keep it?" asked the storekeeper.

"There are two voices inside of me," replied the Indian. "One said, 'Keep it, you found it, and the white man will never know.'"

Then the other voice said, "Take it back! Take it back! It is not yours. You have no right to keep it!"

"The two voices inside me talked all night and would not let me sleep. Here, please take the money. Now the two voices will stop talking. Tonight, I shall sleep."

For I know that in me (that is, in my flesh,) dwelleth no good thing: for to will is present with me; but how to perform that which is good I find not. For the good that I would I do not: but the evil which I would not, that I do. ... For I delight in the law of God after the inward man: but I see another law in my members, warring against the law of my mind, and bringing me into captivity to the law of sin which is in my members. O wretched man that I am! Who shall deliver me from the body of this death? I thank God through Jesus Christ our Lord. So then with the mind I myself serve the law of God; but with the flesh the law of sin. (Romans 7:18-19; 22-25 KJV)

March 3   One Day at a Time

An elderly woman with heavy household cares saw the day when she could carry on no longer. Her strength was waning day by day, and each new day the duties for which she was responsible seemed to mount higher.

One day the physician called on her, and, seeing how little strength she had, told her she would have to give up for a little while, and she became a patient in a hospital. Only then did she realize how exhausted she was.

After a few days, she thought of the affairs at home and became restless. "Doctor," she said, "how long will I have to lie here?" The answer was, "Only one day at a time." That was all he said, but it served to strengthen the virtue of patience in her.

And what lesson do those six magic words teach us? "How long shall I have to pore over books before I can go out and make some money?" "How long shall I have to slave in order that I may provide a livelihood for the family?" "How long shall I have to bend my back to pick and shovel to build highways?" "How long shall I have to stand before the flaming forge to create machinery for the world's work?"

It is not a day's work that breaks us, but a week's work, and a month's work, and a year's work – all crowded into one day. The answer to all these questions is the same the doctor gave to the elderly, exhausted woman: "Only one day at a time."

Will Rogers, the "human philosopher," found that contentment and happiness were to be attained by doing each day's tasks with confidence and laying them down at night without worry. Once a discouraged friend said to him, "Will, if you had but forty-eight hours to live, how would you spend them?" And the indomitable cowpuncher replied, "One hour at a time."

Take therefore no thought for the morrow: for the morrow shall take thought for the things of itself. Sufficient unto the day is the evil thereof. (Matthew 6:34 KJV)

March 4   Let Me Help – I'm Going Your Way

It was sleeting and slushy underfoot. Pedestrians were hurrying along forty-second Street in New York with their coat collars up about their ears, scarcely glancing at passersby. A young black man, carrying a heavy valise in one hand and a huge suitcase in the other, was hurrying toward the Grand Central Station, slipping and skipping as he went.

Suddenly a hand reached out and took the valise, and at the same time a pleasant but positive voice said, "Let me take one, brother! Bad weather to have to carry things."

The young black man was reluctant, but the young white man

insisted, with the remark, "I'm going your way." All the way to the station the two chatted like two old friends.

Years later, Booker T. Washington, who told the story, said, "That was my introduction to Theodore Roosevelt.

We then that are strong ought to bear the infirmities of the weak, and not to please ourselves. (Romans 15:1 KJV)

As we have therefore opportunity, let us do good unto all men, especially unto them who are of the household of faith. (Galatians 6:10 KJV)

March 5   No Room for Self-Pity

Among the students of one of our well-known colleges some years ago was a young man who had to walk with crutches. He was a stumbling, homely sort of human being, but he was a genius for intelligence, friendliness, and optimism.

During his four years in college, this crippled young man won many scholarship honors. During all this time his friends, out of consideration and respect, refrained from questioning him as to the cause of his deformity. But one day his pal made bold to ask him.

"Infantile paralysis," was the brief answer.

"Then, tell me," said the friend, "with a misfortune like that, how can you face the work so confidently and without bitterness?"

The young man's eyes smiled, and he tapped his chest with his hand. "Oh," he replied, "you see, it never touched my heart."

Why art thou cast down, O my soul? and why art thou disquieted within me? hope in God: for I shall yet praise Him, who is the health of my countenance, and my God. (Psalm 43:5 KJV)

In the lore of the Orient there is a story about a good man who built a large business through honest toil and unselfish cooperation with his fellows. As old age crept upon him, he became concerned for the future of his enterprise. His only living relatives were three stalwart nephews. One day he called the young men to him, saying, "One of you shall be my successor." They thanked him, and each promised to do his best if chosen.

The old man continued, "I have a problem. He who solves it best shall have my business." So, saying, he handed each youth a coin. "This is a large room but go and buy something to fill it as nearly full as you can but spend no more than the coin I have given you. Go now, but return at sunset, for I shall be waiting."

All day long the young men went about in the market places and among the tradesmen, and as the shadows lengthened, they made their way back to their uncle's house. He greeted them kindly, and asked to see their purchases.

The first youth dragged into the room a huge bale of straw, which, when he untied it, made a pile so great that it hid two walls of the room. He was complimented by the others as they cleared it away. The second youth brought in two bags of thistledown, which, when released, filled half the room. The other two cheered him.

The third youth stood silent and forlorn, and carried no package. "And what have you?" asked the old man.

"I gave half my coin to a hungry child," he answered meekly, "and most of what remained I gave to alms at the church, where I asked God to forgive my sins." There was no cheering, but the youth continued, "And with the little bit of the coin I had left, I purchased this flint and this small candle." And with that he struck the flint and lighted the candle, which filled every nook of the room.

"'Well done, good and faithful servant,'" quoted the old man; "thou hast been faithful over a few things; I will make thee ruler over many things.'" And while the young man fell to his knees, the old man blessed him, and gave him all of his possessions.

For ye were sometimes darkness, but now are ye light in the Lord: walk as children of light. (Ephesians 5:8 KJV)

Again, a new commandment I write unto you, which thing is true in Him and in you: because the darkness is past, and the true light now shineth. He that saith he is in the light, and hateth his brother, is in darkness even until now. He that loveth his brother abideth in the light, and there is none occasion of stumbling in him. (1 John 2:8-10 KJV)

March 7   Open the Door to Jesus

There is a story about Holman Hunt, the famous artist who painted "The Light of the World." It is a portrait of Christ in a garden at midnight. In His left hand He was holding a lantern, and with His right hand He is knocking on a heavily paneled door.

On the day the painting was unveiled, a group of art critics was present. One of them remarked, "Mr. Hunt, you haven't finished your work."

"It is finished," the artist replied.

"But there is no handle on that door."

"That," said the artist, "is the door to the human heart; it can be opened only from the inside."

Behold, I stand at the door, and knock: if any man hear My voice, and open the door, I will come in to him, and will sup with him, and he with Me. (Revelation 3:20 KJV)

March 8   Name Above All Names

Rutgers University Bookstore, New Brunswick, New Jersey, is a gathering place for many scores of undergraduates and faculty members in the course of a few days. A few years ago, one of the student papers gave these persons an opportunity to make a list of the twelve men, who, in their opinion, have had the greatest influence in the world. One hundred and three lists were made, almost equally divided between students and faculty members. Each was free to use his own judgment and compile his list without outside influence.

All but three of the lists included the name Jesus Christ, and two of the three later stated that they had omitted the name inadvertently. It was therefore almost unanimous that Christ's influence on the world has been greatest.

Next in order came Napoleon Bonaparte; then Caesar, Gautama, Mohammed, Aristotle Mars, Plato, Pasteur, Edison, and Columbus. Those at the bottom of the list with very low numbers were Darwin, Mussolini, Hitler and Stalin, who got three votes. The test was significant among teachers and students in a school of high standing.

I am the Lord: that is My name: and My glory will I not give to another, neither my praise to graven images. (Isaiah 42:8 KJV)

I, even I, am the Lord; and beside me there is no Savior. (Isaiah 43:11 KJV)

I have sworn by Myself, the word is gone out of my mouth in righteousness, and shall not return, That unto Me every knee shall bow, every tongue shall swear. (Isaiah 45:23 KJV)

Wherefore God also hath highly exalted Him, and given Him a name which is above every name: that at the name of Jesus every knee should bow, of things in heaven, and things in earth, and things under the earth; and that every tongue should confess that Jesus Christ is Lord, to the glory of God the Father. (Philippians 2:9-11 KJV)

March 9   Use Your Talent and Keep Improving It

Calling on a successful businessman, an ambitious yet discouraged young man asked the secret of success.

"It's no secret," replied the businessman; "whatever you do, do well; and continually do it better and better."

"But," said the young man, "there isn't anything at all I can do."

"A wise thinker," said the businessman, "once gave us something like this: 'Every man born into the world has his work born with him.' Now, you too have some activity. What is it?"

Hesitatingly the young man answered, "I make soap."

"Well, you can make a success at that as well as at anything else. Go home, young man, and make better soap today than you have ever made before and, tomorrow, improve on that."

The young man followed the advice. He made different bars and added a scent to the soap, which was an innovation. He gradually improved on new product, and the soap he thought unsalable once was quickly absorbed by an eager public.

Today there is not a youth in any part of the civilized world who hasn't heard of the name of the millionaire magnate who at one time considered himself a colossal failure. For that successful soap manufacturer was none other than Gilbert Colgate of New York City, USA!

Whatsoever thy hand findeth to do, do it with thy might; ...
(Ecclesiastes 9:10 KJV)

March 10   Run From God and You'll Get Dirty

I took our white Spitz-Poodle, Crystal, to the kennel for grooming. Being a lap dog, she had always been kept powder puff clean and fresh. Usually I had to pull her out of a cringing position from the corner of the seat when we arrived at the kennel. That time, however, she bounded out of the car and took off homeward at what appeared to be ninety miles per hour.

I ran down the road yelling at her to come back, but she just kept running. The kennel owner's husband came and I got in his truck. He drove fast to catch up with her. In all, it took less than ten minutes to retrieve her, and when we did, she was filthy black from running through plowed fields and drainage ditches, almost unidentifiable. She required extra scrubbing to restore her to her former appearance, if that were even possible.

It is the same way in the Christian's life. As long as he is on the alert keeping his body under control, he can live above reproach before those who are watching. But you let one be careless and become a bit worldly, he will begin to get dirty and the longer he runs the other direction from God he will get more dirty. When he has been caught and is cleaned up again, there may be scars and stains that can never be removed to return that person to his former state.

Think about the Bible character, David, a man after God's own heart. He slew the giant with nothing but faith in God. He became the mighty King of Israel for forty years. During the time he was close to God he lived above reproach among his subjects, family and even his enemies. Then he let down the bars and committed sins of adultery and murder.

Even though David received pardon from God, he was chastened severely. He bore scars of sorrow and regret as long as he lived. He could never achieve the greatness he had enjoyed before his transgression.

The lady at the kennel scolded filthy Crystal saying, "Child, you didn't know how well off you were." In essence God says the same thing to His child who strays from the close-to-God way and gets filthy and has to be scrubbed up again.

Enter not into the path of the wicked, and go not in the way of evil men. Avoid it, pass not by it, turn from it, and pass away. (Proverbs 4:14-15 KJV)

Abstain from all appearance of evil. (1 Thessalonians 5:22 KJV)

March 11   ## Trees are Ripe for Harvest

One day I dropped by my parents' home just to visit, and before I had been seated long, my Dad said "The peaches are ripening fast."

I said "Well, I'll come by later and pick them."

He came back with, "They are so ripe they're falling off, and when they fall, they get bruised and ruined."

I said, "I've got another errand to run first. I'll come back after awhile and pick them."

He started walking toward the tree and called over his shoulder, "Bring that bucket over there and pick the peaches now. It won't take but a few minutes. Then you can run your other errand."

I followed him to the tree and we began to pick the ripened fruit. They were turning loose from the limbs so easily that he said he would pick them and I could catch them before they hit the ground. There were so many I had to go fetch another bucket. Like he said, it didn't take us long, and we were both amazed at the large amount we had gathered.

As I drove away with the aroma of ripe peaches coming from the back seat, I realized how my attitude toward dad's peach tree was like the way we Christians treat the Lord's harvest. No doubt there are souls ripe and ready to be *picked* if we would just take the time. Dad said if the peach falls to the ground it would bruise. How tremendously severe the bruise to the soul that is not picked before it falls!

Dad would not pay attention to anything I said. His only concern was the ripe peaches. Don't you know it is the same way when we go to God with our petty excuses? Can't you hear His voice ring from heaven, "But the harvest is ripe now! Gather the fruit now! It's going to bruise and ruin!"

God help each of us to see the white harvest and the fall and ruination of precious souls if we do not pluck them now.

Say not ye, There are yet four months, and then cometh harvest? behold, I say unto you, Lift up your eyes, and look on the fields; for they are white already to harvest. (John 4:35 KJV)

March 12   Kindness Reciprocal

I opened the door at the post office for a person laden with a package filling both her hands. About a half hour later someone held a door open for me as I held two large sacks of groceries. How glad I was at that moment that I had held the door open for the lady at the post office!

Back in the winter when a car would get stuck in front of my husband's business, a print shop, because of the snow and ice, my husband would turn off the presses and go out and help push the car out. A day or two later my car got stuck in front of another door. Before my tears of frustration began to spill, two men came out of the store and shoved my car out. How glad I was at that moment that my husband had helped push the car out in front of his shop!

I see this as the law of sowing and reaping. Also, it is the law of return for casting your bread upon the waters. It's doing good deeds as the opportunity comes just because it's something you ought to do, and then God turns it around and heaps it back to you when you need it.

I am the recipient of blessings today because some forefather of mine bestowed favors to someone in his day. Because one of my ancestors was faithful to teach somebody's child about the Savior so that that child could be saved, God saw to it that somebody came along at a time in his descendant's life – mine – to explain the way of salvation. Although I may be burdened for a loved one and wish for his salvation, yet not be where I can introduce him to Christ as Savior, I can keep praying and do the witnessing where I am to somebody else's loved ones, and God will see to it that somebody is sent to that place where my loved one is.

Because I have worked with youth all my adult life in the church, I feel confident God will see to it that there will be somebody to work with my grandchildren in their spiritual lives when I'm not around.

Taking time for an elderly person now will mean somebody will return the favor when you are elderly and need a friend. Open that door for somebody when it is within your power to do it, for at the next door you come to, it might be you needing someone to open the door for you.

He that hath pity upon the poor lendeth unto the Lord; and that which he hath given will He pay him again. (Proverbs 19:17 KJV)

Give, and it shall be given unto you; good measure, pressed down, and shaken together, and running over, shall men give into your bosom. For with the same measure that ye mete withal it shall be measured to you again. (Luke 6:38 KJV)

Nutritionists say you should chew your food savoring each morsel and delighting your taste buds. Not one food tastes like another. A bean does not taste like a pea nor a beet like a turnip. Even an acorn squash hasn't the flavor of the yellow summer variety. A white potato differs from a red one.

Consider the diversity of flavors of a chicken. The white meat is not like the dark meat and the egg from the same hen is distinct in taste even more.

Try as you might to make low-calorie butternut squash taste like fattening sweet potatoes, you won't succeed. I'm still wondering how Rebekah seasoned goat meat to make it taste like venison so Jacob could deceive his blind father with it.

In a Sunday School class recently, twins were visitors. They looked so much alike someone asked them "When you two get up in the morning, do you wonder which one you are?" The same day across the hall a substitute teacher was apologizing to the pupils because she could not teach as well as the regular teacher.

As no food is like another, neither is one person exactly like another, even in multiple births. Every person is himself individual with his peculiar personality traits, height, frame, coloring, blood type, down to the setting of his hairs on his head.

From all of this we can see God is an individual Creator. Each food He gives has its own flavor, and each person He makes has his own individuality. God calls for each one's unique service. He takes no pleasure in our trying to copy another. He wants me to render myself with my peculiar characteristics and abilities, and likewise He wants the other fellow to perform in his own manner.

Consider how awful it would be if every food we had tasted like a bowl of oatmeal. What if each person in robot fashion performed like the other? How dull life would be!

There's no one like you! You as a person are as peculiar as the onion!

I will praise thee; for I am fearfully and wonderfully made: marvelous are thy works; and that my soul knoweth right well. My substance was not hid from thee, when I was made in secret, and curiously wrought in the lowest parts of the earth. Thine eyes did see my substance, yet being unperfect; and in thy book all my members were written, which in continuance were fashioned, when as yet there was none of them. (Psalm 139:14-16 KJV)

March 14   Everybody Needs Somebody

There was a little vine in a big green-and-white pot in my house. It refused to grow even though I watered it, pulled back the curtain and let the sunshine in on it, and kept the dirt around it just right. In another pot a plant flourished abundantly so much so that I had to keep transferring parts of it to other pots.

Having run out of pots one day, I stuck one of the vine's roots into the pot with the stunted plant. "That'll slow you down," I thought to myself.

Then one morning weeks later, when I was watering the plants, I noticed something happening in the green-and-white pot. I was not surprised to see the newly rooted one showing vibrant signs of life. But a surprise! I saw a tiny new leaf coming out on the stunted vine! And it looked like it had grown a little taller. I was so pleased I showed it to my husband. I said "Now doesn't that just show you everybody and every living thing needs company."

We talked about it more and could see how this illustrated how one alone does little, if anything, and makes hardly any showing. But two or more associating help each other along and make a showing. We need each other for encouragement, to listen to each other, to laugh together, to shed tears with each other, and, yes, even to criticize each other at times.

I believe Jesus meant this when He said, "Neither do men light a candle and put it under a bushel, but on a candlestick; and it gives light unto all that are in the house." That in essence is saying, a single light or a lone person neither puts out an effective influence, whereas when the single light is put with other lights, or a single Christian joins other

Christians in the church, there is an effective, noticeable influence. Also, Jesus sent His disciples out two by two rather than each one apart from the other. It was for the purpose of companionship that He ordained marriage of man and woman so that all Adams might not be alone.

The idea goes even further, such as in world mission programs for the Lord's kingdom work. One local church would not be able to support missionaries in all the countries of the world, but by cooperating with other local churches also supporting the mission work, the job gets done.

God never intended for man to be a loner. A person needs others all along the journey of his life.

And the Lord God said, It is not good that man should be alone; I will make him an help meet for him. (Genesis 2:18 KJV)

Two are better than one; because they have a good reward for their labor. For if they fall, the one will lift up his fellow: but woe to him that is alone when he falleth; for he hath not another to help him up. (Ecclesiastes 4:9-10 KJV)

Again I say unto you, That if two of you shall agree on earth as touching any thing that they shall ask, it shall be done for them of my Father which is in heaven. For where two or three are gathered together in My name, there am I in the midst of them. (Matthew 18:19-20 KJV)

March 15   Waiting for New Bodies

If you want to see a vivid illustration of what the sin of one man brought upon the human race, just take a walk through the halls of a nursing home. To me, it speaks of the sorrowing results of the Adamic sin more than even the funeral home. There you can see the bodies of mankind wearied out, perishing daily. Some of them are not even sick, that is with any particular disease. They are just slowly dying.

The brow weather-beaten from dawn-to-dawn toil
is now swathed by attendants in white.
Hands quaveringly now folded once handled the soil,
the plow handle, the hoe, a little boy's kite.
Eyes that beheld loved ones' faces with delight,
a sunrise, the green of a thriving field . . .
can no longer read or discern day from night,
but only stare blankly and to darkness yield.

Ears once attuned to a field bird's call,
the cry of a child, the notes of a song,
catch no words now, hear nothing at all—
Intense stillness makes his every day long.
A mouth that shared laughter and spoke words of love
gives a parched stammer and an occasional smile.
'though his shell is useless, his site's far above
where he'll get a new body after a while.

--Carlene Poff Baker

In a moment, in the twinkling of an eye, at the last trump: for the trumpet shall sound, and the dead shall be raised incorruptible, and we shall be changed. For this corruptible must put on incorruption, and this mortal must put on immortality. So when this corruptible shall have put on incorruption, and this mortal shall have put on immortality, then shall be brought to pass the saying that is written, Death is swallowed up in victory. (1 Corinthians 15:52-54 KJV)

March 16 **God Fills Vacancies of His Choice**

At the commencement exercises of the high school my daughter attended, since its beginning, The Battle Hymn of the Republic has been sung by the choir, composed of all members including seniors, where the seniors in caps and gowns would leave their pompous seats and take their places on the risers. The traditional rule of two accompanists at the piano was met—one of them being a junior and the other a senior.

When our daughter was a junior, she played Pomp and Circumstance for the near 300 graduates. Then her graduating senior friend and she played The Battle Hymn of the Republic. When she was a senior, her junior friend played for the more than 300 seniors' processional. Then she took her place on the bench (opposite from the year before) for the last time to play for her class, The Battle Hymn of the Republic.

The junior pianist elevated and someone in the sophomore class moved up to her place the next year.

In like manner, the Lord set His church in the world to perpetuate until His return. He gave her the Commission. One graduating class after another has moved on to greater heights (heaven), leaving those coming behind to sit on the bench perpetuating His work.

The choir director would panic sometimes when at the beginning of the year it appeared there was no one qualified to succeed the present pianist. But one always turned up just the same. It seems the church's light burns low sometimes, with few workers, and many who do not seem to be able to do anything, but there is always someone who rises to the need and gets the work done.

I am confident that the high school my daughter attended has always had someone to play "The Battle Hymn of the Republic." I am undauntedly confident that so long as the Lord's church is in the world someone will be faithful to the task and accomplish as forcefully and effectively as the stalwart soldiers who have already graduated.

Moses My servant is dead; now therefore arise, go over this Jordan, thou, and all this people, unto the land which I do give to them, even to the children of Israel. (Joshua 1:2 KJV)

Go ye therefore, and teach all nations, baptizing them in the name of the Father, and of the Son, and of the Holy Ghost: Teaching them to observe all things whatsoever I have commanded you: and, lo, I am with you alway, even unto the end of the world. Amen. (Matthew 28:19-20 KJV)

But ye shall receive power, after that the Holy Ghost is come upon you: and ye shall be witnesses unto Me both in Jerusalem, and in all Judaea, and in Samaria, and unto the uttermost part of the earth. (Acts 1:8 KJV)

March 17   Produce Fruit for God's Glory

I observed two peach trees growing in my backyard side by side. The young tree stood straight and leafy, but there was only one peach on that tree. The one fruit was large and perfectly shaped and would be very desirable to a hungry person.

The older tree, on the other hand, had limbs drooping to the ground weighted down with its many peaches. There were all sizes, some of them knotty and misshapen, but they were fruit produced by the tree. Each piece of fruit from these trees possessed something to keep a starving person from dying. Within each one there was another seed with the potential of producing more fruit.

I thought how like fruit-bearing Christians these two trees were. There are those who seem to produce more fruits. Then there are those who produce only one fruit, and sometimes that fruit is hard to see. Whether the fruit produced is great or small, God is pleased with fruit bearing and will bless and reward accordingly. Only God knows the extent of the reach of each individual fruit.

Just as the seed in the peach off the young tree may be planted in fertile earth and bring forth a like tree that may produce an abundant fruitage, so the Christian who brings forth only one good fruit or is influential in winning only one person to the Lord, that fruition may in turn become a missionary, writer of a particular Christian book or tract, or speaker on a nationwide radio ministry who will win thousands to the Lord.

I was proud of the two trees, each doing its own work. So is God pleased when each of us is faithful to her task, the seemingly insignificant or the stupendous, and fruit is borne . . . "some a hundredfold, some sixtyfold and some thirtyfold."

Abide in Me, and I in you. As the branch cannot bear fruit of itself, except it abide in the vine; no more can ye, except ye abide in Me. I am the Vine, ye are the branches: He that abideth in Me, and I in him, the same bringeth forth much fruit: for without Me ye can do nothing. (John 15:4-5 KJV)

March 18   The Lord and I Can Leap Any Hurdle

My daughter and I went to see her friend's graduation ceremony in another town. We spent the night and then brought the friend home with us so she could see our daughter's graduation.

The mother in that home was hospitable, warm and radiant. I had known her in years past when she was ill, nervous and extremely unhappy. During our conversations I asked her what had happened that made the wonderful change. She said she learned to "praise the Lord."

She explained, "I stopped trying to change the course of things in my own power. I just gave myself into the Lord's hands to take control." She said she commenced taking each situation as it came and with the Lord's help coped with it. Then in essence she said, "Lord, I'm ready for the next hurdle. We can leap it together."

She is living proof that the scripture, Philippians 4:13, when practiced, works: "I can do all things through Christ which strengthens me." She is an example of 2 Corinthians 12:10: "Therefore, I take pleasure in infirmities, in reproaches, in necessities, in persecution, in distresses for Christ's sake; for when I am weak, then am I strong."

All people are to praise God, and that includes the sick, suffering, those weighted down with problems they cannot solve or circumstances that cannot be turned around.

Both young men, and maidens; old men, and children: Let them praise the name of the Lord: for His name alone is excellent; His glory is above the earth and heaven. (Psalm 148:12-13 KJV)

Let the saints be joyful in glory: let them sing aloud upon their beds. (Psalm 149:5 KJV)

Let every thing that hath breath praise the Lord. Praise ye the Lord. (Psalm 150:6 KJV)

March 19   Why Go to Church? Simple as A, B, C

America as a struggling nation needs her citizens in church.

Battlefield personnel fight with purpose when those for whom they are serving go to church.

Colleges gain courage in their fight against moral decay when their enrollees go to church.

Daughters, little and big, count on their parents going to church.

Educators, religious and academic, find teaching rewarding and with purpose when their students go to church.

Friends know your friendship is sincere when you go to church.

God is delighted, glorified, exalted, and showers with blessings those who go to church.

Hell's Occupants had rather you go to church and learn how not to come to that awful place.

I, myself benefit in all realms of living: spiritual, intellectual, moral, emotional and relational when I assemble with other believers in church.

Judges of Courts would find their task much easier if more who appear before them were church attendants.

Kinfolks, distant and close, are proud to be kin to someone who goes to church.

Lonely shut-ins know you genuinely care about them after you've been to church.

Missionaries scattered across the world take on new strength when they know that the folks back home are going to church.

Neighbors feel a safeness and security living near you because you go to church.

Outcasts to Society know they are not forgotten by those who go to church.

Presidents and other leaders of our land recognize the safety and strength of our nation is brought about by the God of those who attend church.

Questioning Crowds observe the peace and serenity that envelops those who go to church.

Rioters would be defeated by an overwhelming come-back to the church.

Sons become great men when they stay in and with the church.

To sum it *Up*: Go to Church. The *Victory* can be *Won*. *Xert Yourself* with *Zeal*!

Therefore, my beloved brethren, be ye steadfast, unmovable, always abounding in the work of the Lord, forasmuch as ye know that your labor is not in vain in the Lord. (1 Corinthians 15:58 KJV)

March 20   My Body – Temple of the Holy Spirit

When I was born, I had nothing to do with what I looked like. All of my features were designed by God through my parents as instruments. They nurtured me and my physical body began to develop. That living, breathing body was fashioned that I might glorify God in it.

When I became a child of God by the new birth, my body became the temple of the Holy Spirit, who came and made His abode within. Immediately I learned my body was not my own (1 Corinthians 6:19-20). So, with this in mind, I am responsible for the care and keeping of my body until it goes down in death. Thus, I must resolve to keep physically fit.

First, I will use my body in manual labor. In Proverbs 31 we find the industrious woman busy with cares of home and family as well as in the business world. We do our bodies good when we are busy in physical labor.

Also the Apostle Paul advised "And that ye study to be quiet, and to do your own business, and work with your own hands, …" (1 Thessalonians 4:11 KJV)

Second, I must eat and drink properly, in moderation, not over-indulgent or gluttonous (Philippians 4:5 and Proverbs 23:2). Someone aptly said "We dig our graves with our forks and spoons."

Third, I must get ample rest in sleep. Solomon said that sleep is important. So, I must be sure to get sufficient sleep and leave my worries with the Lord. Then, my sleep will be peaceful (Proverbs 3:24). The Psalmist David admonished me not to deprive myself of an appropriate amount of sleep by worrying (Psalm 127:2). Sleep is the best nerve-untangler, a great aid to the process of healing, as well as an energy rejuvenator.

Fourth, I must take time for recreation. It is as needful for the body to rest and play as to work. In Mark 6:31-32 we find Jesus looking upon His physically exhausted, anxious, questioning disciples. "And He said unto them, Come ye yourselves apart into a desert place and rest awhile: for there were many coming and going, and they had no leisure so much as to eat. And they departed into a desert place by ship privately." Each of us has things we like to do for fun. As long as the doing is honorable and does not transgress God's commandments nor cause you to neglect your duty to God, it will serve to give you enjoyment so that you can return to your work refreshed and renewed.

Resolving to care for our physical bodies these ways will help us keep our *temples* in good shape so that we can be used by Him for His glory.

March 21   Moral Purity

Moral purity is synonymous with virtuous, meaning also chaste, unspotted, acting in conformity to the moral or divine law, abstaining from vice.

A compact catalog of moral standards is found in Jesus' Sermon on the Mount in Matthew chapters 5, 6, and 7. To name a few: (1) Do no murder, no, not even to be angry with your brother without cause; (2) Make amends of offense with another before you can worship God; (3) Do not commit the outward act of adultery, nor the inward act of lust toward another; (4) Take your marriage vows seriously, staying married to one spouse so long as you shall live; (5) Turn the other cheek to him who smites the one; (6) If compelled to go one mile, go two; (7) Give, not expecting a return; (8) Do good to your enemies; (9) Do good deeds quietly; (10) Pray secretly; (11) Forgive.

For other rules, read what Paul says in Ephesians 6, Philippians 2 and 4, Colossians 3, and 1 Thessalonians 5. In the latter mentioned chapter, verse 22 summarizes it all: Abstain from all appearance of evil.

One Bible example of a morally good person is Joseph. He turned the other cheek to his brothers and let them do with him what they would. He maintained integrity and honesty when he was enticed to commit adultery. He steadfastly abstained from all appearance of evil, even though he was consequently falsely accused, framed, and imprisoned for wrongs of which he was not guilty. He held no malice toward his enemies. Later, when he controlled the life of his brothers, who had earlier mistreated him, he lovingly forgave and nourished them during the time of famine.

There may be times in each of our lives where we must turn the other cheek rather than retaliate; go the second mile when our going the first one is unappreciated; and lose ties with friends whose activities could fall into the category of *appearance of evil*. But we must strive toward a standard of excellence in moral purity which God expects of us, especially during these dark days of prevalent wickedness.

March 22   Keep Mind Stayed on Christ

We hear much today of mental breakdowns and someone "blowing his mind." Recovery from such is seldom complete and only then with God's help.

The Apostle Paul says to young Timothy, "For God hath not given us the spirit of fear; but of power, and of love, and of a sound mind." (2 Timothy 1:7 KJV) God has entrusted the most of us with a sound mind, and, just like with our physical bodies, we are to glorify God with it. Thus, I must take care of my mind that it might be usable by God.

First, I must know God's Word. I must acquaint myself with scripture. Better still, I must commit as much scripture as possible to memory.

There is a story of a prisoner of war who declared he withstood brainwashing and cruel mental tortures only because he remembered a few scriptures that he kept in the forefront of his thoughts. Also, an elderly Christian woman in a nursing home said she could endure the cries and wails of other residents of the home who were in pain, because she would recall a memorized scripture, which she would repeat over and over during such a time. Also, she was glad she had taken time to memorize scriptures because her eyesight was almost gone and she could not read her Bible.

The Psalmist David knew something of this when he said, "I will delight myself in Your statutes; I will not forget Your word," and "O but I love Your law! It is my meditation all the day."

Paul catalogs the things our minds should dwell on in Philippians 4:8. They are whatsoever things are true, honest, just, pure, lovely, of good report, all to prove virtuous and praiseworthy.

In our society sordid, depressing matters are all around us with which we have to cope. It is trying to the mind, to be sure, but we have Jesus to look to who also lived on earth during a time of extreme degradation. He is goodness, purity, and righteousness personified. He has given us a sound mind, and we have access to His Word and His presence as we go along, so that we can remain mentally sound.

Thy word have I hid in my heart that I might not sin against thee. ... O how love I thy law! It is my meditation all the day. (Psalm 119:11, 97 KJV)

Thou wilt keep him in perfect peace whose mind is stayed on thee, because he trusteth in thee. (Isaiah 26:3 KJV)

March 23   **God Uses Many to Win One**

Have you ever won anyone to the Lord? If you say yes, you are being presumptuous. If you answer no, you may not be saying the truth. That question cannot be answered truthfully by any one of us. It can be made known only at the Judgment Seat of Christ when all things are revealed.

Some who have thought they never made an impression for good on anyone will have a joyful surprise at that time.

When indeed a sinner turns to the Lord for salvation, it is unlikely that one single person won him. Possibly many contributed to his turning from sin to the Lord. One may have planted, another watered, others cultivated, another pulled out weeds from around the sown seed, and others added fertilizer.

One person said her salvation came about because her mother taught her Bible stories as a small child. She was taken to church where Sunday School teachers taught her the scriptures. The ministers expounded from the pulpit words of life. She watched the lives and listened to everyday conversations of dedicated Christians. All these persons were used by the Holy Spirit to bring conviction to that person's heart. When she gave her heart to the Lord as a teenager, neither the evangelist, who had preached that night, nor the woman who knelt by her side in the altar, were the only two to influence her to accept Christ.

Young Timothy, whom Paul referred to as *my son in the ministry*, was not won entirely by Paul. Paul says the godly teaching of his mother and grandmother had made him *wise unto salvation*.

We think Deacon Stephen's sermon was what influenced Paul to become a Christian. But Paul himself said he had an excellent knowledge of the scriptures before his conversion. Paul must have overheard some of the goings-on of the church meetings and observed the peculiar lives of the members whom he hailed to prison when he persecuted the church. No doubt, all of these things were weighing him down upon him when God brought the increase there on the Damascus Road.

We should not become distressed when we do not see friends turn to the Lord before our eyes. We should continue living a godly life, praying secretly, and standing ready to tell the plan of salvation, for who knows what part the Holy Spirit will use to bring that lost soul to Jesus for salvation.

> Now he that planteth and he that watereth are one: and every man shall receive his own reward according to his own labor. For we are laborers together with God: ye are God's husbandry, ye are God's building. (1 Corinthians 3:8-9 KJV)

Preach the word; be instant in season, out of season; reprove, rebuke, exhort with all longsuffering and doctrine. (2 Timothy 4:2 KJV)

March 24   Do My Part to Make the World Better

A man and his little son were in the den of their home. The man was reading the newspaper and his son was playing on the floor. They talked to each other companionably off and on during that time. Soon the man saw his son was tiring of the activity and needed something else to occupy his time.

Finally. he thought of an idea that would keep the boy occupied for at least an hour. He had seen an intricate map of the world in one of his magazines, so he found the magazine and tore the page with the map into tiny pieces and challenged his son to put the puzzle back together. You can imagine his surprise when the little fellow proudly marched back up to his Dad with the picture intact in just a few minutes.

"Why, how did you ever do it so fast, Billy?" his father asked.

"It was easy, Dad," replied his son. "There was a picture of a man on the back of that page. I put the man together and then turned it over to the picture of the world. See, Dad, when you get the man right, the world will be right."

God does not give us power to change our world, but He does give us power to change ourselves. As we change for the better, we in turn affect the world around us and make a difference for the better.

Let your light so shine before men, that they may see your good works, and glorify your Father which is in heaven. (Matthew 5:16 KJV)

Let your speech be alway with grace, seasoned with salt, that ye may know how ye ought to answer every man. (Colossians 4:6 KJV)

Let no man despise thy youth; but be thou an example of the believers, in word, in conversation, in charity, in spirit, in faith, in purity. (1 Timothy 4:12 KJV)

March 25   Youth Into Old Age for God – Best Life

After a silver-haired guest with tranquil manners had left the home of friends, a young daughter, greatly impressed, commented to her mother: "Oh, if I could be an old lady like that, so sweet, serene, lovable and beautiful, I wouldn't mind being old."

The insightful mother replied: "Remember—that kind of person was not grown in a hurry. It took her a long time to make her what she is. And if you are going to be that kind of an old lady, if you are going to paint yourself to be a portrait like she is, you had better start mixing the colors and brushing a few strokes now."

One's conduct is now determined by the person's relation to the divine order. The time to become truly related to God is at the beginning, the days of youth. Then, the whole life will be regulated by the divine will and be lived in the way that will commend the divine favor.

Remember now thy Creator in the days of thy youth, while the evil days come not, nor the years draw night, when thou shalt say, I have no pleasure in them. (Ecclesiastes 12:1 KJV)

I beseech you therefore, brethren, by the mercies of God, that ye present your bodies a living sacrifice, holy, acceptable unto God, which is your reasonable service. And be not conformed to this world: but be ye transformed by the renewing of your mind, that ye may prove what is that good, and acceptable, and perfect, will of God. (Romans 12:1-2 KJV)

But grow in grace, and in the knowledge of our Lord and Savior Jesus Christ. To Him be glory both now and for ever. Amen. (2 Peter 3:18 KJV)

In a McGuffey's Reader there is a story of an old clock that suddenly quit running. The reason: the clock counted the number of times it would have to tick in one year—31,536,000 times. This was just too many ticks for a weary clock, so it lost its morale and stopped. Later it was explained to the clock all that was expected of it was to tick just one tick at a time. With this reflection, the old clock regained its spirit and began running again.

So it is with human beings. Trying to live life in the lump is frightening. All that is necessary is to do your duty moment by moment.

Jesus said He would take care of us "day by day" and asked that we not worry about tomorrow. When tomorrow would come it would be another today. We must trust Him day by day. He knows what He has planned for each day He gives us.

So teach us to number our days, that we may apply our hearts unto wisdom. (Psalm 90:12 KJV)

Take therefore no thought for the morrow: for the morrow shall take thought for the things of itself. Sufficient unto the day is the evil thereof. (Matthew 6:34 KJV)

Vex not at small beginnings. The oak began as an acorn. The oozing through of one drop of water started the proverbial break of the dike. The muscular athlete once had trouble crawling. The university graduate started in kindergarten. The massive international oil industry began with a little shallow well. Today's colossal aviation can be traced back to a most humble beginning. A cent is the beginning of a dollar.

History is packed with stories of little people who launched out and performed stupendous feats. Some of them are found in the scriptures. One was a little shepherd boy named David, the youngest of Jesse, who seemed to have no military traits at all, as did his older brothers. Yet,

God chose him to defeat the giant Goliath. Then, when it came time for someone to succeed King Saul, God chose this lad.

There was also a little Hebrew maiden who served a military officer's wife. When she knew Naaman had leprosy, she told her mistress that if he went to see Israel's prophet Elisha, he would be healed. It came to pass he did at last go to inquire of the prophet, and the strange healing solution to the problem the man finally adhered to, and he was healed.

Then there was Gideon, who felt so insignificant to be used by God. But when he obeyed God, he led the Israelite army of 300 men to defeat the Midianite armies numbering thousands.

In our own country, just think of how little people have accomplished great things—Edison, Colonel Sanders, Walt Disney, to name a few, and in the King of King's ministry, D. L. Moody, Billy Graham, and the list goes on and on. Never think you are too small to be used by God in His kingdom's work!

And Samuel said unto Jesse, Are here all thy children? And he said, There remaineth yet the youngest, and, behold, he keepeth the sheep. And Samuel said unto Jesse, Send and fetch him: for we will not sit down till he come hither. And he sent, and brought him in. Now he was ruddy, and withal of a beautiful countenance, and goodly to look to. And the Lord said, Arise, anoint him: for this is he. Then Samuel took the horn of oil, and anointed him in the midst of his brethren: and the Spirit of the Lord came upon David from that day forward. (1 Samuel 16: 11-13 KJV)

Now Naaman, captain of the host of the king of Syria, was a great man with his master, and honorable, because by him the Lord had given deliverance unto Syria: he was also a mighty man in valor, but he was a leper. And the Syrians had gone out by companies, and had brought away captive out of the land of Israel a little maid; and she waited on Naaman's wife. And she said unto her mistress, Would God my Lord were with the prophet that is in Samaria! for he would recover him of his leprosy. And one went in, and told his lord, saying, Thus and thus said the maid that is of the land of Israel. ... So Naaman came with his horses and with his chariot, and stood at the door of the house of Elisha. And Elisha sent a messenger unto him, saying, Go and wash in Jordan seven times, and thy flesh shall come again to thee, and thou shalt be clean. . . . Then went he down, and dipped himself seven times in Jordan, according to the saying of the man of God: and his flesh came again like unto the flesh of a little child, and he was clean. (2 Kings 5:1-4; 9-10, 14 KJV)

And the Lord looked upon him, and said, Go in this thy might, and thou shalt save Israel from the hand of the Midianites: have not I sent thee? And he said unto Him, Oh my Lord, wherewith shall I save Israel? behold, my family is poor in Manasseh, and I am the least in my father's house. And the Lord said unto him, Surely I will be with thee, and thou shalt smite the Midianites as one man. (Judges 6:14-16 KJV)

March 28   Honesty: The Apex

"Honesty's the best policy," so declared Miguel de Cervantes, who lived from 1547 to 1616. But honesty is more than policy, more than discretion, more than course of action based on entity interest.

While honesty will deal you a better hand in all the affairs of life, it is not engaged in just for gain. It is a principle that is adhered to for honesty's sake because it is right. Doing the honest thing is something the honest person does because he is honest; to be dishonest would be out of character. The honest person is honest, win or lose!

Abraham Lincoln said: "I am not bound to win, but I am bound to be true. I am not bound to succeed, but I am bound to live up to what light I have."

Recompense to no man evil for evil. Provide things honest in the sight of all men. (Romans 12:17 KJV)

Providing for honest things, not only in the sight of the Lord, but also in the sight of men. (2 Corinthians 8:21 KJV)

Now I pray to God that ye do no evil; not that we should appear approved, but that ye should do that which is honest, though we be as reprobates. For we can do nothing against the truth, but for the truth. (2 Corinthians 13:7-8 KJV)

March 29   Known by the Company You Keep

Remember the story of long ago about the old parrot who flew out of a farm house and joined some crows in a watermelon field? The farmer, not knowing this and wanting to protect the fruit of his labors, blasted them with his shotgun. The results were three dead crows and one ruffled parrot with one missing toe.

The farmer tenderly took the parrot home where the excited children gathered around and asked, "What happened to your toe?"

"Bad company! Bad company!" answered the parrot.

He spoke wiser than he knew. His foolish choice of associates had endangered him.

So it is with people—bad days come from bad companions, and better days come from better acquaintances

George Washington said: "'Tis better to be alone than in bad company."

My son, if sinners entice thee, consent thou not. If they say, Come with us, let us lay wait for blood, let us lurk privily for the innocent without cause: Let us swallow them up alive as the grave; and whole, as those that go down into the pit: We shall find all precious substance, we shall fill our houses with spoil: Cast in thy lot among us; let us all have one purse: My son, walk not thou in the way with them; refrain thy foot from their path: For their feet run to evil, and make haste to shed blood. (Proverbs 1:10-16 KJV)

He that walketh with wise men shall be wise: but a companion of fools shall be destroyed. (Proverbs 13:20 KJV)

March 30 Attributes of a Great Ruler

When a man holds dear the rights of men—as George Washington did; and prefers ethics to profit—as Washington preferred; and believes that man was not designed by the All-wise Creator to live for himself alone—as Washington believed; and is courageous enough to stand up to hostility—as Washington stood; and towers above deception and political leanings—as Washington towered; and refuses to be a king—as Washington refused; and trusts in the All-wise Disposer of events—as Washington trusted; and sees heroics in ragged men with a cause—as Washington saw—that man is truly worthy of rulership and a place in the hearts of his countrymen.

George Washington said: "The red coats do look best, but it takes the ragged boys to do the fighting."

Moreover thou shalt provide out of all the people able men, such as fear God, men of truth, hating covetousness; and place such over them, to be rulers of thousands, and rulers of hundreds, rulers of fifties, and rulers of tens. (Exodus 18:21 KJV)

Lord, who shall abide in thy tabernacle? who shall dwell in thy holy hill? He that walketh uprightly, and worketh righteousness, and speaketh the truth in his heart. He that backbiteth not with his tongue, nor doeth evil to his neighbor, nor taketh up a reproach against his neighbor. In whose eyes a vile person is contemned; but he honoreth them that fear the Lord. He that sweareth to his own hurt, and changeth not. (Psalm 15:1-4 KJV)

Corruptible Will Put on Incorruption

Man's only hope of permanence is found in his dual nature—flesh and spirit. This enables him to lay aside the corruptible body for an incorruptible one suited to an everlasting habitation.

Benjamin Franklin, one of the world's brightest and most versatile genius, had this thought in mind, because he had the following epitaph inscribed on his tomb in the old cemetery of Christ Church in Philadelphia:

Like the cover of an old book, its contents torn out, and stripped of its lettering and gilding, lies here for worms; But the work shall not be lost, for it will (as he believes) appear once more in a new and more elegant edition, revised and corrected by the Author.

For this corruptible must put on incorruption, and this mortal must put on immortality. So when this corruptible shall have put on incorruption, and this mortal shall have put on immortality, then shall be brought to pass the saying that is written, Death is swallowed up in victory. (1 Corinthians 15:53-54 KJV)

Pilgrims Just Passing Through

Christians are sustained in the assurance that they are pilgrims passing through this earthly habitat to another shore where loved ones await their arrival. I attribute the fitting poem below to Henry Van Dyke's *Upon the Seashore.*

I am standing upon the seashore. A ship at my side
Spreads her white sails to the morning breeze
And starts for the blue ocean . . .
I stand and watch her
Until at length she hangs like a speck of white cloud.

When someone at my side says, "There! She's gone!"
There are other eyes watching her coming,
And other voices ready to take up the glad shout,
"Here she comes!"

The days of our years are threescore years and ten; and if by reason of strength they be fourscore years, yet is their strength labor and sorrow; for it is soon cut off, and we fly away. (Psalm 90:10 KJV)

Then shall the dust return to the earth as it was: and the spirit shall return unto God who gave it. (Ecclesiastes 12:7 KJV)

April 2   ## Work to Be Done Today

A farmer lay ill in a hospital. For weeks he struggled between life and death, much of the time in a coma. One morning he regained consciousness and asked his nurse what time it was. She replied, "It is springtime, and nature is bursting forth with renewed vigor."

"Springtime," said the patient. "Then I can't die now, for it is time to plow."

For all of us, now is plowing time. The only time to which we are joined is now. With this attitude, today can be yours, and so can tomorrow when it becomes today.

God has always intended for mankind to work, labor with brain and brawn. God is always working and Jesus said He too is working. We know one thing Jesus is doing – He told His disciples that when He would leave them, after His death, burial and resurrection, He would go and prepare places for them in heaven where they would live after this earthly life is over. In the beginning, immediately after God created Adam, every person's ancestor, He told him to tend to the Garden of Eden.

Work is good and honorable. We must be like all of God's creatures – even the little ants – and work while we have this day.

And the Lord God took the man, and put him in the g2arden of Eden to dress it and to keep it. (Genesis 2:15 KJV)

So built we the wall; and all the wall was joined together unto the half thereof: for the people had a mind to work. (Nehemiah 4:6 KJV)

Go to the ant, thou sluggard; consider her ways, and be wise: which having no guide, overseer, or ruler, provideth her meat in the summer, and gathereth her food in the harvest. (Proverbs 6:6-8 KJV)

But Jesus answered them, My Father worketh hitherto, and I work. (John 5:17 KJV)

And that ye study to be quiet, and to do your own business, and to work with your own hands, as we commanded you. (1 Thessalonians 4:11 KJV)

April 3   Right is Always Right

Henry Clay, one of America's most eloquent statesmen, had just proposed a political gesture to an associate.

"It will ruin your prospects for the Presidency," was the lightning response of his friend.

But just as quickly, Mr. Clay remarked, "I had rather be right than be President."

Switching the tags of right and wrong might have switched some votes, but not the right of right and the wrong of wrong.

No matter what other qualifications one has, he can never be the right person on any job unless he does right.

He that justifieth the wicked, and he that condemneth the just, even they both are abomination to the Lord. (Proverbs 17:15 KJV)

Woe unto them that call evil good, and good evil; that put darkness for light, and light for darkness; that put bitter for sweet, and sweet for bitter! (Isaiah 5:20 KJV)

April 4   Aim Higher and Higher

It was the multi-character P. T. Barnum, the circus king, who said, "If I shoot at the sun I may hit a star." We don't always reach our aims, but, O how much higher we rise because we try. Achievement is not something that just drops in an idle person's lap. Having no aim means no success. No ambition sprouts leaden feet.

Every person is capable of raising himself; there are two requirements: first, look up, and, second, walk up. The higher the aim, in keeping with reality, the more transcendent the person becomes.

Now therefore give me this mountain, whereof the Lord spake in that day; for thou heardest in that day how the Anakims were there, and that the cities were great and fenced: if so be the Lord will be with me, then I shall be able to drive them out, as the Lord said. And Joshua blessed him, and gave unto Caleb the son of Jephunneh Hebron for an inheritance. (Joshua 14:12-13 KJV)

I press toward the mark for the prize of the high calling of God in Christ Jesus. (Philippians 3:14 KJV)

April 5   Fashioned in God's Image

There is but one race – human - and to it every man belongs. All have the same lineage, a common ancestry: Adam and Eve. Thus *man* – not *kinds* – is the master race with dominion over every other creature.

And in the gain or loss of one man the whole race is lifted or lowered. Being of the same ancestry, blood should be stronger than prejudice; it is, and in time shall prevail. In this, the rationalism of a common blood, is one hope for civilization.

> And hath made of one blood all nations of men for to dwell on all the face of the earth, and hath determined the times before appointed, and the bounds of their habitation. (Acts 17:26 KJV)

April 6   Scars: Medals for Perseverance

Lumbermen and scientists who examined a big tree in California after it had been cut down found that it began growing 271 years before the birth of Christ. When it was 516 years old it was partly burned, the charred portions of the bark and trunk being visible far inside the giant. Other fires left their marks upon it in 1441, 1580 and 1797. The latter made an enormous scar eighteen feet wide.

That tree is a lesson in patient endurance in overcoming obstacles! Burned, disfigured and partly destroyed, each time it covered up its wounds, broadened out and continued its reach toward the sky. The good persevering man is like a tree planted by the rivers of water.

> And he shall be like a tree planted by the rivers of water, that bringeth forth his fruit in his season; his leaf also shall not wither; and whatsoever he doeth shall prosper. (Psalm 1:3 KJV)

> Therefore, my beloved brethren, be ye steadfast, unmovable, always abounding in the work of the Lord, forasmuch as ye know that your labor is not in vain in the Lord. (1 Corinthians 15:58 KJV)

> We are troubled on every side, yet not distressed; we are perplexed, but not in despair; persecuted, but not forsaken; cast down, but not destroyed; always bearing about in the body the dying of the Lord Jesus, that the life also of Jesus might be made manifest in our body. (2 Corinthians 4:8-10 KJV)

April 7   No Retirement from the Lord's Work

When Longfellow was old, an enthusiastic admirer asked him how it was that he was able to keep so vigorous and write so beautifully. Pointing to a tree clothed in blooms, the aged poet replied: "That apple tree is very old, but I never saw prettier blossoms upon it than those it now bears. The tree grows a little new wood every year, and I suppose it is out of that new wood that those blossoms come. Like the apple tree, I try to grow a little new wood every year."

Yes! Though time cuts furrows in my face, may I ever grow and be fruitful.

> The righteous shall flourish like the palm tree: he shall grow like a cedar in Lebanon. Those that be planted in the house of the Lord shall flourish in the courts of our God. They shall still bring forth fruit in old age; they shall be fat and flourishing; to shew that the Lord is upright: He is my rock, and there is no unrighteousness in Him. (Psalm 92:12-15 KJV)

April 8   No Double-Standards in God's Economy

A baker in a little country town bought the butter he used from a nearby farmer. One day he suspected that the bricks of butter were not full pounds, and for several days he weighed them. He was right. They were short weight, and he had the farmer arrested.

At the trial the judge said to the farmer, "I presume you have scales to weigh your bricks of butter."

"No, Your Honor."

"Then how do you manage to weight the butter you sell?" inquired the judge.

The farmer replied, "That is easily explained, Your Honor, I have balances and for a weight I use a one-pound loaf of bread I buy from the baker."

This illustrates the injustice of many people. They have two standards: one for themselves and another for the other fellow.

It is so necessary to man's well-being and society's good that a person think first of what is right and then practice the right thing.

A false balance is abomination to the Lord: but a just weight is His delight. (Proverbs 11:1 KJV)

To do justice and judgment is more acceptable to the Lord than sacrifice. (Proverbs 21:3 KJV)

April 9   Judge Not

Justice probes beneath appearances, knowing that things are not always what they seem. The Bible says "Judge not according to the appearance, but judge righteous judgment" (John 7:24 KJV). Surface appearance may be so different from the hidden facts. Taking this into consideration, justice is slow to pass judgment.

> Pray do not find fault with the man that limps—
> Or stumbles along the road
> Unless you have worn the shoes he wears—
> Or struggled beneath his load.
> There may be tacks in his shoes that hurt
> Though hidden from view,
> Or the burdens he bears placed on your back—
> Might cause you to stumble too.

Judge not, that ye be not judged. For with what judgment ye judge, ye shall be judged … (Matthew 7:1, 2 KJV)

But why dost thou judge thy brother? Or why dost thou set at naught thy brother? or why dost thou set at nought thy brother? for we shall all stand before the judgment seat of Christ. For it is written, As I live, saith the Lord, every knee shall bow to me, and every tongue shall confess to God. So then every one of us shall give account of himself to God. (Romans 14:10-12 KJV)

There is one lawgiver, who is able to save and to destroy: who art thou that judgest another? (James 4:12 KJV)

April 10 — Just to be Called Brother

A beggar at a street corner, with bony hands and pallid lips, asked for an alms. The passerby searched his pockets and found that he was without money. Then he took the beggar's hand in his and said, "I'm sorry, my brother, but I have nothing with me."

The worn face lighted up, and the beggar said, "But you called me brother – that is a great gift."

That is what mankind needs most of all, a love that extends the heart to another and calls him brother. Neither eloquence, nor knowledge, nor faith, nor sacrifice will serve as a substitute for it.

And above all things have fervent charity among yourselves: for charity shall cover the multitude of sins. (1 Peter 4:8 KJV)

April 11 — Hold Fast Your Rein

An old stage-driver, after thirty years of experience, commented that he had never hurt a passenger nor a horse, simply because he always kept a firm grip on the reins. "The whole secret is in not letting the horses get the start," he said.

Good philosophy for controlling self: Hold the reins; hold yourself back from bad habits. You never become a runaway in a thing you never start. No one is stronger than his will. Unless you have will power, you have no power. For where there is no will, there is no way.

Let us not therefore judge one another any more: but judge this rather, that no man put a stumbling block or an occasion to fall in his brother's way. (Romans 14:13 KJV)

I therefore so run, not as uncertainly; so fight I, not as one that beateth the air: But I keep under my body, and bring it into subjection: lest that by any means, when I have preached to others, I myself should be a castaway. (1 Corinthians 9:26-27 KJV)

April 12   Laugh at Bumps in Your Road

When a little boy on his scooter hit a bump in the sidewalk and took a tumble, he paused and then burst out laughing.

A passer-by who saw him with a bloody, skinned knee, asked: "What's so funny? Why laugh about it?"

The boy replied, "Mister, I'm laughing so I won't cry."

Occasionally we hit a rough place in life and suffer a spill. Now that is a good time to laugh, lest we lose self-possession. Laughing is a safety-valve which lets off the tensions of irritations.

Why art thou cast down, O my soul? And why art thou disquieted within me? Hope in God: for I shall yet praise Him, who is the health of my countenance, and my God. (Psalm 43:5 KJV)

A merry heart maketh a cheerful countenance: but by sorrow of the heart the spirit is broken. (Proverbs 15:13 KJV)

A merry heart doeth good like a medicine: but a broken spirit drieth the bones. (Proverbs 17:22 KJV)

April 13   Kindness Gets the Job Done

"I'll shape you," said the hammer to a piece of iron as his blows fell upon it. But every blow dulled the edge more and more.

"Let me change you," said the saw as he ripped into the cold metal. However, after losing several teeth, the saw had to quit.

Next, the little flame gently said, "Let me try." And it warmly embraced the iron, and there it stayed until the hardness melted. The forging was then an easy task.

There are hearts like this. They resist blows and cuttings, but soften under the warmth of kindness.

Bear ye one another's burdens, and so fulfill the law of Christ. (Galatians 6:2 KJV)

And be ye kind one to another, tenderhearted, forgiving one another, even as God for Christ's sake hath forgiven you. (Ephesians 4:32 KJV)

April 14   The Hub of the Home

One day in our Bible study group, our lesson was about how to live together in the home. As a warm-up, each lady was asked to tell what she remembered as being the best things about her life as a child growing up.

Invariably, every good thing had to do with her mother. She was the central figure in the home, whether the thing remembered had to do with playing, singing, or doing chores.

In spite of all the activity going on in our country today, where groups are trying to take the woman out of her place and put her into another role, the woman in the home – the *mother* – remains the special one. She's the hub of the wheel of activity. She's the sun in the solar system of balance in the home. She's the whole committee on arbitration, encouragement, education, sympathy, health, honor, and integrity.

Gaining praise from her is the goal most sought after; winning her smile brings greatest delight. Her presence makes the worst case of sickness better. Her voice lightens the heaviest load of heartache. Her prayers touch the heart of God.

I was fortunate to have had my mother until she turned eighty-eight. We lived in the same town, and I was able to see and talk with her daily. Whether our mothers are living or dead, there will be a special tenderness in our hearts when we think of them.

Also, may we who are mothers realize the esteemed place in which God has set us, and may we be the right kind of *hub* and *sun* in our homes so that when our children remember the *best things* of their earlier years, *Mother* will be the central figure.

The aged women likewise, that they be in behavior as becometh holiness, not false accusers, not given to much wine, teachers of good things; that they may teach the young women to be sober, to love their husbands, to love their children, to be discreet, chaste, keepers at home, good to their own husbands, that the word of God be not blasphemed. (Titus 2:3-5 KJV)

April 15   Time for Recess

Day by day I hear folks say that time is flying. I never hear anyone say time is dragging. I remember when I was in my youth it seemed days were longer and there was time for everything with a lot of time left over.

I wonder as we scurry along if this is really living the abundant life the Lord has come to give us. Are we filling our lives with too many unnecessary activities and not finishing the necessary ones essential to purpose. Are we squeezing out time for aloneness with God, meditation, seeking His will?

As found in Mark 6, the Greatest Person who ever walked on this earth left the place of much activity now and then where He could have stayed and done many good things, no doubt, but He said to His disciples, "Come ye yourselves apart into a desert place and rest awhile." There had been so much coming and going that they had had no leisure so much as to eat. And they departed into a desert place by ship privately.

Someone once suggested it would be great if all cars, buses, trains, trucks, airplanes, telephones, radios, and machinery (and computers) should be stopped for ten minutes every day to give people an opportunity to sit still and think without interruption.

It is impossible to stop the whole world, but we can stop ourselves occasionally. We can give up rushing for an hour or so, and take time for a mental stock-taking and meditation about God. Whether we have the responsibilities of a large business or a small one on our shoulders, or only the single life to work out, this period of withdrawing from the whirl of business or the clamor of other people's demands on our time can be valuable.

Standing aside we can get a new perspective on our way of life that shows it as a whole. From a distance we can see from the outside the walls that enclose us, as others see them. We see the edifice we have raised in its true proportions against those which stand beside and around it.

These quiet times might enable us to hear the voice of God, to learn the life-giving currents of His will, and to taste His grace. It's high time each of to take time to say "Hold it! I'm going apart to a desert place to rest awhile."

> Rest in the Lord, and wait patiently for Him: fret not thyself because of him who prospereth in his way, because of the man who bringeth wicked devices to pass. (Psalm 37:7 KJV)

> For thus saith the Lord God, the Holy One of Israel; In returning and rest shall ye be saved; in quietness and in confidence shall be your strength: and ye would not. (Isaiah 30:15 KJV)

> Come unto Me, all ye that labor and are heavy laden, and I will give you rest. Take my yoke upon you, and learn of Me; for I am meek and lowly in heart: and ye shall find rest unto your souls. (Matthew 11:28-29 KJV)

April 16   ## Filthy Talk Off-Limits

"I dwell in the midst of a people of unclean lips," Isaiah lamented long ago. Today my lamentation is the same. Everywhere I go—to the grocery store, post office, to the corner mail box—from the garbage collector, the children playing half a block away, across my neighbor's fence—curse words, smutty slang words, foul, filthy language—blasts from every direction, without regard for anyone who might be hearing it.

When I turn on the TV, I hear it. When I turn on the radio, I hear it. When I read books, sometimes even the newspaper, I see it. I hate it! I despise it! I hold no respect for anyone who uses it!

Sometimes I think it is a bird's eye view of what hell is going to be like. At least we have a restraining force in the world now to hold it back somewhat – the Lord's born-again children in whom His Spirit dwells. Imagine how it will be when the Lord's people are not in the midst of this people of unclean lips.

After hearing this sort of talk, my ears feel dirty, and my mind feels unclean. I always get a headache and want to cry (sometimes I do).

Our wonderful Lord knows it is rough on us to live in the evil world. He has a purpose for our being here. He does not take us out of the world but supplies a thorough cleansing agent—His word.

So, when I feel unclean after hearing such filthiness, I must run to the scriptures for cleansing. I return to my tasks refreshed. I know, however, as I go about my duties, I will get my ears dirty again and will feel the need to scrub again with God's word.

Won't it be wonderful when in the place Jesus has gone to prepare for us there will be nothing there to defile? Then it will not be said, "I dwell in the midst of a people of unclean lips." Praise the Lord!

Let the words of my mouth, and the meditation of my heart, be acceptable in thy sight, O Lord, my strength, and my redeemer. (Psalm 19:14 KJV)

Deliver me, O Lord, from the evil man: preserve me from the violent man; which imagine mischiefs in their heart; continually are they gathered together for war. They have sharpened their tongues like a serpent; adders' poison is under their lips. (Psalm 140:1-3 KJV)

And the tongue is a fire, a world of iniquity: so is the tongue among our members, that it defileth the whole body, and setteth on fire the course of nature; and it is set on fire of hell. (James 3:6 KJV)

Some of us can remember when the first REA lines moved into our neighborhoods. How prestigious we felt when they wired our houses and cut holes in the ceilings of all the rooms to install lights. Nobody knew what a wall switch was. Each light had a string hanging down from it to pull it off and on.

Remember how it was when you came home after dark and all the members of the household participated in flailing their hands around over their heads trying to catch hold of the light string? Sometimes you whacked the other fellow in the process. When one latched onto the string and pulled the light on, didn't everybody look funny at their respective stations in the room?

The thing about it, the string hadn't moved. The problem was the seekers were in the wrong places.

Sometimes you and I flail about in the darkness feeling for God awkwardly. Sometimes we whack or hurt each other in the process. One may seek God in an emotional experience. Another tries to attract God's attention to come to where he is by doing good works. Another will try to find Him by turning over a new leaf.

God remains true and stationed in the same place. He never wanders away. We *pull the string* by exercising faith in Him, confessing our sins, and depending upon Him for strength to do our service. Then we can stay in touch with Him, and won't have to flail about, by regular prayer and reading, meditating on and practicing His written Word.

When we come to where He is, and has been all the time, we come into His light. Our ways are then illuminated. We can see where we are going, and our going has definite direction and purpose.

Have not I commanded thee? Be strong and of a good courage; be not afraid, neither be thou dismayed: for the Lord thy God is with thee whithersoever thou goest. (Joshua 1:9 KJV)

Thou art near, O Lord; and all thy commandments are truth. (Psalm 119:151 KJV)

The Lord is nigh unto all them that call upon Him, to all that call upon Him in truth. (Psalm 145:18 KJV)

Let us draw near with a true heart in full assurance of faith, having our hearts sprinkled from an evil conscience, and our bodies washed with pure water. (Hebrews 10:22 KJV)

April 18   God-Guided Leaders a Must

It is a rare privilege to visit the shrine of Valley Forge. The road leads through the glorious Pennsylvania hills, past a majestic boulder upon which is mounted a bronze tablet telling the story of the heroic, ragged, barefoot army which tramped over snow and ice to that strategic range in which nestles Valley Forge. There the father of our country kept his small band of heroes intact at the most serious moment during the War of the Revolution.

Washington was fundamentally a good man. He believed fervently in the power of prayer. There is a tradition that he was seen repeatedly during the early morning hours in the garden of his simple headquarters on bended knee in devotion.

One of his prayers after his inauguration reads: "Almighty God, we make our earnest prayer that Thou wilt keep the United States in Thy holy protection; that Thou wilt incline the hearts of the citizens to cultivate a spirit of subordination and obedience to government (order); to entertain a brotherly affection and love for one another and for their fellow citizens of the United States."

Washington's wisdom has been an inspiration for large numbers of our leading men and women in every decade since his time. He had the mysterious foresight of seeking to build a nation upon the bedrock of strong patriotism, unquestioned integrity, opportunities for all, high ideals, and love of God.

Be wise now therefore, O ye kings: be instructed, ye judges of the earth. Serve the Lord with fear, and rejoice with trembling. (Psalm 2:10-11 KJV)

Blessed is the nation whose God is the Lord; and the people whom He hath chosen for His own inheritance. (Psalm 33:12 KJV)

April 19   Listening Friend Lifts Loneliness

Charles Swindoll told about an ad in a Kansas newspaper that offered to simply listen to someone talk for thirty minutes without comment for five dollars. Swindoll said, "It wasn't long before this individual was receiving ten to twenty calls a day. The pain of loneliness was so sharp that some were willing to try anything for a half hour of companionship.

Life is designed for companionship, not isolation; for intimacy, not loneliness. Some people prefer isolation, thinking they can handle life's problems without the help of others. We are not here on earth, however, to serve ourselves or care just for ourselves, but to serve God and others in His name. Don't isolate yourself and try to go it alone. Seek godly companions and you will find life's journey a whole lot easier.

> There is one alone, and there is not a second; yea, he hath neither child nor brother: yet is there no end of all his labor; neither is his eye satisfied with riches; neither saith he, For whom do I labor, and bereave my soul of good? This is also vanity, yea, it is a sore travail. Two are better than one; because they have a good reward for their labor. For if they fall, the one will lift up his fellow: but woe to him that is alone when he falleth; for he hath not another to help him up. (Ecclesiastes 4:8-10 KJV)

April 20   Christian Soldier Stays His Post

Arlington National Cemetery near Washington D.C. is the site of the Tomb of the Unknown Soldiers from various wars. This memorial is guarded twenty-four hours a day every day. The soldiers performing this duty are volunteers from the elite Third U. S. Infantry, the Old Guard, headquartered in Fort Myer, Virginia.

These guards train and prepare rigorously for this honored task. They serve alternating shifts of twenty-four hours on and twenty-four hours off. Each day the guard is ceremonially changed at thirty-minute-to two-hour intervals. Every guard takes the assignment very seriously and no guard forsakes his post.

Such steadfast devotion in the *Christian* army was in the mind of Jude when he wrote his letter. The faithful Christian soldier never deserts his post. He stays true to the faith even though some abandon it.

Thou therefore endure hardness, as a good soldier of Jesus Christ. No man that warreth entangleth himself with the affairs of this life; that he may please him who hath chosen him to be a soldier. (2 Timothy 2:3-4 KJV)

Beloved, when I gave all diligence to write unto you of the common salvation, it was needful for me to write unto you, and exhort you that ye should earnestly contend for the faith which was once delivered unto the saints. (Jude verse 3 KJV)

April 21   No Quitting – Game's Not Over

In 1929, Roy Riegels, a University of California football player, made Rose Bowl history. In the second quarter, he grabbed a Georgia Tech fumble and headed for the end zone ... the wrong end zone. For a moment, the other players froze. Then Benny Lom, a teammate of Roy's, started chasing him. After making a spectacular sixty-five-yard fumble return, a confused Riegels was tackled by his own teammate, just before he scored for his opponents.

Riegels' team had to punt with their backs at their own goal line. Georgia Tech blocked the punt and earned a two-point safety, which would provide the margin of victory. The final score was Georgia Tech 8, University of California 6.

At the half, the University of California players filed glumly to their dressing room. Spectators and players alike were wondering what Riegels' fate would be in the hands of University of California's Coach

Price. In the dressing room, Riegels slumped in a corner, put his face in his hands and cried uncontrollably.

Coach Price was silent and offered no half-time pep talk. What could he say? As they got ready to go out for the second half, his only comment was "Men, the same team that played the first half will start the second."

The players started for the door, all but Riegels. Coach Price walked to the corner where Riegels sat and said quietly, "Roy, didn't you hear me? I said, the same team that played the first half will start the second." Roy replied, "Coach, I can't do it. I've ruined you, the University of California and myself. I couldn't face that crowd in the stadium to save my life."

Coach Price put his hand on his player's shoulder and said, "Roy, get up and go back; the game is only half over." So Roy Riegels went out to play again, even harder, said the Georgia Tech players afterward, than they had ever seen anyone play before. Makes one think, "What a coach!"

Possibly each of us has made big mistakes causing embarrassment to the degree we wanted to dig a hole in the ground and hide from the world. It is at those times that God comes to you and me in the person of His Son, Jesus Christ, and says, "Get up, my Son (Daughter), and go back in the game—the game is only half over." That's the Gospel of the Second Chance. Makes us exclaim "What a God!"

This reminds us of the Apostle Peter, who acted impulsively in so many ways and spoke rashly at times. The worst thing perhaps he thought he did against Jesus was to vow to never deny Him, and yet he did three times. But Jesus was His Savior, and the One who bestowed second chances to erring followers. He had denied Him three times, but Jesus provided a way to have Peter say "I love You" three times. After that Jesus told Peter of the great task He laid upon him. He would be the staunch leader of the others as they launched out on the Great Commission.

So when they had dined, Jesus saith to Simon Peter, Simon, son of Jonas, lovest thou me more than these? He saith unto Him, Yea, Lord; thou knowest that I love thee. He saith unto him,

Feed my lambs. He saith to him again the second time, Simon, son of Jonas, lovest thou me? He saith unto Him, Yea, Lord; thou knowest that I love thee. He saith unto him, Feed my sheep. He saith unto him the third time, Simon, son of Jonas, lovest thou me? Peter was grieved because He said unto him the third time, Lovest thou me? And he said unto Him, Lord, thou knowest all things; thou knowest that I love thee. Jesus saith unto him, Feed my sheep. (John 21:15-17 KJV)

April 22   God Can Make Any Wall Topple

After the surrender of Germany in 1945, Berlin was divided into two sections. East Berlin was under control of the Soviet Union, while West Berlin was under control of the United States, Britain, and France.

In 1961, the Soviets built a ninety-six-mile wall to prevent East Germans from defecting to the West. Over the next twenty-eight years more than five thousand East Germans did escape to freedom in the West, but more than two hundred were killed while trying.

On June 12, 1987, President Ronald Reagan gave a speech at the Berlin Wall in which he said, "Mr. Gorbachev, tear down this wall." Two years later, the wall was torn down. After a quarter century of suppression to Communism, the people of Germany were finally reunited.

For Christians, real freedom comes when we bow to Jesus in faith that He can tear down any wall He chooses to. David was very familiar with the great power of God in his life. He said on one occasion:

Thine, O Lord, is the greatness, and the power, and the glory, and the victory, and the majesty: for all that is in the heaven and in the earth is thine; thine is the kingdom, O Lord, and thou art exalted as head above all. Both riches and honor come of thee, and thou reignest over all; and in thine hand is power and might; and in thine hand it is to make great, and to give strength unto all. (1 Chronicles 29:11-12 KJV)

A man bought his wife a keepsake box that was supposed to glow in the dark. He turned out the light, but the box was not visible. Disappointed, he complained, "I've been cheated!"

The next day his wife noticed these words on the box: "If you want me to shine at night, keep me in the sunlight all day." So, she put her gift in a sunny window. That evening when she turned out the light, the box had a brilliant glow.

Just like that box, Christians should constantly expose themselves to the Son so they will take on His nature and shine as lights in a dark world.

> Ye are the light of the world. A city that is set on an hill cannot be hid. Neither do men light a candle, and put it under a bushel, but on a candlestick; and it giveth light unto all that are in the house. Let your light so shine before men, that they may see your good works, and glorify your Father which is in heaven. (Matthew 5:14-16 KJV)

> For ye were sometimes darkness, but now are ye light in the Lord: walk as children of light. (Ephesians 5:8 KJV)

April 24   Trustworthy Father

A family was hiking at a place where there was a Falls. As they neared the top of the Falls, the husband and father of the family heard a voice above him yell, "Hey, Dad! Catch me!"

He turned to see his eight-year-old son joyfully jumping off a rock straight at him. He had jumped first and then yelled for his dad to catch him. Fortunately, he landed in his dad's arms, and both fell to the ground.

For a moment after the father caught him, he could hardly talk. When he found his voice, he gasped in exasperation, "Son, can you give me one good reason why you did that?"

Without missing a beat, he said, "Sure, because you're my dad." His whole assurance was based on the fact that his father was trustworthy. He felt he could live life to the fullest because his father could be trusted.

Many Bible characters portray this kind of trust in their God. One in particular was Job who said, "Though He slay me, yet will I trust Him" (Job 13:15).

If ye then, being evil, know how to give good gifts unto your children, how much more shall your Father which is in heaven give good things to them that ask him? (Matthew 7:11 KJV)

For as many as are led by the Spirit of God, they are the sons of God. For ye have not received the spirit of bondage again to fear; but ye have received the Spirit of adoption, whereby we cry, Abba, Father. The Spirit itself beareth witness with our spirit, that we are the children of God: And if children, then heirs; heirs of God, and joint-heirs with Christ; if so be that we suffer with Him, that we may be also glorified together. (Romans 8:14-17 KJV)

April 25   Never Cause One to Stumble

A man had his nine-year-old daughter, Molly, in the car with him when he went to the bank to cash a check. As they sat in the drive-through lane waiting their turn, the man told Cindy that a good way to end their errand-running day would be a couple of servings of rich chocolate ice cream.

But as they later stopped at the ice cream drive-through, the man noticed the bank had given him a hundred dollars too much money, so he turned around and headed back toward the bank to return the excess. His daughter pleadingly said, "But, Dad, we could buy lots more ice cream with that money."

Undeterred he went back to the bank, and told the teller of the mistake. Although he did not know her, she knew him. She told him that she realized her mistake as they drove off, and she wondered if he would be an honest man.

Then it hit the man. He could have sold his integrity that day for only one hundred dollars. Not only that, but his dishonesty would have affected the faith of two people: the bank teller and his nine-year-old Molly.

Let us not therefore judge one another any more: but judge this rather, that no man put a stumbling block or an occasion to fall in his brother's way. (Romans 14:13 KJV)

But take heed lest by any means this liberty of yours become a stumbling block to them that are weak. (1 Corinthians 8:9 KJV)

April 26   Power Inside Clay Vessels

A minister enjoyed his hobby of gardening. During those years he acquired a large number of clay pots. They were of the reddish brown in color with a small hole in the bottom. However, not one of them would last. They cracked easily. Some would even disintegrate when they fell to the soft soil of the garden. They even crumbled in his hands.

Somewhere along the way, while holding one of these clay pots in his hands, a verse of the Apostle Paul in his letter to the Corinthians came to his mind (*see below*). We are easily breakable, like the clay pot. But the Apostle does not leave us there. He goes on to say we have a treasure in our earthen jars. We carry a treasure within our mortal being. The treasure is the Holy Spirit who has taken up residence in our mortal bodies the moment we received Jesus as Savior into our hearts. He is the one who gives us power and capacity to be more than merely human in our reach toward the life to which Jesus invites us. We have a hope, a gift which we carry in our bodies. We are indeed vessels of God to be used by Him for His glory.

But we have this treasure in earthen vessels, that the excellency of the power may be of God, and not of us. (2 Corinthians 4:7 KJV)

       Forsake Not Corporate Worship

A man told his pastor, "Pastor, I don't have to go to church to worship," as he placed his hands on his hips. The pastor thought a few minutes and then replied, "You don't have to go home to be married either, but is sure enhances your relationship if you do."

For a person to be rightly related to God, worship is essential. Worship is an expression of our love for God. It reveals our hearts.

Hundreds of years after God instructed the Israelites as recorded in Leviticus about worship, He reminded believers to hold fast to His promises and not to forsake gathering for worship. Relating to God in worship makes all the difference in our lives.

Appropriate worship involves commitment, thanksgiving, confidence in God, and repentance. God wants His children to be active in worship.

As Christians, we should show the world that our Savior deserves our best in worship. He is worthy of our deepest expressions of praise and our best proclamation of the Bible in teaching and preaching. He gave nothing less than His best. He deserves nothing less than ours.

O come, let us worship and bow down: let us kneel before the Lord our maker. For He is our God; and we are the people of His pasture, and the sheep of His hand. Today if ye will hear His voice. (Psalm 95:6-7 KJV)

Let them exalt Him also in the congregation of the people, and praise Him in the assembly of the elders. (Psalm 107:32 KJV)

I was glad when they said unto me, Let us go into the house of the Lord. (Psalm 122:1 KJV)

And let us consider one another to provoke unto love and to good works: Not forsaking the assembling of ourselves together, as the manner of some is; but exhorting one another: and so much the more, as ye see the day approaching. (Hebrews 10:24-25 KJV)

A vine clings to an oak tree and in so doing endures times that threaten its survival. If a violent storm arises and the vine is on the side of the tree away from the wind, the vine is protected. If the vine is on the exposed side of the tree, the wind serves only to press the vine closer to the tree it already clings to.

In the storms of life God will at times set Himself between us and the fury of the storm and so protect us from it. At other times He will expose us to the storm so that its ravages will press us closer to Him.

From the earliest records of God's people, violent winds have tested their faith. But spiritual heroes, like Job and Joseph, have found that even as they wrestle with life's challenges, they are pressed closer to God. They are examples of trusting God in all circumstances of life, especially the painful ones.

The eleventh chapter of the book of Hebrews is the "Hall of the Faithful," listing many who met the tests of faith victoriously. They stood up to evil rulers, lived righteously, clung to the promises of God, even when circumstances made those promises seem obscure. They stood undaunted against persecution and fought valiantly.

During times of testing we are often tempted to seclude ourselves. Like a wounded animal, we want to retreat and lick our wounds. But the command of Jesus to be the light of the world is not for the good times alone. You shine your brightest when surrounded by darkness.

Impressive testimonies are not built by wealth and prosperity. They are earned in the valley of the shadow of death. Once others realize the depth of your faith, God will use your suffering for His glory. The ultimate aim of the Christian life is to point others to Christ, and nothing will do that like enduring hardships.

> And not only so, but we glory in tribulations also: knowing that tribulation worketh patience, and patience, experience; and experience, hope. (Romans 5:3-4 KJV)

> Who through faith subdued kingdoms, wrought righteousness, obtained promises, stopped the mouths of lions, quenched the

violence of fire, escaped the edge of the sword, out of weakness were made strong, waxed valiant in fight, turned to fight the armies of the aliens. (Hebrews 11:33-34 KJV)

April 29   Rugged Road to Godly Maturity

Some flowers, such as the rose, must be crushed for their full fragrance to be released. Some fruits, such as the sycamore, must be bruised if they are to attain ripeness and sweetness. Some metals, such as gold, must be heated in the furnace to become pure.

The attaining of godliness – the process of becoming a mature Christian – requires similar special handling. It is often through pain, suffering, trouble, adversity, trials, and even temptation that we develop spiritual discipline and become refined and enriched.

Where do troublesome times come from? Either through the devil's role in the Fall and the resulting curse on all of creation, or through personal attack, Satan brings them into our lives. But only with *God's* permission. And during every time of sorrow God watches over us.

Your suffering has a purpose. God is constantly testing and shaping your faith. His desire is for you to be conformed to the image of His Son.

God loves you so much that He will do whatever it takes for you to become your best. Instead of whining during your suffering, turn to and trust in God.

When a wood sculptor wants to create a work of art, he starts with a log and begins to fashion it with a sharp chisel. The log, which might otherwise have been burned in a fireplace, becomes a beautiful masterpiece to display on the mantle. God's working in our lives may sometimes be painful, yet His ultimate purpose is to produce a masterpiece in us.

So, expect to be crushed as the rose as you go about serving Jesus Christ, knowing that the perfume will spill out into the air and God will see that others take notice, all for His glory. Also, as God uses His sculpting tools on you, realize He is creating in you're a masterpiece that will bring glory to Him and delight and peace in your heart.

And we know that all things work together for good to them that love God, to them who are the called according to His purpose. (Romans 8:28 KJV)

I beseech you therefore, brethren, by the mercies of God, that ye present your bodies a living sacrifice, holy, acceptable unto God, which is your reasonable service. And be not conformed to this world: but be ye transformed by the renewing of your mind, that ye may prove what is that good, and acceptable, and perfect will of God. (Romans 12:1-2 KJV)

April 30   The Other Side

When a person has gotten from the doctor the words, "There is nothing else we can do for you. All we can do is make you as comfortable and pain-free as possible." Then, that person begins to focus on his or her death. Often questions are asked of how will it be on the other side.

And no one knows, but sometimes dying persons say words or show facial expressions of things. For instance, when my mother was near death, and she came to after being in a coma, she looked up at me beside her bed and said, Oh, I thought I'd be with Daddy and Edward."

When Grandpa Poff died, his daughter Barbara was beside his bed, and she said just before he died, his wrinkled face spread with a big, toothy smile, like he had seen someone.

Another story I heard long ago was when on the battlefield a soldier and his best buddy were involved. One of them died, but as the unharmed one held him in his arms, the one dying grasped his friend's hand, and said, "Oh, what a beautiful place! Come and go with me!"

And though after my skin worms destroy this body, yet in my flesh shall I see God: Whom I shall see for myself, and mine eyes shall behold, and not another; though my reins be consumed within me. (Job 19:26-27 KJV)

Blessed be the God and Father of our Lord Jesus Christ, which according to His abundant mercy hath begotten us again unto a lively hope by the resurrection of Jesus Christ from the dead, To an inheritance incorruptible, and undefiled, and that fadeth not away, reserved in heaven for you. (I Peter 1:3-4 KJV)

May 1   God's Kind of Forgiveness

During the Korean war, an American soldier left behind his loving wife to go fight for his country. They daily wrote of their love for each other, but then his letters stopped. She continued to write in hopes that all was well. But one day the sad news came; her husband had found a Korean woman whom he loved. He planned to stay with her in that country after the war. The brokenhearted wife remained faithful to her husband, and sought to keep in contact with him as best she could.

Then news came from the Korean woman. She first told of the husband's illness. Her next communication told of his death and his astonishing request. Would the American wife let the Korean woman and her two children (by the husband) live with her in America? The problem was their rejection in Korea because of the illegitimate nature of his relationship with the Korean woman. The husband wanted them to have a better life in America. He had continued to trust his wife, even though he had betrayed her.

Could the American wife possibly take them to live with her? With a prayer in her heart, she sent the plane fare for the Korean woman and her husband's two sons. But how would it be when they met? The plane landed with the Korean woman and her two boys. The miracle of God's grace took place. Both women wept as they embraced. An outcast woman and her two small boys found a new home through the godly forgiveness of an American woman.

Put on therefore, as the elect of God, holy and beloved, bowels of mercies, kindness, humbleness of mind, meekness, longsuffering; forbearing one another, and forgiving one another, if any man have a quarrel against any: even as Christ forgave you, so do ye. And above all these things put on charity, which is the bond of perfectness. And let the peace of God rule in your hearts, to the which also ye are called in one body; and be ye thankful. (Colossians 3:12-15 KJV)

May 2   Time Invested in Eternity

Each morning we receive one brand-new, shiny, golden day, set with twenty-four jeweled hours. Every one of us receives precisely the same amount of time each day. Today some of us will use our hours to God's glory and the betterment of humankind. Others will waste them, and still others will use these for evil. What we do with this day will have eternal consequences.

Time is an irreplaceable asset. Once it is gone, we can never get it back. Scripture says that one day time will end and eternity will begin. When that happens, we will have to account for how we spent the time God gave us.

So, what are wise investments of our time? We invest our time wisely when we concern ourselves with the things that concern God – when our hearts break with the sorrows that break God's heart. And what breaks God's heart more than lost people? Jesus came to seek and to save the lost. He gave His life looking for us. He died to redeem us. This was His joy. Christ finished the work God gave Him, and He sends us into the world to do the same. As we invest our time in people and the great work of Christ's kingdom, we invest in eternity!

Create in me a clean heart, O God; and renew a right spirit within me. Cast me not away from thy presence; and take not thy Holy Spirit from me. Restore unto me the joy of thy salvation; and uphold me with thy free spirit. Then will I teach transgressors thy ways; and sinners shall be converted unto thee. (Psalm 51:10-13 KJV)

Now then we are ambassadors for Christ, as though God did beseech you by us: we pray you in Christ's stead, be ye reconciled to God. (2 Corinthians 5:20 KJV)

Wherefore He saith, Awake thou that sleepest, and arise from the dead, and Christ shall give thee light. See then that ye walk circumspectly, not as fools, but as wise, redeeming the time, because the days are evil. (Ephesians 5:14-16 KJV)

May 3   Little Folks Become Big with God

"You're a dunce!" That's what she said. "You 're a dunce and I'm going to fail you." And the teacher failed Einstein in mathematics.

"I'm sorry. We don't want you in our choir. You can't sing, so don't come back." But Jerome Hines became the greatest basso instrumentalist the Metropolitan Opera has ever known.

Many of us have horrible self-images because we believe lies rather than the truth of God. Often, we've heard from parents or misguided authorities that we have no worth. "You can't do it. You tried before, and you blew it."

As the old maxim puts it, "God don't make no junk."

We should learn from the *successful failures*. Walt Disney went broke seven times before he succeeded. Thomas Edison made fourteen thousand experiments that failed before he developed the incandescent light. Babe Ruth recorded the most strike outs in the history of baseball, yet he became one of the greatest hitters of all time. When these people were told they couldn't hit the mark, they just kept on shooting.

"I can do all things through Christ which strengthens me." (Philippians 4:13) Who made that claim? Paul the Apostle, with his thorn in the flesh and his weak eyes, who was *contemptuous* in his speech. The same Paul who turned the world upside down for Christ.

When we have doubts about our abilities to accomplish something, let's ask God to tell us the truth about Whose we are. He wants us to do a great work in Him.

I am the Vine, ye are the branches: He that abideth in Me, and I in him, the same bringeth forth much fruit: for without Me ye can do nothing. (John 15:5 KJV)

And He said unto me, My grace is sufficient for thee: for My strength is made perfect in weakness. Most gladly therefore will I rather glory in my infirmities, that the power of Christ may rest upon me. Therefore I take pleasure in infirmities, in reproaches, in necessities, in persecutions, in distresses for Christ's sake: for when I am weak, then am I strong. (2 Corinthians 12:9-10 KJV)

May 4   Don't Let Possessions Possess You

Many of us have read writings of Dr. Peter Marshall, the famous Senate chaplain of many decades ago. There was even a movie about him, titled "A Man Called Peter." A particular story where he was involved had to do with giving tithes and offerings. I want to relate it here:

A man started out well. He succeeded in business. He lived his life as John Wesley encouraged: "Make all you can, save all you can, give all you can." This man tithed regularly, and God blessed him as he did so.

But as this man became more and more prosperous, he found tithing more and more difficult. One day he came to Peter Marshall, the famous Senate chaplain of decades ago, and said, "Dr. Marshall, I have a problem. I've tithed now for some time. It wasn't too bad when I made $20,000 a year. I could give the $2,000. But, you see, I now make $500,000 a year, and there's just no way I can afford to give away $50,000 a year."

Dr. Marshall said, "Yes, sir, I see that you do have a problem. I think we ought to pray about it. Dear Lord, this man has a problem, and I pray that you will help him. Lord, reduce the salary back to the place where he can afford to tithe."

This man started out having mastery over things, but ultimately things had mastery over him. Money makes a wonderful servant but a terrible lord.

But godliness with contentment is great gain. For we brought nothing into this world, and it is certain we can carry nothing out. And having food and raiment let us be therewith content. But they that will be rich fall into temptation and a snare, and into many foolish and hurtful lusts, which drown men in destruction and perdition. For the love of money is the root of all evil: which while some coveted after, they have erred from the faith, and pierced themselves through with many sorrows. (1 Timothy 6:6-10 KJV)

May 5   Do It for God's Glory

A gentleman was walking down the street, and he passed a large construction site where a group of men were laying brick. He asked one of the workers, "What are you doing?"

The man answered, "I'm laying bricks, stupid. What does it look like I'm doing?"

The gentleman asked another man, "What are you doing?"

The second replied, "I'm making a wall."

The passerby asked a third man, "What are you doing?"

He said, "I am building a magnificent cathedral to the glory of God."

What's the difference between the narrow vision of the first two men and the great vision of the third man? The third man saw the ultimate purpose of his work to glorify God.

Whatever God has called us to do, we should pursue excellence both professionally and personally. We should make it our end to glorify God in all we do, and God will help us achieve the highest quality of which we are capable. Even the simplest, most mundane task will ultimately result in a magnificent cathedral of glory to our God.

Whether therefore ye eat, or drink, or whatever ye do, do all to the glory of God. (1 Corinthians 10:31 KJV)

And whatsoever ye do in word or deed, do all in the name of the Lord Jesus, giving thanks to God and the Father by Him. (Colossians 3:17 KJV)

May 6   Dispel Darkness with Your Light

Sir Henry Lauder, a famous Scotsman of the turn of the century, watched a lamplighter one evening at the Hotel Cecil. "I was sitting in the gloaming (dusk), and a man passed the window. He was the lamplighter. He pushed his pole into the lamp and lighted it. Then he went to another and another. Now I couldn't see him. But I knew where he was by the lights as they broke out down the street, until he had left a beautiful avenue of lights."

Jesus told His disciples that He is the light of the world, and the ones who follow Him would no longer walk in darkness but would have the light of life (John 8:12).

When talking to Nicodemus, Jesus again spoke of light coming into the world, but that men loved darkness rather than light because of their evil deeds (John 3:19). Therefore, the followers of Jesus, the Light of the World, are the ones who must let their lights shine brightly before those who sit in the shadow of darkness, so that they too would want this wondrous light of life. We are the lamplighters. The darkened lamps are the lives and souls of lost men and women who sit in sin's dark night, far apart from God's life and light. The flame is Jesus Christ burning within our hearts through His Spirit. The light pole is the presentation of Jesus Christ as Savior.

The world will know where we are, *what we believe*, by the lights we have lit.

Scottish Missionary to Africa John Mackenzie, prayed: "O Lord, send me to the darkest spot on earth!"

Let your light so shine before men, that they may see your good works, and glorify your Father which is in heaven. (Matthew 5:16 KJV)

For ye were sometimes darkness, but now are ye light in the Lord: walk as children of light. (Ephesians 5:8 KJV)

May 7   Thank God for His Blessings

Growing weary in body from working eighteen hours day after day, I almost worked myself into a state of self-pity. A man came into the shop where I worked. He had changed drastically. His hair was thin and his eyes looked haggard. I learned he had been taking chemotherapy. Did he complain about being weary in body? No, instead he smiled and said, "We're having a great revival meeting at our church! You ought to come and see!"

I sweated under the load of bills that kept piling up, especially the gasoline, insurance and garage charges to keep up our two vehicles. Very soon I recognized a car sitting on the bank lot with a "For Sale" sign on it. I learned the one who had owned it had lost his job and the bank had to repossess his car.

Standing in my own backyard looking up at the rainless sky and then below at the brown grass infested with army worms, I wanted to murmur. I thought of the retire coupled who had worked all their lives for their home and then they were not able to stay in it because their income was not enough to keep it. After dividing up their *keepsakes* among family members, they had to move into an efficiency apartment.

When I considered these things, I repented of my grumbling and thanked God for being so blessed. So what if I worked long hours. I was blessed with work to do and good health and energy to do it! So what if my lawn was a shaggy brown. I was blessed as being resident at that address! So what if the bills strained our budget. We enjoyed the conveniences those expenses afforded! And, oh! To have a Heavenly Father who was so mindful of me as to show me how blessed I was, the selfishness of my thinking, and to cause me to put the right value on things was the greatest blessing of all!

Bless the Lord, O my soul: and all that is within me, bless His holy name. Bless the Lord, O my soul, and forget not all

His benefits: who forgiveth all thine iniquities; who healeth all thy diseases; who redeemeth thy life from destruction; who crowneth thee with lovingkindness and tender mercies; who satisfieth thy mouth with good things; so that thy youth is renewed like the eagle's. (Psalm 103:1-5 KJV)

May 8   Redeem the Time

I have been made aware of the frailty of life more vividly lately as some of my friends and loved ones have been leaving this world frequently. Our church has experienced deaths of many of the members within the last few weeks and others are bedridden never to get up again.

But outside the church, among our townspeople, numerous business friends and acquaintances are going to meet God day by day. As recently as Friday we lost one of our business friends suddenly in unexpected death and the town is still stunned. He came by our shop often and we will miss his thunderous voice.

Life is indeed but a vapor which today is and tomorrow is gone. This realization alerts me to the fact that what I must do for Jesus I must do now while I have breath and mobility. Also, it causes me to place priceless value on being with my friends and loved ones lest death should separate us.

Let us take time to visit one more time that person we have been putting off a visit. Let's pay a compliment to the deserving now while with him to encourage him. Let us only say kind things so there won't be regrets later. We should settle all matters amiss between ourselves and others while there is opportunity.

Most of all, let's show an interest in a lost soul and let God use us through prayer, speaking and living before the lost to lead him to Christ our Savior.

The Lord God hath given me the tongue of the learned, that I should know how to speak a word in season to him that is weary ... (Isaiah 50:4 KJV)

As we have therefore opportunity, let us do good unto all men, especially unto them who are of the household of faith. (Galatians 6:10 KJV)

May 9   ## Influence Not Fenced In

There is a median with grass growing on it between our neighbor's yard and ours. Half of the median is the neighbor's and half is ours. However, whichever of us mows first in the week that one mows all of the median.

Another neighbor has a garden with nice vegetables right across the fence. When she waters her garden, she also waters my roses and tomato plants on my side of the fence.

The neighbor behind me has some tame blackberries growing on his side of the fence. He nurtures the plants on his side of the fence but they steal through the holes in the fence to our side here and there. He says we can take all we want.

This is an excellent illustration of how God's blessings upon His children overlap into others' yards. His manifold blessings toward His children cannot be contained within the bounds of where His children may be, but they shower all around on others, too. In return, when one of God's children honors God with his life, that deed will be *sprinkled over the fences* of those around him.

He that hath pity upon the poor lendeth unto the Lord; and that which he hath given will He pay him again. (Proverbs 19:17 KJV)

Give, and it shall be given unto you; good measure, pressed down, and shaken together, and running over, shall men give into your bosom. For with the same measure that ye mete withal it shall be measured to you again. (Luke 6:38 KJV)

There's a story someone told me about woman sitting in her wheelchair near her window. She saw on the very tip end of a long elm bough a beautiful oriole's nest. It was shaped like a pear and was fastened to a crotch of the limb by strong cords woven of horsehair and woolen threads. She thought it probable that no man living could weave that nest of like materials and make it so beautiful. Two little golden creatures had woven it, not for themselves but for other golden creatures of their own kind.

That day the nest swung idly in the wind. It was empty and capped with a white bonnet of snow. It would never be used again, and in time its cords would break and it would tumble down to earth. But for the woman looking at it, it still had a mission in life.

The nest had been the home of the good and the lovely. Above it had flashed the golden wings of parent birds. Beside it, the air had thrilled with the liquid sweetness of the oriole song. Within it, three little creatures had come to light and life with a mission of joyfulness in their hearts: three little messengers of harmony and sincerity, destined to carry, on swift wings, tuneful notes of love and happiness to the hearts of men.

The woman in the wheelchair recognized a shrine of beauty that made her sigh with joy. Each time she saw the oriole's nest swinging in the wind, she saw the flash of glorious wings, and heard the silver flutelike melody of a song long sung.

Like that woman, those of us who appreciate such splendor pay silent tribute to the spots where beauty has come to life: a deserted nest, a withered stem of last year's rose, a fallen tree, a torn and broken book, a fragment of a great painting, the birthplace of a noble man or woman. And we, too, sigh with joy.

Remember the days of old, consider the years of many generations: ask thy father, and he will shew thee; thy elders, and they will tell thee. (Deuteronomy 32:7 KJV)

The works of the Lord are great, sought out of all them that have pleasure therein. His work is honorable and glorious: and His righteousness endureth forever. (Psalm 111:2-3 KJV)

Remove not the ancient landmark, which thy fathers have set. (Proverbs 22:28 KJV)

May 11   Claim the Lord's Promises

A pastor and wife, Cal and Ruby, lived and served in a country church, whose congregation were farmers with little cash flow. Whatever amount the money received as offering on the first Sunday of each month was the pastor's salary for the money. Most of the time, they did well, spending frugally. However, one month, half way through the month, Ruby noticed her pantry shelves were getting emptier than usual.

While thinking on this, she walked over to the window and looked out. She saw about a dozen birds on the ground pecking the ground and eating. She remembered the scripture in Matthew 6:25-34, where Jesus said He would provide food for His children. She prayed, "Lord, I'm going to claim your promise, that just as you take care of the birds You will take care of us. I know You will provide for us somehow." She walked away from the window with a peace in her heart.

She was busying herself with dusting furniture when she heard Cal come in.

"Ruby, who has been here today?" He asked.

"Nobody; I've been here all day by myself," She replied.

"Well, somebody's been here and left three boxes of groceries on the porch. Come and see."

She was amazed at the sight! "Who could have done this, Cal?"

"Ah, here's a note," He said, taking it out of the box. "It's from Lee and Betty Burns. He reads: "We are moving out of our rental house, and we must have it ready for the new renters, our landlord says. We have all of this food that is still boxed up, and we are going to spend three months with our daughter in another state. We don't need it. We know you are pastor of the church, and sometimes people need food, and we've heard how they are provided for by your church. Please use this for someone in need."

Cal turned to see Ruby wiping tears from her cheeks.

"Well, you're not sad, are you?"

"Oh, no, Cal. I had just prayed this morning for God to supply us with some groceries, as what we bought the first of the month is almost gone. And I claimed His promise. But. I didn't expect Him to answer so quickly. Praise His wonderful name!"

And it shall come to pass, that before they call, I will answer; and while they are yet speaking, I will hear. (Isaiah 65:24 KJV)

O taste and see that the Lord is good: blessed is the man that trusteth in Him. (Psalm 34:8 KJV)

Trust in the Lord, and do good; so shalt thou dwell in the land, and verily thou shalt be fed. Delight thyself also in the Lord; and He shall give thee the desires of thine heart. Commit thy way unto the Lord; trust also in Him; and He shall bring it to pass. (Psalm 37:3-5 KJV)

Trust in the Lord with all thine heart; and lean not unto thine own understanding. In all thy ways acknowledge Him, and He shall direct thy paths. (Proverbs 3:5-6 KJV)

May 12   Your Smile Can Lift a Despairing Heart

The Big City is a lonely place. A person had stood wearily on the corner and watched the people as they boarded the streetcars. This particular time she was boarding a trolley and fortunately found a seat near a window. She settled comfortably. She then looked out and saw faces of tired, discouraged men and women, no one smiling.

Then, among the crowd, she saw a tall woman standing on the sidewalk a little to one side of the jostling crowd of commuters. She too wore a sad, lined face, and seemed to be totally unaware of her purpose. Her eyes seemed to be searching for a fortress.

Slowly her searching deep-set eyes swept the scene as though seeking to grasp some value, or searching for a friend, or for some meaning to what she saw. There seemed to be yearning in those steady grey eyes for the hills of home, for something somewhere that might make the worthwhile difference between just breathing and living.

The woman in the trolley could not take her eyes from that face. Suddenly, the woman outside looked into the trolley window and their eyes met. The woman in the window smiled at the one outside, and she smiled back. Tears began to run down the cheeks of both of them. The one in the trolley car felt in some small measure she had helped the other one, by no more than an exchanged greeting, though nothing more than a warm smile.

As the trolley car clanged away, the woman had no way of knowing how the other woman's day would be, but she knew in her heart her day was brighter. In smiling at this total stranger she had learned the secret of happiness, unlocking my calloused heart to let a little compassion into some life so desolate.

> Finally, be ye all of one mind, having compassion one of another, love as brothers, be pitiful, be courteous: not rendering evil for evil, or railing for railing: but contrariwise blessing; knowing that ye are thereunto called, that ye should inherit a blessing. (1 Peter 3:8-9 KJV)

May 13   Just Like You

A young man contracted to teach in a rural school, determined to spare no effort to do his best by his pupils. With qualms of misgivings, however, he began his work, since every teacher in recent years had been a failure at the job. Not one of them had been able to control the pupils, and two teachers had actually been driven forcibly away from the school by unruly boys.

Determining to rule his school by love and friendship instead of force, the new teacher soon noticed that some of the worst pupils had begun to like him and to respond favorably to his efforts to win their confidence and respect. Finally, every pupil was won over by the teacher's love and understanding except one big rowdy boy who persisted in ignoring the teacher's efforts to be friendly and fair, in continually disrupting the work by his unruly behavior.

At the end of the year the teacher resigned, discouraged with his failure to win the boy's respect. Going to his room to make out his final reports, feeling gloomy, disheartened, and disappointed, he found a rumpled piece of paper thrust under his door. Picking it up, he saw that it was a scrawled note from the school's "bad boy." It read:

"Dear Teacher – I am sorry I have caused you all the trouble I have this year. It hurts me because you are going away and not coming back. But when I get to be a man, I wanna be just like you."

The teacher's eyes were moist as he looked up from the paper. Suddenly the heaviness seemed lifted from his heart and a trace of a smile played across his lips as he used: "Perhaps, after all, I haven't been such a dismal failure as I thought I had been."

In the schoolrooms of the nation are many such as this young teacher. "The most potent of all indirect influences in the development of our citizenry is the influence of a good teacher," wrote Armand J. Gerson.

Let no man despise thy youth; but be thou an example of the believers, in word, in conversation, in charity, in spirit, in faith, in purity. (1 Timothy 4:12 KJV)

May 14   My Permanent Home

We had recently had our house repainted inside. When the painters had gone, we had to "move in" again. We were trying to make it look prettier for a few years when it would have to be done over again.

One night when all of my bones and muscles were aching from lifting all that heavy furniture, I remembered Jesus' wonderful words: "In my Father's house are many mansions: if it were not so, I would have told you. I go to prepare a place for you. And if I go and prepare a place for you, I will come again, and receive you unto Myself; that where I am, there ye may be also" (John 14:2-3).

Just think! The Master Designer has fashioned permanent residences for His beloved believers!

Not like our house that requires repainting and redecorating, I read in Peter's letter: "To an inheritance incorruptible, and undefiled, and fadeth not away, reserved in heaven for you, who are kept by the power of God through faith unto salvation ready to be revealed in the last time" (1 Peter 1:4-5).

I thank God for our earthly home, although it is nothing elaborate, but I look forward to the permanent place promised me because I have placed a saving trust in the Lord Jesus.

For the Lord Himself shall descend from heaven with a shout, with the voice of the archangel, and with the trump of God: and the dead in Christ shall rise first: Then we which are alive and remain shall be caught up together with them in the clouds, to meet the Lord in the air: and so shall we ever be with the Lord. (1 Thessalonians 4:16-17 KJV)

May 15   With Color and Joyful Song

Thrusting themselves upward through the snow, the first blazing spears of the crocus herald *Hallelujah!* Bulbs and seeds which last autumn appeared dry and lifeless are swelling and flowering with a new burst of *Hallelujah!* Trees that have shivered unclothed though the chill of the year are putting forth buds and leaves, ready for their appointed mission to proclaim their *Hallelujah!*

The pure white of the dogwood and the warm pink of the redbud are adorning the awakening hills with *Hallelujah!* Everywhere is a parade of colors from the palette and brush of the Master Artist.

Birds are merrily practicing their songs declaring there is new life. This is resurrection time, and all nature is answering the summons to awake and live

When we see nature reviving and flowering in the newness of life, it is reasonable to believe that we who have put our faith in the Risen Christ can claim the resurrection for ourselves!

> In a moment, in the twinkling of an eye, at the last trump: for the trumpet shall sound, and the dead shall be raised incorruptible, and we shall be changed. For this corruptible must put on incorruption, and this mortal must put on immortality. (1 Corinthians 15:52-53 KJV)

May 16   Knuckle Down and Plunge On

Samm Sinclair Baker said, ". . . knuckling down instead of knuckling under often distinguishes pro from amateur." This was directed to struggling writers. The Apostle Paul said something like that to struggling Galatian Christians and also to the Christians at Corinth. We are admonished to be mature, to grow up, to *knuckle down* to the service of the Lord. The life of a Christian is not easy, but it is profitable, pleasant, and satisfying to the soul. The abundant life is not achieved by knuckling under the load but by plunging on against seemingly insurmountable odds. We must walk, live and serve by faith, not by sight.

Satan delights to see a Christian fall under the load. Let's not give him that delight. God will provide everything we need for our journey through this world. Let's knuckle down to the job at hand, looking to Him for leadership, strength and courage to endure so that we may discharge our role duties, for His glory, the good of others, and the gladness it brings to our souls.

> Though he fall, he shall not be utterly cast down: for the Lord upholdeth him with His hand. (Psalm 37:24 KJV)

> Therefore, my beloved brethren, be ye steadfast, unmovable, always abounding in the work of the Lord, forasmuch as ye know that your labor is not in vain in the Lord. (1 Corinthians 15:58 KJV)

Watch ye, stand fast in the faith, quit you like men, be strong.
(1 Corinthians 16:13 KJV)

May 17 — Heavenly Rejoicing

The flags were flying high over my home town one day. I was one in the crowd of Boy Scouts, Air Force Base officers, representatives of other military branches, veterans and ex-prisoners of war of both world wars, and others of the citizens of our town who gathered on the court house lawn to watch the heart-tugging ceremony honoring the release of our fifty-two hostages.

A strip from a long, yellow streamer was cut each time one of the hostages was named. Eight yellow roses were laid on the grave on the lawn of a World War 2 hero in memory of the eight men who gave their lives in the rescue mission.

It was a day of rejoicing, and I felt those of us there, as well as all over our nation, appreciated our liberties more than ever.

As I watched, I thought of another type of celebration: one in heaven. Jesus said that there is rejoicing in the presence of the angels when a sinner repents. These words, in essence, mean there is rejoicing in heaven when a sinner is set free from a more terrible, vicious captor than the Iranians or any other world power. Satan has the sinner bound and there is only One who can set the sinner free: Jesus!

The sad thing about it, Satan has blinded the eyes of them who do not believe, so that many are not aware they are bound. When a sinner realizes his stand and his destiny,

Jesus stands ready to release him. No negotiations are necessary, no money must be exchanged. However, there was a great cost involved of more value than all the multiplied trillions that could be fathomed. The price has been paid by the Deliverer Himself, Jesus, with His own precious blood.

If the Son therefore shall make you free, ye shall be free indeed.
(John 8:36 KJV)

My nephew Dewayne, who was then about twelve years old, helped me mow and rake my yard. I compensated him for his work well done, for which he grinned, and I treated him to a chocolate milk shake at the Big T, which broadened his grin even more. But it was when I told his mother and others, in his hearing nearness, what a magnificent job he had done, that made him the happiest.

That just proves once again that there is far more hunger for love and appreciation in the world than there is hunger for bread. It takes such little effort to bestow love and appreciation. How often we fail to do so.

May we this day be careful to say a good word, compliment a good deed, smile at someone who looks cloudy, extend a hand in appreciation, and make the way better for someone else! And throw in a chocolate milkshake once in a while!

> Withhold not good from them to whom it is due, when it is in the power of thine hand to do it. (Proverbs 3:27 KJV)

> A man hath joy by the answer of his mouth: and a word spoken in due season, how good is it! (Proverbs 15:23 KJV)

One night I was desperately anxious over a business problem. The next day I was to meet the appointment that would decide the outcome, and I could only speculate whether it would be complimentary or adverse to me. Heavy foreboding hovered over me during the night as I tried to sleep. Then I talked to my husband and we prayed diligently for God's intervention.

The next morning was gray and rainy. I expected the somber heaviness to greet me the moment I awoke. To my utter surprise, it had vanished! The problem was yet to be faced that very morning, but I was readily equipped with courage to meet it head-on.

I felt the assurance that God was by my side as I faced the day's appointment. I felt His strength, which lent me courage. The problem was worked out, and I left the business office with confidence and a spring in my step.

When there come days and nights of anxiety and temptation, loneliness and suffering, we must harbor every resource to see as Tennyson said, "the best that glimmers through worst."

Wait on the Lord: be of good courage, and He shall strengthen thine heart: wait, I say, on the Lord. (Psalm 27:14 KJV)

For His anger endureth but a moment; in his favor is life: weeping may endure for a night, but joy cometh in the morning. (Psalm 30:5 KJV)

Casting all your care upon Him; for He careth for you. (1 Peter 5:7 KJV)

May 20   Walk in the Best Tracks

My husband, driving the truck, pulled up behind our place of business the morning after a seven-inch snowfall. Seeing the drifts were higher than my boots, and not higher than his, he said "Get out on the driver's side and I'll tromp a path for you to the door."

He bounced out and commenced tromping and I followed in the trench he made with not a dab of snow getting inside my boots.

It made me think of something Jesus has done for us. When He came to earth robed in flesh and walked among men, He came into contact with and was victorious over every type temptation with which any of us will ever be confronted. He saw the drifts of sin that we would have to walk through and knew the distresses and problems that would be ours if we got *over the boot tops* in sin, so He tromped out a trench for us so we could avoid yielding to temptation.

In Hebrews 4:15, we read "For we have not an High Priest which cannot be touched with the feeling of our infirmities; but was in all points tempted like as we are, yet without sin." And in 1 Corinthians

10:13, Paul writes, "There hath no temptation taken you but such as is common to man: but God is faithful, who will not suffer you to be tempted above that ye are able; but will with the temptation also make a way" – tromped out trench – "to escape, that ye may be able to bear it" - wade through it without getting any in your boots.

May 21   God's Masterpiece: the Human Body

The most famous temple of olden times was Solomon's temple, the marvel of the age for design and splendor. A vast army of men spent several years in building it.

But more wonderful in design and more beautiful in architectural structure than any column, arch, pillar, ancient ruin or even Solomon's temple is the human body.

While the body is not to be worshiped, it is to be held as a sacred trust. The proper care of it is just as much a part of the service due to God as is prayer or the giving of alms.

This rare and beautiful temple, the human body, dates back to the first week of creation. From Adam to the present day there has been a continuous, uninterrupted succession of living temples. Though the human temple has been marred by fierce tempests without and sullen fires within, by ignorance and superstition, by sin and sickness, and though it has passed through raging storms of passion and disease, yet it has weathered these elements of disintegration. Marred and defaced as it is, it still stands a monument of beauty to the Master Architect who in the beginning fashioned it after the divine similitude.

Up and down the corridors of the human temple and in all the various apartments, everywhere are groups of cells, all exceedingly busy, and working with an intelligence that impresses one deeply that they are under the guidance of the Master Architect.

These cell workers are the builders of the body. They work with the most mathematical precision, and with infinite skill. There is nothing more beautiful in all creation than a healthy and symmetrically developed human body, with a well-balanced intellect expressing itself through every feature.

In the beginning, man, crowned with glory and honor, was made upright, able to talk face to face with his Maker. Man towers above all other creatures. The human smile cannot be imitated or duplicated. The human hand, with its flexibility, adaptability, gracefulness, strength and dexterity is marvelous beyond compare. The human foot is a masterpiece.

A dead body is held in reverence and awe, even by uncivilized tribes, and it is against the law of nations to mutilate a body slain in battle. How much greater respect should be paid to a body which throbs with life and intelligence and to which we have unmistakable evidence that the Divine Power is at work!

May we always dedicate our temples to Him for His best use and His glory!

So God created man in His own image, in the image of God created He him; male and female created He them. (Genesis 1:27 KJV)

What? know ye not that your body is the temple of the Holy Ghost which is in you, which ye have of God, and ye are not your own? For ye are bought with a price: therefore glorify God in your body, and in your spirit, which are God's. (1 Corinthians 6:19-20 KJV)

May 22   Pray Specifically

The Lord is faithful to answer our prayers, but He does it in His own way.

During one drought season I prayed for rain in general. Then I decided to get more specific. I told my husband, "I'm going to pray for two inches of rain."

His reply was, "Make it three inches," so I did just that.

In a few days it began to rain. It only rained a little over an inch. A few days later it rained some more, enough to make above two inches total. After a longer interlude, to allow the water to soften the stony ground somewhat, there came a mushy soaker!

I said "Well, we got the three inches we prayed for, except in small portions."

My husband stated matter-of-factly, "If we had received the whole three inches at one time, it would have flooded our town we're so low above sea level."

I was shown once more that God hears the prayers of His children and answers at the time and in the manner it will do the one praying, and others to be affected by the answer, the most good. He knows exactly how and when to answer!

And all things, whatsoever ye shall ask in prayer, believing, ye shall receive. (Matthew 21:22 KJV)

Therefore I say unto you, What things so ever ye desire, when ye pray, believe that ye receive them, and ye shall have them. (Mark 11:24 KJV)

May 23   Grandeur of Grandparents

I am grandmother of four and great-grandmother of six, and I am one of the more fortunate in that they all live close by so that I can see them often. I always look forward to spending time with them, and enjoying their various activities

God is surely delighted with grandparents being involved with their grandchildren. And He put that delight in the hearts of human beings. I imagine Adam and Eve delighted in seeing their grandchildren beginning with their son Seth (Genesis 4:25-26; 5:4.). We know Jacob was proud of his grandchildren, and we have the account of the two born to his son Joseph (Genesis 48:9-14). Naomi was so pleased when Ruth and Boaz made her a grandmother of Obed (Ruth 4:13-17), who grew up to be the father of Jesse, who grew up to be the father of David.

In the New Testament we read about Timothy's Grandmother Lois, who helped to bring him up in the nurture and admonition of the Lord (2 Timothy 1:5).

Growing up, I too had the privilege of living close to my paternal grandparents, and I spent so much time with them. I found I could talk about sensitive things and they listened and gave good advice. We always went to the same church where they were active teachers. They were there when I made my profession of faith and saw me get baptized.

I've heard all sorts of stories of how grandparents have been so involved in their grandchildren's lives. One example is of two sets of grandparents, both having retired from public work. The first half of the year one set of grandparents take an apartment near the grandchildren and attend every activity in which they are involved – sports, music recitals, and others events – and always being available to baby-sit if needed. Then that couple goes back home, several states away, and the other set of grandparents do the same thing: leave their far-away home to come, take a close-by apartment, and do the same sort of activity the first ones did.

Recently I heard of a grandmother who wanted to see her grandson play baseball. As it was so cold that day, she wore four layers of clothing to brace herself against the cold wind as she sat in the bleachers. Then, because she had an allergy issue, her nose started bleeding. She left the bleachers, went to the restroom and sought to stop the bleeding. When it didn't stop, and knowing she was likely to miss her grandson's time to bat, she stuffed her nose with tissue and arranged a scarf over her nose so that only her eyes were seen. She went back to the bleachers and arrived just in time for her grandson's turn at batting, and he made a base hit. He never knew what the scarf was covering!

I remember one time in my daughter's life when her grandfather, my dad, attended a musical where she played the piano. The music was all classical, and he was a blue-grass fan, but he sat there big-eyed with a grin as she performed – only because she was a special granddaughter.

Only take heed to thyself, and keep thy soul diligently, lest thou forget the things which thine eyes have seen, and lest they depart from thy heart all the days of thy life: but teach them thy sons, and thy sons' sons. (Deuteronomy 4:9 KJV)

After this lived Job an hundred and forty years, and saw his sons, and his sons' sons, even four generations. So Job died, being old and full of days. (Job 42:16-17 KJV)

May 24   Forgiveness Beyond the Norm

She and he had been married more than twenty-five years and had had what she thought was a wonderful marriage. Then one day, out of the blue, her husband told her he wanted a divorce because he had found someone else who met his romantic needs.

Her heart was broken. And there was no way she could persuade him to reconsider, to seek counseling, and other solutions. Nothing prevailed with him. So, they separated and the divorce came to pass. He soon married the other woman.

The divorced woman began a life of her own, relocating to an apartment, because their home had been sold and proceeds divided between them, going to work for the first time, and dealing with the shame of what her husband had done. She spent a lot of time with God who helped her make discernments and granted a portion of comfort for her grief. She kept a good relationship with their children.

Then one day, out of the blue, she received another horrendous declaration: Ex-husband and new wife were divorcing because he had just been diagnosed with cancer, and the current spouse did not want to deal with it. The doctor said the cancer was so far advanced that there would be no surgery nor treatment, except to medicate to relieve pain.

What to do, Lord? She found she still loved him. After the divorce was final, she and he remarried. She moved into a larger apartment and took him in, where she bestowed all the loving care she could as she watched him fade day by day. Of course, their children came alongside her to assist.

He died. She felt a loss, but she also knew the peace of having forgiven him. Years later someone asked her would she have done it again. "Yes," she replied!

Let all bitterness, and wrath, and anger, and clamor, and evil speaking, be put away from you, with all malice: And be ye kind one to another, tenderhearted, forgiving one another, even as God for Christ's sake hath forgiven you. (Ephesians 4:31-32 KJV)

May 25   Keep on Talking – Somebody Might Listen

Often, I wonder what's the use to keep on trying to get people to forsake their sinful ways and turn to the Lord for salvation. It seems old hearts get harder and even the young hearts that are supposed to be tender cannot be penetrated.

When I think such thoughts, the Lord chides me with various scriptures. One He brought to my mind lately was in Isaiah chapter six. The Lord had asked "Whom shall I send, and who will go for us?" To this question Isaiah answered "Here and I, send me."

The Lord continued to tell Isaiah that most of the people would not listen to his message. To this Isaiah asked how long should he continue to preach to a non-listening crowd.

The Lord's answer to Isaiah, and to me, was "Until the cities be wasted without inhabitant and the houses without man." So, my responsibility to tell the world about Jesus does not diminish merely because no one seems to listen.

Along this same time, I found an outline in an old backless Bible that set me straight and renewed my zest to keep to my task in hope and faith. The title was "And I was left," taken from Ezekiel 9:8. The one left was the living among the dead and the faithful living among the faithless.

Other points were the fact that a person that has life and breath is no oversight of God. He is here in order that God's will be done in his life. The saved person is left here to complete his assigned service and to witness to sinners both by mouth and deeds. The sinner is yet living here to be warned again so that he may have opportunity to repent and to be saved.

Also I heard the voice of the Lord, saying, Whom shall I send, and who will go for us? Then said I, Here am I; send me.

And He said, Go, and tell this people, Hear ye indeed, but understand not; and see ye indeed, but perceive not. Make the heart of this people fat, and make their ears heavy, and shut their eyes; lest they see with their eyes, and hear with their ears, and understand with their heart, and convert, and be healed. Then said I, Lord, how long? And He answered, Until the cities be wasted without inhabitant, and the houses without man, and the land be utterly desolate, And the Lord have removed men far away, and there be a great forsaking in the midst of the land. (Isaiah 6:8-12 KJV)

May 26   Appreciate Verbally

I had heard all my life that it was right to pay someone a compliment when one is due and to do it in season, but I did not know there was a scripture to prove it. Then I came upon Proverbs 3:27, which says "Withhold not good from them to whom it is due, when it is in the power of thine hand to do it."

I realize this also infers doing a good deed to someone when you have occasion to do so, but often I think paying tribute or honor or praising someone for a job well done is the best deed that could be rendered someone. Everybody wants to be appreciated.

It isn't enough that we fill our minds with silent praise. Instead, it's going right up to the man himself and telling so that counts.

Here is a little poem that says the same thing:

> If a man does a work that your rightly admire,
> Don't leave a kind word unsaid
> In fear that to do so might make him vain,
> And cause him to "lose his head."
> But reach out your hand and tell him "Well done!"
> And see how his gratitude swells.
> It isn't the flowers we strew on the grave—
> It's the word to the living that tells!

A businessman and his wife took a few days of relaxation at an ocean-front hotel. One night a violent storm lashed the beach, sending massive breakers thundering against the shore.

The wind finally died down, and early the next morning the man slipped out of bed and took a walk along the beach to see what damage had been done. As he strolled, he saw that the beach was covered with starfish that had been tossed ashore and helplessly stranded by the enormous waves. Once the morning sun would begin to burn through the clouds, the starfish would dry out and die.

All at once the man saw an interesting sight. A young boy was picking up the starfish, one at a time, and flinging them back into the ocean.

"Why are you doing that?" the man asked the lad, as he got near enough to be heard. "Don't you know you'll never be able to get all those hundreds of starfish back into the water? What difference can you make when there are so many?"

The boy sighed as he picked up another starfish and flung it into the water. Then as he watched it sink, he looked up at the man, smiled, and said "I sure made a difference to that one. I know he is glad I picked him up and put him where he can live." And he began picking up another and another starfish and threw them into the water!

The businessman then bent down and picked up a starfish, reared back, and threw it into the ocean. He kept on doing it. The little boy grinned at him.

True, one person or even two cannot beat the odds. There will always be more people to reach than time or energy or commitment can provide. But the truth is that each one of us can touch a few.

We, as followers of Jesus Christ, are to be fishers of men, or ones who pick up hopelessly stranded people like the starfish on the beach. The Lord is with us in this commission. He calls us and then gears us to accomplish His kingdom's work. Yes, you and I can make a difference. Because we can, we must. We can count on the Lord to honor and multiply our best efforts, even though they may seem small.

It was to fishermen, Peter, Andrew, James and John, Jesus said

"Follow Me, and I will make you fishers of men" (Matthew 4:19). No doubt they had never caught over a hundred at one time in their fishing business, and they likely figured that's about how many lost men they would ever be able to catch. But, look what happened on the Day of Pentecost! More than 3,000 were *caught*, and on another occasion after a sermon, over 5,000 had come into the salvation net!

> Herein is My Father glorified, that ye bear much fruit; so shall ye be My disciples. . . .Ye have not chosen Me, but I have chosen you, and ordained you, that ye should go and bring forth fruit, and that your fruit should remain: that whatsoever ye shall ask of the Father in my name, He may give it you. (John 15:8, 16 KJV)

> Now then we are ambassadors for Christ, as though God did beseech you by us: we pray you in Christ's stead, be ye reconciled to God. (2 Corinthians 5:20 KJV)

May 28   Bask in the Rays of the Son of God

The first warming rays of spring's sun do amazing things to a person. Suddenly there is a pulsating urge to get outdoors and breathe deeply, to dig in the rich, fertile soil, to plant a garden. A man sees the exterior of his house for the first time in a long time and notices the paint peeling. The woman of the house becomes aware of cluttered closets, dirty windows, and how much the kids have grown and are needing new clothes.

And the kids doing outside things, biking, climbing trees, bouncing on trampolines, bunching together at somebody's basketball goal post. It's a marvelous time of the year.

In like manner, the warming rays of the Son of God in the heart of His child brings about much activity. That person sees things differently: a lost soul, a needy neighbor, the problem in a fellow-Christian's life and ways to help. That one sees the dirty windows and cluttered closets and peeling paint of his or her own life that need to be made right. The urge to dig into the rich earth of God's Word and plant seeds of what is learned into the eager heart's surfaces.

As we warm to the rays of spring's sun, let's also allow the rays of the Son of God to warm our hearts.

Thou wilt shew me the path of life: in thy presence is fulness of joy; at thy right hand there are pleasures for evermore. (Psalm 16:11 KJV)

He that hath My commandments, and keepeth them, he it is that loveth Me: and he that loveth Me shall be loved of My Father, and I will love him, and will manifest Myself to Him. (John 14:21 KJV)

May 29   Always Safe in the Hands of God

This past year has given each of us blessings and misfortunes. The blessings outnumbered the misfortunes and always do. God is good to each one of us in so many ways, even in the tragedies. He is there undergirding us with His strong arm.

In winter He has driven us inside with the snow and ice, but He is inside with us, and what a wonderful opportunity to have some lengthy conversations with Him. Ah, there is so much to talk about an He is interested in everything about you and me. Talk about your happiness and don't be afraid to tell Him your fears. He is bigger than our fears.

"I said to the man who stood at the gate of the year: 'Give me a light that I may tread safely into the unknown,' And he replied, 'Go out in the darkness and put your hand in the hand of God. That shall be better than a light and safer than a known way.' Better than a light! How those words come back to me this year, and I say Happy New Year to my fellows! May all of you put your hands in God's hand and know that you have something far better than light, and far safer to guide you through every day of the year, no matter what kind of day it may be." (King George VI of England)

What time I am afraid, I will trust in thee. In God I will praise His word, in God I have put my trust; I will not fear what flesh can do unto me. (Psalm 56:3-4 KJV)

Fear thou not; for I am with thee: be not dismayed; for I am thy God: I will strengthen thee; yea, I will help thee; yea, I will uphold thee with the right hand of My righteousness. (Isaiah 41:10 KJV)

May 30   The Light in Our Scary Darkness

As children afraid of the dark, so are adults as well. We become apprehensive of the unknown. There lurking around any corner might be something to dread. The year stretches forth like a great road, or dark alley, with fears to beset us. Death, sickness, soul-searching decisions, disappointments, loneliness, to name a few, will likely attack us.

But cheer up! There is One who sees around the bends and marks the steps of His followers. He is the Lord Jesus Christ, the Light of the World. Inviting Him to go with us day by day will dissipate our fears.

The steps of a good man are ordered by the Lord: and He delighteth in his way. Though he fall, he shall not be utterly cast down: for the Lord upholdeth him with His hand. (Psalm 37:23-24 KJV)

Then spake Jesus again unto them, saying, I Am the Light of the world: he that followeth Me shall not walk in darkness, but shall have the light of life. (John 8:12 KJV)

May 31   God Owns Even Our Money

God owns everything. He created everything that is or ever has been. Then the last of His creation was His masterpiece: the human being. He made him in the likeness of Himself, and He expressed His purpose for that being: to rule over His created earth. That was the main *likeness* of man to God, to be Ruler. While God would ever rule over everything in His universe, including mankind, He endowed this His best created person to rule. Of course, we know how Satan came along and targeted God's masterpiece, and we know the results, all becoming sinners by nature and practice. But we also know, praise the LORD, that He provided a remedy of redemption through His Son, the Lord Jesus Christ, for all who would repent of sin and accept Him as Lord and Savior.

Because God owns everything, that includes all the gold, silver, all manner of gems, indeed all the wealth. Yet, he allows mankind to use that wealth to meet their needs. He gives each person the ability, talent and skill to earn the wealth. Yet, the Bible says much about the unwise attitude and use of wealth. The person comes to think "I earned this money and it's mine to do with as I please." That is different from God's perspective. He expects the person with money to thank Him for it, for his career or manner in which it was earned as a favor from God, and that person is expected to return a portion of it in worship to God. God does not need the money; He owns it already. But a person's gift back to God glorifies Him in worship. It seems that ministers are reluctant to preach about money for fear of losing some of the congregation. It seems every church is "in the red" for lack of funds to carry on the various godly ministries of the church. When a church treasury suddenly gets in the *black* financially, it stuns leaders in the church, especially the pastor.

There is a story about a man who suddenly became ill. He had such a massive heart attack that the doctor told his family "Don't say or do anything to excite him, because to do so would cause him to drop dead with another heart attack. Don't give him either bad news or good news.

The family was cautious to keep the doctor's advice. Then one day, out of the blue, an attorney sent the sick man a letter saying a distant uncle had died and left him one million dollars, as he was the closest of kin. The ill man's wife read the letter and shared it with their adult children, wondering what they should do. They knew they needed to tell the sick man of the good news but feared it would so excite him he would die, as the doctor had suggested.

Finally, they came up with the idea that they would let the pastor of their church break the news to the sick man, because the pastor knew how to tell him tactfully and carefully so he could receive it. The pastor agreed to do it, and went to the man on his sick bed. They talked about mundane things that were not disturbing before the pastor said to him, "What would you do if suddenly out of the blue you received a million dollars?"

His reply, "I'd give half of it to the church." Someone passed out all right, not with a heart attack, but by fainting: the pastor.

Behold, the heaven and the heaven of heavens is the Lord's thy God, the earth also, with all that therein is. (Deuteronomy 10:14 KJV)

For every beast of the forest is mine, and the cattle upon a thousand hills. I know all the fowls of the mountains: and the wild beasts of the field are mine. If I were hungry, I would not tell thee: for the world is mine, and the fulness thereof. (Psalm 50:10-12 KJV)

Every man according as he purposeth in his heart, so let him give; not grudgingly, or of necessity: for God loveth a cheerful giver. (2 Corinthians 9:7 KJV)

June 1   Safe and Secure

The airplane in which a businessman was a passenger suddenly became bouncing and swaying to his dismay. The flight attendant came out immediately and told them they were experiencing some unexpected turbulence and asked that they buckle their seat belts and try to remain calm. She assured them the captain knew what he was doing and would have everything under control soon.

But the rocking and bumping continued and seemed to the businessman to be getting worse. All others around him wore fearful countenances. Some were twitching their hands and leaning against each other and whispering. Some began to cry.

Except for one little girl who sat in a seat by herself near the window. He figured her to be about eight years old. She was reading, her feet in the seat, and she wore a peaceful, calm expression, absent of the slightest fear as the plane dipped and flung things out of seats noisily into the aisles.

As he watched her, the man thought "She must be disabled or handicapped mentally for showing no fear."

At length, he got out of his seat and sat down beside the little girl. She moved her feet out of the seat and smiled at him.

"Aren't you frightened with the plane tossing about so violently?"

Smiling at hm, she replied, "Oh, no. My Daddy is the pilot and he is taking me home." And she began to read her book again.

How like the little girl ought we to be when tossed about in the storms of life, with perils looming on every side. Our Heavenly Father is steering the airplane of our life, and He will always take care of us during the whole journey. Bumps, dips, plunges, and all sorts of fears may assail us, His children, but we can remain calm through it all. He is taking us safely home!

I will both lay me down in peace, and sleep: for thou, Lord, only makest me dwell in safety. (Psalm 4:8 KJV)

Thou wilt keep him in perfect peace, whose mind is stayed on thee: because he trusteth in thee. (Isaiah 26:3 KJV)

 June 2   **Hear the Author's Voice**

Although authors do their literary work quietly, with pen or keyboard, yet each one has his or her own *voice*.

I have met authors during my lifetime at writers' conferences and conventions. After meeting and talking with one, and I then bought that author's book for autograph, when I read it, I could hear the voice of the author.

One I met was Mary Higgins Clark at our book store in my home town in Arkansas. I was an avid fan of hers for years before meeting her. When my turn came to stand before her at the table where she was to autograph the book I had bought, we talked. I told her I too was a writer. She asked what genre and I told her. I told her I had written three biographies plus had done some features for newspapers and magazines of "unsung heroes," plus other stuff. She said she started out in writing for newspapers. Although the people in line behind me kept making "hurry up" sounds, she took time to chat with me.

After I left and went home to begin reading her book, I heard her voice between the lines.

Other writers I have met and whose books I have bought do the same thing with me. I hear their voices.

Likewise, as I read the Bible, I have met the Author: God Himself. I have accepted His Son as my Savior, and God is now my Heavenly Father too. All of the Bible is God's Word, but He used His own picked-out writers to pen it. After reading and studying the Bible, I have recognized each writer's peculiar pen. David writes a certain way; so do Paul and Peter. When I hear their writings being read from the pulpit, I soon can tell who the writer is – maybe not the exact chapter and verse or even the particular book – but that one's voice has its own resonance.

The Best Author and the Best Book in all the world is the *BIBLE*, as it holds the way to live, work, love, know joy and peace, and how to prepare for eternal life to be spent with this Great Author!

The grass withereth, the flower fadeth: but the word of our God shall stand forever. (Isaiah 40:8 KJV)

And when He putteth forth His own sheep, He goeth before them, and the sheep follow Him: for they know His voice. (John 10:4 KJV)

All scripture is given by inspiration of God, and is profitable for doctrine, for reproof, for correction, for instruction in righteousness. (2 Timothy 3:16 KJV)

God, who at sundry times and in divers manners spake in time past unto the fathers by the prophets, hath in these last days spoken unto us by His Son, whom He hath appointed heir of all things, by whom also He made the worlds. (Hebrews 1:1-2 KJV)

Many Times in John's Gospel, Jesus said, "My Father Sent Me" (All in KJV)

"For God sent not His Son into the world to condemn the world; but that the world through Him might be saved," John 3:17, enlightening Nicodemus.

"Jesus saith unto them, My meat is to do the will of Him that sent me, and to finish His work," John 4:34, telling His disciples after talking to the Samaritan woman.

"I can of mine own self do nothing: as I hear, I judge: and my judgment is just; because I seek not mine own will, but the will of the Father which hath sent Me," John 5:30, stating to the Jews who sought to persecute Him for healing on the Sabbath.

"But I have greater witness than that of John: for the works which the Father hath given Me to finish, the same works that I do, bear witness of Me, that the Father hath sent me," John 5:36, answering the Jews who objected to Him.

"Jesus answered and said unto them, This is the work of God, that ye believe on Him whom He hath sent," John 6:29, declaring to the multitude after He fed more than 5,000 with five loaves and two fishes.

"For I came down from heaven, not to do mine own will, but the will of Him that sent Me. And this is the Father's will which hath sent Me, that of all which He hath given Me I should lose nothing, but should raise it up again at the last day. And this is the will of Him that sent Me, that every one which seeth the Son, and believeth on Him, may have everlasting life: and I will raise him up at the last day," John 6:38-40, adjuring the multitudes.

"As the living Father hath sent Me, and I live by the Father: so he that eateth Me" – as Bread of Life – "even he shall live by Me," John 6:57, speaking to the multitudes.

"Jesus answered them, and said, My doctrine is not mine, but His that sent Me," John 7:16, addressing the self-righteous Jews.

"Then cried Jesus in the temple as He taught, saying, Ye both know

Me, and ye know whence I am: and I am not come of Myself, but He that sent Me is true, whom ye know not. But I know Him: for I am from Him, and He hath sent Me" John 7:28-29, teaching in the temple to unbelieving Jews.

"And yet if I judge, my judgment is true: for I am not alone, but I and the Father that sent Me," John 8:16, informing the religious Pharisees.

"I am One that bear witness of Myself, and the Father that sent Me beareth witness of Me," John 8:18, answering the Pharisees.

"I have many things to say and to judge of you: but He that sent Me is true; and I speak to the world those things which I have heard of Him," John 8:26, explaining to the Pharisees.

"Jesus said unto them, If God were your Father, ye would love Me: for I proceeded forth and came from God; neither came I of Myself, but He sent Me," John 8:42, responding to Pharisees.

"I must work the works of Him that sent Me, while it is day: the night cometh, when no man can work," John 9:4, emphasizing to His disciples.

"And I knew that Thou hearest Me always: but because of the people which stand by I said it, that they may believe that Thou hast sent Me," John 11:42, praying to His Heavenly Father in the hearing of His disciples and crowd before raising Lazarus.

"Jesus cried and said, He that believeth on Me, believeth not on Me, but on Him that sent Me. And he that seeth Me seeth Him that sent Me," John 12:44-45, declaring to a multitude.

"For I have not spoken of Myself; but the Father which sent Me, He gave me a commandment, what I should say, and what I should speak," John 12:49, explaining to multitudes.

"Verily, verily, I say unto you, He that receiveth whomsoever I send receiveth Me; and he that receiveth Me receiveth Him that sent Me," John 13:20, educating his disciples.

"He that loveth Me not keepeth not My sayings: and the word which ye hear is not Mine, but the Father's which sent Me," John 14:24, expounding to His disciples.

In conversation with a veteran of the Marines of decades ago, he said he was told as an infantry soldier by his superior officer to "Take care of your weapon and your feet." He grinned at me and said, "I took care of my rifle and ammunition all right, but I did not look out for me feet as I should. Now I have Gout, and, man do I have awful pain every once in a while."

In Paul's writing to the Ephesians, he listed the armor that soldiers in the Lord's Army needed when going to war against the devil's forces. Among them is the kind of boot for the feet and the type of weapon to be used. The feet must be shod with the preparation of the gospel of peace, and the weapon used must be the Word of God.

As infantrymen in the Lord's Army, we must adorn our feet with the proper boots. They must be comfortable enough so that nothing would make them sore to the point of causing the wearer to be unable to focus due to the discomfort. Yet, they need to be sturdy enough so that they could trudge through any manner of terrain on the battlefield. The soldier would take special care in preparing by studying God's Word so that he could go out into whatever terrains the Lord sends him to spread the gospel of peace.

The only weapon the soldier needs is a deep, meditative knowledge of the scriptures, as the Author is The Commander of the Army. So saturated with the knowledge of this sword, and how to wield it to accomplish his Commander's instructions, this soldier is bound to put the battle against the enemy to flight. Also, he must have it at the ready when the enemy assails him.

> Wherefore take unto you the whole armor of God, that ye may be able to withstand in the evil day, and having done all to stand. Stand therefore, having your loins girt about with truth, and having on the breastplate of righteousness; And your feet shod with the preparation of the gospel of peace; Above all, taking the shield of faith, wherewith ye shall be able to quench all the fiery darts of the wicked. And take the helmet

of salvation, and the sword of the Spirit, which is the word of God. (Ephesians 6:13-17 KJV)

Preach the word; be instant in season, out of season; reprove, rebuke, exhort with all longsuffering and doctrine. (2 Timothy 4:2 KJV)

June 4   Compassion in Kind

The owner of a pet shop heard the entrance doorbell clang one summer morning and looked up to see a man and a little boy enter. The little boy had a grin on his face and his eyes were shining. The owner reasoned the boy was about seven or eight years old.

"My son Stevie wants to buy a dog, sir," the man said. "He has been saving money from his allowance a long time and he is ready to buy now."

The owner took them into the back part of the shop where there were all manner of woofs and yips and loud barks of the horde of dogs in cages. They looked at all of them. Finally, Stevie pointed to a little black and white one, a mutt of some sort, which had only three legs. The right front leg was missing.

"I want that one if I have enough money for it," He said, looking up at the owner.

"But why don't you choose one with four legs, son? This one couldn't run and play with you since he just has three legs," his Dad asked.

"Aw, but Daddy, he really wants to be mine. Can't you see how he's really looking at me and wagging his tail really fast?"

"If you really want that one, then let's see if you have enough money."

The price was even less than the amount the boy had to pay, and the sale went well. The shop man took the dog out of the cage and placed him in the outstretched arms of Stevie. As they made their way toward the door, the owner saw that below the shoe of Stevie was the end of a steel brace, and he noticed he had a limp. A lump surged to his throat. Tears rushed to his eyes. "Those two are going to have a joyful summer!" he thought to himself.

Rejoice with them that do rejoice, and weep with them that weep. Be of the same mind one toward another. Mind not high things, but condescend to men of low estate. Be not wise in your own conceits. (Romans 12:15-16 KJV)

Finally, be ye all of one mind, having compassion one of another, love as brethren, be pitiful, be courteous. (1 Peter 3:8 KJV)

June 5   This Man Reached Your Heart

One of England's leading actors was being banqueted. In the after-dinner ceremonies, the actor was asked to recite for the pleasure of his guests. He consented, and asked if there was anything special anyone in the audience would like to hear.

There was a moment's pause, and then an old clergyman spoke up. "Could you, sir," he said, "recite the Twenty-Third Psalm?"

A strange look came over the actor's face, but he was speechless for only a moment.

"I can, sir. And I will, on one condition, and that is that after I have recited, you, my friend, will do the same."

"I?" replied the surprised clergyman, "but I am not an elocutionist. However, if you wish, I will do so."

Impressively, the great actor began the Psalm, holding his audience spellbound. As he finished, a great burst of applause erupted from the guests.

After the applause had ceased, the old clergyman arose. The audience sat in tense silence. The Psalm was recited, and when it was done, there was not the slightest ripple of applause, but those in the audience, whose eyes were yet dry, had their heads bowed.

The great actor, with hand on the clergyman's shoulder, his voice trembling, exclaimed, "I reached your eyes and ears, my friends, but this man reached your hearts. I know the Twenty-Third Psalm; this man knows the Shepherd."

The Lord is my Shepherd; I shall not want. (Psalm 23:1 KJV)

I am the good shepherd, and know my sheep, and am known of mine. (John 10:14 KJV)

June 6   ## With God's Help, Yes You Can

You can muster hopefulness in the midst of despair by remembering "This too will pass."

Tell yourself, "Today is the first day of the rest of my life."

Say this and mean it: "At some point in my life I have to give up all hope for a better yesterday."

Consider this: Suppose you had never been born. How many lives would be less complete because you are not around?

Persistence pays: Abe Lincoln lost eight elections before becoming president. Colonel Sanders suffered 1,000 rejections before he sold his first chicken recipe. Don't be afraid to fail – Abe and the Colonel weren't!

True inner peace comes from a permanent connection with God. Let Him govern your life.

I can do all things through Christ, which strengtheneth me. (Philippians 4:13 KJV)

June 7   ## Pray Without Ceasing

"A godly man is a praying man. As soon as grace is poured in, prayer is poured out. Prayer is the soul's traffic with heaven. God comes down to us by His Spirit, and we go up to Him in prayer," proclaimed Thomas Watson.

"If you are a stranger to prayer, you are a stranger to power," said Billy Sunday.

Hudson Taylor professed, "You must go forward on your knees."

"Prayer will make a man cease from sin, or sin will entice a man to cease from prayer," John Bunyan warned.

When the Lord's people realized they had sinned against Him, they asked Samuel to pray for them. His response was that he would do so. Else, he would be sinning against God. "Moreover, as for me, God forbid that I should sin against the Lord in ceasing to pray for you." (I Samuel 12:23 KJV)

June 8   God is Looking for a Few Good Men

God seeks out brave men like Moses who dare to stand boldly before the lords of government, and demand "Let my people go!"

God calls for wise men like Caleb, who spurn the smooth way and turn toward the habitat of giants, saying "Give me this mountain!"

God searches for moral men like Joseph, who staunchly resist passion's lure, and choose to suffer wrongfully, declaring, "How can I do this great evil against God?"

God desires men of leadership like Solomon, who, when applauded as richest and wisest in all the world, acknowledge "The God of heaven is my Counselor in government."

God delights in immovable men like Job, who refuse to abandon their commitment to God, and vow for all the world to hear, "Though He slay me, yet will I trust Him!"

God is most greatly pleased with accomplishing men like His Son Jesus, who, in the face of being spurned, forsaken, and bearing the load of sin of the whole world upon Himself, lifted His eyes to His Father and prayed humbly, "Not My will, but Thine be done!"

Now the days of David drew nigh that he should die; and he charged Solomon his son, saying, I go the way of all the earth: be thou strong therefore, and shew thyself a man; And keep the charge of the Lord thy God, to walk in His ways, to keep His statutes, and His commandments, and His judgments, and His testimonies, as it is written in the Law of Moses, that thou mayest prosper in all that thou doest, and whithersoever thou turnest thyself. (1 Kings 2:1-3 KJV)

June 9   The Prince of Scottish Hymnists

Horatius Bonar was one of eleven children born of his Scottish parents in early 1800's. After studying for the ministry at the University of Edinburg and serving an internship at Leith, Horatius was ordained and began pastoring in Kelso. Later he moved to Edinburg where he became one of Scotland's famous evangelists.

He and his wife had many children, but five of them died in rapid succession. Whether because of those losses or another reason, he had a unique gift for connecting with children. He began writing hymns while at Kelso, many of which were for children. Later, in his church at Edinburg, where only the Scottish version of the Psalms were allowed to be sung in the adult services, two of his church's most devout leaders stomped out of the church building in stormy protest when a hymn he had written was announced to be sung. The children never protested. They loved his visits to Sunday School when he would lead them in joyful singing.

One of his most famous hymns was "I Heard the Voice of Jesus Say," which he wrote in 1846. He based his three stanzas on three promises of Jesus, in Matthew 11:28, John 4:14, and John 8:12. The first of each verse echoes the Lord's promise, and the last had fitting words for the singer's response.

Many years later, one of his daughters, who had been widowed and had had to return to live with her parents, brought along five children. Horatius was elated to have these five living in his home. He wrote to a friend expressing "God took five children from life some years ago, and He has given me another five to bring up for Him in my old age."

Horatius was nearly eighty when he preached for the last time in his church. Among his last requests was that no biography be written of him. He wanted all glory to be Christ's alone. In spite of his request, his name lives on in his works. Those who loved and appreciated him, especially the children ascribed to him to title, "The Prince of Scottish Hymnists."

> And I heard a voice from heaven saying unto me, Write, Blessed are the dead which die in the Lord from henceforth: Yea, saith the Spirit, that they may rest from their labors; and their works do follow them. (Revelation 14:13 KJV)

June 10   Majestic, Omnipotent God

The Sunday School teacher of a group of pre-school children was telling them about God's creation of all things, using the first chapter of Genesis. The little ones listened with wide-eyed fascination as she told of His created things day by day: light, darkness, sun, moon, stars, plant life, animal life, and the human being.

After expounding on all of it, she asked the children if they had any comments. One little girl raised her hand.

"Yes, Mary, do you have a question?"

"No," she replied, "But I just wanted to say. God made all things, everything, and He did it with just His left hand."

Perplexed at Mary's statement, she asked, "What do you mean, He did it all with His left hand, Mary?"

The youngster looked up at the teacher with such an awe-struck expression, and answered, "Because Jesus is sitting on His right hand."

Understanding what Mary had said, the teacher's heart swelled with praise to God.

"You know, Mary, He does not really need to use either of His hands. He has all power. Nothing is impossible with Him. He just has to speak the words and whatever He commands comes to pass."

> Ah Lord God! Behold, thou hast made the heaven and the earth by thy great power and stretched out arm, and there is nothing too hard for thee. (Jeremiah 32:17 KJV)

But Jesus beheld them, and said unto them, With men this is impossible; but with God all things are possible. (Matthew 19:26 KJV)

June 11   God Knows Right Where You Are

The guillemot is a small arctic sea bird that lives on the rock cliffs of northern coastal regions. These birds flock together by the thousands in comparatively small areas. Because of the crowded conditions, hundreds of females lay their pear-shaped eggs side by side on a narrow ledge, in a long row. Since the eggs all look exactly alike, it is incredible that a mother bird can identify those that belong to her. Yet studies show that she knows her own eggs so well that when even one is moved, she finds it and returns it to the original location.

Sometimes life can make you feel like one of those eggs. The air around you is bitterly cold. Your shell is thin and fragile. Adverse circumstances have moved you away from where you feel you should be. However, God knows right where you are! He is anxious to receive you and comfort you. He is as close as a prayer. For lasting comfort, speak regularly with the Father. He has enough comfort to get you through all the struggles of life.

O Lord, thou hast searched me, and known me. Thou knowest my downsitting and mine uprising, thou understandest my thought afar off. Thou compassest my path and my lying down, and art acquainted with all my ways. (Psalm 139:1-3 KJV)

Are not two sparrows sold for a farthing? And one of them shall not fall on the ground without your Father. But the very hairs of your head are all numbered. Fear ye not therefore, ye are of more value than many sparrows. (Matthew 10:29-31 KJV)

A young boy carried the cocoon of a moth into his house to watch the fascinating events that would take place when the moth emerged. When the moth finally started to break out of its cocoon, the boy noticed how hard the moth had to struggle. The process was very slow and painful. In an effort to help, he reached down and widened the opening of the cocoon. Soon the moth was out of its prison.

But as the boy watched, the wings remained shriveled. Something was wrong. What the boy had not realized was that the struggle to get out of the cocoon was essential for the moth's muscle system to develop. In a misguided effort to relieve a struggle, the boy had crippled the future of this creature.

Trials are necessary for a healthy Christian life and growth. When you suffer, you might be tempted to give up, but remember that the *process* is just as important as the *finished product* of your faith.

God allows Satan to tempt His children, but with the temptation God always provides an available aversion that the one tempted can choose. Satan's ultimate goal is not to get you to sit on the sidelines of life. He wants you out of the game completely. He does not want to just rob you of your effectiveness as a Christian; he wants you to turn your back on God.

Each time the Christian confronts a temptation and with God's help resists and flees from it, he becomes stronger. Satan never knocks once and leaves. He repeatedly pounds on the door of your heart and life. Spiritually, you are in the fight that will last your entire lifetime. But each time he comes to you with one of his many tactics or lures, when you resist and overcome, your faith becomes stronger and stronger in the service of the Lord.

> There hath no temptation taken you but such as is common to man: but God is faithful, who will not suffer you to be tempted above that ye are able; but will with the temptation also make a way to escape, that ye may be able to bear it. (1 Corinthians 10:13 KJV)

For in that He Himself hath suffered being tempted, He is able to succor them that are tempted. (Hebrews 2:18 KJV)

For we have not an High Priest which cannot be touched with the feeling of our infirmities; but was in all points tempted like as we are, yet without sin. (Hebrews 4:15 KJV)

My brethren, count it all joy when ye fall into divers temptations; knowing this, that the trying of your faith worketh patience. (James 1:2-3 KJV)

June 13 — Unconditional Love

A father was tucking in his six-year-old son for the night when he asked him, "Son, when does Daddy love you the most? When you've been fighting with your sister and getting into a lot of trouble, or when you've been real helpful to Mommy and nice to everyone?"

The son thought for a moment and said, "Both times."

"Right," the father said, "and do you know why?"

"Because I'm your special guy," replied the boy. The boy knew his father loved him no matter what because he was daddy's *special guy.*

God loves us the same way, unconditionally, because we belong to Him. When you hurt, tell God how you feel. He is not distant or uncaring. When you have something you are happy about, tell Him. He is always eager for you to come to Him. He knows you better than you even know yourself. How great it is for us to have such a wonderful loving Father!

The Lord hath appeared of old unto me, saying, Yea, I have loved thee with an everlasting love: therefore with lovingkindness have I drawn thee. (Jeremiah 31:3 KJV)

The Spirit itself beareth witness with our spirit, that we are the children of God: And if children, then heirs; heirs of God, and joint-heirs with Christ; if so be that we suffer with Him, that we may be also glorified together. (Romans 8:16-17 KJV)

Behold, what manner of love the Father hath bestowed upon us, that we should be called the sons of God: therefore the world knoweth us not, because it knew Him not. (1 John 3:1 (KJV)

June 14   Greatest Beyond Comprehension

In 1715, King Louis XIV of France died after a reign of seventy-two years. He had called himself *the Great*, and was the monarch who made the famous statement, "I am the state!" His court was the most magnificent in Europe, and his funeral was equally spectacular. As his body lay in state in a golden coffin, orders were given that the cathedral should be very dimly lit with only a special candle set above his coffin, to dramatize his greatness.

At the memorial, thousands waited in hushed silence. Then Bishop Massilon began to speak. Slowly he reached down and snuffed out the candle, and said, "Only God is great!"

For thou art great, and doest wondrous things: thou art God alone. (Psalm 86:10 KJV)

I am the Lord: that is my name: and my glory will I not give to another, neither my praise to graven images. (Isaiah 42:8 KJV)

Fear ye not, neither be afraid: have not I told thee from that time, and have declared it? Ye are even my witnesses. Is there a God beside me? Yea, there is no God; I know not any. (Isaiah 44:8 KJV)

During the 1800s, George Mueller was a pastor who operated an orphanage in Britain. In 1870 his wife, Mary, contracted an illness and died after months of suffering. Mueller said at her funeral, "I miss her in numberless ways and shall miss her yet more and more. But as a child of God, and as a servant of the Lord Jesus, I bow. I am satisfied with the will of my Heavenly Father. I kiss continually the hand that has thus afflicted me."

Mueller went on to minister to more than 30,000 orphans during his ministry. Out of his loss, God gave him one of the largest families the world has ever known, along with the undying love of grateful children.

Instead of wallowing in your pain, allow God to restore you. Trust Him with your life and see what amazing things He can accomplish through you.

But none of these things move me, neither count I my life dear unto myself, so that I might finish my course with joy, and the ministry, which I have received of the Lord Jesus, to testify the gospel of the grace of God. (Acts 20:24 KJV)

For which cause we faint not; but though our outward man perish, yet the inward man is renewed day by day. For our light affliction, which is but for a moment, worketh for us a far more exceeding and eternal weight of glory. (2 Corinthians 4:16-17 KJV)

June 16 Hang on to Hope

In 1965, naval aviator James B. Stockdale became the first American pilot to be shot down during the Vietnam War. As a prisoner of the Vietcong, he spent seven years as a P.O.W. He was frequently tortured in an attempt to break him and get him to denounce the United States' involvement in the war. He was chained for days at a time with his hands above his head so that he could not even swat the mosquitoes. His captor broke his leg and never reset it. Today he still cannot bend his left knee. Worse than everything else, he was held in isolation away from the other American prisoners of war and was allowed to see only his guards and interrogators.

How could anyone survive seven years of such treatment? Stockdale says that it was hope that kept him alive, hope of one day going home, hope that each day could be the day of his release. Without hope, he knew that he would die, as others did.

Hope comes from walking with your Lord through daily life and through death. Don't give up hope. Look to God. Hope in Him and you will triumph. Hope is an anchor of the soul!

Happy is he that hath the God of Jacob for his help, whose hope is in the Lord his God. (Psalm 146:5 KJV)

Which hope we have as an anchor of the soul, both sure and steadfast, and which entereth into that within the veil. (Hebrews 6:19 KJV)

June 17   Words Fitly Spoken

During the football season preceding Super Bowl I, quarterback Bart Starr had an incentive scheme going with his oldest son. For every perfect paper Bart Jr. brought home from school, Starr gave him ten cents.

After a particularly rough game against St. Louis, in which Starr felt he had performed poorly, he returned home worn and battered, late at night after a long plane ride. But he couldn't help feeling better when he reached his bedroom.

There attached to his pillow was a note: "Dear Dad, I thought you played a great game. Love, Bart Jr." Taped to the note were two dimes.

That day, Bart Starr learned that words are important, especially from someone who loves you.

A man hath joy by the answer of his mouth: and a word spoken in due season, how good is it! (Proverbs 15:23 KJV)

A word fitly spoken is like apples of gold in pictures of silver. (Proverbs 25:11 KJV)

Let your speech be alway with grace, seasoned with salt, that ye may know how ye ought to answer every man. (Colossians 4:6 KJV)

June 18   **Appropriate Worship**

An irate man left church one Sunday morning in a terrible mood. As he hurried past an usher he exclaimed, "I didn't get anything out of that worship service!"

The usher wisely and gently replied, "The focus in worship, my friend, is not you, but God. What do you think God got out of you in worship today?"

Appropriate worship begins with a recognition of God's worthiness. We must shift our focus from ourselves to Him. We must recognize who He really is and what He has graciously done for us. Right worship focuses first and foremost on God's glory and majesty. It exalts God's agenda instead of our agenda. We must worship with commitment to God's plan for our lives. Always we must worship with thanksgiving for all His many blessings. He is worthy of our deepest expressions of praise. He gave nothing less than His best. He deserves nothing less than ours.

O come, let us worship and bow down: let us kneel before the Lord our Maker. For He is our God; and we are the people of his pasture, and the sheep of His hand. (Psalm 95:6, 7 KJV)

Make a joyful noise unto the Lord, all ye lands. Serve the Lord with gladness: come before His presence with singing. (Psalm 100:1-2 KJV)

Then saith Jesus unto him, Get thee hence, Satan, for it is written, Thou shalt worship the Lord thy God, and Him only shalt thou serve. (Matthew 4:10 KJV)

June 19   Bow Before an Awesome God

Two brothers grew up in a small farming community. One went to a university, earned a law degree, and became a prominent lawyer. The other stayed on the family farm and assumed responsibility there. One day the lawyer asked his brother, "Why don't you make a name for yourself as I have done?"

His brother gently replied, "See that field of wheat. Look closely. Only the empty heads stand up straight and erect. Those that are full always bow low."

When you are full of God's Spirit, you bow in gratitude for His blessings. You offer Him your best gifts. You want to worship God with a humble spirit.

For thus saith the high and lofty One that inhabits eternity, whose name is Holy; I dwell in the high and holy place, with him also that is of a contrite and humble spirit, to revive the spirit of the humble, and to revive the heart of the contrite ones. (Isaiah 57:15 KJV)

He has shewed thee, O man, what is good; and what doth the Lord require of thee, but to do justly, and to love mercy, and to walk humbly with thy God? (Micah 6:8 KJV)

And whosoever shall exalt himself shall be abased; and he that shall humble himself shall be exalted. (Mathew 23:12 KJV)

An evangelist was preaching in a revival service in a town away from his home when he became painfully ill. His head throbbed, his back ached, and waves of nausea poured over him. For nearly five minutes he had talked about Jesus as Savior who makes people more than conquerors. Suddenly he could no longer continue.

He extended the invitation and asked the pastor of the church to greet those coming forward to make decisions. He stumbled outside, and a deacon rushed him to the hospital emergency room. The doctors quickly diagnosed his problem as acute kidney infection.

About an hour later the pastor visited him at the hospital. "Thanks for letting the Lord use you," he commented. "Sixteen people trusted Christ as Savior tonight."

What the evangelist viewed as a failure and an embarrassment, God had turned into triumph for His glory. He realized he had obeyed God in preaching the message. God then took charge and by His Spirit moved the message into the hearts of listeners. God's purpose was accomplished.

But God hath chosen the foolish things of the world to confound the wise; and God hath chosen the weak things of the world to confound the things which are mighty; And base things of the world, and things which are despised, hath God chosen, yea, and things which are not, to bring to nought things that are: That no flesh should glory in His presence. But of Him are ye in Christ Jesus, who of God is made unto us wisdom, and righteousness, and sanctification, and redemption: That, according as it is written, He that glorieth, let him glory in the Lord. (1 Corinthians 1:27-31 KJV)

June 21   The Cross Leads Home

A little four-year-old was playing in his wire-fenced back yard. Suddenly a yellow cat came through a hole in the fence, and the little boy was delighted. He chased it around in the yard, laughing at the cat's antics. Then the cat went to the fence and crawled through the hole. The little boy wanted to follow the cat, so he began climbing the fence, putting his tennis-shoed feet in the fence holes. He reached the top and looked for the cat.

Running to the front of the house and to the sidewalk he looked both ways. Then he espied the yellow cat near the end of the block. He ran in that direction calling "Come back kitty. I want to play with you." But the cat kept going and so did the boy. The distance between the cat and the boy grew farther apart, and the little boy stopped chasing it.

Hot and thirsty, the boy looked around him. He did not recognize any of the houses. He became frightened. He knew he was lost. He began to cry. A man raking leaves in the yard of the house at which the boy had stopped heard him crying and rushed to him.

"What's the matter?" he asked. "Where is your mother? Are you here by yourself? Where do you live?"

"I saw a cat," the boy whimpered, "and it ran away and I wanted it to come back to play with me, and . . ."

"Oh, my! Did you run away from your home?" the man asked, stooping down and wiping the boy's face with a big handkerchief.

"Yes . . . and I don't know where my house is now," he bellowed.

"Well, come with me, and we'll go back the way you came and we'll find your house," the man said, taking him by the hand.

As they walked along slowly, the man asked "What is your name?"

"Billy."

"What is your last name?"

"Just Billy."

"What is your Daddy's name?"

"Mommy calls him Jim."

"What is the color of your house?"

"Yellow, I think."

The man seemed to be making no progress at all. He hoped a policeman would come along. For sure he was not going to let go of the hand of this little boy if it took him hours to find his home. Wondering what else he needed to do, suddenly the little boy gripped the man's hand, looked up at him, and exclaimed, "If you can get me to the street where the church with a cross on top of it is, then I'll know how to get home. My house is on that street."

The man immediately knew the street where the church stood with a cross on top, and he and the boy hurried toward it, five long blocks away. The closer they came to the street, the boy walked faster, and finally, he turned loose of the man's hand and began to run. The man jogged along with him. They reached the church, and as they turned toward the boy's home, they were met by his weeping mother and other neighbors.

After being hugged by his mother, the boy looked up at the man and said "Mama, he found me and brought me home. I got lost, 'cause I ran after a cat."

She reached out and shook the man's hand. "Oh, thank you, sir, thank you."

Then the man told her, "It was when he told me if I could get him to the cross, he would then know his way home, and I knew the right way."

And being found in fashion as a man, He humbled Himself, and became obedient unto death, even the death of the cross. (Philippians 2:8 KJV)

And, having made peace through the blood of His cross, by Him to reconcile all things unto Himself; by Him, I say, whether they be things in earth, or things in heaven. (Colossians 1:20 KJV)

Looking unto Jesus the author and finisher of our faith; who for the joy that was set before Him endured the cross, despising the shame, and is set down at the right hand of the throne of God. (Hebrews 12:2 KJV)

June 22   God <u>Do</u> Love You

During the years when D. L. Moody was evangelist in many areas of the world, his name and work was known far and wide. In some of the descriptions of this popular preacher people made jokes about him.

They especially laughed at his vocabulary. He did not always use proper grammar, did not put the right verb with the noun. He did not speak with eloquence.

Because of this problem with his speaking, people would sometimes go to his crusades merely to be entertained, laughing at his poor use of grammar. Such were some American soldiers stationed near the place one of the revival meetings was going on. Several of the soldiers went one night and sat in a section where they could hear and make fun of him, by guffawing at certain points.

It was a first time for one of the soldiers, and he was there to jeer along with his fellows. His opportunity came when, after the choir sang a hymn about how Jesus so loved sinners, that Moody took the podium. He looked out over the crowd and said with such persuasion, "Oh, how God do love you! He *do* love you! Yes. He *do!*"

The soldiers laughed aloud and clapped their hands in derision. All during the sermon they kept up their taunting. In spite of their rudeness, Moody kept on with his sermon. At the end when the invitation was extended, many went forward, knelt and gave their hearts to Jesus.

The crowd dispersed. The soldiers made it back to their barracks, and got into their bunks, some of them still rehashing the Moody *entertainment.* At length all were asleep and much snoring was going on. Except for one fellow. The one who had gone to the meeting for the first time. The words "God do love you" kept running through his mind. He tossed and turned and could not sleep. Finally, he found himself sobbing. Then down beside his bunk he prayed to the God who *do* love him, repented of his sins, and received Jesus as his Lord and Savior.

God uses all types of persons, each one with his or her personality traits and mannerisms to accomplish His purpose.

> How beautiful upon the mountains are the feet of him that bringeth good tidings, that publisheth peace; that bringeth good tidings of good, that publisheth salvation; that saith unto Zion, Thy God reigneth! (Isaiah 52:7 KJV)

> So shall my word be that goeth forth out of My mouth: it shall not return unto me void, but it shall accomplish that which

I please, and it shall prosper in the thing whereto I sent it. (Isaiah 55:11 KJV)

So then faith cometh by hearing, and hearing by the word of God. (Romans 10:17 KJV)

June 23   Simply, Like a Child

Except you become as a *little child*, Jesus said. So, I began to watch the doings of little boys and girls. A little boy chose a narrow path to walk on, and he squatted to finger a little yellow wildflower. Seeing a dandelion, he flopped down on his stomach and blew the fuzz away. On his knees he put his face close to an ant hill to watch the ants scurrying about. He tilted his face to the rush of wind and giggled when it tugged at his blond curls.

Trotting along the path, he caught sight of a ladybug on a blade of grass. Pointing to it, he blurted: "Look, it's got dots!" Then he spun to chase a yellow butterfly.

Following him back to his home, I noticed he hurried to a little corner, and sat in a little chair there. Then, he hopped down and skipped to a book case where he picked up a little book with frayed corners and chocolate smears. Toddling to where I sat, he ordered, "Read to me." He looked up and listened with trusting eyes and ears as I began to read the book to him.

Then I understood at once something of what Jesus meant when He said, "Except you ... become as a little child." I learned that I too must choose the simple things. I need to pay attention to lowly matters and take pleasure in tiny sights and sounds all around me. Most especially, I must trust God, my Father, simply and unwaveringly, and I must listen to and obey His Word without complicating it with dissecting and analyzing, merely accepting it, simply like a little child.

Better it is to be of an humble spirit with the lowly, than to divide the spoil with the proud. (Proverbs 16:19 KJV)

And Jesus called a little child unto Him, and set him in the midst of them, And said, Verily I say unto you, Except ye be converted, and become as little children, ye shall not enter into the kingdom of heaven. Whosoever therefore shall humble himself as this little child, the same is greatest in the kingdom of heaven. (Matthew 18:2-4 KJV)

But He giveth more grace. Wherefore he saith, God resisteth the proud, but giveth grace unto the humble. (James 4:6 KJV)

June 24   God is Looking for Such Women

God is looking for a woman like *Eve* who kept herself lovely in Adam's eyes. Her love for her mate made their garden home a continually pleasant Paradise.

God wants to find a woman like *Sarah* who followed Abraham wherever God sent. She never complained, 'though all her life through her dwelling was a tarpaulin tent.

God searches for a woman like *Hannah* who lent her son to Him without regret. She praised God for hearing her petition, grateful that her heart's desire He had met.

God is seeking a woman like *Esther*, who to her people's cries was not deaf. Determined to deliver her kin from harm, she willingly risked the life of herself.

God favors one like Bethany's *Mary*, at whose table Jesus would often eat. She worshiped, anointing Him with spikenard, and sat raptly listening at His feet.

God is pleased with one such as *Lydia*. For the church's meeting, her home she lent. She often lodged preachers like Paul and Silas as on journeys they came and went.

All these women have finished their courses; there is nothing more they can say or do, But God still seeks out women to serve Him— mothers, teachers, and, someone like *you*.

Of course, you are not Eve, Sarah, Hannan, nor Esther with her beauty and grace, But wherever the Lord wants you to serve Him, you will make this world a lovelier place.

Even every one that is called by my name: for I have created him for my glory, I have formed him; yea, I have made him. (Isaiah 43:7 KJV)

For we are His workmanship, created in Christ Jesus unto good works, which God hath before ordained that we should walk in them. (Ephesians 2:10 KJV)

Who gave Himself for us, that He might redeem us from all iniquity, and purify unto Himself a peculiar people [a people for His own possession], zealous of good works. (Titus 2:14 KJV)

June 25   Fogs Across Our Paths

Once when driving to an appointment in an early morning, fog entombed my car and me in suffocating gray. Alongside the road on both sides leaf-bare trees cast eerie silhouettes. The car's headlights' pale glow pushed against the dense, murky drape, and the drape flounced ahead into a like tunnel room.

Then glorious sunshine punctured through, unwrapped the bindings, and lifted my car and me out of the crypt.

Another time, in like fashion, fear entombed my heart in purple shadows. Corners leered ever closer. Time ticked loud. With fists of panic I pushed against the smothering curtain, and the curtain flounced ahead to a thicker curtained room.

Then I cried unto the Lord with full-throttled trust in Him, and peace punctured through, drove back dark corners, quietened the tick of time, and lifted my heart out of the pit.

He brought me up also out of an horrible pit, out of the miry clay, and set my feet upon a rock, and established my goings. And He hath put a new song in my mouth, even praise unto our God: many shall see it, and fear, and shall trust in the Lord. (Psalm 40:2-3 KJV)

What time I am afraid, I will trust in thee. (Psalm 56:3 KJV)

Fear thou not; for I am with thee: be not dismayed; for I am thy God: I will strengthen thee; yea, I will help thee; yea, I will uphold thee with the right hand of my righteousness. (Isaiah 41:10 KJV)

June 26   Daily Provider

Our Heavenly Father owns the cattle on a thousand hills and all the gold of this planet. Why then, as His children, need we doubt His promise to provide our daily bread?

Yes, He commands that we ask for it. Why? Perhaps it is because He wants us to realize we must rely upon Him for our every day's sustenance. Or, could it be He just wants to hear our voices daily, each one's voice having its own resonance.

It's like He makes a date with us to meet with Him and talk about things pertaining to that particular day. If we slip up and fail to meet Him, I wonder if He feels we've stood Him up?

We don't want to disappoint Him, so we must take care to talk to Him each morning, and ask for what we need, even though He already knows before we ask. He has already started connecting the dots to bring our requests to pass.

Over and over, the Lord has provided this same way for all we have needed, and He still does, from the enormous to the wee. He never gives less nor more than we need.

Yes, He is our Daily Sufficient One, and we who love Him look forward to meeting Him every morning to talk about what that day holds, and all during that day He delights in our sharing the moment-by-moment happenings.

At close of day, we then can say, "Goodnight Lord," knowing He will stay awake and watch over us while we sleep.

There shall not any man be able to stand before thee all the days of thy life: as I was with Moses, so I will be with thee: I will not fail thee, nor forsake thee. (Joshua 1:5 KJV)

He will not suffer thy foot to be moved: He that keepeth thee will not slumber. (Psalm 121:3 KJV)

But thou, when thou prayest, enter into thy closet, and when thou hast shut thy door, pray to thy Father which is in secret; and thy Father which seeth in secret shall reward thee openly. (Matthew 6:6 KJV)

As the Father hath loved Me, so have I loved you: continue ye in my love. (John 15:9 KJV)

June 27   You are Important in God's Economy

I read the following lines somewhere and copied them. I like them. And hope you do too!

- A rooster minus a hen equals no baby chick.
- Kellogg minus a farmer equals no corn flakes.
- If the nail factory closes, what good is the hammer family?
- Beethoven's genius wouldn't have amounted to much if the piano tuner hadn't shown up.
- A cracker maker will do better if there's a cheese maker.
- The most skillful surgeon needs the ambulance driver who delivers the patient.
- Just as Rodgers needed Hammerstein, you need someone and someone needs YOU!

For none of us liveth to himself, and no man dieth to himself. (Romans 14:7 KJV)

For to one is given by the Spirit the word of wisdom; to another the word of knowledge by the same Spirit; To another faith by the same Spirit; to another the gifts of healing by the same Spirit; To another the working of miracles; to another prophecy; to another discerning of spirits; to another divers kinds of tongues; to another the interpretation of tongues: But all these worketh that one and the selfsame Spirit, dividing to every man severally as he will. (1 Corinthians 12:8-11 KJV)

Only Luke is with me. Take Mark, and bring him with thee: for he is profitable to me for the ministry. (2 Timothy 4:11 KJV)

June 28   Good Men in Place

> When men hold roles of prominence
> And take charge of making the rules,
> Fewer homes are plundered,
> And order reigns in our schools.
> When in the halls of government,
> Voices heard are mostly of males,
> Power exudes against corruption
> And integrity primarily prevails.
> With men as managers of business,
> Commerce will thrive and abound.
> Their credence prompts top performance
> And pride in one's job is found.
> Husbands and fathers are pillars
> In churches that take root and grow,
> Their steadfastness sways their watchers
> To worship the God they know.
> When men assume God-designed places,
> Wives and mothers know contentment and mirth.
> Their children rise to heights of achievement,
> And the bests of life encompass the earth.
>   --Carlene Poff Baker

Her husband is known in the gates, when he sitteth among the elders of the land. (Proverbs 31:23 KJV)

But I would have you know, that the head of every man is Christ; and the head of the woman is the man; and the head of Christ is God. (1 Corinthians 11:3 KJV)

For the man is not of the woman; but the woman of the man. Neither was the man created for the woman; but the woman for the man. (1 Corinthians 11:8-9 KJV)

For the husband is the head of the wife, even as Christ is the head of the church: and he is savior of the body. (Ephesians 5:23 KJV)

But I suffer not a woman to teach, nor to usurp authority over the man, but to be in silence. For Adam was first formed, then Eve. (1 Timothy 2:12-13 KJV)

June 29   The Widow's Mite

Seeing out her window the hunched man set down his burlap sack to pick up a cola can, she hurried to the closet, where her box of empty cans sat, that she had planned to sell when she had enough to buy a new broom.

Dashing to the front door, she opened it and hollered, "Wait, sir, I have some cans I need to get rid of." Taking an armload of cans to the curb, she dropped them in his burlap sack. He gave her a wide, toothless grin, and a nod of his head. Then he shuffled on down the street.

Watching two squirrels scavenge in her back yard, without a find on the frosty ground, she scooped two bowlfuls of her store of last year's pecans and flung them toward the startled critters. At her kitchen window she watched delightfully as they skittered along the high line wire back to their hollow tree somewhere, their cheeks pooching fat.

Noticing the big-eyed boy in ragged jeans, who she knew lived two blocks down the street from her, kicking up dirt from the asphalt street as he trudged past her house, his eyes searching for coins. After he had gone farther down the street in his search, she donned coat and scarf and filled her pocket with pennies and nickels she had been saving to buy herself a pair of new shoes. She walked along the street past the boy's home, trickling the coins from her gloved fingers, delighting in hearing them clink and bounce against the curb, where she hoped the boy might find them tomorrow.

Circling the block to return home, she passed the Woodruff's house, and noticed a telling wreath on the door. So, Mr. Woodruff must have died, she mused. She remembered he had been ill so long.

What can I do to help? She wondered. I can fix a dish of food, she reasoned. Recalling her cupboard was down to a one-meal serving of beef, a few pieces of bread, a tad of milk, and two eggs, she knew there was not much left until her monthly check would arrive in three days. But . . .

Donned once more in coat, scarf and gloves, in late afternoon, hoping to be in readiness for the evening meal, she made her way up the Woodruffs' doorsteps, with her prettiest covered dish in her gloved hands. The aroma of the warm meat loaf wafted deliciously in the frosty air.

She stretcheth out her hand to the poor; yea, she reacheth forth her hands to the needy. (Proverbs 31:20 KJV)

Let him that stole steal no more: but rather let him labor, working with his hands the thing which is good, that he may have to give to him that needeth. (Ephesians 4:28 KJV)

But to do good and to communicate forget not: for with such sacrifices God is well pleased. (Hebrews 13:16 KJV)

June 30   Sterling Words of Great Patriots

Thomas Jefferson: "When a man assumes a public trust, he should consider himself as public property."

Wendell Phillips: "One on God's side is a majority."

Carl Schurz: "Our country, right or wrong. When right, to be kept right; when wrong, to be put right."

Patrick Henry: "Is life so dear, or peace so sweet, as to be purchased at the price of chains and slavery? Forbid it, Almighty God! I know not what course others may take, but as for me, give me liberty, or give me death!"

Abraham Lincoln: "I am not bound to win, but I am bound to be true. I am not bound to succeed, but I am bound to live up to what light I have. I must stand with anybody that stands right, stand with him while he is right, and part with him when he goes wrong."

John D. Rockefeller, Jr.: "I believe in the supreme worth of the individual and in his right to life, liberty, and the pursuit of happiness. I believe that the law was made for man and not man for the law, that government is the servant of the people and not their master. I believe in the dignity of labor, whether with head or hand; that the world owes no man a living, but that it owes every man an opportunity to make a living. I believe that truth and justice are fundamental to an enduring social order. I believe in the sacredness of a promise, that a man's word should be as good as his bond, that character – not wealth or power or position – is of supreme worth. I believe in an All-Wise and All-Loving God, and that the individual's highest fulfillment, greatest happiness, and widest usefulness are to be found in living in harmony with His will. I believe that love is the greatest thing in the world; that right can and will triumph over might."

Benjamin Franklin's Creed: "I believe in one God, the Creator of the Universe; that He governs it by His Providence. That He ought to be worshipped. That the most acceptable service we render to Him is doing good to His other children. That the soul of man is immortal, and will be treated with justice in another life respecting its conduct in this."

Blessed is the nation whose God is the Lord; and the people whom
He hath chosen for His own inheritance. (Psalm 33:12 KJV)

    The American Creed as Applied to My Heart

I am persuaded that my country, the United States of America, is a prefecture of the people, the governed, who by their ardor set in effect unshakable powers.

I am assured that my country is a state of body prudent, a sovereign entity of fifty sovereign entities, fraternally linked and bonded.

I am convinced that my country will stay undauntedly fixed upon those precepts of liberty, parity, fairness, and altruism for which her benefactors gave their very lives and fortunes in yielded sacrifice.

Henceforth, I am indebted to my country, The United States of America, to cherish her, to shore up her statutes, to perform her doctrines, to reverently hail her flag, and to put to flight all her enemies.

"God, bless America, land that I love; Stand beside her and guide her, through the night with a light from above. From the mountains, to the prairies, to the oceans white with foam, God bless America, my home sweet home!"

    What America Needs

+ *Leaders*, like Moses, who refused to be called the son of Pharaoh's daughter but was willing to go with God.
+ *Army Generals*, like Joshua, who knew God and could pray and shout things to come to pass rather than blow them to pieces with atomic energy.
+ *Food Administrators*, like Joseph, who knew God and had the answer to famine.
+ *Preachers*, like Peter, who would not be afraid to look people in the eye and say, "Repent or perish," and denounce personal as well as national sins.
+ *Mothers*, like Hannah, who would rather pray for a child that she might give him to God, rather than women who are delinquent mothers of delinquent children.
+ *Physicians*, like Luke, who would care for the physically sick and minister to the spiritual soul.

- *Children*, like Samuel, who would talk to God in the night hours.
- *A God*, like Israel's instead of the dollar god, the entertainment god, and the auto god.
- *A Savior*, like Jesus, who could and would save to the uttermost.

For ye are bought with a price: therefore glorify God in your body, and in your spirit, which are God's. (1 Corinthians 6:20 KJV)

July 3   Not Home Yet

A missionary and wife, who had been on a mission field for several years, were returning to the United States for a one-year furlough. They were to rest visit with their family members from whom they had been separated all those years. They had contacted their family, and, of course the churches who had supported their mission work, of the date they would arrive by ship at the sea coast.

Their excitement mounted as they neared the port where they would dock. They wondered who all would be there to welcome them. When at last they arrived, they were stunned to hear a band playing loud music on the shore. As they made their way toward the exit gate, they saw an enormous crowd of people.

"Ah, wife, just look at all those people! And somebody got together a band to welcome us!"

Then, they heard over a loud speaker the announcement that a government dignitary had arrived from his trip abroad, and the crowd was to make way for his departure down the ramp.

All other passengers on the ship had to wait for the departure of the person named to leave the ship. They watched as the crowd followed. The band ceased to play and band members were making their way with the crowd.

Finally, the ones left on board were then permitted to leave the ship. The missionary and his wife looked out on the shore and saw no one they recognized. Not a single person rushed to welcome them. The wife of the missionary looked at him and saw his face had begun to show somber disappointment. Then, awe-struck, she noticed a slow, changing expression on his face. Watching him wipe tears off his face with his handkerchief, she then saw the most radiant smile spreading over his face.

"Dear, I just received the most wonderful news. I sensed the Lord saying to me, 'My child, you've not come home yet.' Oh, how wonderful will be the time when you and I do go home! What a welcoming event that will be! First, we'll see Jesus, and then angels, no doubt, and then all those loved ones who have gone on ahead of us."

> Then Abraham gave up the ghost, and died in a good old age, an old man, and full of years; and was gathered to his people. (Genesis 25:8 KJV)

> And Isaac gave up the ghost, and died, and was gathered unto his people, being old and full of days: and his sons Esau and Jacob buried him. (Genesis 35:29 KJV)

> And when Jacob had made an end of commanding his sons, he gathered up his feet into the bed, and yielded up the ghost, and was gathered unto his people. (Genesis 49:33 KJV)

 July 4   What Do They See?

After Jesus had ascended back to heaven, having completed His purpose for coming to the earth – death, burial and resurrection, His sacrifice to pay the penalty for the sins of all mankind – He left His church in the world to evangelize the message of salvation.

The larger the church grew, the angrier the devil became, and he and his crowd set out to make an end of the church. The devil used every means and everyone he could convince to do the work, including the political powers.

The political powers did accordingly, and there began a mass persecution of the Lord's people. Among the means of death was fastening a believer in Jesus to a pole in a recreation-type field, with bleachers all around for spectators to watch, as lions were turned loose on the ones tied to the poles to attack them until they died. Others were put on poles and a brush fire would be set under the poles so that the believers would burn to death.

The persons watching in the bleachers enjoyed the event as if it were a sporting or festive occasion. Even emperors were among the crowd who watched. What stunned the spectators, however, was how the believers who were being tortured sang psalms as they were dying, and it seemed that each one lifted his or her head heavenward with a look of hope on their bleeding faces.

On one occasion an emperor noticed the expressions of serenity on the tortured ones' faces and said, "Wonder what they are looking at when they look up. Do they see someone? I just don't understand how they could look so at peace."

We have one account of a like event in the Bible. It was during the time when the devil's crowd stoned Stephen to death because he preached about Jesus the Savior. As he was near death, he looked up and said, "I see heaven opened and the Son of Man standing on the right hand of God. ... Lord Jesus, receive my spirit. ... Lord, lay not this sin to their charge."

> But he, being full of the Holy Ghost, looked up steadfastly into heaven, and saw the glory of God, and Jesus standing on the right hand of God, And said, Behold, I see the heavens opened, and the Son of man standing on the right hand of God. Then they cried out with a loud voice, and stopped their ears, and ran upon him with one accord, And cast him out of the city, and stoned him: and the witnesses laid down their clothes at a young man's feet, whose name was Saul. And they stoned Stephen, calling upon God, and saying, Lord Jesus, receive my spirit. And he kneeled down, and cried with a loud voice, Lord, lay not this sin to their charge. And when he had said this, he fell asleep. (Acts 7:55-60 KJV)

I drive into Nashville, Tennessee as I go to my work site. There are billboards and other signs all along the roads declaring it "Music City." There is even a new, extravaganza of a building named Music City Center. Street buses advertise with huge, colorful writing and designs that the whole area is the Music City. Recently I was following a big truck, and on its whole back was a painting of two pair of cowboy boots: a man's pair and a woman's pair. When I drove up behind it closer, I read "Boots worn by Dale Evans and Roy Rogers."

I enjoy all the logos and exciting musical phrases as I go up and down the streets. Another really peculiar thing I have noticed is many young adult men walking along the streets, and sitting on corner benches, wearing guitars strapped around their shoulders. It seems to me they have the aspiration that just being under the dome of the sky over Music City they will become great musicians and maybe even a star. If that be their thinking, they are far off track. There must be some action on their part to achieve.

Then I thought how similar it is to persons who want to be attendants in church services, under the dome of a sanctuary for worship, but they don't want to come to know the Lord Jesus as Savior. They don't want to surrender to Him and become committed to serving Him. Well, just like the guy with a guitar strapped on his shoulders, walking around under the Music City sky, the person who is sitting in the pew with no interaction between him and the Lord is just as foolish.

We read of the religious leaders during Jesus' ministry on earth who felt they were righteous by merely being Hebrews. They enjoyed their positions, but they wanted nothing to do with accepting Jesus as their Messiah.

Environment does not change the person. It takes the person coming to grips to who he is and what he needs to do about it, and then pursuing. In the case of the church goer in the pew, he or she needs to take care of the situation by coming to Jesus and accepting Him as Lord and Savior, and then that one and the environment will agree.

Ye hypocrites, well did Esaias prophesy of you, saying, This people draweth nigh unto Me with their mouth, and honoreth Me with their lips; but their heart is far from Me. But in vain they worship Me, teaching for doctrines the commandments of men. (Matthew 15:7-9 KJV)

July 6   Special in God's Universe

Do you ever wonder how important you are in God's eyes? He knew about each human being before he or she was born. In fact, He designed that person in the mother's womb. He created each one for His glory and purpose. So, you are special!

Let's just think about it! There are twelve entities in which you are involved:

1. The Number of your Residence
2. The Name of the Street on which you live
3. The City in which your Street is located
4. The District in which your City is fixed
5. The County in which your District is located
6. The State in which all of the above are contained
7. The Nation in which your State is mapped
8. The Continent which owns your Nation
9. The Hemisphere that claims your Continent
10. The Planet on which your Continent is placed.
11. The Galaxy in which your Planet is fixed.
12. God's Great Universe which envelopes all of the above components.

The one who receives Jesus as Savior becomes a child of God, and that means an heir of God, and joint-heir with Jesus. Yes, you are indeed very special to the One and Only Living God!

Even every one that is called by my name: for I have created him for My glory, I have formed him: yea, I have made him. (Isaiah 43:7 KJV)

July 7 — Omnipresent, Sovereign God

Many of us have heard the expression, "God's in His heaven, all's right with the world." That's a line from Robert Browning's "Pippa's Song," about an orphan girl who lived in Italy and was forced to labor long hours in horrific conditions. Despite her miserable life, Pippa with optimism claims that because one can believe that God is ever present with that person no matter the circumstances, all is right with the world.

Sometimes we wonder why harsh and unjust things happen to God's faithful people. Only God knows the whys of everything. Nothing is a surprise to Him. In fact, He orchestrates the events of everybody's life and of every activity in His universe. Like Pippa, we just have to trust Him, for He always knows what is best. He has a purpose and reason for every happening.

Yes, with faith in the Sovereign God of the universe, no matter whatever situation we find ourselves in, He is alongside and taking care of us in the midst of it all. Hallelujah!

The steps of a good man are ordered by the Lord: and He delighteth in his way. Though he fall, he shall not be utterly cast down: for the Lord upholdeth him with His hand. (Psalm 37:23-24 KJV)

For as the heavens are higher than the earth, so are My ways higher than your ways, and My thoughts than your thoughts. (Isaiah 55:9 KJV)

A favorite song of many people is "The Love of God." The lyrics expound on the magnitude of God's love for the whole sinful human race. The way the words to "The Love of God" came to be known was they were found written on the wall of an insane asylum in Germany. Someone set the poem in music in 1917. Apparently, no one knows the author of the poem.

All through God's Word the Lord tells of His immeasurable love for sinners and His desire to have them come to know Him in forgiveness of their sins and to have peace and the accessibility to the abundant life here on this earth and in the ages to come.

The most often quoted scripture pertaining to God's love is John 3:16 in which the words "For God so loved the world" is found. Can anyone measure the word *so*? It is beyond comprehension!

I'll quote the first words of the wonderful hymn below. You can find them in many hymn books as well.

> The love of God is greater far
> than tongue or pen can ever tell
> It goes beyond the highest star
> and reaches to the lowest Hell.
> The guilty pair, bowed down with care,
> God sent His son to win.
> His erring child He reconciles
> and pardons from his sin.

For God so loved the world, that He gave His Only Begotten Son, that whosoever believeth in Him should not perish, but have everlasting life. (John 3:16 KJV)

But God commendeth His love toward us, in that, while we were yet sinners, Christ died for us. (Romans 5:8 KJV)

Love Above and Beyond

We all know God loves human beings above and beyond comprehension in intensity. But there are those among us who have a like love for others. In fact, we are to love others as ourselves, so say the Scriptures. That can be accomplished only when we know Jesus as personal Savior and the Holy Spirit has come to live within us.

There are at least two examples of this kind of love in the Scriptures. One is that of Moses who had such an intense love for the rebelling Israelites, and the other is the Apostle Paul, who spoke of his love for his Israelite brethren.

In the case of Moses, he had just come down from the Mount where he had been with God and had received the Ten Commandments. When he came down, he found the Israelites worshiping the golden calf idol that Aaron had made. After an awful battle ensued where about three thousand died, Moses told the people he would make an atonement for them. He prayed to God, saying "Oh, this people have sinned a great sin, and have made them gods of gold. Yet now, if You will forgive their sin--; and if not, blot me, I pray You, out of Your book which You have written." He was willing to take the people's sins as a curse upon himself to save the people he loved.

We read of the Apostle Paul's deep love for his people in his letter to the Romans. He expressed his great sorrow for his people, the Jews, by saying he would wish himself accursed from Christ if it took that to get his loved ones to come to know Christ as Savior.

History of God's people down through the ages is full of accounts of those who loved their people so much, they confronted all sorts of perils in their fields, some even to the risk of losing their lives, so that the people they loved could hear the message of redemption. I remember reading a story of a missionary's wife, who awoke in the middle of the night to find her husband not in the bed. She saw no light anywhere, and the fire had gone out and the house was cold. She got up and made her way through the house. She found her husband on his knees with his head on his folded arms at the sofa. He was cold and his face was wet with tears. She begged him to come back to bed. He said he could not because his heart was so heavy for the lost ones to whom he had been sent. She wrapped a blanket around him, and seeing he wanted to be alone, made her way back to their bed.

And Moses returned unto the Lord, and said, Oh, this people have sinned a great sin, and have made them gods of gold. Yet now, if thou wilt forgive their sin –; and if not, blot me, I pray thee, out of thy book which thou written. (Exodus 32:31-32 KJV)

That I have great heaviness and continual sorrow in my heart. For I could wish that myself were accursed from Christ for my brethren, my kinsmen according to the flesh. (Romans 9:2-3 KJV)

July 10   Salt of a Different Savor

I realized a new factor about salt one day. I had whacked down a peach tree that had quit producing fruit, but I could not take up the stump and roots. My neighbor who lived back of me gave me an idea. He was an old, stooped-over white-haired man, who was always working in his yard, so I reckoned he knew about such things.

"Wet the ground around the stump and pour a lot of salt around it," he advised. "In time the stump will come out on its own."

I thought, well, it's worth a try. My skepticism grew, however, when as the months passed, when I had kept watering the stump and dumping salt around it, the stump had not budged. I continued to have to mow around that stump. That stump stayed in its place a whole year.

The next summer, however, when I was mowing, my mower bumped against the stump, and the whole thing gave way and came out of the ground. I thought, well, my back-door neighbor knew what he was talking about.

The Lord said in Matthew 5:13, "You are the salt of the earth," and I had always taken that to include qualities of preservative, seasoning, healing, cleansing, moisture retention, but never as a destroyer. For me that summer, salt destroyed something that had hindered.

Could it be that we who are the Lord's people can so persist or persevere against evil or a hinderance to the point that the problem will give way in time? Keeping applying salt on a hanging-on ungodly habit will in due time give way and disappear. Persistent praying might move old stumps of doubt and unconcern in the hearts of loved ones we want to see saved. It's worth a try!

> For ye have need of patience, that, after ye have done the will of God, ye might receive the promise. (Hebrews 10:36 KJV)

July 11   No Greater Friend than Jesus

Nearly every hymn writer we read about came to the point of writing his or her poem after a vivid, sometimes traumatic event in that one's life. My Sunday School teacher told of one such person, whose name was Joseph Scriven, a young Irish immigrant. He and his sweetheart had made plans for their wedding. But shortly before the wedding day the bride-to-be drowned. For a long time, Joseph Scriven was angry and embittered, and had even gotten to the point of great depression.

Cornered in his despair, he at last turned to Christ, and through His mercy and grace, he found peace and comfort. Knowing such heartbreak and loss, and then having turned to the and compassionate Lord and Savior Jesus Christ, he was able to write the lyrics to "What A Friend We Have in Jesus." The words of that hymn have blessed, and continues to bless, so many people who have found themselves in a feeling of utter loss as he, and who were lifted from despair when finding genuine friendship in Christ.

> God is our refuge and strength, a very present help in trouble. (Psalm 46:1 KJV)

> A man that hath friends must shew himself friendly: and there is a friend that sticketh closer than a brother. (Proverbs 18:24 KJV)

Ye are my friends, if ye do whatsoever I command you. Henceforth I call you not servants; for the servant knoweth not what his lord doeth: but I have called you friends; for all things that I have heard of my Father I have made known unto you. (John 15:14-15 KJV)

July 12   Idleness Makes Shoulders Sag

A friend of mine said she thanked God every morning when she got up that she had something to do which must be done. In fact, she said she kept an errand undone sometimes so she would have that errand to tackle next morning. Being forced to work, and forced to do your best, will breed in you temperance, self-control, diligence, strength of will, content, and a feeling of accomplishment, which slothful folks never know

God works. Genesis chapter one states that emphatically! He created everything. In fact, the Three Persons of the Godhead were at work in creation. God spoke, the Holy Spirit moved, and Jesus, the Son of God, created, Jesus said God His Father continued to work and that He Himself was continually working. The Holy Spirit is busy throughout the whole world, everywhere present and everywhere powerful.

When God created the first man, Adam, He told him to work, to tend to the Garden of Eden. And after Adam and Eve sinned He said they were to work by the sweat of their brows. The Apostle Paul said that, if a person does not work, he cannot expect to eat. In Proverbs, wise Solomon said much about the idle, even showing the lazy that the ant was smarter than they.

We are to work, and in every work we do we are to do it as to the Lord, only do the kind of work or occupation that is pleasing in His sight. He is the One who makes each of us the way He wants, and He is the One who equips us with talents and skills to do our work.

Let's be busy doing good things in our world to make it a lovelier place, helping others, and glorifying our Lord. Then we won't be seen with sagging shoulders!

In the beginning God created the heaven and the earth. And the earth was without form, and void; and darkness was upon the face of the deep. And the spirit of God moved upon the face of the waters. And God said, Let there be light: and there was light. (Genesis 1:1-3 KJV)

And the Lord God took the man, and put him into the garden of Eden to dress it and to keep it. (Genesis 2:15 NKV)

But Jesus answered them, My Father works hitherto, and I work. (John 5:17 KJV)

For even when we were with you, this we commanded you, that if any would not work, neither should he eat. (2 Thessalonians 3:10 KJV)

July 13   Jesus was Really Asking

When Jesus asked the lame man, "Do you want to be made whole?" He was really asking, "Do you really want to give up your luxury of being waited on?" (John 5:6)

When Jesus stopped abruptly in the jostling procession and asked, "Who touched Me?" He was really asking, "Who showed unrelenting persistence to reach out to Me at any cost?" (Mark 5:31; Luke 8:45)

After the crowds dispersed because His sayings were too hard, Jesus asked the twelve, "Will you also go away?" He was really asking, "Do you not enjoy just being with Me as much as I enjoy your fellowship?" (John 6:67)

On the Jericho Road, hearing Bartimaeus' bellow above the crowd's din, Jesus asked, "What is it you would have Me do for you?" He was really saying, "Don't hedge, Bartimaeus, be specific." (Mark 10:51)

After praying in the Garden of Gethsemane and finding His disciples asleep, Jesus asked "Could you not watch with Me one hour?" But He was really telling them, "I do not demand your whole day. I just want you to stand with Me one hour." (Matthew 26:40; Mark 14:37)

When King David said, "Go in peace, my son," he was not aware of the deception

that Absalom had schemed to take his throne and win all of Israel's reception.

He stole the hearts of Israel's throng with cunning and crafty deceit,

deliberately doing his father wrong; hatefully plotting the King's defeat.

When a messenger brought King David news that his son planned his horrid plight,

the king left his palace, rather to lose all he had gained than his beloved to fight.

The king prayed and wept, ever fearing, not for his kingdom or loss of his life.

His yearning was for the son of his rearing whose rebellion had affected this strife.

"No truce!" Absalom shouted, deficient of ration; the king geared for battle, Joab in command.

As they left, the king pleaded with compassion, "Deal gently with the young man."

In the woods of Ephraim, they battled; Absalom's army could not Joab withstand.

He hurried to meet Joab's men astraddle a mule footing the craggy, wooded land.

Absalom staunchly refused to surrender and return to his father's due will,

Trampling underfoot a love, kind and tender, preferring his vindictive, egotistical thrill,

wielding his mule to keep his feet tangle-free, he pursued with speed and conquering vim.

But he failed to see the spreading oak tree with a jutting, forked limb.

The branch snagged his long, golden hair; his animal kept clomping on.

He wailed in pain and terror hanging there. "Help me, somebody! I'm King David's son!"

Joab saw this as victory as he pierced his body through, forgetting "Don't hurt my boy!"

Joab reasoned it an honorable war act to do, seeing himself as victor with
a right to feel joy.

Joab sent this message to the king at his seat: "Battle's over, enemy met
his death."

One messenger ran and fell at the king's feet, but scarcely could speak,
so out of breath.

"Is my son safe?" the king kept prodding. Before the man could answer,
another man came.

"You're avenged, O King! It's cause for applauding!" The king's question
to him was the same.

"Is the young man Absalom safe," I ask. "Please tell me what it is you
are saying."

"Absalom is dead, the one who took you to task. For this victory you
have been praying."

With shoulders drooping, his countenance paling, the king went away
so no one could see.

Those outside heard his heartbroken wailing, "Oh, my son, Absalom,
my son, my son, would to God I had died for thee!"

July 15   Author's Psalm Twenty-Three, Personalized

The Exclusively Specific One, who holds the position of Highest Person
of Preeminence, present here this moment, and each succeeding moment,
is the One whose sheep I am, whom He knows by name.

He leads me in only right places for my good and for His glory, He
give me the just right rest when I am weary to the core. He refreshes and
renews me with His constant Presence.

He envelopes me in peace and provides a regal feast, while my
enemies look on glaring. I rely on His boundless mercy all the while,
and I claim His promise that I will live with Him in His house forever.

I had been visiting my kinfolks in Tennessee, and was on my way home in Arkansas, driving my Pontiac car. I had never had any problem with the vehicle, and was so pleased with it. But that day, suddenly I heard a shrill screaming noise coming from under the hood. The car's motor kept running, but I knew something was terribly wrong.

Fortunately, not long after the noise began, I saw an exit sign and took it, and even more fortunately, I saw a service station-convenience store not far away. I parked beside the station, turned off the ignition, and the noise stopped. I pulled the handle that lifted the hood, got out and looked under the hood. Nothing looked amiss, no smoke or fire or anything like that.

I went inside the station where a woman was the one at the counter. I asked if there was a mechanic there. She said no but she could call one for me. While thinking about it, I saw a gray-haired man sitting in a booth looking at me. He had a little bag of stuff, probably bought there at the station. I asked him if he knew anything about cars and why one would just start making a loud noise out of the blue. He said, "I might, but I'm waiting for a taxi to come and take me home."

I asked if he would just come and look under the hood and see if he could tell what was wrong. He followed me to the car. I got in and turned on the ignition. The noise began. He came to my window and said, "Turn it off. I can see what is wrong."

Then he said, "There is a loose screw in a really close place that needs to be tightened. Do you have any tools?" I took him to the trunk and we looked at tools. No wrench the size he needed. So, we went back into the station.

I asked the counter lady, "Do you sell wrenches here?"

"No, but I can call someone," she said again.

The little man had gone back to sit at the booth with his sack. The cab not come yet. While I wondered what I should do, suddenly the driver of a TV cable van dashed in the front door with a thermos in his hand. He asked the lady for a soft drink which, apparently, he would put in his thermos.

I dared to sidle up to the van driver and asked, "Sir, do you have tools in your van, like certain wrenches?"

He said he did. Then I took him over to the little man in the booth and he told him what size wrench was needed. They both went to the van and the little man had the right wrench. I followed the two men to my car where the man tightened the screw. Then he told me to get in and turn on the ignition. I did, and, glory be, there was no noise. The motor purred perfectly.

The little man grinned at me with such a big grin that his eyes almost disappeared in his wrinkles. The younger man took his wrench and went back into the store to get his soft drink.

I felt I needed to pay these two guys for their work on my behalf, but I had only fifteen dollars. I knew I could make it home without any money, so I told the men, "I'll give you fifteen to be divided between yourselves. That's all I have." The van man shook his head with a grin and said he was just glad he happened by at the right time. He got in his van and left with the thermos in his hand. I followed the other man back into the station – his cab still not having arrived. I said "Sir, I am so glad for what you did for me. I want to pay your taxi cab fare." He refused. But I left a ten-dollar bill on the table in front of him.

When I got back in my car, I thanked God for His intervention. I felt like He had sent these two men, perhaps angels unawares, just for me. He was taking care of me again, as He so did all the time.

After that day, every time I took that road going to and from my daughter's home in Tennessee, I slowed down to look at the service station-convenience store. It became a hallowed spot for me!

The angel of the Lord encampeth round about them that fear Him, and delivereth them. (Psalm 34:7 KJV)

What time I am afraid, I will trust in Thee. (Psalm 56:3 KJV)

For He shall give His angels charge over thee, to keep thee in all thy ways. (Psalm 91:11 KJV)

People who climb mountains always fascinate me. I see it as a daring endeavor surrounded by myriad hazards. I knew a mountain-climbing family once, who spent some time every summer in climbing the high Ozark Mountains. I would always sit spellbound when they told of their ventures.

They were a family of husband, wife, two sons and a daughter. All of them were actively adept. Then, one summer their youngest son fell from a lofty peak to his death. That was their last time to climb a mountain.

While I don't know all the things one has to know and be trained for to mountain climb, I learned at least one thing that has stayed with me. My friend said, "When climbing a mountain, you need to always have three of your extremities stationed firmly. When you reach with one of your arms to take hold of the next crag, the other arm and both feet must be anchored. Then, to take a step upward with one foot, both hands and the other foot has to be placed in firm, unmovable places."

I have compared mountain climbing to the journey of one's life. It is not always on even ground. There are little ridges, blind curves, rutted holes, and then there are the huge things we confront: the mountains. None of us knows what God has orchestrated along our journey.

We must tackle every circumstance that comes our way – a little hill, a bumpy side road, a holey terrain that could cause one to fall. We have to cope with the situation to achieve the goal on the other side. The high craggy mountains are the ones where there is the most danger, and, like the mountain climber, we must see that we have at least three firmly placed footholds to reach the summit of accomplishment.

The One we get our instruction from is the Creator of the mountains: God Himself. He knows where and when our mountains will loom up. He is ready to equip us for the climb. One of the footholds is Faith in Him. Faith is the substance of things hoped-for, the evidence of things not seen. We won't know where all the rough, unsafe places are on our mountain, so we have to have faith in Him, knowing He will mark each step.

Hope is another foothold or hand-grasp. We are told in God's Word that hope is an anchor of the soul, sure and steadfast. We can launch out, or climb up, knowing He will keep us safe.

Perseverance is a third stronghold that will see that we endure the climb. Sometimes when attempting to reach a peak of one of life's hurtful ordeals, we feel ourselves slipping or getting weary with the struggle, but that's when perseverance kicks in. We take a deep breath and pause briefly, and then proceed to reach our goal.

For all our journey's traveling, and meeting and dealing with whatever size mountain we find in our path, God is always with us. He wants us to look to Him, because nothing is impossible with Him. He delights to have us accomplish our tasks of life, whether they're personal, familial, financial, in health, or career-related. He wants to be involved in our every activity.

Yes, we all have our mountains, but let's always remember we have a God who can and will gear us for the climb. We'll enjoy the trip, and He will get the glory!

The righteous also shall hold on his way, and he that hath clean hands shalt be stronger and stronger. (Job 17:9 KJV)

I can do all things through Christ which strengtheneth me. (Philippians 4:13 KJV)

July 18   Wearers of Uniforms

People in uniform have always impressed me. When I was a young girl, we lived in a town with an Army Base nearby. One of my favorite things to see was to sit in our Model A Ford on Main Street and watch the uniformed soldiers who had come to town to shop. They always looked so *creased* with shiny shoes, and I liked to hear their laughter as they passed by in twos or threes. I had an awe-struck admiration of each one!

As I grew up that fascination continued toward the military men. My Dad never had to go into the military, even during the years of World War 2, but an uncle did. I thought he was so *polished* when he came home on furlough in his uniform. Of course, as time has gone by, many of my family were clad in one or the other of the military branches, whether cousins, husband, son-in-law, or nephews. My reverence for them has not abated over time.

When our town had a parade of any sort down Main Street, I always made it a point to get there for the start of the parade, because the color guard with our flag was first in line. In fact, one time I found myself shedding tears when they passed my spot at the curb.

Another uniformed person I had great respect for was the city's policeman. I always felt protected when he was nearby. That admiration continues for him wherever I see him as I go about life. I feel protected.

There are other uniformed special people: judges in black robes, nurses clad in white, sports referees in black and white, and so many more. In the Old Testament priesthood, the High Priest wore significant clothes.

Thus, it is a fact, a person's uniform identifies his career. We know his or her occupation by the uniform.

Likewise, the Christian wears the uniform that identifies to whom he belongs. His or her clothing acclaim his or her calling.

> I put on righteousness, and it clothed me: my judgment was as a robe and a diadem. (Job 29:14 KJV)

> I will greatly rejoice in the Lord, my soul shall be joyful in my God; for He hath clothed me with the garments of salvation, He hath covered me with the robe of righteousness, as a bridegroom decketh himself with ornaments, and as a bride adorneth herself with her jewels. (Isaiah 61:10 KJV)

July 19   Laughter's Language

A foreign dignitary visiting the United States of America was asked one time what he thought was the most unique trait he observed in the American people. He quickly replied, "The people laugh." Apparently in some countries their people wore only solemn faces, according to him.

Laughter is contagious. My husband had an Uncle W who liked

to tell funny stories. He seemed to have a whole treasure of tales of his boyhood. His story-telling was such fun that when in a family gathering, especially with children among them, someone would ask Uncle W to tell a funny story.

He always was ready. And he would begin with something like "There once was this man," and then *he* would laugh. He would describe the man in the story with a few words and then he would laugh. He kept this up, a few words, followed by his laughter. He was a portly man, and as he would laugh, his stomach would shake. As the story progressed, his listeners began to laugh along with him. By the time the tale ended, everybody was in a fit of laughter. Later, when anyone reflected on what was so funny about the story, they could not come up with anything. We all laughed because Uncle W was laughing, and it made everybody feel good. Next time there was a family reunion, sometime during the day or night Uncle W was asked to tell a tale, and his listening audience surrounded him.

What causes someone to laugh? Many things. The one main thing is joy. When joy has filled your whole being, laughter erupts. Everyone's laughter has its own resonance. A person is known by the sound of his or her laughter. How delightful to the heart of a mother when her little infant's smile makes a laughter sound. Laughter is associated with everything in a person's life in growth to maturity in all the areas of endeavor.

Don't you know the Lord delights in hearing us laugh with joy as we go about life, enjoying His presence? I believe Jesus laughed along with His apostles during His personal ministry. For example, I feel sure He chuckled when He saw wee Zacchaeus running ahead and climbing up in a sycamore tree to watch Him as He came along. I'm sure there was much laughter at the wedding at Cana of Galilee. There were other times as well.

The Christian has the most reason for laughter. No matter the situation or circumstance, grim or pleasant, that person's joy remains, and in due time bubbles up and overflows. And it being contagious, before long those close by laugh too!

Then was our mouth filled with laughter, and our tongue with singing: then said they among the heathen, The Lord hath done great things for them. The Lord hath done great things for us; whereof we are glad. (Psalm 126:2-3 KJV)

These things have I spoken unto you, that My joy might remain in you, and that your joy might be full. (John 15:11 KJV)

July 20   Afflicted to Help the Afflicted

When I was married and my husband was alive and well, I could not understand the depth of loss of a woman who had become a widow. I felt a pity for her, and could only imagine how it would feel to in her shoes. But it was not until my husband died and the lonesomeness, emptiness, *half-ness* came to me that I could fully understand.

Also, I had been a healthy person all my life, and never had a single surgery. I was in the hospital to have a baby, and it was a natural birth, no surgery involved. When I was in a crowd of people who were lamenting their various ills, I often got into a frustrated mood listening to all the complaints. Then, as I grew older, I began to have stiffness here, pain in another spot, difficulty bending and squatting, so I went to the doctor who told me I had Arthritis and Osteopenia and a Sciatic nerve impingement. Wow! I began dealing with all of it, and after several years found myself using a cane and, now, I use a walker.

Until I experienced various difficulties, I could not relate to others who had had them. I sternly became in the know. And my sympathies for my fellows with ailments kicked in. Not every affliction that hits us is always for the benefit of understanding the hurts of others, but, I believe, God allows this to happen sometimes.

Likewise, there are issues not related to health or bereavement that God brings into our lives, and our having dealt with them, we sometimes get the opportunity to help a fellow Christian with similar problems, such as rebellious children, financial problems, relationship issues, and other things. That's one of the reasons the Lord left His church here, so we could assemble, share our joys and sorrows, help each other if we have *been there, done that.*

So, maybe this particular problem currently going on in my or your life God has allowed to happen because somewhere along our journey there may be someone who needs our help to cope and we can lend encouragement and help somehow to restore that one.

We can be assured the Lord is with each of us in whatever circumstance, and He has our best interest for our good, the good of a fellow-traveler, and for His glory!

Blessed be God, even the Father of our Lord Jesus Christ, the Father of mercies, and the God of all comfort; Who comforteth us in all our tribulation, that we may be able to comfort them which are in any trouble, by the comfort wherewith we ourselves are comforted of God. (2 Corinthians 1:3-4 KJV)

July 21   Even the Worldly Seek Christian Neighbors

As a real estate sales associate for over two decades, I learned many things in dealing with home buyers. Prospective buyers always ask questions, about the house, and the community, as well.

Amazingly, one of the questions I was asked was "Do the people who live in this neighborhood go to church?" Of course, I did not always know who the neighbors were, nor their lifestyles, occupations, or religious affiliations. And just as startling was their statement: "We are not avid church-goers, but we always like to live close to families who are. We feel safe. God is sure to bless them, and in so doing, we feel we will get some of the blessing."

That dialogue brought me to the conclusion that, in spite of worldly people wanting nothing to do with church-going or with Jesus as Savior, deep down in their hearts they preferred them over the ungodly sort. And I, too, believe God's blessings on His faithful people will spread out on others who live in the proximity of His own.

And Moses said unto Hobab, the son of Raguel the Midianite, Moses' father in law, We are journeying unto the place of which the Lord said, I will give it you: come thou with us, and we will do thee good: for the Lord hath spoken good concerning Israel. And he said unto him, I will not go; but I will depart to mine own land, and to my kindred. And he said, Leave us not, I pray thee; forasmuch as thou knowest how we are to encamp in the wilderness, and thou mayest be to us instead of eyes. And it shall be, if thou go with us, yea, it shall be, that what goodness the Lord shall do unto us, the same will we do unto thee. (Numbers 10:29-32 KJV)

July 22   Mean It When You Say It

God makes promises and He always keeps them! He expects His followers to do the same. Furthermore, everyone likes to be able to count on a person who makes a promise. Even liars and otherwise unreliable people expect the persons they deal with to be true to their word. They even hold an esteemed respect for such a person.

An example of this is when former President Ronald Reagan died. Who would have expected the former leader of the Soviet Union, Mikhail Gorbachev, to board a plane headed for Washington D.C. and come to pay his respects to the former United States President. In recounting his relationship with Mr. Reagan, Mr. Gorbachev stated what won him over was Mr. Reagan was a "man of his word."

Promises, vows, oaths, pledges and commitments are kinship words. They are all words to be kept, and to not do so brings about harsh consequences.

Vows include the Wedding Vow, where the ones being united in marriage say with devoted meaning that they will keep themselves together for as long as they live and to be true to each other in every respect. Look at what happens when those vows are broken. Heartache ensues, and many are affected, especially if there are children involved.

An oath is a promise to tell the truth such as is given, with right hand raised, and sometimes with the other hand on a Bible, as a witness in a court trial. When a lie is found out in a testimony, a perjury charge is filed against that one.

A pledge is usually taken when elected government officials, of all ranks, take office. My husband was in city government and after each time he was elected he was sworn in, with right hand raised and verbal *I do*, to be faithful to his duty in office. To fail would cause him to be ousted from office, and would carry a shadow on his integrity for a long time.

A commitment covers a lot of territory, such as agreeing to do the required tasks in a career when hired in a position. Also, it is committing to pay the lien for purchase of home or car or student loan, etc. On these commitments, often the Notary Public or some other person witnesses the signature and signs and seals the document.

Once upon a time, a man's word was his bond. The parties involved shook hands in agreement and the business was settled. Not even anything in writing.

God expects His children to keep all promises to the maximum degree. Anything short of that is lying. Jesus said that Satan is the father of lies. To not keep one's word makes Satan happy, especially if one of the Lord's people is doing the lying. Satan knows he cannot get the soul of the Christian after that one has trusted Jesus as Savior, but he begins at once to trip up the Christian so that his or her influence for Jesus will be ruined.

Let's all keep our vows and pledges and promises to the hilt. If, for some reason, we run into a problem in the ability to do so, by all means, let's run to the Savior who is our Mediator and tell Him of our predicament. He is always on hand to keep His promise to keep us on track. He always has a solution!

When you shall vow a vow unto the Lord thy God, thou shalt not slack to pay it: for the Lord thy God will surely require it of thee; and it would be sin in thee. (Deuteronomy 23:21 KJV)

All things God has created acclaim His majesty and excellence. All was created for His honor and glory. Last of all He created the human being, His masterpiece, breathing into his nostrils the breath of life, making him to become a living soul, which would live eternally. All the marvels of His creation He wanted this masterpiece to enjoy and praise Him for each one. Everything that exists has come to be by God's hand. His fingerprints are on all.

But the magnificent heavens He created display His handiwork that no human being has been able to satisfactorily and eloquently describe. Perhaps it is because mankind cannot touch the heavens. They are beyond reach of even the highest spaceship.

He put the sun, the moon, the stars in place, and so fixed them to do their duties, and since their creation they have kept to their assignments according to His commands. While the earth is only one of many planets in one galaxy, there are myriads of galaxies unreached by man. The stars are without number, and God has named each one!

How awe-struck we find ourselves when we see the sun rise in the morning and its setting in the evening! At night we look with wonder into the star-lit sky and at the moon at its particular appearance – quarter, half, full, harvest, etc.

In the scriptures the Psalmist David had more to say about the heavens, likely because as a shepherd he was outdoors at all hours of the day and night.

Let us, like David, day by day enjoy the heavens above us, and thank God for these great provisions, all for our good and delight, but especially for His glory!

Some writers have given various views of the heavens:

"The moon rode silver over the lake."

"The stars stretched into an awesome celestial awning."

"The clouds framed clusters of stars."

"Deep orange of sunrise was just candling the tops of the oaks."

"Twilight had faded and the stars winked one by one in the mauve heaven."

"Under a star-stippled sky."

"The sky was freckled with stars."

In the beginning God created the heaven and the earth. ... And God made two great lights; the greater light to rule the day, and the lesser light to rule the night: He made the stars also. (Genesis 1:1, 16 KJV)

The heavens declare the glory of God; and the firmament sheweth His handywork. (Psalm 19:1 KJV)

July 24   Lift Your Voice in Song

For certain, the Lord loves music. He is the designer of music. The scriptures are full of references to singing and accompaniment with instruments. There are five Old Testament books cataloged as Books of Poetry or Music: Job, Psalms, Proverbs, Ecclesiastes, and Song of Solomon. Other places in scriptures have songs ascribed to certain people.

When Jesus and His Apostles had finished the Lord's Supper in the Upper Room, they left singing a hymn, as they walked on their way to the Garden of Gethsemane.

Music has been a part of worship of God all down through time, and it continues to be in worship services today. Often the hymns correspond with the of the pastor's sermon of that day.

Having gone to church all my life, as a child I learned words of tunes of the hymns. Amazingly, sometimes I have forgotten parts of the pastor's sermon that day, but I carried the words of the songs we sang with me. Over the years I have memorized so many songs and their tunes. So much so, I have found myself waking up mornings with a song in my heart. It just comes on naturally. And it lasts throughout the day.

I know the Lord gets glory out of our voices singing songs in celebration and worship of Him and His goodness. I believe the Holy Spirit uses those songs to bring conviction as well. The invitation hymn being sung when I gave my heart to Jesus as as a young girl was "Jesus Is Tenderly Calling Thee Home."

I remember hearing the story of a lady in a nursing home. She had been a faithful Christian all her 90-plus years, and over that time had sang hundreds of hymns in worship. She said as she lay in her bed in the nursing home, she often heard the cries and wails of discomfort of others in the nursing home. She said, first she prayed for that person, and then she thought of words of a hymn she loved and she let those words drown out the discomforting noises of her fellow residents.

In the New Testament Paul wrote in his letters that followers of Jesus were to sing and make melody in our hearts to the Lord.

Yet the Lord will command His lovingkindness in the daytime, and in the night His song shall be with me, and my prayer unto the God of my life. (Psalm 42:8 KJV)

And when they had sung an hymn, they went out into the mount of Olives. (Matthew 26:30 KJV)

July 25   With God Alongside

It had been another Sunday like so many other Sundays of late. The minister felt he had accomplished so little to bring the people of his congregation closer to God, having tried to teach them the meaning of love and faith and kindness to each other. Feuds between neighbors, greed, and jealousies continued among them.

He had preached for decades, and in his aging had grown tired and ill. The doctor had told him he had possibly less than a year to live. He was pondering the fact of retiring from the ministry due to his failing health and seeming non-accomplishment as pastor. One day, while thumbing through his Bible in his study, it fell open to the passage where the resurrected Jesus joined the disciples on the Road to Emmaus, and as they walked and talked with Jesus, the hour grew late. As recorded in Luke, He was invited to come into one's home for it was evening, and the day far spent.

Pastor Henry Francis Lyte read and reread those familiar words. He felt it was the Lord telling him, "Yes it's toward the evening of your life, but if you abide with Me, there is yet work you can do." Suddenly he no longer felt depressed. Hope surged. He knew with God alongside him, there was something he could yet do. At once he began to pen words on paper, and that very evening he had written one of the most inspiring songs that would comfort and encourage millions in ensuing generations. The fitting title of the hymn: "Abide With Me." We find this song in nearly all Hymn Books.

When a famous nurse went before a German firing squad, she whispered the words of "Abide With Me." When the *Stella* was sinking with over one hundred victims during World War Two, an unidentified noble woman stood on the bridge and sang the hymn, and soon others were singing with her, and they sank courageously.

So God used a dying man, who thought his life's work was finished, to pen this great hymn, to inspire and lend hope to others after him, who would need to be shored up by asking the Lord to abide with them.

The main thing to learn about this experience is that, even when a person thinks his work has ended for the Lord, he needs at once to look around and listen for God's voice, for as long as there is breath in one of His child's nostrils, God has a work planned just for him or her, even if the day is far spent as far as that one's life is concerned.

Be strong and of a good courage, fear not, nor be afraid of them: for the Lord thy God, He it is that doth go with thee; He will not fail thee, nor forsake thee. (Deuteronomy 31:6 KJV)

But they constrained Him, saying, Abide with us: for it is toward evening, and the day is far spent. And He went in to tarry with them. (Luke 24:29 KJV)

July 26   Someone Passed This Way Before

The whole world racked is racked by storm. War rages, crime soars, famine prevails. Fear, insecurity and unsettling grip hearts. Through it all, we are going along, living our lives, experiencing joys and sorrows.

When we look about us, we realize the experience we are undergoing is one, in the end, that will make us bigger and better.

The above words sound like those of a Twenty-first Century author. But they are not. They were penned in December, 1943 by someone who did not sign his or her name. Thousands of fathers, sons, and sweethearts were on a distant battlefield during that time, and the gift everybody wished for was the return of that loved one.

How encouraging to know others have gone this way before, and we are experiencing today no *new* thing. Someone else before us had to deal with like economic, political, religious, educational, and criminal problems. During all these times God's men and women have risen to meet and solve the issues head-on. He still counts on us, His people, in this our time, to come to the front, and with His help handle the crises.

Let us not succumb to the idea, "There is nothing anybody can do now." God is still on His throne! His arm is not shortened! His power has not diminished! He knows exactly where we are in time! And He is in perfect control! Let us just trust Him, do our assigned tasks faithfully, and leave the outcome of everything to Him.

> The thing that hath been, it is that which shall be; and that which is done is that which shall be done: and there is no new thing under the sun. (Ecclesiastes 1:9 KJV)

> Behold, the Lord's hand is not shortened, that it cannot save; neither His ear heavy, that it cannot hear. (Isaiah 59:1 KJV)

July 27   My Personal Great "I Am"

Jesus said "I am the Bread of Life," providing sustenance that satisfies my soul's deepest hunger. He said "I am the Light of the World," and when I walk in that Light, all dark shadows fall behind me. In another place He said "I am the Door of the Sheep," and as one of His fold I feel His touch each time I go for fellowship or go out to pasture.

"I am the Good Shepherd" He told His flock. As one of His sheep I am familiar with His rod and His staff, and I know His voice when

He speaks to me. I claim the promise He made to Martha, "I am the Resurrection and the Life," knowing the same assurance that, though this frame returns to dust someday, when His trumpet sounds, I will rise in an immortal body. I have come to find His answer to questioning Thomas, "I am the Way, the Truth and the Life," as my foundation for living. He is the source of every facet of my make-up, physical, mental, intellectual, emotional, and spiritual.

Shortly before His crucifixion, He said "I s, the Vine," and when I abide in Him, He can surge sap into my being, a branch, or a mere twig, so that I will be able to produce fruit for His glory. In the Bible's last book, the writer John quotes Jesus saying "I am the Alpha and the Omega, the First and the Last," names which stun me into the realization that He is my Everything. He is my All in All. He is my Foreverness. How blessed am I to belong to the GREAT I AM!

> O the depth of the riches both of the wisdom and knowledge of God! How unsearchable are His judgments, and His Ways past finding out! ... For of Him, and through Him, and to Him, are all things; to whom be glory forever. Amen. (Romans 11:33, 36 KJV)

July 28   Good Intentions Too Late

> I said "I'll go to see him,
> Right now he needs a friend,
> Someone to share his burden,
> On whose care he can depend."
> I said "I'll call tomorrow
> And talk to him by phone.
> Perhaps our chat will cheer him;
> He'll not feel so alone."
> I said "I'll send a postcard
> To let him know I care,
> And understand his heartache
> Because I've too been there."

My good intentions idled;
I did not visit at all.
I never wrote the postcard,
Nor made the telephone call.
I did go by to see him
Where he lay in state one night.
He never knew that I cared—
His soul had taken flight.

--Carlene Poff Baker

Withhold not good from them to whom it is due, when it is in the power of thine hand to do it. (Proverbs 3:27 KJV)

July 29 **Generation After Generation**

Generation after generation, since Satan's encounter with our first parents, war has marshaled brother against brother, family against family, kingdom versus kingdom.

Generation after generation the gallant has fallen before the sword, the gun, and the bomb, on ships sinking to the ocean's floor, from aircraft hurled into the firmament in millions of pieces, and cut down bleeding in murky foxholes.

Generation after generation bereft women and children and old men weep, while war-enders sign pacts and strike hands – until one brother seeks his own over the good of his brother – and war erupts again, brother against brother.

Generation after generation, so it shall be, until the King of Kings usurps over all others His rightful throne on earth, putting down for all time Satan and his crusade.

Then brother and brother shall beat their swords into plowshares and live in peace: brother with brother, generation after generation.

For nation shall rise against nation, and kingdom against kingdom: and there shall be famines, and pestilences, and earthquakes, in divers places. (Matthew 24:7 KJV)

And He hath on His vesture and on His thigh a name written, KING OF KINGS, AND LORD OF LORDS. ... And I saw thrones, and they sat on them, and judgment was given unto them: and I saw the souls of them that were beheaded for the witness of Jesus, and for the word of God, and which had not worshipped the beast, neither his image, neither had received his mark upon their foreheads, or in their hands; and they lived and reigned with Christ a thousand years. (Revelation 19:16; 20:4 KJV)

July 30   Devotion to One's Master

Certain pets have such devotion for their masters that it sometimes boggles the minds of human beings. One's horse has such an avid devotion for its master. Perhaps the dog is the one that shows its undying devotion to its master more than any other creature. While some dogs are used as work animals, as those that pull sleds or service dogs as seeing-eye dogs, but I believe the main purpose for God giving dogs to His human beings is to be affectionate, loyal companions for life.

A dog knows his master, and that is the most important person in his life. He wants to be where his master is and to do what his master asks. The dog is so pleased when his master touches him and talks to him, calling his name. He shows it by face and tail.

Even when the master has to discipline the dog, he cowers in humiliation, and then he is so pleased when he and the master are back in good fellowship.

There is a fascinating story about a dog many decades ago. It had been in the household of its master from puppy to almost senior in dog years. He was so devoted to his master. When his master became ill, the dog laid beside his bed all the time. Then the man died, and the dog saw when his master's body lay in state in the home. Again, the dog laid on the floor beside the coffin. Because the funeral and burial were to be in another state, the coffin was taken to the railroad and put on a train for going to that designated place. The dog followed the hearse that took his master in his coffin to the train. He was not allowed to go on the train, but he watched as the doors closed on the train and the engine started and the train moved away.

The dog stayed at the depot until nightfall and then returned to the house. There he was restless and could not be becalm calm or comforted by any means the others of the household tried. They noticed, however, every day at the same time the train had left from the depot taking his master away, he arose, trotted in haste to the depot and waited, wagging his tail. His daily presence became a ritual, which the train station people took notice of. He never stopped coming and awaiting the return of his master until he died.

That is a graphic illustration of how it is with a devoted Christian to his or her Master, the Lord Jesus Christ. He knows each of us by name. He loves to have us with Him for talking and fellowshipping. He delights when we do good things. When He disciplines us, we do what is necessary to get back in fellowship with Him. Unlike the dog and His master situation, our Master went away all right, into heaven to become our Intercessor, seated at His Father's right hand, but He left His Holy Spirit with us, who lives within us constantly. Also, unlike the dog's master never returning to him, one day our wonderful Master will indeed return in person and call us unto Himself, and we will ever be with Him, no more parting!

> The Lord hath appeared of old unto me, saying, Yea, I have loved thee with an everlasting love: therefore with lovingkindness have I drawn thee. (Jeremiah 31:3 KJV)

> Herein is love, not that we loved God, but that He loved us, and sent His Son to be the propitiation for our sins. ... We love Him, because He first loved us. (1 John 4:10, 19 KJV)

July 31 — A Turn in the Road

After dinner in the home of Mary Pickford, she and her evening guests moved to the library where they chatted. At first they talked of lively happenings, but then the conversation took a turn for personal maladies, and of a need for fortitude and jauntiness to overcome such hindrances.

Suddenly the group's hostess spoke up. "I have a philosophy that I've proven workable over the years. It has helped me through every heartbreak and discouragement, has stood by me through every unhappy experience."

Her audience begged her to tell them about it. She responded, "What looks like the end of the road is only the turn in the road, the beginning of a new and more beautiful journey. I have found this to be so in my life."

Among her the hostess' guests was an editor of a magazine, who asked her to write an article for his magazine, expressing her views. Reluctant at first, she at last agreed. As she began to think about what she would say, the first thing would be the emphasis of her faith in God, and how faith in Him gave her courage to meet all trials of life. She would explain how she looked upon unhappy times as a turn in the road: an end, but also a beginning, that life had promise, and that there was always another opportunity no matter how hopeless things might seem. So she wrote that each day is new, and we'll get out of it what we put into it. Despite mistakes, there is always another opportunity. One can fall down, but the greater failure is staying down.

As Mary Pickford said, all of us fail time and again. But we are not to become despondent. We ought to say, "I've messed up again, Heavenly Father, but You've helped me up, and here I am again. Show me what to do next."

Another person said "Our greatest glory is not in never falling, but in rising every time we fall."

For a just man falleth seven times, and riseth up again; but the wicked shall fall into mischief. (Proverbs 24:16 KJV)

Rejoice not against me, O mine enemy: when I fall, I shall arise; when I sit in darkness, the Lord shall be a light unto me. (Micah 7:8 KJV)

The visitation program of one church had members go out two by two to invite people who had just moved into the community. A man and his wife went to a house whose address they had been given. They found a little boy about eight years old playing in the yard. The man asked if his parents were home.

He replied they were but his dad was sleeping as he had been working hard moving furniture into the rooms. His mother was inside but she too was busy unboxing things. That's why he was outside playing, to get away from all that bustle.

The couple decided they would not pay a visit to his parents that day but would come back at another less busy day. But they decided to talk to the little boy about the church, about the many activities offered to children.

"We will come back to visit you and your parents later," the man told him. "Would you like to come to our church?"

"No," the boy answered and kept playing with his truck on the ground.

"Well, here is a little book that shows some of the things boys your age can enjoy if you do come to our church," the woman said, handing him the colorful book. He looked at it and handed it back to her.

"Would you like to come and do some of these things with other children?" she asked.

"No," he replied again, returning to his truck.

"Do you have any questions about what we've talked about?" the man asked.

"Yes," the boy answered; "if I come, will you be there?"

"Sure, we will be there. We always go to that church. We love to go!"

"Then, if you are there, I would like to go there too."

The couple bade farewell to the boy, promising they would return so they could visit the whole family. In their car, making their way to their next assigned visit, they realized what made the difference and talked about it. It's okay to invite somebody and even to pass out pamphlets advertising the church, but it's of no value to the one invited if the one who visited them won't be present to greet them and mix and mingle with them in person.

Be kindly affectioned one to another with brotherly love; in honor preferring one another. (Romans 12:10 KJV)

My little children, let us not love in word, neither in tongue; but in deed and in truth. (1 John 3:18 KJV)

August 2   Practical Visitation Format

My husband and I became involved in the visitation of newcomers ministry of our church. We met at the church first with others of the visiting team. After prayer and the assigned ones we were to visit, we left. Also we did not go out haphazardly. The pastor gave us a format which worked. We were to use it in orderly fashion to accomplish our goal.

The format was an acrostic of the word FORM:

"F – Family; O – Occupation; R – Religion; M – Message"

When we approached the house we were to visit, we looked at the outside. If there were playground things in the yard, we figured there were children in the home. If there was a boat in the back yard, we surmised the man was a fisherman perhaps. When we were invited into the home and introduced ourselves and the reason of our visit, we then began using the format. We talked about their family, kids' ages, even names. Noticing a photo of someone, perhaps military person, and asking about that one could be included.

After that, then the topic of occupation or career of the man and/or woman of the home would be talked about. Seeing a piano in the room would be a way to begin talking about musical interests. Next, ask if they attend church anywhere in town. If they do, we were to encourage them to continue. If not, we presented the various ministries of our church. Last of all, the message. If they are happy in their own church, tell them how glad you are for them. If they have no church involvement, invite them to your church. Then, leave, thanking them for your visit. Never stay over thirty minutes at any address.

Next, there comes into focus the format GIVE:

"G – Greet; I – Introduce; V – Visit; E – Encourage"

If one of the people whom we visited came to our church, my husband or I, or both of us, enthusiastically greeted them. Then we introduced them to the pastor and others. If they came for Sunday School or Connect Group, we introduced them to various leaders of classes, especially children group leaders. If that person by himself or with family members returned to the church in succeeding weeks, then we invited them to our home for a social on a Sunday evening. We also invited other members of their age.

We enjoyed fellowship and got better acquainted. We did that to encourage them in their spiritual walk. Over time, it was our added joy to see them join our church, become active in various places – in the choir, playing an instrument, teaching, and, yes, even teaming up with us in the visitation ministry.

Although my husband and I were involved in other places in our church, being a part of the visitation team was one of the most enjoyable of ministries.

Also I heard the voice of the Lord, saying, Whom shall I send, and who will go for us? Then said I, Here am I; send me. (Isaiah 6:8 KJV)

And the lord said unto the servant, Go out into the highways and hedges, and compel them to come in, that my house may be filled. (Luke 14:23 KJV)

Now then we are ambassadors for Christ, as though God did beseech you by us: we pray you in Christ's stead, be ye reconciled to God. (2 Corinthians 5:20 KJV)

August 3   Be Up and Doing

I've always been an avid reader from the time I read my first-grade book about "Tom and Nancy." My teacher also had us memorize poetry, so

I've always enjoyed reading poetry, especially the classics. I've even tried my hand at writing poetry, and some have been published.

It has always amazed me how some poems have touched the lives of others for good, and after so doing over a hundred years, it is looked upon as a classic. One in particular is the poem written by Longfellow, which he titled "Psalm of Life."

Longfellow was a Harvard professor, and, in fact, lived in the very room President Washington had had his headquarters. The young professor had become utterly lonely after his wife had died. Although he was a poet, he had lost interest in everything, even writing poetry. Life was empty for him.

But he suddenly realized he was nursing his despondency, and that thought stirred him so strongly that he told himself that life is not an empty dream! He must be up and doing! Being so invigorated, he at once began to pen the poem, "Psalm of Life." After writing it, he set it aside because he felt it was to give solace to only his own heart. But in time he allowed it to be published.

It moved directly to hearts of a myriad of readers. Over time it was translated into many languages. Some school children were required to memorize all nine stanzas. For over a hundred years this poem has lifted weary, downtrodden people to rouse up, stand up, and get moving to make things happen. Courage, daring, optimism became the premise, and gloom dissipated from their lives. Here are only the first and last stanzas of that classic:

> Tell me not, in mournful numbers
> Life is but an empty dream—
> For the soul is dead that slumbers,
> And things are not what they seem.
> Let us then be up and doing,
> With a heart for any fate;
> Still achieving, still pursuing,
> Learn to labor and to wait.

See, I have set before thee this day life and good, and death and evil. (Deuteronomy 30:15 KJV)

Yet now be strong, O Zerubbabel, saith the Lord; and be strong,
O Joshua, son of Josedech, the high priest; and be strong, all ye
people of the land, saith the Lord, and work: for I am with you,
saith the Lord of hosts. (Haggai 2:4 KJV)

Wherefore He saith, Awake thou that sleepest, and arise from
the dead, and Christ shall give thee light. See then that ye walk
circumspectly, not as fools, but as wise, redeeming the time,
because the days are evil. (Ephesians 5:14-16 KJV)

August 4   Big Yields from Small Starts

The left mirror on our car had been bumped and it was out of kilter. But
our family went on vacation as planned. My husband became frustrated
often coping with the mirror as he drove. He said that, as soon as we
arrived at our motel, he would locate the Chevrolet company nearby and
get the mirror fixed. And he found one.

While the mechanic was replacing the mirror, my husband and
he talked. Among other subjects they talked of where we lived. The
mechanic said, "That's the town with the Air Force Base where my
son is." When they parted, the new mirror in place, my husband had
promised to contact the man's son and to invite him to our church.

After our return from vacation, my husband did contact John, the
Air Force guy. He accepted the invitation to attend our church. He was
there the next Sunday, and, as was our custom, we invited him home
with us for lunch and the afternoon. He accepted. This continued after
that, and soon John began bringing buddies with him. And one Sunday
we had John, Charles and Tim at our dining table. As time went on, John
married pretty Rhonda, a member of our church.

Good things continued to happen. John made known that God had
called him into the ministry. He began to preach his first sermons at our
church, and then he was called to do so elsewhere. When he had finished
his Air Force term, he and Rhonda moved to his home town, and they
began a family. Rhonda's parents were dead, and she had a sister in a
wheel chair and a younger brother. John moved them to where they lived

and provided for them – the one in the wheel chair becoming a happy resident in a facility close by.

We kept in touch awhile, but then my husband died, and I lost touch completely, until one day I received a letter from John. He wanted to let me know how the Lord had used him, and was still using him as youth pastor in a church in Oklahoma.

I could see all along how God puts little incidents across our paths that turn out to be big and grow even bigger. Our God is not a God of coincidence. He orchestrates the doings of it all to the end He intends to achieve. Even if the little thing be a mere car side mirror!

Lead me, O Lord, in thy righteousness because of mine enemies; make thy way straight before my face. (Psalm 5:8 KJV)

The Lord God hath given me the tongue of the learned, that I should know how to speak a word in season to him that is weary: He wakeneth morning by morning, He wakeneth mine ear to hear as the learned. (Isaiah 50:4 KJV)

August 5   Kindness Math: Add and Multiply

It has been proven over and over, when a kindness is shown by one person to another, it spreads on from the recipient to another and on to another from that recipient. In time, the kindness returns in reciprocity to the first one who showed kindness.

For example, one day I went to the gas station to get gas, intending to get ten dollars' worth. At the pay counter, I opened my wallet and found only four dollars. I had some gas in my tank, so I decided to just use the four dollars to get me by driving in town, and then would get more tomorrow, using cash I had at home. I gave the man my money and returned to the pump and began filling my tank. It did not stop at four dollars but kept going. I said, "Oh, my! I am getting more than I paid for. The man surely made a mistake!" Then I saw him coming toward me with a smile on his face.

"The lady behind you in line paid six dollars for you so you could get ten dollars' worth."

"Oh, but I must repay her. Where is she?" I replied.

"She has already driven away."

"Oh, if she is your customer, I will leave money here for her for you to give to her," I persisted.

"She would not take it," He said. "She is a kind person."

I knew I had to use that six dollars of mine somewhere to show a kindness, to pass it on. The opportunity came the next Sunday. In Sunday School Class they were handing out Bible study books, and we were to pay the teacher for them. I had cash in my wallet and paid for mine. Then I noticed a lady did not buy one. I knew she had financial straits, so I got out my wallet and anonymously paid for Linda's book. Know what the price of the book cost? Exactly six dollars

Later on, I learned indirectly that the person for whom I had bought the book had taken a wheel-chaired person to the grocery store. In the store the she helped her get her groceries. When they got to the check-out counter, the disabled woman lacked some funds to pay for her items. Linda added her own money to pay the difference.

Another, of many like events, was when I stopped at a convenience store to get a coffee. I filled my cup and waited in line at check-out to pay for it. I had my money in hand. When my turn came, the clerk said "Your coffee has been paid for by the lady in front of you." She was a stranger. I looked back and she was outside making her way to her car.

I decided I'd pay for somebody's purchase in like order. I paid for my coffee and for the stranger's purchase who was immediately behind me. I had not gotten out of the door before I heard her holler, "Oh, how wonderful! Nobody has ever done a kind thing like that for me!" She followed me to my car and kept on thanking me. It did her good all right, but it was my blessing too.

No one knows the author of the following gem, nor when it was said. But it took hold, impelling untold numbers of people to be kinder to their fellow human beings. It is as vital as ever, a little gold nugget of inspiration:

"I shall pass through this world but once. Any good therefore that I can do, or any kindness that I can show to any human being, let me do it now. Let me not defer nor neglect it, for I shall not pass this way again."

It is a reminder that we do not live for ourselves alone, that we must do what we can to help others, to lighten a burden or comfort a grief whenever the need arises.

Thou shalt not avenge, nor bear any grudge against the children of thy people, but thou shalt love thy neighbor as thyself: I am the Lord. (Leviticus 19:18 KJV)

See that none render evil for evil unto any man; but ever follow that which is good, both among yourselves, and to all men. (1 Thessalonians 5:15 KJV)

August 6   Can't Do Wrong and Get By

I was driving on a two-lane highway between two small towns in Arkansas. No car was in front of me, nor was there one behind. The highway was full of pot holes so deep my car bounced, and I feared I would have a tire to blow out. Seeing no traffic, I began dodging the pot holes, so I was going from one side of the highway to the other and even driving off on the right-hand shoulder as well.

I thought "I'm breaking the law all right, weaving from one lane to the other and onto the shoulder, but there is no traffic in front of me or behind me, so I'm in no danger to anyone."

But all of a sudden, out of nowhere, a car was behind me with its blue light flashing. Uh, oh! I pulled over onto the shoulder. The car pulled over behind mine. I got really panicky. I lowered my window and the officer said, "I just wondered if you were all right." Knowing he was in essence seeing if I was drunk, I told him I was all right. Then I said "I was driving all over the road trying to avoid hitting the pot holes."

He actually laughed, which eased my panic somewhat. "The Highway Department is scheduled to begin filling them and resurfacing the highway," he said. Then he walked away, saying "Drive in your proper lane, just drive slowly and maybe there will be no damage to your car." Smiling, he returned to his car.

Rolling up my car window, I started my car and pulled back onto the pot-holey highway. I stayed in my proper lane, drove slowly, and bumped my car the rest of the way. The officer did not even follow me. He turned around and drove back, probably to a smoothly paved road.

That is a picture of how we as Christians sometimes think we can sin and nobody will see us. We may even reason we are doing a wrong thing because it can cause damage to our person or property if we do the right thing. But, not so! Even if no other person in the world knows I am sinning, God does. He sees everything. And He catches up with me. He never allows one of His to sin and get by with it.

Like the police officer, God is merciful. He cares about me. Then He says "Do the right thing regardless of the unpleasant situation." Because of His mercy and grace, after reminding me of my proper duty, He watches me get back into the bumpy situation, but, unlike the officer, He watches me lovingly as I go my way. He delights in our fellowship being restored after forgiving me, and so do I.

> Against thee, thee only, have I sinned, and done this evil in thy sight: that thou mightest be justified when thou speakest, and be clear when thou judgest. (Psalm 51:4 KJV)

> O God, thou knowest my foolishness; and my sins are not hid from thee. (Psalm 69:5 KJV)

> He that covereth his sins shall not prosper: but whoso confesseth and forsaketh them shall have mercy. (Proverbs 28:13 KJV)

August 7   ## Under His Wings

When I was a child we lived on a farm, and we kept many animals and fowls. In the barn were the milk cow, mules, Sam and Shorty, and many hogs. In another spacious fenced-in place was the chicken yard, which had a roosting house and nests on the sides of the house where the hens laid their eggs and hatched chicks. However, there was a hole in the fence to allow the chickens to go outside the fenced area into other places.

One summer day a rainstorm came with a cascade of rushing water.

The yard was flooded, and most of the chickens took shelter in the chicken house. When the storm had abated, my Mother went out to see about the chickens and to feed them on some of the less-wet places. She noticed one hen which had just hatched six baby chicks was missing, as well as the little ones. Mom pulled off her shoes and went barefoot in the flooded cotton field rows hunting for the hen and her chicks. She feared the little ones had drowned.

My sister and I watched from the back porch as she sought the chickens. Ah, at last, we saw her bend over and she began filling her apron with little chickens. Here she came, with a grin on her face, her apron full of peeping chickens, with the rain-drenched hen scolding her as she followed behind. Mom told us she found the mother hen soaking wet sitting on the top of a row with the little ones under her wings. We all rejoiced that not a one of the little chicks was missing.

Although the mother hen fussed and pecked at her hands repeatedly, Mom dried off her feathers as much as she could, took her inside the hen house with her chicks and fed her some chops.

In the Bible God speaks of sheltering His children under His wings, where He provides safety and refuge, because He so loves His own! Especially when the storms of life come from all sides. He will not force anyone to come. He graciously invites all to come. Under His wings, whatever is happening all around them, there is peace and contentment.

Keep me as the apple of the eye, hide me under the shadow of thy wings. (Psalm 17:8 KJV)

How excellent is thy lovingkindness, O God! Therefore the children of men put their trust under the shadow of thy wings. (Psalm 36:7 KJV)

He shall cover thee with His feathers, and under His wings shalt thou trust: His truth shall be thy shield and buckler. (Psalm 91:4 KJV)

A Good Method to Pray

We are always learning better ways to serve our Lord. One way I learned to pray back when I was a young person, in line with Jesus' Model Prayer, was taught me in an acrostic: ACTS. In our prayers we are taught in God's Word to cover these areas when we pray.

A – *Adoration* – At the start of every prayer, we should address our Heavenly Father reverently. Jesus said we should "Hallow" His name at the start (Psalm 8:1; 9:1-2; Romans 11:33-36).

C – *Confession* – Ask for forgiveness of any sin you are guilty of since last praying. While doing so, be sure there is no grudge or unforgiveness toward anyone else (Psalm 51:8-10; 1 John 1:8-9).

T – *Thanksgiving* – Thank God for blessings, especially His answers to prayers previously prayed (Psalm 50:14; Psalm 100:4; Ephesians 5:20; 1 Thessalonians 5:18).

S – *Supplication* – Ask for needs, as in the Model Prayer, for daily needs, for deliverance from temptation, interceding on behalf of others, and for His will to be done, whatever it be (1 Samuel 12:19, 23; Ephesians 6:18; Colossians 1:9; 1 Timothy 2:1-4).

And always, before saying "Amen," say "In Jesus' Name."

We Sow and Water, God Brings to Fruition

As a Sunday School teacher of Junior High age children, I became so concerned about the souls of two young boys who had confessed that they were lost. The lesson for that day was about Jesus standing on the outside of the door of one's heart and wanting to enter, and that the one on whose heart He was knocking would have to let Him come in. I so prepared that lesson with the hope that God would have me use the right words to touch the hearts of those two boys.

The two seemed to listen to my teaching that morning, and I prayed they would respond by accepting Christ as Savior.

The pastor's sermon was along the same line as the Sunday School lesson, so I prayed that the two boys would listen and respond. When the invitation was given, neither of the two boys I had aimed at came forward, but another boy in my class that morning walked down the aisle, saying he gave his heart to Jesus. When the pastor asked if he wanted to make a statement, he said, "When Mrs. Baker told us how Jesus was wanting to come into my heart and save me from my sins, I invited Him to come in and forgive me, and He did, and I am saved."

I had focused on two particular guys, sowing seeds and watering them, but God was working on another person. Yes, indeed, we must keep on sowing and watering, not knowing in what soil the seed will take root. God does that particular work Himself, and He is the One that accomplishes His purpose.

So shall my word be that goeth forth out of my mouth: it shall not return unto me void, but it shall accomplish that which I please, and it shall prosper in the thing whereto I sent it. (Isaiah 55:11)

I have planted, Apollos watered; but God gave the increase. So then neither is he that planteth any thing, neither he that watereth; but God that giveth the increase. (1 Corinthians 3:6-7 KJV)

Preach the word; be instant in season, out of season; reprove, rebuke, exhort with all longsuffering and doctrine. (2 Timothy 4:2 KJV)

August 10   More than Almost

Being a female driver of a vehicle, I have to run to a mechanic or other person when the least thing goes wrong with my car. Recently when I turned on my ignition a light on my dash read "Oil Change Required." I knew I had only a couple of months ago had the car serviced which included an oil change, of course. So, I immediately drove to the oil change service place, and showed the service man there. He knew how to fix it.

"Turn on your ignition, but do not start the motor. Press with your left foot the brake and with the right foot the accelerator all the way to the floor, and hold those positions."

The young man said, looking at my dash, "Keep on just a little bit more, you are almost there. Come on, just a little bit more time holding your feet that way on the pedals."

I did so, and then he exulted, "There, you did it! The light won't come back on your dash."

I thanked him and told him I'd return in a couple of months to get the car serviced again when it was the proper time. He smiled and told me to have a great day. As I drove away, I thought again that had I not persisted when I was almost there, I would have gone away with the light still coming on my dash every time I turned the ignition on. I felt so at peace knowing I would not have to fret about it anymore.

It also reminded me of an incident in Acts, where the Apostle Paul was speaking to King Agrippa and Festus, testifying as to what God had done for him in saving him and calling him into the ministry.

In response to Paul's message King Agrippa said "Almost thou persuadest me to be a Christian. And Paul said, I would to God, that not only thou, but also all that hear me this day, were both almost, and altogether such as I am" (Acts 26:28-29). We have no record of whether King Agrippa ever became altogether persuaded to be a Christian. Almost won't get the job done! One must totally be persuaded to receive Jesus as Savior to become a Christian.

He that believeth on Him is not condemned; but he that believeth not is condemned already, because he hath not believed in the name of the only begotten Son of God. (John 3:18 KJV)

August 11   A Picture of Grace

A story has been handed down of what happened decades ago when corporal punishment was conducted in school. The teacher or principal had the right to whip with a belt or razor strap a child who broke a rule of the school's laws.

Children brought their lunches from home in sacks or pails and they sat them on shelves in the room where coats were hung during winter. One boy came every day without his lunch. When asked why, he said "I just don't get hungry." Folks doubted it because he was often seen watching others eating their lunches with a longing on his skinny face.

One day this boy asked to go to the outside rest room, and the teacher allowed him to go. On the way he went into the cloak room and took down the pretty blue lunch pail of someone. He ran outside, but not to the rest room. He ran to a big tree and sat behind it so that no one from the school could see him. He opened the pail and began to eat the food inside. He meant to hurry back before the noon bell rang and put the pail back without anyone knowing what he had done. But the bell rang while he was still eating.

He just hoped he would not be found out. But that was not to be. Soon the owner of the lunch pail and the principal were looking down upon him.

"Is that your lunch, Johnny?"

"Yes, sir, it is. He stole my lunch!"

"Billy," the principal said, "You know you are not to steal at this school, don't you?"

"Yes, sir." Billy replied.

"You will come with me. You know the rules, that if you steal something, you will get a whipping."

"Yes, sir. I know it. I deserve it."

The way it was done back then, the one who had broken a rule would strip off his shirt and the principal would give him about five hurtful lashes across his bare back. Not only was that humiliating, with other students hearing the lashes and the cries of pain, but the one who had been stolen from could watch it being done.

When Billy took off his shirt, the principal and Johnny saw scars all over the boy's back which had come from someone else.

"Billy, who has beaten you so badly?" the principal asked.

"My Dad," he said, almost in a whisper.

"Well, Billy, I hate to do it, but if I don't punish you for your stealing then other kids will think they can get by with breaking the rules too."

"I know, sir."

Suddenly Johnny marched to where the principal stood.

"I'll take his beating, sir, because my back has no scars," he said.

"But you're the one he stole from," responded the principal.

"But I want to do this. I'll take his lashes. Let him go free."

And the principal gave Johnny the lashes deserved by Billy. Johnny's cries were loud, but not as loud as Billy's, who knelt at the feet of Johnny while he was being whipped. After that day, Billy loved Johnny, and Johnny felt a tenderness to the one for whom he was punished.

That's a perfect picture of what Jesus has done for every sinner. Each sinner has broken the rules that God has laid out. Not a single one is without guilt. And each one deserves severe punishment for sinning against a loving God. But Jesus took the punishment for each one of us.

But He was wounded for our transgressions, He was bruised for our iniquities: the chastisement of our peace was upon Him; and with His stripes we are healed. All we like sheep have gone astray; we have turned every one to his own way; and the Lord hath laid on Him the iniquity of us all. (Isaiah 53:5-6 KJV)

For He hath made Him to be sin for us, who knew no sin; that we might be made the righteousness of God in Him. (2 Corinthians 5:21 KJV)

August 12   Querulous Folks

In every crowd there are the querulous folks. No matter how pleasant a situation, there is always one who will find something to be critical about. Ever the fault-finding sort!

My husband owned a print shop, and the church we attended had no printing machine, so the pastor of our church would bring his draft of the next Sunday's bulletin to us for me to type and for my husband to run off on the press. We always took the finished printed and folded bulletins to the church on Saturday evening before so early arrivals could get their copies.

The church did purchase a copier, but the pastor continued to have me type his draft and then my husband and I went to the church Saturday night and printed next day's bulletin. That continued until we had a pastor who wanted me to do the bulletin except his short greeting at the top. I agreed to do so and enjoyed doing it, having gotten news from members of events. Then my husband died, and I was left with typing bulletins and running them off the Saturday night before, and would have them ready for early readers.

In one bulletin I wrote "This Sunday will be one of our charter member's ninety-fifth birthday." Her name was Mrs. Pearl Jones, and she was in a nursing home. I lauded her with her faithfulness and love for the Lord and the church.

When I got to church that Sunday morning, one after another of the early arrivals came to me and said "Mrs. Jones is ninety-four, not ninety-five." I apologized to each one. Finally, I asked the deacon who always gave the greeting and made announcements at the start of worship service to make the announcement that I had made an error and that he correct it, giving Mrs. Jones' true age. He did so.

When the pastor got up to speak, he looked at me and said "That just shows you, Mrs. Baker, that they do read the bulletin you write. It proves you are doing a good work. I for one certainly appreciate your doing it in my stead."

Let your speech be alway with grace, seasoned with salt, that ye may know how ye ought to answer every man. (Colossians 4:6 KJV)

August 13   Not for Himself, But for Me

Jesus allowed His perfect brow to be jabbed with hurtful thorns so that my brow might be free of worry lines. He let them whip His shoulders raw so that I could stand straight and tall.

He gave His skin to caked, dried blood, nasty human spittle, and fist-made bruises, so that my face might glow radiantly free of sin's blemish. His tongue stuck to the roof of

His mouth in feverish thirst, so that He might provide living water to satiate my parched soul's thirst.

His sandaled feet trudged wearily as soldiers cruelly pushed and shoved Him from Pilate's judgment hall to Golgotha, so that I might claim His promise of rest. He stretched out His arms and to the spikes in His hands, that my sin-guilty hands deserved, thus penning with His blood on my sin-debt page: Account Paid in Full.

Then, oh, then, Heaven's Dearest died! Then, oh, then, Heaven's Most Precious One's body was placed in a tomb! But Heaven's Darling did not stay there! On the third day, as He had promised, He burst forth from that tomb, never to die again!

Alive forevermore, He has established and assured me that, because I have claimed Him as my personal Lord and Savior, I have everlasting life, and will spend my eternity with Him. My loudest shout of "Thank You, Lord!" would be less than a whisper compared to the magnitude of what Jesus, God's Dearest, God's Most Precious One, God's Darling accomplished for me, and for me only, but for every sinner who comes to Him for salvation from sin!

For even hereunto were ye called: because Christ also suffered for us, leaving us an example, that ye should follow His steps: Who did no sin, neither was guile found in His mouth: Who, when He was reviled, reviled not again; when He suffered, He threatened not; but committed Himself to Him that judgeth righteously: Who His own self bare our sins in His own body on the tree, that we, being dead to sins, should live unto righteousness: by whose stripes ye were healed. (1 Peter 2:21-24)

August 14   Love is a Must

Love propels one to step outside of self, and to become absorbed with another. Love stirs a need to bestow some gift of self to another. Love surfaces in traits of kindness, tenderness, and patience toward the one loved.

The mother of a newborn loves the red, wrinkled, squalling little person, even though it may be weeks before he even focuses his eyes on her. She dotingly spends herself to protect and cuddle him, not concerned with whether this child will ever love her in return.

The wife of an unfaithful husband refuses undauntedly to allow her love for him to ebb, and, at every turn, she stokes dying embers of the low-burning fire, hoping for a return. Yet, whether he comes back or not, she delights in loving him still.

When one's child turns from his parents' good values, choosing hurtful companions instead, even expressing to his parents, "I want to do things m way with no reprimand from you!" The wept-dry hearts of those parents still love that child unconditionally, and say "Oh, my precious child, how can I let you go?"

Billy's old dog, Shag, could no longer hear, see, nor walk up and down the back steps. Once when his Dad suggested they let the vet put Shag mercifully out of his misery, Billy sobbingly pleaded, "No, Daddy. Shag needs somebody to love him. That somebody is me. He knows it is me when I touch him, and he knows I am close by."

Hatred stirreth up strifes: but love covereth all sins. (Proverbs 10:12 KJV)

This is My commandment, That ye love one another, as I have loved you. (John 15:12 KJV)

And now abideth faith, hope, charity, these three; but the greatest of these is charity. (1 Corinthians 13:13 KJV)

August 15   Jesus Prepared for Scoffers

Because All-wise Jesus Christ knew twenty-first century scoffers would taunt maliciously: "Noah and the ark and Jonah and the whale are not true; they are mere myths," He authenticated those great events by words from His own lips in the hearing of witnesses during His personal ministry on earth.

I can see Jesus make eye-contact with, and nod to, Apostle Matthew to jot down verbatim the words He spoke. Matthew jubilantly obeyed, penning the words Jesus spoke about Noah. (Matthew 24:37-39)

Jesus had Matthew also pen what He said about Jonah. (Matthew 12:38-41)

Jesus Christ, who knows all things, including the malicious jeers twenty-first century scoffers would employ, made sure to have His words in place, using these two Old Testament accounts against that future time.

August 16   Ugliness Transformed

There is a tale that, when a man saw Abraham Lincoln for the first time, he said to him, "Mr. Lincoln, I've been called ugly all my life. I said to myself, I'd rather die than be so ugly. I hope I could find somebody uglier than I before I die. I have to say, Mr. Lincoln, I believe I have found such a person. You are uglier than I am. So now I have reached my goal."

Never to be outdone, Mr. Lincoln looked at him and grinned, and said: "I don't blame you. If I could not find someone uglier than you, I wouldn't want to live either."

I'm not sure that is an exact tale. But Mr. Lincoln was not handsome from all the pictures we have of him. But, oh, history reflects he was a good-looking person on the inside.

History tells us the Apostle Paul was not a handsome man either. He is described by historians as short in stature, bow-legged, bald-headed, with scarred face, eyes close together and a hook nose. But, despite that, his audience included Jews, Gentiles, even kings, and when he spoke, people listened.

Other descriptions said about less-than-acttractive people are "Her bony face was redeemed from ugliness by bright black eyes;" and "The wrinkles in her face folded into each other;" and "On his face the years had scored with a heavy pen;" and "She wore a make-up that was a hundred percent improvement on nature."

I am confident when God created the first man, Adam, he was the most handsome creature. Then when He made a wife for Adam, I feel sure she was the most beautiful female. When sin entered, we know that their appearances changed. Their bodies began to die, as God said would happen. Every human being since that time has had to deal with the appearance God gave us. And yes, some of you are better looking than the rest of us in outward appearance, but that is not the important thing! The person we are inside, adorned with the fruits of the Spirit, will exude to the outside and that person will radiate.

God loves us in whatever shape, size, color of skin, color of eyes, color of hair – He knows the number of hairs on every head, remember - even to the crooked toes and floppy ears, and He delights in us. Most importantly, He sees what is on the inside of us, and He sees all things beautiful about us when we are in the right relationship with Him.

So, let's not pay all that much attention to what a person looks like on the exterior, but rather focus on how much handsomeness or loveliness with which that person glows from his or her interior framework.

And it came to pass, when they were come, that He looked on Eliab, and said, Surely the Lord's anointed is before Him. But the Lord said unto Samuel, Look not on his countenance, or on the height of his stature; because I have refused him: for the Lord seeth not as man seeth; for man looketh on the outward appearance, but the Lord looketh on the heart. (1 Samuel 16:6-7 KJV)

Woe unto you, scribes and Pharisees, hypocrites! for ye are like unto whited sepulchres, which indeed appear beautiful outward, but are within full of dead men's bones, and of all uncleanness. (Matthew 23:27 KJV)

August 17   Feeling Desperately Cornered

I was so concerned about a lost friend during my teenage years after I had become a Christian. She admitted she was a lost sinner but said "Oh, I have time to become a Christian. I'm young yet." I witnessed to her often and told her I was praying for her. She would shrug and sneer and sometimes avoid me when we would meet.

I spent so much time praying for her that I seemed to be neglecting others who needed my prayers. So, when I saw June one day, I said "I'll not bother talking to you about becoming a Christian. I won't pray for you anymore. It seems to do no good."

And I kept my word. I cared for her but she seemed to be getting more and more worldly and not interested in becoming a Christian at all.

Then one day I learned from a mutual friend, "Hey, did you hear? June got saved during a revival meeting a few weeks ago." I rejoiced, praising God, but I wondered why June had not told me. I got in touch with her soon after that and told her how glad I was she had become a Christian.

She answered, with tears running down her cheeks, "As long as I knew you were praying for me, I felt I had time to make a decision. But when you said you would not talk to me about the Lord anymore and would not pray for me, I suddenly felt afraid, and like I was backed into a corner. The only way out of that corner was to acknowledge I was a sinner and receive Jesus as my Savior. I did that right there in my bedroom, and I came to know peace in my heart." We hugged, rejoicing together.

Years passed and she married a Christian man and he became a deacon in the church and she was very active in so many places in her church. She had two sons and they became Christians. More years passed, and she became ill and was in a nursing home many years until she died. We lived in separate states, but one time when I was in that area, I made it a point to visit her in the nursing home. She was bedridden, but bright-eyed and joyful. She said she knew she was going home to be with Jesus soon. We parted, and her last words to me were, "I love you. I'm so glad you pointed me to our Lord and prayed for me." I'm so glad she finally responded with placing her faith in our Savior.

> Moreover as for me, God forbid that I should sin against the Lord in ceasing to pray for you; but I will teach you the good and the right way. (1 Samuel 12:23 KJV)

> For what is our hope, or joy, or crown of rejoicing? Are not even ye in the presence of our Lord Jesus Christ at His coming? For ye are our glory and joy. (1 Thessalonians 2:19-20 KJV)

He stooped with a basin of water
And washed each disciple's feet,
Preparing them with tender affection
For anguish they soon would meet.
In Gethsemane He groaned in agony
Within hearing of His closest three.
He wailed under the weight of the sin load,
"If possible, let this cup pass from me."
Surrendered to do His Father's will,
He submitted to the kiss of a friend,
And allowed the mob to bind and hurl Him
Where cruelties before Sanhedrin would begin.
He gave His face to slaps and spittle;
To the whip He offered His back.
Blood oozed down His face from thorn pricks,
And rising fever made His parched lips crack.

He stretched out His hands to the mallet,
And yielded His feet to the spikes too.
Looking down on the crowd He said gently,
"Forgive them; they know not what they do."
Though His physical pain was beyond measure,
His mental anguish insurmountable agony,
The most severe hurt He revealed when He languished,
"My God, My God, why have You forsaken Me?"
His reason for dying was to satisfy God--
The Holy for the unholy was He.
His blood paid for the sinner's ransom--
Now by faith in Him the sinner goes free!
He did not stay on the rough-splintered cross;
In the tomb of Joseph neither did He stay.
The third day He arose to be alive forever.
He is indeed The Truth, The Life, and The Way!

-- Carlene Poff Baker

Watching her sleeping infant in her arms, I wonder if Mary touched His soft brow and thought about someday that brow would sweat great drops of blood and soon after wear a crown of thorns.

Holding Him to her breast, and feeling His hand reach up and touch her chin, I wonder if she ever thought that someday that dimpled hand would be pierced with nails until blood ran down.

Watching Him toddle about at her knee, wearing little brown sandals, I wonder if Mary watched those precious feet and thought that someday they would walk up a hill to die.

Getting Him dressed for school, where He and other Hebrew boys would sit at the feet of a Rabbi, and wrapping the colorful tunic she had made for Him around His shoulders and back, I wonder if she surmised that someday that dear smooth back would be beaten brutally.

As she watched her teenager Son sleeping on His mat, I wonder how many times she tiptoed to watch Him sleep and thought that in due time this Sinless Young Man would bear in His own body the sins of the whole world.

At dusk, when she called Him in for supper, and He obediently rushed to her and poured water in a basin at the door to wash his feet. I am sure Mary signed happily and pondered, "This is God Himself washing His feet in my home!"

And when He became a young adult, and He sat around their supper table, with His half-brothers and half-sisters, and the main course was roasted lamb, when she saw Him pause to touch the flesh of His own arm. And He shuddered. She ached in her own heart as well, knowing He was reminded again that He Himself was God's Lamb of God to be slain for the whole world, including herself, her husband Joseph, his siblings, all his kinfolks, and every human being all over the world.

But Mary kept all these things, and pondered them in her heart. (Luke 2:19 KJV)

To get a picture of the *omni* or *all-sufficiency* of God, read Psalm 139 for starters and then run references in other places in both Old and New Testaments of our Bible. All scriptures cited below are KJV.

+ God is Omniscient: All-Knowing - Thou knowest my down sitting and my uprising; thou understandest my thought afar off. (Psalm 139:2)
+ God is Omnipresent: Everywhere Present - Whither shall I go from thy Spirit, or whither shall I flee from thy Presence? (Psalm 139:7) God is not limited to time or space.
+ God is Omnivisual: Sees All Things at One Time - Yea, the darkness hideth not from thee; but the night shineth as the day; the darkness and the light are both alike to thee. (Psalm 139:12)
+ God is Omnific: All-Perfect - I will praise thee; for I am fearfully and wonderfully made: (Psalm 139: 14(a) I am God's Masterpiece.
+ God is Omnipotent: All-Powerful - And marvelous are thy works; and that my soul knoweth right well. (Psalm 139:14b)

O Lord our Lord, how excellent is thy name in all the earth! who hast set thy glory above the heavens. (Psalm 8:1 KJV)

O the depth of the riches both of the wisdom and knowledge of God! how unsearchable are His judgments, and His ways past finding out! ... For of Him, and through Him, and to Him, are all things: to Whom be glory forever. Amen. (Romans 11:33, 36 KJV)

August 21   **Endure and Persevere**

Never has a man achieved his God-glorifying goal without obstacles! At times it is an uphill climb with rocks and traps all along the way, or it is the fighting against an up-stream current. Those forward challenges leave their scars, but those are the marks of having done the job well.

Once a man who was forced to take shelter in a barn from a thrashing storm noticed a spider on the wall climbing upward. The wind from the storm coming through the cracks of the barn kept knocking the spider down to the ground. But that eight-legged bug began the climb upward after falling. The man watched and counted each time the spider fell. It helped him get over the fear of the storm outside. It fell twelve times! But up it went again, and reached the top of the wall where it took its place on a shelf. By then the storm had subsided, and the man felt sure that spider was about to begin weaving its web!

Yes, like the spider, sometimes we will fall, but we are not to stay down. As soon as we can, we are to take up where we left off, or even start over, but never, never, never give up. Among other things, others are watching the life of a Christian. When they see the endurance and getting back on track and proceeding, it is a great testimony which sometimes wants those watching to want to do likewise.

And the one continuing to achieve for the Lord's glory will always have the Lord alongside to help. For without Him we can do nothing. That person will grow and mature in his Christian journey. The Lord will be glorified by that person's life.

I can do all things through Christ which strengthenth me. (Philippians 4:13 KJV)

Therefore, my beloved brethren, be ye steadfast, unmovable, always abounding in the work of the Lord, forasmuch as ye know that your labor is not in vain in the Lord. (1 Corinthians 15:58)

August 22   Home Sweet Home

Home means so many things: abode, habitat, residence, dwelling, lodging, quarters, chambers, space, digs, place to stay, and others. But perhaps the best would be *family*. One who lives alone without family for whatever reason is bound to be empty and so lonesome at times. God didn't intend for people to be alone.

Home also means: where my stuff is, where I can rest, where I can be at peace, where I can rejuvenate, where I can interact with others I love. It means security, too.

A friend who had moved from Northwest USA where she grew up and lived until her advanced senior years, when she moved to Southwest USA made the remark, "I'm always lonesome for home." She meant her former home. I too live in another area from which I had grown up, married, and reared family. And I too have feelings of lonesomeness for the old home soil at times. Being a widow, and my husband being buried in my former home state, I will be placed beside him someday.

Did you know Abraham's wife Sarah probably never had a built house? They were on the move, always traveling, and when they stopped, they lived in a tent. Abraham was rich, but, based on search of the scriptures, there's no indication they lived otherwise.

Do you reckon the Jewish people longed for their homeland of Israel when they had been taken away by the Babylonians? They did return seventy years later. Although they were scattered to all corners of the world after that, I see and read and hear comments from them that they are hurrying back to Israel as fast as they can. Going home!

No matter the shape, size or condition of the building that houses the home, here is a great description penned by an anonymous person: "The mellow old house had a look of brooding tenderness, as though in its warm embrace it had soothed heartaches, laughed with youth, welcomed visitors, celebrated births and bridals, and cared lovingly for the aged."

Jesus knows home is special to us. He told His apostles shortly before He was crucified that He would be going back to heaven and would prepare places of abode for them, so that someday they would be living in the same place with Him. After building all those manses or rooms or homes for His believers, He said He would return and take all with Him to that place.

The good part about going to that wonderful dwelling-place, there will never be any parting, no moving, never to be lonesome any more. Down here on earth, the most magnificent home, be it even a palace, is subject to ruin, deterioration, erosion by weather, possibility of being burned or flooded or swallowed by an earthquake. Not there in Jesus' Place!

Another grand thing about being in that territory, we will be with all our fellow brothers and sisters in Christ, never to part again. What a wonderful reunion. But most of all, we will be in the presence of our Redeemer, our Home Builder, our Magnificent Lord, where we will participate in joy unspeakable and full of glory!

> By the rivers of Babylon, there we sat down, yea, we wept, when we remembered Zion. We hanged our harps upon the willows in the midst thereof. For there they that carried us away captive required of us a song; and they that wasted us required of us mirth, saying, Sing us one of the songs of Zion. How shall we sing the Lord's song in a strange land? (Psalm 137:1-4 KJV)

> In My Father's house are many mansions: if it were not so, I would have told you. I go to prepare a place for you. And if I go and prepare a place for you, I will come again, and receive you unto Myself; that where I am, there ye may be also. (John 14:2-3 KJV)

August 23   ## To Your Own Self Be True

One of my former pastors said "If you have no respect for yourself, you will never have respect for another person." Nothing in life will bring genuine satisfaction unless one has self-respect.

President James Garfield had this to say about self-respect for himself: "There is one man whose respect I must have at all hazards, and his name is James A. Garfield – for I must room with him, work with him, eat with him, commune with him – live with him."

To have self-respect, a person must be honest with himself about everything. He must be able to lie down at night in peace within himself. Shakespeare expressed it just right in one of his poems:

This above all: to thine own self be true;
And it must follow, as the night the day,
Thou canst not then be false to any man.

One's integrity comes from always being honest with self and all other people. It means keeping to the truth without compromise. It is one of the virtues found in the heart and life of the person who has accepted Jesus as Savior and follows Him.

Satan is the father of lies, Jesus said, and he has many followers. But let us, who have come out from under Satan's dominion, and have become the children of God by our receiving the Lord Jesus as Savior, never veer from keeping ourselves honest in all matters and conditions. So doing, we will know peace in our hearts, and will be able to show forth the light of our Lord's presence through the way we live.

All the while my breath is in me, and the spirit of God is in my nostrils; My lips shall not speak wickedness, nor my tongue utter deceit. God forbid that I should justify you: till I die I will not remove mine integrity from me. (Job 27:3-5 KJV)

Finally, brethren, whatsoever things are true, whatsoever things are honest, whatsoever things are just, whatsoever things are pure, whatsoever things are lovely, whatsoever things are of good report; if there be any virtue, and if there be any praise, think on these things. (Philippians 4:8 KJV)

August 24   Sometimes, Just Listen

One day while eating my sack lunch in the break room at work, a co-worker joined me. She said she was so glad to find me because she needed to ask my advice about a situation. As the two of us sat facing each other, she eating her sack lunch, and I munching on my tuna fish sandwich, she talked constantly, laying out the *mess* that she had gotten into. Tears streamed down her face.

I reached over and touched her hand, but she just kept ranting.

239

When she asked me something, she'd say "You see what I mean?" All I did was nod yes.

Her long, emotional tirade continued until we were both wadding up our sacks of finished lunches. She pushed back her chair and said, "I'm so glad I had this time with you. You have helped me so much with your thoughts and advice."

She left the room ahead of me. I sat there a bit longer and smiled to myself. I had not said one word to her, not given her one single word of advice. She had not realized it. She needed someone to listen and I was her sounding board. I'm glad I was there. One thing I did determine to do, and I did it right there as I walked back to my desk. I would pray for her that the mess would clear. I felt sure God would help her straighten it out.

I learned something else. She trusted me as her friend. She knew I would keep her words to myself, and not spread to anyone else. That was a compliment to me!

Sometimes we can help a person, who is baffled with a problem, more by listening rather than by saying a word. We ought to always be ready to lend our ears and listen, for, who knows when it might be, that we find ourselves needing to be listened to.

Whoso stoppeth his ears at the cry of the poor, he also shall cry himself, but shall not be heard. (Proverbs 21:13 KJV)

August 25 **Right Place, Right Time**

One morning an aged woman, who since becoming a widow had to move in with her daughter and son-in-law, prayed, "Lord, what will you have me do today? I cannot walk without my walker. I cannot do any strenuous house cleaning. I cannot even go out in the yard and pull weeds out of the flowers, because I cannot bend. I feel so useless."

She could fix her own meals, using her walker, cooking by microwave. So, after she sat down at her breakfast that day of a two-egg omelet from the microwave, a cup of orange juice, a bagel with apple butter on it, and a cup of coffee, her daughter came in and said, "Oh, Mom, we need you today. You know we have the two grandchildren with us because their mother had to go to a meeting. Here is our problem. I have to go to a meeting until 10:30. And hubby has to go to his doctor appointment at 10:45. If I am delayed at my meeting and he has to leave early, there needs to be someone here to mind the two boys for that little time gap. If you aren't available, I can call our neighbor to watch the boys."

She said, "Oh, I'll be glad to do that." She knew she would park herself in a seated position where she could hold the four-month-old baby or lie him down at times on the sofa beside her, and she would watch his older brother play in the spacious room. She breathed a prayer of thanks to her Heavenly Father for giving her something important and helpful to do.

She finished her breakfast, put her dishes in the sink for later washing, and readied herself to take that position on the big sofa.

And it turned out to be splendid timing! There was a time gap of half an hour when she was alone with the children. She held the little one in her lap, and he grinned at her and made cooing sounds. The older boy, who was currently taking martial arts classes, performed for her some of his movements. The baby also watched his brother and even let out a giggle.

Having filled her role, and seeing gratitude on her daughter's face, she made her way back to her own room, delighted that the Lord answered her prayer this way.

This shows how God can use us in various ways, some even seeming so insignificant, but they turn out to be blessings for everybody involved. We just have to be always "at the ready!"

She hath done what she could: she has come aforehand to anoint my body to the burying. (Mark 14:8 KJV)

But now hath God set the members every one of them in the body, as it has pleased Him. ... Nay, much more those members of the body, which seem to be more feeble, are necessary: And those members of the body, which we think to be less honorable, upon these we bestow more abundant

honor; and our uncomely parts have more abundant comeliness.
(1 Corinthians 12:18, 22-23 KJV)

August 26 Sometimes God Lets Me See an Answered Prayer

A man I knew who had an alcohol-drinking problem lived in a distant state, but his relative asked prayer for him that he would give up his drinking and return to his family. I prayed for that person, knowing I would never see him nor have any contact with him. But I knew God answers prayers and I felt He would send someone to that person to help him.

One day while eating lunch in a crowded restaurant, I sat alone at a table. Facing the entrance, I saw a man come in and stand at the hostess's place waiting to be seated. I thought, that man looks like the one I've been praying for, but surely not, because he has been gone out of state a long time.

Then I saw the hostess making her way from table to table trying to find a spot for him. She looked my way and moved toward my table.

"Do you mind if this gentleman sits with you?" she asked. "This place is so crowded, and your table has room for another person."

I agreed, and the man sat at my table. Yes, he was the one for whom I had been praying! We had not seen each other in many years, but we carried on catching-up conversation. He told me he had been away but had returned to his home. He said he had been in a facility to help him overcome a health problem. I just let him talk, not admitting I knew about his problem. I somehow came up with encouraging words and told him how delighted I was he had come home. Whatever words I used surely came from God. I realized God was using me to answer one of my own prayers.

He left first, and, as I watched him make his exit, I praised the Lord for planning this appointment that special day. Later I learned he had begun going to church again with his wife, and that he had become a sponsor for other men with alcoholic problems through the AA Program.

Yes, I knew God heard my prayer for him, but He also wanted to

use me somehow with personal encounter and conversation to serve
His purpose.

Therefore I say unto you, What things so ever ye desire, when
ye pray, believe that ye receive them, and ye shall have them.
(Mark 11:24)

I exhort therefore, that, first of all, supplications, prayers,
intercessions, and giving of thanks, be made for all men.
(1 Timothy 2:1 KJV)

August 27 — Homesick for God

Hubert Van Zeller said, "The soul hardly ever realizes it, but whether
he is a believer or not, his loneliness is really a homesickness for God."

When God created man and breathed into him and he became a
living soul, I believe God gave a space inside that man that wanted to be
ever yoked up with God, his Creator. He wanted to fellowship with God
and enjoy all that God had in store for him.

Then when sin entered the world through that first man's sin, that
space became so alarmingly empty inside the man. That emptiness
passed down with his descendants. God made a remedy for that space to
be filled again by His redemptive plan of salvation through Jesus Christ.
But mankind has sought all manner of ways to fill that emptiness:
worship of other gods, good works, exalting himself among his peers,
achieving a revered name. But he finds none of these give complete
satisfaction. That thirst for God still lingers.

The wonderful invitation of God still stands. He wants that longing,
yearning, emptiness of soul to come to Him, so that man can find
fullness, purpose, and fellowship again with his God. His ear is attentive
to the cry of those who long for that satisfaction.

But I am poor and needy; yet the Lord thinketh upon me: thou
art my help and my deliverer; make no tarrying, O my God.
(Psalm 40:17 KJV)

Since thou wast precious in my sight, thou hast been honorable, and I have loved thee: therefore will I give men for thee, and people for thy life. (Isaiah 43:4 KJV)

August 28   The Best Book, Authored by God

Someone said "Other books were given for information; the Bible was given for our transformation."

A knowledge of the Bible is essential to scholarship in many fields. It is a library within itself. Divided into two Testaments, the Old Testament which told of the coming of Jesus, and the New Testament which recorded His coming to the earth, His ministry, His death, burial, resurrection, organizing His church, and His ascension back into heaven. In the Old Testament, there are 66 books, composed of five books of the Law written by Moses; twelve books of history of the Jewish nation; five books of poetry; five major prophets' books, and twelve minor (or shorter) books of prophecy. In the New Testament there are four Gospels, one book of history, letters of the Apostle Paul, and general epistles, with the Book of Revelation ending the Testament.

The Bible is inexhaustible, as described by Leroy Brownlow, in his book, *Today Is Mine*, as "dipping up the ocean with a spoon."

Although penned by men, God is the Author of it all, from cover to cover. God gave His message to sinful mankind, telling of so many mighty things, but the main thing intended is that sinful man will believe God's message and believe on Jesus as Savior from sin, and then that one will be marvelously transformed to begin to live the abundant life.

But it is not merely a book to be placed on a shelf and admired, but to be read, yea, to be memorized, to be meditated upon, and then to be practiced in the reader's life.

Thy word is a lamp unto my feet, and a light unto my path. (Psalm 119:105 KJV)

The entrance of thy words giveth light; it giveth understanding unto the simple. (Psalm 119:130 KJV)

So then faith cometh by hearing, and hearing by the word of God. (Romans 10:17 KJV)

For the word of God is quick, and powerful, and sharper than any two-edged sword, piercing even unto the dividing asunder of soul and spirit, and of the joints and marrow, and is a discerner of the thoughts and intents of the heart. (Hebrews 4:12 KJV)

August 29 Spend Time Meditating with God

In our fast-paced world of activity, sometimes we miss out on separating ourselves from all commotion to spend quality time with our Lord. Most of us plan to do so, and do it haphazardly, squeezed in between events. I'm speaking for myself. It is like I have a date with God and then stand Him up.

Special things take place when I am alone with God, away from everybody else. One place I can do this is on the back deck of our house in my glider. There is nobody else around. I can even talk out loud. I enjoy knowing He is there with me listening and giving me thoughts, answering my questions, always with scriptures. Sometimes the words of a hymn will surface. It never gets dull, but, in fact, causes me to want to stay awhile longer. When duty calls, I bid Him farewell, and look forward to our next time together. I surely do hope He enjoys our time together as much as I do.

I am not alone in this experience. Friends have told me they experience like delights when they spend time alone with our God.

Some of the world's greats have always sought solitude for musing. It has been said that Leonardo de Vinci, the renowned artist, would sit almost motionless for days at a time meditating and getting the inspiration for his masterpieces.

I am sure the Psalmist David spent hours and hours, perhaps while tending his father's sheep, meditating on the ways of God, because he penned them in his Psalms.

Jesus Himself stole away often to spend time alone with His Father. He is an example for us.

> Let the words of my mouth, and the meditation of my heart, be acceptable in thy sight, O Lord, my strength, and my redeemer. (Psalm 19:14 KJV)

> This book of the law shall not depart out of thy mouth; but thou shalt meditate therein day and night, that thou mayest observe to do according to all that is written therein: for then thou shalt make thy way prosperous, and then thou shalt have good success. (Joshua 1:8 KJV)

August 30   Not Expected, But Selected

While we have many children born into our extended family, at a surprising last count, I discovered we have eleven who have been adopted into the family. And we are so glad to have them with us. They belong to us!

Children are a heritage from the Lord. He loves children. He wants them to have loving parents from conception forward. That is His divine intention. But sometimes little ones are not wanted by natural parents, and likewise there are couples who cannot have children of their own, so how wonderful when the end results are the placing of children where they can be cared for.

The amazing thing I have observed in families with adopted children, the little ones begin to look and act like their parents or siblings. They seem to fit. Another factor in belonging.

Yes, it is so good to belong to someone, to take someone's name, and to feel the homeness of being a part of a family. Legally, an adopted child can never be disowned by the adoptive parents.

In the Bible there are references to the blessing of being adopted into the family of God.

Our newest addition to the family by adoption is my great-grandson Ethan Thomas, the Thomas named in honor of my deceased husband, his great-grandfather. My granddaughter and husband have one son born to them, age eight, and they wanted another child, but have not been able to have it happen, and Ethan fits just right.

The Bible speaks of adoption into the family of God.

For as many as are led by the Spirit of God, they are the sons of God. For ye have not received the spirit of bondage again to fear; but ye have received the Spirit of adoption, whereby we cry, Abba, Father. (Romans 8:14-15 KJV)

But when the fulness of the time was come, God sent forth His Son, made of a woman, made under the law, To redeem them that were under the law, that we might receive the adoption of sons. And because ye are sons, God hath sent forth the Spirit of His Son into your hearts, crying, Abba, Father. (Galatians 4:4-6 KJV)

August 31   Remove Not the Ancient Landmarks

I have read recently that two of the historical buildings in my old home town have begun to deteriorate dangerously, with parts of the ceilings and other structural places falling. Both places have served mankind within their walls for decades, and nostalgic memories surface in the hearts and minds of thousands of people.

Also, in driving down a street in Nashville, I saw the tall, multi-storied Lifeway building had been razed. Heavy equipment machines were removing the debris. I learned a hotel will be built in its place. Of course, the Lifeway facility and staff have moved to another building. No doubt, because Lifeway – formerly Broadway Publishing Company – housed hundreds of writers of Biblical literature for use in churches around the world, God surely visited that place daily, with His Spirit moving in the hearts and minds of writers as they completed their assignments. And I'm sure a lot of prayers went up through the top of that tall building into heaven from the writers.

While I know old things have to be replaced, it just seems that a certain hallow never goes away from the place. I even saw an old dilapidated barn recently and atop the tin roof I saw a crow. I wondered if maybe others of nature long for the old places.

More than hanging onto old relics, the most important entity we need to hang onto is what God has written in His Word, the Bible. While things of wood and stone will have to perish and vanish, God's Word will never vanish or pass away. It will always stand. It is relevant in every generation, no matter how drastically Satan and his crowd seek to erode or completely eradicate it.

It's okay to hold onto in our memories the places and events of fond yesteryears, because they will vanish visibly from our landscapes, but never, never ought we let go of the tried and proven true written word of God, a library of 66 books, penned by men whom He selected to accomplish its completion. Not only ought we read it, but we should memorize as much of it as we can, so the right words will surface as we deal with situations in our life and we have to make decisions.

I felt a sadness seeing the Lifeway building gone, but I also knew the work begun there was being continued in another place, its business being the printing of lessons of study from God's never-passing-away Word, the Bible!

Remove not the ancient landmark, which thy fathers have set. (Proverbs 22:28 KJV)

The grass withereth, the flower fadeth: but the word of our God shall stand forever. (Isaiah 40:8 KJV)

September 1   Keep to the Narrow Path

A few times as I left the house and made my way over the concrete sidewalk to the car, I noticed a narrow crack in the concrete and ants were hurrying in one direction from one side of the sidewalk to the other side. It was narrow, and only one or maybe two could walk beside another. They were so orderly and traveled at the same pace. Then, I saw a wider place in the concrete. Ants were there too, but they were going every direction. Some were even going in reverse to the others. Some acted drunkenly.

As I reflected on that scene, the scripture came to mind where Jesus said that there were two ways to travel. One had a strait gate and narrow way and the other had a wide gate and a broad way. He said the strait gate led to life and few found that way, but that the wide gate led to destruction and many found it.

Those ants hurrying in the narrow crack were going one way and they marched orderly and seemed eager with purpose. They seemed to know where they were going. The ones in the wider scruffy place seemed to just be idling along, running this way and that, without purpose.

I could see how Jesus used this illustration. The ones who have come to Him for salvation know what road they are on, the narrow way, and they know their destination. They keep on the move on with joyful purpose while making the journey. Those people who have not received Jesus as Savior reel and wobble from one thing to another, seeking to fill their soul's emptiness, and never finding contentment. They move from this scenario to that, constantly changing directions.

Those on the broad road have many traveling companions but they are never satisfied. When one on that road comes to the end of himself, seeing nothing he can do or be can bring peace in his soul, and he turns to Jesus Christ and asks Him to become his Savior, then salvation happens, and he changes from the broad to the narrow, and gets in step with fellow travelers on the road to glory!

Enter ye in at the strait gate: for wide is the gate, and broad is the way that leadeth to destruction, and many there be which go in thereat: Because strait is the gate, and narrow is the way, which leadeth unto life, and few there be that find it. (Matthew 7:13-14 KJV)

God made human beings with the built-in ability to laugh. That factor proves itself as early as in infancy. Of course, the newborn comes into the world crying when the doctor slaps him on his bottom. And for days, weeks and maybe months, parents hear him crying and see him puckering his little lips. But, lo and behold, one day they rejoice when they see him spread his little toothless mouth in a wide, dimpled smile, and before long, they hear a bubbly giggle.

All during his growing-up days laughter occurs at every turn. Happiness exudes at the slightest happening in which the child is involved. It continues into teen-hood, adulthood, and to the end of that one's life. Each person's laughter is as uniquely his as is his fingerprints and voice resonance.

In the Bible we read of numerous events where either single persons or whole crowds rejoiced. Of course, there are many times in God's word when a person or many persons wept over happenings. But even after harsh times of weeping, when it was finished, there was rejoicing.

I imagine Jesus did a great deal of laughing. One example possibly was when He saw the wee man Zacchaeus running and climbing up in the sycamore tree so he could see Jesus as He passed under the tree. We know He saw him because, when He got to the tree, He called the wee man to come down and He told him He was going to be a guest at his house for a meal that very day.

Possibly another time Jesus must have chuckled was when the crowd at Peter's house where Jesus was teaching and healing people was so large that four men had to make a hole in the roof over Jesus' head so they could let down a crippled man on a cot through the hole in front of Jesus. We also know He spent so much time during His three-year ministry with His Twelve, in all sorts of weather, situations, and places, that I can hear them talking and laughing together.

Laughter is good for all of us, even in harsh trying times. The Book of Philippians has many scriptures where Paul uses the word *rejoice*, and the Psalms are full of happy words. We as children of God have so much rejoicing to do, and laughter is bound to burst its way out. Let's not smother it. It's good for the laughing one, the ones who hear the laughter, and especially God, who equipped us with the ability to laugh!

Then was our mouth filled with laughter, and our tongue with singing: then said they among the heathen, The Lord hath done great things for them. (Psalm 126:2 KJV)

Rejoice in the Lord always: and again I say, Rejoice. (Philippians 4:4 KJV)

September 3   **Time with Dad**

I saw a man with a group of about eight boys in a park once. All except one were about the same age, but the youngest was three or four. The man was father of one of the older boys and the youngest. They were all running and playing in the park, ahead of the man. Then, I saw the youngest look back at his dad. He left the big boys and came running to his dad. His dad held his hand awhile. Then he hoisted him upon his shoulders as he walked behind the other boys. The little one had the happiest grin on his face! He had more fun with his dad than with the whole gang of bigger boys.

It reminded me of one occasion with my own dad. Back in my youth, I asked if I could spend the night with my grandparents, my dad's parents. He not only agreed, but (not owning a car back in those days) he walked with me the eight miles to my grandparents' home. We got there about mid-afternoon, and he stayed there until near dark and then left to go back to our home. I looked around and saw he was gone, and suddenly I had the most *lost* feeling. So, I told my grandmother, "I'm going back home. I've got to go now and catch up with him." I began to run back along the road we had traveled, and hollered, "Daddy! Daddy!" at intervals. At length, I saw him stop and look back at me. "I changed my mind. I want to go back home with you." He just grinned at me, and we began our walk, side by side, back to our house.

We lived on a farm, and Dad was always on the premises or in the field close by. I especially liked his presence when there was a thunderstorm with high winds and lightning and thunder. He stayed outside the storm cellar watching the cloud while we huddled inside with Mom. We were afraid until he stepped inside with us and shut the door. Fear disappeared.

Children are happiest if they have a close relationship with their fathers growing up. If it should be that a dad has died, the absence is so great to the children. In those cases, it is always good to have a grandfather, uncle, or other male relative to come alongside to lend the father touch.

We know God the Father and God the Son had the best and closest relationship possible. They did all things together. God the Father called His Son, His "Only Begotten," and "Beloved Son in whom He was well pleased." The redemptive plan of both God the Father and God the Son necessitated the Son leaving Heaven where His Father was to come to the earth as a human being, yet without sin, that He might provide salvation for sinful mankind, but during His personal ministry, we read of times when Jesus prayed to His Father. Sometimes He prayed in the presence of others, like before He raised Lazarus from the grave, and in the presence of His apostles before going to the Garden of Gethsemane (John 17) as well as in the Garden afterward. But the scriptures also say at times He slipped away just to talk to His Father all alone. Those must have been such delightful, loving times.

Because God the Father is our Heavenly Father as well, since we have accepted Jesus as Savior, we too have the privilege and invitation to slip away apart from others and talk to our Heavenly Father about anything and everything. He delights in our coming to Him. Jesus is there listening to us too, and we are told to always give Him our prayers "in Jesus' name." Like the little boy riding on his Dad's shoulders, enjoying the experience to the full, so can we when we spend time with our wonderful Heavenly Father!

> And when He had sent the multitudes away, He went up into a mountain apart to pray: and when the evening was come, He was there alone. (Matthew 14:23 KJV)

And it came to pass in those days, that He went out into a mountain to pray, and continued all night in prayer to God. (Luke 6:12 KJV)

September 4   I Just Want to Be a Man

Once a school teacher of fourth graders, after having talked about various careers that her students might pursue when all grown up, asked each one "What would you like to be when you grow up?" All types of careers came back in answer. When she came to one, she asked, "What do you want to be when you grow up, Johnny?" He sat silently, seeming to ponder.

Then he looked straight at her and solemnly responded, "I just want to be a man." It was such a startling answer, she let it stand at that.

A man is a special person. The first person God created was a man – not an infant, but a full-grown man. God made him in His own image, in His own likeness. He Himself breathed into his nostrils, face on face, and made him a living soul. After that, because the man Adam was alone and needed a helpmeet, God made a woman. And He fashioned that woman from one of the man's ribs. His purpose for her was that she would always be subject to the man. They were to unite as one in marriage and produce children, whose children would produce children, and fill the world with human beings. The children were to be subject to the parents. Humans were to rule over the animal kingdom. So the order of rank with God has been and always will be: 1) God the Father; 2) Jesus Christ the Son; 3) Man/Husband; 4) Woman/Wife; 5) Child; and 6) Animals.

Anyone who steps out of that rank makes the whole atmosphere or situation chaotic. This is proven when a woman runs the house instead of the man. It is really disastrous when a child runs the parents. But there are even some households where the household pets are more important than their children.

When governments are run by men, progress comes about. When men are leaders in a church, the church flourishes. When men head up companies and businesses, growth and expansion results.

God loves both man, woman and child equally with all His heart, but He has designed roles for all. Adhering to those straits bring forth fulfillment, contentment and delight because those are the right ways. To do the opposite is costly to a person, a family, a business, a church, a country.

Oh, that all little boys growing up would say "I just want to be a man when I grow up," and little girls would say "I just want to be a woman, who stands behind the man, and be his helpmeet in all the ways I can."

So God created man in His own image, in the image of God created He him; male and female created He them. (Genesis 1:27 KJV)

Now the days of David drew nigh that he should die; and he charged Solomon his son, saying, I go the way of all the earth: be thou strong therefore, and shew thyself a man; And keep the charge of the Lord thy God, to walk in His ways, to keep His statutes, and His commandments, and His judgments, and His testimonies, as it is written in the law of Moses, that thou mayest prosper in all that thou doest, and whithersoever thou turnest thyself. (1 Kings 2:1-2 KJV)

But I would have you know, that the head of every man is Christ; and the head of the woman is the man; and the head of Christ is God. ... For the man is not of the woman; but the woman of the man. Neither was the man created for the woman; but the woman for the man. (1 Corinthians 11:3, 8-9 KJV)

Children, obey your parents in the Lord: for this is right. Honor thy father and mother; which is the first commandment with promise; that it may be well with thee, and thou mayest live long on the earth. (Ephesians 6:1-2 KJV)

Once when I was asked to pray for a loved one in a distant state who was facing a big issue. She had gone to college, and although had been brought up in a Christian home and had made a profession of faith and was a believer herself, she had gotten caught up in an anti-Bible cult. I prayed and prayed, but it did not seem to be enough. I had a photo of that person, and I set it out so I could look at her image often when I prayed. I still felt I needed to do something more.

One night when I could not sleep, I recalled the scripture in the book of James where prayer was mentioned, and the ones praying were to anoint the one for whom they were praying with oil. So, I went to my pantry and took out the bottle of olive oil. I walked back to the picture, opened the olive oil, dabbed some on my fingertips, and smeared it on the face of the person in the photo. I was saying in essence, "Now, Lord, I don't know what else to do, so it is totally in Your hands." At once, I felt peace. I knew God had heard me. I trusted Him to bring the answer to pass.

As I waited for Him to work things out in that situation, the mother of that person called and asked me to write a letter to the one for whom I had prayed. I had also learned along the journey of my Christian life that sometimes God uses the one doing the praying to bring about His answer. I agreed to write a letter to the person. I labored over the wording with God giving me discernment. I mailed it and waited again.

No answer came from the addressee. Nor did I hear from the mother, until about four months later. She was so exuberant! Her child had left the anti-Bible cult, had even left that college, had returned home, and would enroll in a community-Vo-tech type college. She immediately went to her church and rededicated her life to the Lord. Very soon she was happily active more than ever in her church service. They continued to live in a distant state from me, but we kept in touch over the years. She is still serving the Lord in even greater ways—teaching a children's class, leading in the college ministry with her peers, and in other ways.

I too rejoiced over the answer to my prayer. I don't know if my anointing of oil on the photo made any difference with God. I know now

I did it because I had come to the end of myself, and I was desperate to hear from God.

> And all things, whatsoever ye shall ask in prayer, believing, ye shall receive. (Matthew 21:22 KJV)

> Is any sick among you? let him call for the elders of the church; and let them pray over him, anointing him with oil in the name of the Lord. (James 5:14 KJV)

September 6   **Let There Be Music**

My life has been permeated by music. As a toddler I remember Mom singing little songs to me, and when she was doing her household tasks, she was always humming a tune. Daddy played the guitar or fiddle at front-porch socials when friends came over in summer. Grandpa was the song leader at church and either Grandma or one of my aunts played the piano or organ. When our extended family gathered for a reunion, before the event ended, someone sat down at the piano, and another led the group in singing hymns.

As I grew up, songs continued to envelop my life. At school we sang the National Anthem after reciting the Pledge of Allegiance. The Music Teacher worked with us all year and then we participated in a big song fest near the end of the school year. Crowds of folks came to see and hear us. In high school, we were invited to sing in glee club or to play an instrument in the band. At birthdays there was singing. At graduation there was fitting music, especially "Pomp and Circumstance." Favorite love songs were on the program at weddings, plus the Wedding March. And, of course, there were funeral hymns at a death.

When we had a daughter, she started piano lessons when in second grade. She also sang in the school choir. Her four children were involved in music all through their school years, some singing and some playing an instrument in the band. I sang songs to my daughter as I rocked her to sleep. Then I sang songs to my grandchildren when I rocked them, and later to my great-grandchildren. Gideon liked me to sing "God

Bless America" as his lullaby, and lately, when rocking the youngest, five-month-old Ethan, he quieted down when I sang "Nearer My God to Thee."

God designed music. It has a purpose. Sometimes a hymn sung at a church worship service will hang on in one's heart and mind longer than the pastor's sermon. Music touches one's mind, heart, soul and spirit. The Psalmist David has much to say about music, singing and playing of instruments, all for the glory and praise of God. In the New Testament we are encouraged to participate in songs, hymns and spiritual songs. God the Father sings over us. He said so! We have one account of Jesus singing with His apostles after observing the Lord's Supper and as they walked toward the Garden of Gethsemane.

We are instructed to memorize scriptures (Psalm 119:11), so that when faced with an issue, the Holy Spirit will nudge a particular scripture to the surface to address it. Likewise, I believe we are to memorize hymn lyrics and learn their tunes, because I have found myself faced with a malady of some sort, and the tune and words of a song will come to quell and allay.

Yes, music is as essential to living as dining, learning, working, and it continues to do God's purpose toward His people. So, let the music roll on as we journey through this life!

> Then sang Moses and the children of Israel this song unto the Lord, and spake, saying, I will sing unto the Lord, for He hath triumphed gloriously: the horse and his rider hath He thrown into the sea. (Exodus 15:1 KJV)

> And He hath put a new song in my mouth, even praise unto our God: many shall see it, and fear, and shall trust in the Lord. (Psalm 40:3 KJV)

> The Lord thy God in the midst of thee is mighty; He will save, He will rejoice over thee with joy; He will rest in His love, He will joy over thee with singing. (Zephaniah 3:17 KJV)

A couple took a walk for their health every morning at 5:00, no matter the weather. It was a quiet, little-traffic time, and it started their day out right. One morning as they were walking, it was raining, and the held their umbrellas and proceeded along the usual route. When they came to one house, the residence of a neighbor they did not know, they noticed the car was parked in the drive. It was a car with a window in the top, a sun-roof or moonlight-roof, and the window was open. Rain was pouring into the car through the window.

The couple stopped and talked about the situation. He said, "The house is dark. They're probably still asleep. We don't know who they are. Might be dangerous for us if we knock on their door." She agreed.

They resumed their trek down the street, but when they had gone no more than a hundred feet, they stopped again. She said, "I've been praying asking God what we ought to do, Ted. And I just got His answer. He said 'Love your neighbor as yourself.' Ted, if that were our car, I'd want someone to wake me up and tell me the roof was letting in the rain."

They turned around and walked up the drive and onto the porch. Ted knocked on the door. At once, they heard dogs barking and rushing toward the door. No one responded. Ted knocked again. The dogs added snarls to their barking. The couple started down the steps to leave, when they heard a man's voice from inside. He called the dogs to hush and they did.

"Who is it?" he asked. Ted told him what they had seen happening to the car. The man opened the door with the chain still intact. "Thank you; I'll come out and close the window." He shut the door again.

The couple left and continued their walk. "I'm so glad we did that, Ted" she said. "It would have ruined my whole day had we not done what God wanted us to do."

"Honey, it sure was scary for me at first, but, I'm with you. If God gave you the response to be kind to this unknown neighbor, He surely would protect us against any harm."

Thou shalt not avenge, nor bear any grudge against the children of thy people, but thou shalt love thy neighbor as thyself: I am the Lord. (Leviticus 19:18 KJV)

Therefore all things whatsoever ye would that men should do to you, do ye even so to them: for this is the law and the prophets. (Matthew 7:12 KJV)

For all the law is fulfilled in one word, even in this; Thou shalt love thy neighbor as thyself. (Galatians 5:14 KJV)

September 8   Called <u>Bird-Brain</u> is Complimentary

I always look forward to seeing marten birds congregate on electric high line wires at busy intersections, as they seem to be making plans for a group migration for the winter.

I've noticed other things about birds. They do not mate outside their species. Mother birds take of their little ones, and their male mates help with feeding the newly-hatched. The parents know the right time to nudge their progeny out of the nest, to begin to fly and, eventually, make their own way.

I saw one spring day two adult ducks and three little ones swimming in a shoot off the Cumberland Pond near where I work. They formed a line, one behind the other as they swam. One adult – perhaps the male – was at the head leading; the three little ones behind that one, and the other adult was behind the three. It looked to me like they were out for a family trek.

I'm always amazed at how skillful birds are in building their nests. Also, it is interesting to me that all birds do not like the same food. I doubt that any bird except the crow likes corn.

Isn't it something to think about that of all the animals and fowls in the ark, Noah chose two birds to check out how well the flood waters had receded? As soon as Noah saw the tops of mountains, he sent out a raven. The raven never returned to the ark, so we suppose it found food consisting of floating stuff in the water, and it perhaps found refuge somewhere atop one of the mountains. Noah waited a few more days and sent out a dove to check out the scenario. The dove found no place to land, so it flew back to the ark. Seven days later Noah sent the dove out again, and this time it returned with an olive leaf in its beak. Noah knew that meant the flood waters were receding more rapidly. A week later he sent out the dove, and this time it did not return to the ark, so he knew soon they would be exiting the ark on land.

We know God created fish and fowl on the fifth day of creation. Birds were used by the priesthood in some of their offerings. The Holy Spirit descended upon Jesus in the form of a dove when He was being baptized by John.

God gave these little winged creatures sense to do what they were supposed to do. They have always kept to their same purpose. So, birds have more sense, with their wee brains, than some human beings who are supposed to be more highly intellectual. Thus, if somebody calls you a *bird brain*, consider yourself markedly scholarly, as it indeed is complimentary.

> He causeth the grass to grow for the cattle, and herb for the service of man; that he may bring forth food out of the earth. ... The trees of the Lord are full of sap; the cedars of Lebanon, which He hath planted; where the birds make their nests: as for the stork, the fir trees are her house. (Psalm 104:14, 16-17 KJV)

> Yea, the stork in the heaven knoweth her appointed times; and the turtle and the crane and the swallow observe the time of their coming; but my people know not the judgment of the Lord. (Jeremiah 8:7 KJV)

September 9   Mother's Personal Touch

When my daughter's seventh birthday was approaching, I planned a get-together for her with some of her friends. As I discussed with her games and prizes, we agreed on things. Then I said, "Mrs. Edge at the Bake Shop makes really pretty birthday cakes. I'll ask her to bake your cake. What color frosting and what design do you want on it?"

She did not answer. I asked her again. No response. Then, looking straight at me across the table where we were sitting, she said "I want you to make the cake for me, Mommy."

I argued, "But you know I usually make messes when I try to decorate a cake. You have seen some of my messes. So why do you want me to make you a messy cake?"

Quietly she said, "Because you are my Mommy."

Tears welled up in my eyes. I took her by her hand and said, "Then I will make your cake, and if it is a mess we can all laugh at it."

The day of her celebration came. Several of her little friends were guests. They played games, and she opened gifts. I cut that cake after she blew out the candles, and nobody said anything derogatory about it. It wasn't as pretty as Mrs. Edge's would have been, but if my cake made my child's day joyful, then I was pleased. I realized then, she just needed her Mommy's special touch on her special day.

That thought stayed with me in ensuing events, when I could see she needed my presence, my input, yes, my touch, for special times in her life, I determined to be in touching nearness.

She looketh well to the ways of her household, and eateth not the bread of idleness. Her children arise up, and call her blessed; her husband also, and he praiseth her. (Proverbs 31:27-28 KJV)

September 10 — Previous Five Words

One of the first scriptures children learn from their parents or in Sunday School is "The Lord is my Shepherd," the first words of Psalm 23. Then in time they go on to learn the whole Psalm. Only five words but with magnanimous meaning. Let's look at them one by one.

The means "One and Only, Sole, Complete, Absolute, Whole, Total, Full."

Lord means "Person Who is Superior, Exemplary, Above All, Noble, Majestic, Regal, Resplendent."

Is means "Have Being, Now, the Present, Subsisting, Staying, Remaining."

My means "whatsoever I Myself personally own or possess."

Shepherd means "One who cares for His sheep." As such Shepherd, He sees that his sheep has no wants. He goes ahead of His sheep to find non-rushing watering places where the sheep can drink without fear. He finds best pastures where His sheep may eat. He defends His sheep against all enemies. He stays close beside His sheep, in touching distance, and He talks to His sheep, calling that one by name. When His sheep is tired, He finds a good resting place. When His sheep strays, He goes out at once to rescue and bring that one back to the safety of the fold. When His sheep gets a sore or is in pain or discomfort, He applies whatever salve is needed to bring healing. He is always gentle. His voice makes the sheep not afraid. He guards His sheep during the night with His own self stationed at the gate. He even lays down His own life for His sheep.

Of course, this speaks of Jesus, our Good Shepherd, who is ever watching over and caring for His beloved sheep. His sheep respond to His voice, and they delight in following Him.

The Lord is my Shepherd; I shall not want. (Psalm 23:1 KJV)

I am the good shepherd: the good shepherd giveth his life for the sheep. (John 10:11 KJV)

September 11   Absences

My husband owned a print shop for twenty-one years and he had worked in printing for other companies many years prior to that. He knew all about the workings of the printing industry: various printing paper, type setting, running all sorts of presses, and inks.

I helped out as receptionist, but I knew nothing about the other things of printing. One day we were talking about colors of ink. He had all colors but there was no white ink. I asked him why. He said "White is not a color; White is the absence of color." That stunned me and gave me something to think about.

I came to realize that was so. In the same vein, I recognized there were other absences. Darkness is the absence of light. Arid is the absence of wetness. Death is the absence of life. Evil is the absence of God.

As sinners we are stained with all manner of bold colors, such as crimson and scarlet. God said that although a sinner's sin be so stained, when that sinner comes to Him, the bold colors will be gone and the color would then be white as snow. Likewise, as sinners we are thirsty with parched souls, but when we receive the water of life from Jesus, our thirst is quenched forever. As sinners we are dead in our trespasses and sins, but when we come to Jesus for salvation, we become alive, quickened by His Spirit. As sinners we are in total darkness, but when we come to Jesus, the Light of the World, we are lit and our light will never be extinguished.

Wherever evil exists and runs rampant, hurting, destroying, ruining, and causing all manner of harm, God is not there. Where God is, there is righteousness, holiness, love, joy, life, peace, comfort, delight, heights of achievement, and so much more. Ah, how thankful ought we to be who know Jesus Christ as Savior and Lord that He is ever present with us, never absent, and in Him we don't walk in darkness. We rejoice that our sins have been removed, and we have the hope of eternal life.

Come now, and let us reason together, saith the Lord: though your sins be as scarlet, they shall be as white as snow; though they be red like crimson, they shall be as wool. (Isaiah 1:18 KJV)

Then spake Jesus again unto them, saying, I am the light of the world: he that followeth Me shall not walk in darkness, but shall have the light of life. (John 8:12 KJV)

September 12   Love Scars

There is a story about a little girl who grew up seeing her mother's hands and arms with horrible looking red scars from her elbows down into her fingers. They stayed that way and never changed. She never wondered about the scars as a small child. Her mother could use her hands and arms like all other adult women she knew.

As the girl grew up into puberty and into her teen years, when her family was in public, she began to notice how others looked with puzzlement and sometimes with pitying expressions. This began to bother the girl, and in time she was ashamed of her mother's hands and arms. It was after one of her visiting girlfriends was in their home, and the visitor said "Ooh," when she saw her mother's hands, that she got up the courage to ask her mother to wear gloves on her hands and long sleeves when they were out in public.

"Why do you have such ugly arms and hands, Mother?" she asked one day.

"I was in a fire once. It was our home when you were a baby. It was night time, and we were asleep upstairs in our beds. Your Dad and I in our bed and you in your crib. I grabbed you out of your crib and wrapped you up in a quilt so you would not get burned. Your Dad and I got burned. His legs and feet got burned bad, but he took most of the heat and hurried me with you in my arms down the stairs to the outside. My arms and hands got burned really bad. So that's why I have the scars. But," she laughed, "I'd do it again and would have been glad to be burned even more, because I loved you so."

Suddenly the little girl, burst into tears, ran to her mother and hugged her. "Oh, Mother, I'm so sorry. I love you so. You have the most beautiful arms and hands in all the world. Thank you for saving my life!"

And one shall say unto Him, What are these wounds in thine hands? Then He shall answer, Those with which I was wounded in the house of my friends. (Zechariah 13:6 KJV)

And when they were come to the place, which is called Calvary, there they crucified Him ... (Luke 23:33 KJV)

And after eight days again His disciples were within, and Thomas with them: then came Jesus, the doors being shut, and stood in the midst, and said, Peace be unto you. Then saith He to Thomas, Reach hither thy finger, and behold my hands; and reach hither thy hand, and thrust it into my side: and be not faithless, but believing. And Thomas answered and said unto Him, My Lord and my God. (John 20:26-28 KJV)

The person who breaks any one of the Ten Commandments does so because of selfishness, thinking only of himself.

To break "Thou shalt have no other gods before me," the person will not reverence the One and Only True God, but will debase Him by focusing on some other person or thing to worship.

The person breaks "Thou shalt not make unto thee any graven image," when surrounding himself with animate or inanimate objects he places reliance on for guidance, comfort, apart from trusting in the True God. Again, he focuses on himself and his own selfish choice of whom to worship.

To defame, debase, dishonor the Majestic Name of the God of Heaven, the person uses that name to vent his emotions for not getting his own way, so he thus refuses to obey the command "Thou shalt not take the name of the Lord thy God in vain."

Deciding to make every day of the week's seven days a day to do his own thing, he puts to naught the command "Remember the Sabbath to keep it holy."

When the person fails to "Honor thy father and thy mother," he loves himself more than he loves the parents to whom he belongs.

When the person breaks the Commandment "Thou shalt not kill," he thinks only of getting revenge for himself. He cares not for the person whom he slays, nor does he care about the loved ones of the one slain, whose hearts are broken, nor does he even think about the hurt he causes the ones who love him.

The one who breaks the command, "Thou shalt not commit adultery," thinks only of satisfying his own sexual passion, thinking not of his own mate, his innocent children, nor the person's family with whom he is involved.

When the person disregards the command "Thou shalt not steal," again he is thinking only of what he himself wants, even though it belongs to another. He cares not a whit for the loss to the one from whom he stole.

"Thou shalt not bear false witness against your neighbor," the person scoffs at when he lies against anyone to bring about gain for himself.

When a person breaks the rule, "Thou shalt not covet," he is actually saying, "Well, I deserve that item or position or recognition." In essence he is saying "I am not content with what I already have."

Yes, every sin we commit is because we are selfish, we want our own way, and choose to suit ourselves. It was that way when Adam and Eve sinned. They chose to disregard God's command and do the opposite. Look what happened!

Jesus Christ was not selfish. He always pleased His Father. He fulfilled the Law we humans could not live up to, so that when a "commandment- breaking sinner" comes to Him, confessing sins, and accepting Him as Lord and Savior, then we have the Holy Spirit living within us to help us stay on track, in thinking of God first and of others more than ourselves.

> But this thing commanded I them, saying, Obey my voice, and I will be your God, and ye shall be my people: and walk ye in all the ways that I have commanded you, that it may be well unto you. (Jeremiah 7:23 KJV)

September 14   Good Samaritans Still Exist

My friend Sandy told me, "My chest felt crushed where it had hit the steering wheel. The knot on my head where it hit the door frame throbbed every time I tried to more it. I was so very scared. I had been told not to move by an off-duty paramedic, who had stopped at the wreck. I sat frozen, gasping for a deep breath, as I waited for the ambulance.

"Then a woman was at my driver's side window. She was attractive, distinguished, sweet-looking with salt and-pepper hair, maybe sixty years old. She reached inside the car and took hold of my left hand in both of hers. She encircled it with her own and smiled at me. She asked "Are you okay?" and I told her I didn't know. She asked "Do you mind if I pray?" I shook my head no, and she bowed her head, kissed the hand she held, and began to pray. When she finished, she kissed my hand again, and smiled. She asked my name and then said "Sandra, you are going to be okay. I'll keep praying for you." Then she left.

"I have no idea who she was; I didn't get a chance to ask. The ambulance came and things got hectic. But I wasn't scared any more. I felt safe and at peace, in spite of the horrible pain. Since that day I've wished so many times that I knew who she was. I wanted to tell her how very thankful I was that she stopped. I needed someone to stop, hold my hand, and seem to care, and, yes, I did need the prayer.

"I hope the need never arises, but if it does that I can help someone as she helped me, I want to be able to repay my debt by easing up to the driver's side, hold the hurt one's hand, and say a prayer that that one will not have fear and will know the peace I experienced that day when my Good Samaritan came my way."

> And Jesus answering said, A certain man went down from Jerusalem to Jericho, and fell among thieves, which stripped him of his raiment, and wounded him, and departed, leaving him half dead. … But a certain Samaritan, as he journeyed, came where he was: and when he saw him, he had compassion on him, And went to him, and bound up his wounds, pouring in oil and wine, and set him on his own beast, and brought him to an inn, and took care of him. (Luke 10:30, 33-34 KJV)

September 14 — Son is Such a Special Word

Some children in our world do not know the blessedness of belonging to their dads. I believe their lives have an empty place being in that position. I know some have fathers who have died, but so many never know who their male parent is.

I knew someone whose natural father died when he was a toddler, but he was fortunate enough to have a stepfather for a while. Then he died. This person longed for somebody to just call him "Son." With my husband's permission, I wrote a poem about his feeling.

> I was just a tyke when my own Daddy died;
> A toddler, I was learning to run.
> Too young to remember Daddy talking to me,
> I wish I'd heard him say "Son."

My brothers were all much older than I
Too big to play with me and have fun.
They teased me with names like "Bohunkas,"
When I yearned for them to call me "Son."
I watched other boys with their Daddies;
Romping after their day's work was done.
I'd have gladly swapped places with any of them,
Just to hear a Dad say "Hey, there, Son."
When I was five, Mama married again,
which brought to our home much joy.
I silently wished for Dad to say "Son,"
But he called me instead "Billy Boy."
Then my new Dad died eight years later
At an age when a fellow needs a dad so.
I had to help Mama make a living
And the ways of the working man go.

I worked hard to please my employer,
And to learn how his business was run.
I talked to him as if he were my father,
Hoping he'd slip up and call me "Son."
I earned the title "Pitcher" in baseball;
In hunting "Old Dead-eye" with a gun.
I answered to "Private Baker" in the Army,
But nobody ever called me "Son."
I hope when I go to meet my Savior
That He will say more than "Well done;"
I want Him to look straight at me,
And say, "Welcome home, "My Son."

                                    --Carlene Poff Baker

I am sure Jesus treasured the knowledge that His Heavenly Father
recognized and devotedly loved Him as His Son. We have scriptures
that tell us so. We can sense the endearment the Father had toward
His Son Jesus.

I will declare the decree: the Lord hath said unto Me, Thou art my Son; this day have I begotten thee. (Psalm 2:7 KJV)

And Jesus, when He was baptized, went up straightway out of the water: and, lo, the heavens were opened unto Him, and He saw the Spirit of God descending like a dove, and lighting upon Him: And lo a voice from heaven, saying, This is My beloved Son, in whom I am well pleased. (Matthew 3:16-17 KJV)

And as He prayed, the fashion of His countenance was altered, and His raiment was white and glistering. And, behold, there talked with Him two men, which were Moses and Elias. ... And it came to pass, as they departed from Him, Peter said unto Jesus, Master it is good for us to be here: and let us make three tabernacles; one for thee, and one for Moses, and one for Elias: not knowing what he said. While he thus spake, there came a cloud, and overshadowed them: and they feared as they entered into the cloud. And there came a voice out of the cloud, saying, This is my beloved Son: hear Him. (Luke 9:29-30, 33-35 KJV)

September 16   Just a Touch

When Jake saw smoke swelling above the trees, he ran all the way home from school, but it was too late. Papa and Mama had died in the blaze. A lad of twelve, he left school to rebuild on the sooty shambles. As he lay on his mat in the still night, he yearned to hear someone's breathing besides his own.

Jake hoed and raked and cut wood to earn wages. Eating biscuits and taters for supper, he longed for another hand to brush his hand. Balmy nights he fixed himself to a spot behind the center field fence, his pale blue eyes watching the stretch, the pitch, the run. As he trudged home, he pined for the coach to hug his skinny shoulders the way he had seen him do the boys on the team.

By young manhood, he had walled-up and roofed a building where his old home had burned. He painted the hut sunshine yellow, and even put a glass window in the front door. Sitting on the steps waiting for the night to cool, he ached for a woman to sit on the steps with him, and to hear her praise him for their painted house. Hearing children's laughter bouncing from somewhere, he signed, wishing for a yard full of whooping children to call him "Papa."

Jake's beard turned gray. His legs trembled under the load of wood he carried toward the porch. He felt himself falling. He awoke in a world of whiteness.

"I'm your nurse, Jake," he heard the hovering face say. "What can I do to make you comfortable?"

Tears slid down Jake's wrinkled cheekbones. The nurse bent low to catch his whisper: "Kiss my cheek, will you, nurse? Nobody's kissed me since my Mama did before she died. Lay your hand on my brow, nurse. Then, just hold my hand. It's so good to feel somebody's touch."

Two are better than one; because they have a good reward for their labor. For if they fall, the one will lift up his fellow: but woe to him that is alone when he falleth; for he hath not another to help him up. Again, if two lie together, then they have heat: but how can one be warm alone? And if one prevail against him, two shall withstand him; and a threefold cord is not quickly broken. (Ecclesiastes 4:9-12 KJV)

And Jesus put forth His hand, and touched him, saying, I will; be thou clean. And immediately his leprosy was cleansed. (Matthew 8:3 KJV)

And when Jesus was coming to Peter's house, he saw his wife's mother laid, and sick of a fever. And He touched her hand, and the fever left her: and she arose, and ministered unto them. (Matthew 8:14-15 KJV)

September 17   Sometimes I Wonder

Sometimes I wonder WHY I am still here;
I know God has designed it so.

Silvering years are taking their toll,
Curbing my launches to do and to go.
Sometimes I wonder WHO I am,
Having worn many hats during my years—
As daughter, sister, student, wife, mother—
And have filled various titled careers.
Sometimes I wonder WHAT is my purpose
As I enter and exit each given day.
What is my task? What deed I'm to perform?
Lord, I trust you to show me the way.
Sometimes I wonder WHERE TO from here?
Is this place my rightful abode?
My stuff is here—my bed, my chair,
But, oft my yen is for a different road.
Sometimes I wonder about WHICH to choose—
The one better than the other bests?
Choices bring along their consequences,
And, now and then come with tedious tests.
Sometimes I wonder about a challenge of HOW
Against a mountain of "cannot be done."
Then God shows me a path at the bottom—
After the climb, atop the peak, there's the sun!
Sometimes I wonder about my WHEN
After all my life's ventures around every bend.
I know this fragile temple will come to a halt.
Then I'll go home to God, my greatest venture to begin!

Trust in the Lord with all thine heart; and lean not unto thine own understanding. In all thy ways acknowledge Him, and He shall direct thy paths. (Proverbs 3:5-6 KJV)

But this thing commanded I them, saying, Obey my voice, and I will be your God, and ye shall be my people: and walk ye in all the ways that I have commanded you, that it may be well unto you. (Jeremiah 7:23 KJV)

For I know the thoughts that I think toward you, saith the Lord, thoughts of peace, and not of evil, to give you an expected end. (Jeremiah 29:11 KJV)

September 18 — He Always Sees His Own

A man named Wayne took his daughter to the college where she was registered. It was her first time to live away from home, in a dormitory with other girls. After settling her in her assigned room, with many bags of her things, they walked outside and hugged each other farewells. As he drove away, looking back he saw the blend of blue jean-clad girls. With hair styles much the same, they made up one dappled montage. Yet, his own child stood out conspicuously from the crowd. Through tear-filled eyes, he saw only one, his very own.

God likewise sees the teeming multitudes scurrying about the campuses of this planet. He is acutely aware of the minute details of the make-up of each one, because He created each one. He longs to be Lord of every one of them. But His eye is distinctly and peculiarly upon each child of His, the one who has chosen Jesus as personal Savior and has made Him Lord of that one's life. Because God is omnipresent, He is different from the father of the college girl who had to be apart from her: God never leaves His child.

The college girl, knowing how much her father loves her, feels tremendously secure and content, and even though they are distanced from each other, she will honor him by keeping all the principles set forth all of her life in their home. She won't want to disappoint him. Likewise, God's child, knowing His great love for him or her, and knowing He is constantly watching, will always feel loved, safe, and confident, and will delight in pleasing Him.

And the Lord, He it is that doth go before thee; He will be with thee, He will not fail thee, neither forsake thee: fear not, neither be dismayed. (Deuteronomy 31:8 KJV)

The Lord is thy keeper: the Lord is thy shade upon thy right hand. The sun shall not smite thee by day, nor the moon by night. The Lord shall preserve thee from all evil: He shall preserve thy soul. The Lord shall preserve thy going out and thy coming in from this time forth, and even for evermore. (Psalm 121:5-8 KJV)

September 19   **You Are Somebody**

As I sat in a waiting room, ready to go to my appointment when my name was called, I was constantly greeted by acquaintances who came and went. Then I heard a young man sitting across from me say, "I wish people noticed me like they do you." At first, I didn't know he was talking to me. Then I looked up and saw only he and I left in the room.

He continued, "Even when I walk down the street, and I've lived here all of my twenty-one years, nobody speaks. Nobody cares."

Before I had a chance to respond, his name was called and he left the room. His words jarred me, and I thought, how awful he must feel to think nobody cared for him. After my appointment, on my drive home, his words kept surfacing in my thoughts. What would my response have been had I another chance to talk with that young man? After a lot of musing, I decided what I would say.

"Go outside on a sunny day and stand or walk in the sun. If you make a shadow, you are somebody. Go by the fenced-in-yard of a couple of Dobermans, or any kind of dog, and if they bark ferociously at you, you are somebody. When you approach a bush where a cardinal or blue jay mama is sitting on her nest, if the male bird comes out fluttering and squawking at you, you are somebody. On a warm day, pack yourself a picnic lunch. Take it outside, to the park, or just out under the tree in your yard. Begin to eat, and if a fly, a mosquito, a gnat, or a bee appears and starts coming between your mouth and your food, you are somebody.

"Now, if the solar system, the animal kingdom, the winged fowl world, and any species of insect folk notice you, then why in the world would you care if people do not notice you? By the way, the receptionist called your name, so that tells me you are somebody. And as far as people noticing you is concerned, why don't you begin to notice other people. Take an interest in some other somebody, and show you care about that one.

"However, there is One who notices you and cares about you, more than any form of other living creations, and that Person is God. He has known you from your conception until now. He designed you. He loves you. He even knows the number of hairs you have on your head."

I likely will never see that young man again, but in case there is anyone who has similar feelings as he did, this is for you! You are Somebody! Recognize it! Admit it! Act on it!

Even every one that is called by my name: for I have created him for my glory, I have formed him; yea, I have made him. (Isaiah 43:7 KJV)

Are not two sparrows sold for a farthing? and one of them shall not fall on the ground without your Father. But the very hairs of your head are all numbered. Fear ye not therefore, ye are of more value than many sparrows. (Matthew 10:29-31 KJV)

More Than a Statistic

I am more than a statistic; I am a thumbprint.
My palm lines define me uniquely.
Blood coursing through my veins has components
distinctively mine.
I am more than a number; I am a pigment.
My teeth settings mark me singularly.
I am more than a noise; I am a voice.
My tongue modulates with my vocal cords
so that I may talk and laugh and sing
in my own vernacular and resonance.
I am more than a mortal body; I am an immortal soul,
exceptional to God my Creator, who made me
intricately for His purpose, to bring honor and glory
to His Majestic Name.

--Carlene Poff Baker

Sitting on my front porch in a wooden rocking chair,
I ate my bowl of oatmeal and watched wake-ups everywhere.
Then I glimpsed a morning glory decked out in pastel blue,
seeming to say "God, here I am, ready for what You'd have me do."
Every morning thereafter, dining in my rocking chair,
I searched for a morning glory to view as I ate my fare.
Yesterday's flower had vanished, but another bloomed in its place,
preening its dress in splendor, and adorning the lawn with grace.
I gleaned a sterling sermon, seeing the morning glory's beauty.
It gave its best to its one-day span to fulfill its God-planned duty.
No matter what my day's forecast, be it joy or intense sorrow,
I've this God-given day to bloom, not certain about tomorrow.
Making my world a lovelier place should be me everyday story.
God wants me to embellish my own spot like the jaunty morning glory!

--Carlene Poff Baker

Serve the Lord with gladness: come before His presence with singing. (Psalm 100:2 KJV)

This is the day which the Lord hath made; we will rejoice and be glad in it. (Psalm 118:24 KJV)

And whatsoever ye do in word or deed, do all in the name of the Lord Jesus, giving thanks to God and the Father by Him. (Colossians 3:17 KJV)

The best thing I discovered when I started to school in first grade was how to read. No longer did someone have to read to me. I could do it myself. I have continued to find reading enhances all facets of life. It opens the doors to education, career, relationships, and its doors remain open.

Centuries ago, not everyone could get an education and, thus, never learn to read. How limited were their spheres! I am so thankful for developments since then that gives people the opportunity to read now.

I know God intended for people to learn to read, because He speaks of it in His written word. His prophets urged people to read and those who did read were lauded for their seeing the necessity for it. God has meant for people to read, because He has had His Word written in many different manners – on papyrus, parchments, walls of homes, etched in stone, and on different kinds of paper. Today His scriptures have been published in all languages so that every person can readily have access to them. He wants all people to know the message of salvation in the scriptures, so that sinners can read the message of salvation and all of His promises to His people.

My young adult grandson, Andy, is an avid reader as well as a collector of some of the classics of great authors. Sometimes I go with him to book sales at the local library. Not only do I enjoy watching him delve into the books on the tables and shelves, but I delight in seeing whole families with young children also selecting books with enthusiasm. They seem to have a spring in their steps when they leave the sale carrying bags of books.

I have noticed in waiting rooms of various facilities that some people are thumbing their I-Phones and Kindles and Tablets, but there are still those who are reading magazines as they wait. I love to read books and hear pages turn.

Seek ye out of the book of the Lord, and read: no one of these shall fail, none shall want her mate: for my mouth it hath commanded, and his spirit it hath gathered them. (Isaiah 34:16 KJV)

Thus speaketh the Lord God of Israel, saying, Write thee all the words that I have spoken unto thee in a book. (Jeremiah 30:2 KJV)

Search the scriptures; for in them ye think ye have eternal life: and they are they which testify of Me. (John 5:39 KJV)

Till I come, give attendance to reading, to exhortation, to doctrine. (1 Timothy 4:13 KJV)

The cloak that I left at Troas with Carpus, when thou comest, bring with thee, and the books, but especially the parchments. (2 Timothy 4:13 KJV)

September 22   Everyone Needs a Friend

A little girl named Molly was invited to a play party at a classmate's home. It was summertime and they were to play some outdoor games and them go inside for indoor games. The one invited said, "I will come if I can bring someone." When asked who, she responded, "Peggy has just moved into the house across the street from me. She is shy and when I talk to her, she just nods her head and looks sad. I don't ever see her playing outside. I don't think she has even one friend. If I can get her to come with me, I think she might, and then maybe she would not be so sad looking."

Her request was granted. Peggy agreed to come with Molly. Although she kept close to Molly's side, she began to play games with the others, and for the first time, Molly saw Peggy smile.

God never intended for a person to be alone. Even when He created the first man, Adam, it was not long before He created someone else, Eve, so he would not be alone. Even Jesus, in the presence of His Father and all the host of angels, wanted to have human beings to be with Him. Of course, because all human beings are sinners, He paid the price for every person's sin, so that whosoever of humans accepted Him as Savior would be with Him and belong to Him.

We all know how awful it would be to live in a world without a single friend. We start out early making friends: in childhood with kinfolks, in Sunday School with other children, with school classmates, and in adulthood making friends in the work place, in the neighborhood and in many other places.

In the days of America's Old West, horse owners said there were two types or horses: runners and standers. At the first sign of trouble, the runner would bolt, abandoning you to whatever peril you were facing. But a stander would stick with you no matter the circumstances. The stander is the true, loyal friend. These two types of horses could be compared to friends. One can be counted on as a friend until a traumatic crisis comes along. Then, that one will run. But the true friend will stand with you, alongside you, and go with you through it all to the finish.

It takes time to make and hold friends. To make friends each one must show himself friendly, to be sincere, considerate, courteous, truthful, sympathetic and helpful. During friends of adversity we need friends we can rely on, be a stander. And when we have reason to rejoice, we know our friends will rejoice with us. May we be the kind of friend who won't run when a friend is in need, knowing that when we find ourselves in need, a true friend will come along side us to help us cope.

A friend loveth at all times, and a brother is born for adversity. (Proverbs 17:17 KJV)

Thine own friend, and thy father's friend, forsake not; neither go into thy brother's house in the day of thy calamity: for better is a neighbor that is near than a brother far off. (Proverbs 27:10 KJV)

Rejoice with them that do rejoice, and weep with them that weep. (Romans 12:15 KJV)

September 23   You Emit a Fragrance

A man visited a rose garden, where there were all manner of roses, in every color, and each one giving off its unique fragrance. After spending about an hour there, he went to his appointment in a building close-by. Being a visitor from another city, he knew no one except the business associate he was to meet. However, as he sat in the room awaiting his call to his appointment, others in the room with him began to look at him and smile. He had no idea why they were doing that.

Finally, one person asked, "Did you enjoy the rose garden?" He replied that he did. Before long another person asked, "Wasn't the rose garden amazing with acres of such beauty?" Again, he agreed that it was. When the third person asked "Isn't the rose garden a delightful place?" then his curiosity surfaced. He replied, "I didn't see anyone else in the rose garden when I was there. How did you know I had gone there?"

"The fragrance of the roses has given your clothing their aroma. You cannot spend any time among the roses without their fragrances touching you," she answered.

The Christian has an aroma like that. That one has been born again and is no longer a lost sinner. He has a new life. The Holy Spirit lives within him. When he follows Jesus as he goes about his various activities, wherever he happens to be, others are aware he has changed and has marks of knowing Jesus. He does not have to wear a sign announcing he is a follower of Jesus. It will show in his demeanor.

When Jesus was here on earth, His followers were always in close proximity to Him, and they learned His ways and followed in His footsteps. Wherever they went, people could see they had been with Jesus. They emitted His fragrance, as the roses to the man who walked in the rose garden. Not only people know this about followers of Jesus, but one in particular knows about it and gets angry. That one is Satan. He does not like to lose any sinner to accepting Jesus as Savior. The evil one knows the saved person can never be lost, but he tries to contaminate the beautiful aroma so that one's fragrance will be no good.

The closer a person is to Jesus, the greater the emitting perfume to those with whom he comes in contact.

But the path of the just is as the shining light, that shineth more and more unto the perfect day. (Proverbs 4:18 KJV)

Now, when they saw the boldness of Peter and John, and perceived that they were unlearned and ignorant men, they marveled; and they took knowledge of them, that they had been with Jesus. (Acts 4:13 KJV)

For we are unto God a sweet savor of Christ, in them that are saved, and in the that perish: To the one we are the savor of death unto death; and to the other the savor of life unto life. And who is sufficient for these things? (2 Corinthians 2:15-16 KJV)

September 24 God Blesses Nations with Godly Leaders

A person has merely to read true history of a nation to find the country prospered in all ways when its leaders of government followed the leadership of the God of the universe in all their dealings. We have read where our first president, George Washington, was seen on his knees praying often. Others as well. But here let's just look at four – three presidents and one statesman.

Benjamin Franklin said, "And have we now forgotten that powerful Friend? Or do we imagine we no longer need His assistance? I have lived a long time, and the longer I live, the more convincing proofs I see of this truth: that God governs in the affairs of men. And, if a sparrow cannot fall to the ground without His notice, is it probable that an empire can rise without His aid?"

Grover Cleveland said, "I know there is a Supreme Being who rules the affairs of men and whose goodness and mercy have always followed the American people, and I know He will not turn from us now if we humbly and reverently seek His powerful aid."

Abraham Lincoln said, in his farewell address, "My friends, No one, not in my situation, can appreciate my feeling of sadness at this parting. To this place, and the kindness of these people, I owe everything. Here I have lived a quarter of a century, and have passed from a young to an old man. Here my children have been born, and one is buried. I now leave, not knowing when or whether ever I may return, with a task before me greater than that which rested upon Washington. Without the assistance of that Divine Being who attended him, I cannot succeed. With that assistance I cannot fail. Trusting in Him who can go with me, and remain with you, and be everywhere for good – let us confidently hope that all will yet be well. To His care commending you, as I hope in your prayers you will commend me, I bid you an affectionate farewell."

Ronald Reagan said: "I believe with all my heart that standing up for America means standing up for the God who has so blessed our land."

And thou shalt do that which is right and good in the sight of the Lord: that it may be well with thee, and that thou mayest go in and possess the good land which the Lord sware unto thy fathers. (Deuteronomy 6:18 KJV)

If my people, which are called by my name, shall humble themselves, and pray, and seek my face, and turn from their wicked ways; then will I hear from heaven, and will forgive their sin, and will heal their land. (2 Chronicles 7:14 KJV)

Blessed is the nation whose God is the Lord; and the people whom he hath chosen for His own inheritance. (Psalm 33:12 KJV)

September 25   I Think You're Trustworthy, Sir

Allen lived alone after his wife died. His four children lived in other states with their families. One of his favorite pastimes was to take a folding chair, put it in his pick-up truck, go to the sports field near the park, and watch whatever game happened to be taking place. This was where his sons played games and he had been a spectator and avid fan of them back then. That was over forty years ago.

He found himself a good place for his chair behind the screen so he could see all bases and especially the pitcher. He knew not a single young one on either team. He merely liked to attend, with his bag of peanuts and his thermos of water. The game that day was two elementary school teams. He would be rooting for neither, merely watching and enjoying.

He watched as they warmed up. Then he noticed one of the boys was standing close to him. He did not know him, but the boy seemed to want to talk to him.

"Son, you want to talk to me?" he asked.

"Yes, sir. I've seen you at bunches of our games. I'm always glad to see you. I've got this problem, Sir. I have some change in my pants pocket left over from what I've spent, and I'm afraid I might lose it when I am playing ball, like if I have to slide to a base, you know. I just wondered if you would keep it for me while I play?"

"Why trust me with your money, son?" the man asked.

"I don't know you, but I believe you go to church every Sunday, and I believe you pray, and I believe you read the Bible. I can just tell from looking at you. So, I know I can trust you to keep my money for me." The boy began bringing out his coins from his pocket and handed them into the old man's open hand. Then he scurried off to where his team was. He did not even look back. If he had, for sure he would have seen the wrinkled face of the man wet with tears, but wearing a wide toothless grin. Lifting his eyes heavenward, the old man thanked His Heavenly Father for this blessed day.

But the path of the just is as the shining light, that shineth more and more unto the perfect day. (Proverbs 4:18 KJV)

Having your conversation honest among the Gentiles: that, whereas they speak against you as evildoers, they may by your good works, which they shall behold, glorify God in the day of visitation. (1 Peter 2:12 KJV)

September 26   I'm on Your Level

Back in post-Great Depression years, the Walters family farm had been hit hard with drought and hail and low prices for the cotton harvested. They had not been able to buy some things they had wanted, especially for their two daughters, Laura and Elizabeth. To make matters worse, it was near the end of school, and a musical festival was to be performed by the school. Their daughters were so excited to be a part of it.

Then Laura showed them a note from the music teacher that they would need to wear new dresses and new shoes for the event. Their parents discussed it. Their mother could make them a new dress apiece from some left-over material, even with lace and rick-rack. But there was no way they could afford new shoes.

Mr. Walters went to the school in person and talked to the music teacher, explaining his daughters would have new dresses, but the shoes would have to be the ones they had worn all winter – high-top tennis shoes. Otherwise, they would not be able to participate in the festival. The teacher replied, "Oh, yes, they will be able to participate in the musical, so make plans for them to be here. It will be okay if they wear their tennis shoes."

The night of the event arrived. Laura and Elizabeth were clad in their new dresses and their old tennis shoes. They were excited to be there, but their excitement reached its apex, when they saw that every one of their fellow students were also wearing high-top tennis shoes!

But their joy could not match that reflected on the faces of their parents in the audience! Because they noticed, as the music teacher sat down at the piano to begin playing for their singing, the foot she placed on the pedal was also clad in a high-top tennis shoe!

> For though I be free from all men, yet have I made myself servant unto all, that I might gain the more. ... To the weak became I as weak, that I might gain the weak: I am made all things to all men, that I might by all means save some. And this I do for the gospel's sake, that I might be partaker thereof with you. (1 Corinthians 9:19, 22-23 KJV)

September 27   God Shows His Reminders

I live in a place where there are many airports and one International Airport. I see at least one airplane every day. I love to watch them. There is one special sight I enjoy in cool weather when the planes make vapor trails. They seem to be sky-writing. One type of design I see often in the azure blue sky of autumn is that of a cross. Last week I saw where planes had made several crosses – white in the blue-blue sky! I said "Thank You, Lord, for directing them to do that."

Amid all the ways the evil powers are working toward causing people to turn from God, and in some instances trying to convince people there is no God, God always shows up to veto all their evil schemes. He always shows Himself the Sovereign Almighty. Jesus said that the gates of hell will never prevail against Him and His Kingdom. He said He will forever get glory for Himself. There is no power that can prevent all He has promised to accomplish!

The heavens declare the glory of God; and the firmament sheweth His handiwork. (Psalm 19:1 KJV)

Be still, and know that I am God: I will be exalted among the heathen, I will be exalted in the earth. (Psalm 46:10 KJV)

Kings of the earth, and all people; princes, and all judges of the earth: both young men, and maidens; old men, and children: let them praise the name of the Lord: for His name alone is excellent; His glory is above the earth and heaven. (Psalm 148:11-13 KJV)

I am the Lord: that is My name: and My glory will I not give to another, neither My praise to graven images. (Isaiah 42:8 KJV)

And I say also unto thee, That thou art Peter, and upon this rock I will build my church; and the gates of hell shall not prevail against it. (Matthew 16:18 KJV)

September 28 — How to Know Right from Wrong

I ask myself the following:

Is it of the world?

> Ye adulterers and adulteresses, know ye not that the friendship of the world is enmity with God? whosoever therefore will be a friend of the world is the enemy of God. (James 4:4 KJV)

Is it a weight upon my soul?

> Wherefore seeing we also are compassed about with so great a cloud of witnesses, let us lay aside every weight, and the sin which doth so easily beset us, and let us run with patience the race that is set before us. (Hebrews 12:1 KJV)

Is it a stumbling block to others?

> But take heed lest by any means this liberty of yours become a stumblingblock to them that are weak. ... But when ye sin so against the brethren, and wound their weak conscience, ye sin against Christ. (1 Corinthians 8:9, 12 KJV)

Can I do it for the glory of God?

> Whether therefore ye eat, or drink, or whatsoever ye do, do all to the glory of God. (1 Corinthians 10:31 KJV)

Can I do it in the name of Jesus?

> And whatsoever ye do, do it heartily, as to the Lord, and not unto men; knowing that of the Lord ye shall receive the reward of the inheritance: for ye serve the Lord Christ. (Colossians 3:23-24 KJV)

What would Jesus Himself do?

> For even hereunto were ye called: because Christ also suffered for us, leaving us an example, that ye should follow His steps: Who did no sin, neither was guile found in His mouth. (1 Peter 2:21-22 KJV)

When Jesus comes, would I want to be found doing it?

> And now, little children, abide in Him; that, when He shall appear, we may have confidence, and not be ashamed before Him at His coming. (1 John 2:28 KJV)

I arrived at my work place parking lot. As I walked toward the ramp to enter the building, I noticed it had been re-concreted, and the concrete was wet. I use a walker, so I knew I could not wheel up the ramp that day. Every other place to get to the door required a high step, and I could not do it with the walker. Looking down as I walked, I was thinking of how to get to the door. When I looked up again, there at the edge of the wet concrete stood a young Mexican man, and he was smiling at me. He saw my predicament, and offered me his arm, like an usher to escort me. I set the walker upon the dry spot, and took his arm. He had to use both arms to push me up. All the time he and I were giggling.

Safely in the dry spot, I turned to say "Gracious," but he was gone. I looked in all directions across the parking lot, but he was nowhere in sight. There was no place he could have hidden. Then, I knew what it was all about. God had seen my dilemma, as He knows all things, and He placed that young man there to help me. I knew He had sent one of His angels.

> Because thou hast made the Lord, which is my refuge, even the most High, thy habitation; There shall no evil befall thee, neither shall any plague come nigh thy dwelling. For He shall give His angels charge over thee, to keep thee in all thy ways. (Psalm 91:9-11 KJV)

> Are they not all ministering spirits, sent forth to minister for them who shall be heirs of salvation? (Hebrews 1:14 KJV)

After I became a widow, and all the funds from life insurance had been spent, at times money for my needs became scant. I continued to work at two jobs, but both were paid by commissions at closings. As I had to travel at times, I allotted amounts for motel – with senior discount – gas for car, and meals. I carried the total amount of cash needed for those items.

One day I had a long lunch hour at my job, and someone said for me to go to the cafeteria at the hospital, about a walking block away from work site, as I would pay according to my portions. So, I went. I chose selected items off the buffet, where prices were shown. It was a noisy place, and behind me there were five or six young adult men who were wearing surgeon uniforms, so I reasoned they had been interns or at least medical students who had come from watching a surgery done. They held their trays piled high with food, I noticed.

When I reached the check-out place, my total was twice the amount I had figured. I hesitated. "That's much more than I thought it would be," I said quietly to the girl at the register. I heard her sigh, like she wanted me to pay and move on. I paid her and made my way to a table. I figured I'd have to eat from the vending machine at the motel for a couple of meals. Then, I thought no more about it.

As I sat enjoying the vegetables from the buffet, suddenly one of the uniformed interns walked to my table. He grinned at me and began taking money out of his two pants pockets. He placed handfuls of coins on my table. "This belongs to you," he said, grinned again, and spun around to join his fellows as they exited the dining room.

With tears streaming down my face, I began to count the money. There was enough for at least two more meals! I knew those precious guys must have discussed the situation (that I didn't know they even were aware of), and took up a collection from among them. I thanked God for them right then and there. I didn't know their names, but God did. Like so many other times, God took care of me. He saw that I would have the food I needed, and would not have to ask for it as a beggar.

I have been young, and now am old; yet have I not seen the righteous forsaken, nor his seed begging bread. (Psalm 37:25 KJV)

But my God shall supply all your need according to His riches in glory by Christ Jesus. (Philippians 4:19 KJV)

My little six-year-old daughter unclutched my hand to enter the big room that smelled of crayons. My watery eyes met the perceptive expression on her teacher's face. Oh, how I ached for her when I returned home.

Twelve years later, her Dad and I unloaded her and all of her college necessities in her new dorm room. We lingered longer than was expedient before we left her to return to our home. She hugged us both quickly, amidst the bustle of other college peers arriving. Her Dad and I rode home quietly. Then we walked back into the heavy vacancy of the house. Hurting loneliness made tears stream down my cheeks. Her Dad looked at me, with sad eyes, and I read there, "Oh, how I miss her!"

Daughter got married. This time she took all of her belongings. I found even her giggles had vanished out of the cracks and crevices of her room. But beginning the next year, she reactivated echoes in the corners, as she brought a grandson into our house. After that, every few years she added another, and another, and another, until there were four: two boys and two girls. Their own special noise spilled into every room when they came to visit. Then, when they left for their own home, I combed room by room searching for heart-tug evidence of their having been there, glad to find granddaughter's dog-eared book or grandson's stuffed "B-Bear" with its one eye missing, which I picked up and hugged.

Years added on top of years, and then, the most lonesome parting came: the death of my beloved husband. In robot-like steps I said and did all the fitting things. And then one night his being gone stabbed my chest with staggering force. I realized he was never, never, never coming back! I missed his voice, his hugs, his laughter, the endearing way he spoke my name.

All of these partings validated the fact that I held each one and the time spent with each one invaluably treasured. I thanked God for each one. To genuinely let them go was the only right thing to do, and I had to stand still, and just let the bittersweet happen.

And when Jacob had made an end of commanding his sons, he gathered up his feet into the bed, and yielded up the ghost, and was gathered unto his people. ... And Joseph fell

upon his father's face, and wept upon him, and kissed him.
(Genesis 49:33; 50:1 KJV)

And when he had thus spoken, he kneeled down, and prayed
with them all. And they all wept sore, and fell on Paul's neck,
and kissed him, sorrowing most of all for the words which
he spake, that they should see his face no more. And they
accompanied him unto the ship. (Acts 20:36-38 KJV)

October 2   Seeking the Perfect Church

A minister who had pastored churches for thirty years was distressed
when he learned that his son and family, who lived in a distant state, had
not joined a church, and would attend one church awhile, and then quit
that one, and attend another. That had been going on for nearly a year.

Having brought his children up in a Christian home, the son having
been saved at the age of twelve, and his having participated in various
activities of the church avidly all his into adulthood, his father and
mother made a trip to visit him because of their concern.

When the time came for them to discuss why the family had not
joined a church for such a long time, his son said, "Well, Dad, it's like
this. I've been searching and searching for a perfect church, and when
we visit a church a few times, it seems okay, but then we begin to notice
members of the church just don't seem holy. So, we leave that church and
go to another, looking for the perfect church. We haven't found one yet."

Surprisingly, the son's minister-father began to laugh. He laughed
so long and hard tears began to run down his cheeks.

"Dad, are you all right?" the son asked.

"Sure, I'm all right. Son, don't you realize that Christians are not
perfect. When a sinner gets saved, the inner part of the person is saved
and does not sin, but he lives in the same old body that continues to have
all the appetites as before. The two natures war against each other. The
Holy Spirit in the Christian keeps him on track but the fleshly nature
keeps on doing wrong. The person has this battle within himself as long
as he lives. After he dies the old sinful nature is finished. That's one of

the reasons Jesus wants us to become a member of His church, because we need each other to pray for each other, to encourage each other, and fellowship with each other along the way."

"But Dad, I don't remember when growing up that there were bad people in the church."

"Oh, son, there were. But the more they stayed in the church and learned how to live to glorify God, the more they whipped the old fleshly nature."

The discussion went on until it was time for the minister and his wife to leave. After saying their goodbyes, his son said, "Well, Dad, I'm still looking for maybe not the perfect church but one that is as near perfect as I can find, and then we'll become members."

Again, his dad leaned back and let out a roar of laughter. "Well, son, when you find that perfect church, when you join it, it won't be perfect anymore."

> For I know that in me (that is, in my flesh,) dwelleth no good thing: for to will is present with me; but how to perform that which is good I find not. For the good that I would I do not: but the evil which I would not, that I do. Now if I do that I would not, it is no more I that do it, but sin that dwelleth in me. I find then a law, that, when I would do good, evil is present with me. For I delight in the law of God after the inward man: but I see another law in my members, warring against the law of my mind, and bringing me into captivity to the law of sin which is in my members. O wretched man that I am! who shall deliver me from the body of this death? I thank God through Jesus Christ our Lord. So then with the mind I myself serve the law of God; but with the flesh the law of sin. (Romans 7:18-25 KJV)

October 3   ## Where Can I Serve You, Lord?

Mary had been a nurse all her life, and loved her work. She had never married but helped raise her nieces and nephews. She worked far past her retirement years, but at length, the beginning of failing health caused her to decide to leave her lifelong career. She owned a little house on a big lot, on which she had set a small mobile home, in which she housed one or the other of her nieces and nephews over the years.

After her income had ceased except for her retirement money, she found she could not keep her house, so she sold it, but she kept the trailer and had it moved to a trailer park. She began living in the trailer. She still had her car and could drive herself to appointments.

One night she could not sleep. Her life seemed empty. She had always served others and now she had no place to serve. The nieces and nephews had all grown up and had fulfilled lives of their own. She prayed to the Lord about the situation. "What would you have me do now, Lord?" she prayed. "I feel so useless." Strange to her, she felt at peace and went to sleep.

The Lord had already begun to bring into her life how she could serve Him and others. It began with the pastor calling and asking, "Mary, would you have time this morning to take Thelma to her doctor's appointment? She asked me to, and both my wife and I have already committed to two other matters."

Mary quickly said yes. He told her Thelma's appointment time and that he would tell Thelma that she would pick her up. She dressed for going out with a spring in her step. That day was the beginning of a delightful service enjoyed by Mary and the ones she helped. After she had begun using her car to take widows to doctor appointments, going to the grocery store with them, and even taking some to the park to feed the squirrels and ducks on the pond, she told the pastor's wife, "I have set each day for doing things for certain people. Retha needs me on Monday. Thelma's day is Tuesday. Lily likes Wednesday. Thursday is my day to give Joyce a pedicure after soaking her feet in Epsom Salt water. Friday, I take Bessie to the beauty parlor and afterward she treats me to a lunch somewhere, my choice. Oh, I am so glad the Lord has given me this wonderful life! I know that somehow I'm making a difference, and I know He is pleased!"

Withhold not good from them to whom it is due, when it is in the power of thine hand to do it. (Proverbs 3:27 KJV)

For God is not unrighteous to forget your work and labor of love, which ye have shewed toward His name, in that ye have ministered to the saints, and do minister. (Hebrews 6:10 KJV)

October 4   Crown of Rejoicing

A story has been handed down of an event that occurred scores of years ago. A man had acquired a fortune in the gold-fields of Australia, and was aboard a ship returning to England, when suddenly the ship sprang a leak and soon, many people were without hope.

This strong man thought he could fight through the waves to the island, and he was about to go, when a little girl asked of him, "Sir, will you save me?"

He looked alternately at his bag of gold and at the anguished face of the child. Then quickly, he stripped his belt of gold and threw it into the water. He took the child on his back, and threw himself into the sea. He struggled hard before he reached the land. His body took a beating. The next day, when his consciousness returned, the little girl put her arms around his neck, and said, "I am so glad you saved me, and I love you." Needless to say, that was worth more to him than all the gold of Australia.

Homecoming day will soon be here, and it will be joy unspeakable to have just one person meet us and say, "I'm here, too, because you explained the way of eternal life to me." There is no thrill on the face of the earth like that which shivers in the innermost being when we see the heavenly peace upon the face of the boy or girl whom we have just led to the Lord. Are not these our crowns of rejoicing?

He that goeth forth and weepeth, bearing precious seed, shall doubtless come again with rejoicing, bringing his sheaves with him. (Psalm 126:6 KJV)

And they that be wise shall shine as the brightness of the firmament; and they that turn many to righteousness as the stars forever and ever. (Daniel 12:3 KJV)

For what is our hope, or joy, or crown of rejoicing? Are not even ye in the presence of our Lord Jesus Christ at His coming? For ye are our glory and joy. (1 Thessalonians 2:19-20 KJV)

October 5   Your Godly Glow Speaks Volumes

At the head of the New York harbor stands the colossal Statue of Liberty, a gift from France to America. At night, the outstretched hand of the figure holds forth a magnificent display of bright electric lights, which guide the ships to safe anchorage. What that statue in New York harbor is to the ocean-plying vessels, Christians are to the masses of the world. The consistent Christ-like life of the believer, day in and day out, is the steady light of the Gospel against which there is no argument. That light must shine through our own hearts and lives. In this present world, with all its superficial front, let us ever live in the will of God, so that Christ shall be seen more, that Christ shall be heard more, that Christ shall be known more, and that we, His weak, earthen vessels, shall be seen less, heard less and known less. We shall then be effectually "holding forth the word of life," as our witness will be backed by the ways of our life.

One morning, centuries ago, the well-known St. Francis of Assisi said to a brother, "Let's go down into the town and preach." The two walked slowly along the road, and eventually reached the town. Francis, however, did not stop anywhere for a preaching appointment, but gradually guided the way back from the town toward their starting place. His companion asked if he had forgotten the preaching.

Francis replied, "My brother, it is no use walking to preach unless we preach as we walk." Yes, we must preach by our walk, as well as by our talk.

Let your light so shine before men, that they may see your good works, and glorify your Father which is in heaven. (Matthew 5:16 KJV)

I therefore, the prisoner of the Lord, beseech you, that ye walk worthy of the vocation wherewith ye are called. (Ephesians 4:1 KJV)

Let no man despise thy youth; but be thou an example of the believers, in word, in conversation, in charity, in spirit, in faith, in purity. ... Take heed unto thyself, and unto the doctrine; continue in them: for in doing this thou shalt both save thyself, and them that hear thee. (1 Timothy 4:12, 16 KJV)

October 6   God's Angels Always on Call

Sandy's husband Gary had ordered a special exercise bicycle for his use after his surgeries. It arrived late, after dark, by the deliverer and was set on the front porch. She knew she had to get it inside the house that night, and proceeded to try to move it. She was a petite woman, herself having just recovered from breast cancer surgery, and the box with the bike in it was at least one hundred pounds.

While deliberating what to do, and with there being no one else in the house except her physically disabled husband, and with it being far past any neighbor's bedtime, she felt helpless. She prayed, "Lord, how can I get this big thing into the house?" as she wiped tears off her cheeks.

Then, suddenly, she heard a jingle. There approaching the front porch steps was a man and a dog. The jingle she heard was from the dog's collar.

"May I help you?" the man asked. "I was taking Benjy for a walk and I could see you seemed to be having trouble with that big package."

"Oh, yes; thank you. This is the exercise bike we ordered for my husband, and the delivery man left it here. I cannot get it inside the house."

"Here, hold Benjy's strap, and I'll set it inside for you," he replied, handing her the leash, and stepping upon the porch. He pulled and tugged, twisted and bent, and lugged it over the threshold into the house. She told him where to set it and thanked him. He smiled and said "It was my pleasure. You know, I have never taken Benjy for a walk this late at night, but he was so restless and would not settle down in his bed to go to sleep. I decided to take him for a walk so he would settle down and I could go to bed myself." Then he and Benjy walked down the steps back to the sidewalk, Benjy's collar jingling.

Sandy burst into tears of joy! "Thank You, Lord, for sending Your angel to our house at just the right time!"

> But to which of the angels said He at any time, Sit on my right hand, until I make thine enemies thy footstool? Are they not all ministering spirits, sent forth to minister for them who shall be heirs of salvation? (Hebrews 1:13-14 KJV)

October 7   **Clad Yourself Modestly**

When I was a young teen, in the summertime, I decided to dress like I knew my friends were dressing. I was given a pair of short shorts from one of them. I donned those shorts and tied the bottom of my blouse in a knot to show my midriff. One day, when so clad, I went to one of my farm chores, that being pumping water, by hand, into the trough for the mules and cow.

As I pumped in my *cool* clothes, suddenly a hand reached over my shoulder and took the pump handle. I looked back into the face of my Daddy.

"I'll pump while you go inside and change out of those clothes into something decent. Then come back and finish pumping," he ordered. I wanted to sass him, but the hurt look on his face stopped me.

I obeyed, but tears were streaming down my cheeks when I got to my bedroom. I found long jeans and kept the same shirt but took out the knot. As I made my way toward the back door through the kitchen, Mama said "Your Daddy didn't want men and boys passing on the road to see you with so much of your bare body showing." Again, I wanted to sass, but Mama was wearing a solemn face too.

I went back to the pump and Daddy grinned at me. I resumed my chore. I began to understand his great love for me. He didn't want others to see me so bare and say bad things about me. In fact, it brought to mind something the preacher had said recently, that we ought not to make a weaker person stumble.

All my life I didn't wear short shorts ever again. When I married my husband had some of the same ideas as Daddy. One year for his birthday someone gave him a pair of short shorts as a gift. After all, his birthday was in July. He wore those shorts one time in only my presence. He never wore them again. I asked him why. "I didn't want anybody to happen to drop in unexpectedly and see me in them," was his reply. I didn't give him a sassy response either.

I find in the scripture God wants us to dress modestly. The first time clothing is mentioned is in Genesis. Before Adam and Eve sinned, the were naked and felt no guilt. After they sinned, they tried to cover themselves with fig-leaf attire. Did not work. God came along and made clothing out of animals' skins to cover their nakedness. Also, in the New Testament, there was a demon-possessed man who lived among the tombs and never wore clothes. Jesus cast out the demons and saved his soul. Afterward, he was in his right mind and clothed.

> And He answered and spake unto those that stood before Him, saying, Take away the filthy garments from him. And unto him He said, Behold, I have caused thine iniquity to pass from thee, and I will clothe thee with change of raiment. (Zechariah 3:4 KJV)

> And when He was come out of the ship, immediately there met Him out of the tombs a man with an unclean spirit, who had his dwelling among the tombs; and no man could bind him, no, not with chains. ... But when he saw Jesus afar off, he ran and worshiped Him. ... For He said unto him, Come out of the man, thou unclean spirit. ... And they come to Jesus, and see him that was possessed with the devil, and had the legion, sitting, and clothed, and in his right mind: and they were afraid. (Mark 5:2-3, 6, 8, 15 KJV)

Let us not therefore judge one another anymore: but judge this rather, that no man put a stumblingblock or an occasion to fall in his brother's way. (Romans 14:13 KJV)

There was a Welsh preacher named Henry Morehouse whose every sermon was from John 3:16: "For God so loved the world, that He gave His only begotten Son, that whosoever believeth in Him should not perish, but have everlasting life." The Holy Spirit used that message every time he preached it, and lost sinners were drawn to the Savior and became saved.

There was an evil man named Ike Miller, who frequented saloons to get drunk and sought the company of prostitutes. When he came home in a drunken state, he would whip his wife and children. They ran to hide when he entered their home.

When he heard Henry Morehouse was to hold a revival meeting in his town, he threatened, "I will pistol him out of town." Those who heard him warned Henry Morehouse of the threat, they asked him not to preach. The preacher would not back down, because he knew that God had called him to preach.

Ike kept his promise and entered the church building. He flashed a pistol. Sighs and gasps went up all over the building from the congregation. He sat on the front row and glared at the preacher. As he always did, Henry Morehouse took his text from John 3:16 and told how God loved sinners and that whosoever received Him as Savior would be saved and would never perish.

More gasps went up from the congregation when Ike stood up. He walked toward the pulpit with the pistol in his hand, and then, to everyone's astonishment, he turned and walked down the aisle to the entrance door. He walked down the steps and made his way toward his home. As he passed the saloon, his old buddies invited him to come in, but he paid on mind and kept walking toward home. Prostitutes leaned out their windows and begged him to come to them. He kept walking.

When he entered the door to his home, the children scurried to hide, and his wife backed away from him.

Then he spoke. "Woman, don't be afraid. We are going to pray. Get the kids out and bring them close." Ike kneeled and tried to pray. The only prayer he knew was one his mother had taught him when he was a child. He prayed "Gentile Jesus, meek and mild, look upon a little child. Forgive my simplicity and suffer me to come to thee." Ike Miller was saved right then and there. His life was totally and wonderfully changed. No longer were his wife and children afraid. In fact, because He knew Jesus loved him, who had been so mean, he began to show love toward his family. All because he realized that as awful as he was, Jesus loved him and invited him to come to Him. Oh, the great love of Jesus!

For God sent not His Son into the world to condemn the world; but that the world through Him might be saved. (John 3:17 KJV)

And hope maketh not ashamed; because the love of God is shed abroad in our hearts by the Holy Ghost which is given unto us. (Romans 5:5 KJV)

October 9   We Both Deserved to Get Zero for a Grade

During high school, I did rather well in writing essays and other literary assignments in English. My friend did not do so well. So, when we were given a *hurried* writing assignment, announced on Friday to be turned in on Monday, my friend asked for my help. We spent Saturday afternoon on our articles.

I turned from my activity to my friend from time to time and noticed she was biting her fingernails, and had written nothing but the title on her page. I made suggestions to get her started. Nail biting and fidgeting, and looking out the window continued. Finally, she asked, "Would you write the piece for me? I cannot do it."

Having finished mine, I agreed. She suggested a subject, and my literary juices flowed, and before long I had finished her assignment. She grinned at me and began to write, copying my words on her pages.

Monday arrived and we turned in our assignments. The teacher, Ms. Lee, said she would read them overnight and grade them, and would return them to us next day. Tuesday came and Ms. Lee handed out our papers with grades on them. To my astonishment, I got a D on mine and my friend got a C. I was flabbergasted! I had always gotten at least a B, and more often an A for my writing works.

When the end-of-class buzzer sounded, Ms. Lee called my name and asked me to wait, that she had something to say to me. I had some questions for her too, about such a low grade.

"You wrote two assignments, didn't you? Yours and someone else's?" she asked.

"Yes, Ma'am, I did."

"Why?"

"She couldn't even get started, so I thought I'd help her."

"You did more than help her. She did absolutely nothing toward the assignment, right?

"Yes, Ma'am."

"Don't you know, both of you cheated. She cheated by doing nothing, and you cheated yourself by using your skills and not allowing her to try. I recognized your manner of writing in both pieces and I could see what you did. I considered giving both of you Zeros as your grades. Then, I decided to give you both a second chance. Actually, the piece you wrote for her was better than yours. Please don't do this anymore."

"I won't, Ms. Lee. I promise." And I kept that promise. The next day, my friend was called by Ms. Lee to wait, and she met the same explanation. Even though I saw her struggling with succeeding writing assignments, I just shrugged at her when her expression indicated she needed help. We both passed that class. That experience has perpetuated over after-graduating date years in all my endeavors. I can show a person how and encourage them, but the person has to do his own work!

Recompense to no man evil for evil. Provide things honest in the sight of all men. (Romans 12:17 KJV)

And that ye study to be quiet, and to do your own business, and to work with your own hands, as we commanded you. (1 Thessalonians 4:11 KJV)

Set Your House in Order

Should my doctor tell me "You have one month to live," I would at first feel sad to leave this earth where I enjoyed life to the brim. My next focus would be to confirm that all is well between me and God, so that I could echo the Apostle Paul's words: "I have finished my course; I have kept the faith."

Then I would set in order my estate, so that my heirs would have no snags. I would see that my living will was intact. Since Dr. Smith spanked me into taking my first infant breath, I have remained alert to enjoy all stages of my life, and so, at the end of my life, I desire to be fully alert when I let go of my last breath.

My next stop would be at the funeral parlor, where I would choose music: grand old hymns exalting the Giver of Life, all tuneful, nothing mournful. My monument need not be ornate except to have an urn to hold a bouquet. Perhaps someone would recall how much I liked fresh-picked flowers.

I would ponder solemnly if any wrongs needed to be righted between me and another. I would dole out my treasured keepsakes, piece by piece, fitting each gift, according to a shared memory.

My last few days I would spend with the ones I love best: my darling daughter and her family – my husband already having died – and my sisters. I would listen elatedly to their voices as they sound out their plans and dreams for a future in which I would no longer have a part.

So, since life is short, as best only a vapor, my Giver of Life being the only One who knows what date will be etched on my stone with the urn, it is only reasonable that I so conduct myself every day as if my doctor had just told me, "You have one month to live."

In those days was Hezekiah sick unto death. And Isaiah the prophet the son of Amoz came unto him, and said unto him,

Thus saith the Lord, Set thine house in order: for thou shalt
die, and not live. (Isaiah 38:1 KJV)

For I am now ready to be offered, and the time of my departure
is at hand. I have fought a good fight, I have finished my course,
I have kept the faith. (2 Timothy 4:6-7 KJV)

October 11   A Place of "No Mores"

The Paschal Family of three, father, mother, and daughter, always
attended Sunday School and church every Sunday. But one Sunday the
man of the house had to stay home because he was recovering from leg
surgery. His wife and eight-year-old daughter went to church. When
they returned, the man called his daughter to where he was reclining
and asked what the pastor's sermon was about.

"Daddy, it was about heaven, and did you know, that is a place where
there will be a lot of no mores?"

"What do you mean by that," he asked.

She plopped down on the sofa beside his recliner and said, "Well,
there will be no more tears, no more death, no more sorrow, no more
crying, no more pain. There won't even be a temple there. And there will
be no more need for the sun or the moon, and there will be night there.
And there will be no evil persons there. And you know what? It is all
found in Revelation chapter twenty-one."

"Sounds like you really got a lot out of that sermon," he replied.

"It was all so good, Daddy. I wish you could have been there too."

"But, just seeing the joy on your face as you tell me about it makes
me rejoice just thinking about it. Heaven is surely a wonderful place for
us to be going someday."

And God shall wipe away all tears from their eyes; and there
shall be no more death, neither sorrow, nor crying, neither shall
there be any more pain: for the former things are passed away.
And He that sat upon the throne said, Behold, I make all things

new. And He said unto me, Write: for these words are true and faithful. (Revelation 21:4-5 KJV)

October 12   Soar Above Your Circumstances

Having lived on a farm in the country all of my childhood, I was familiar with how animals and birds reacted to storms. Chicken would go to their night roosts early if the storm came during the day. If barnyard and pasture animals could make it to the barn in time, they would hasten to do so. But if caught out in the pasture, two mules would stand beside each other, one facing the storm and the other facing the opposite direction. Of course, we humans hurried to our storm cellar.

I always noticed birds would hurry to the barn seeking a hole under the eaves into the loft. I read somewhere that the only bird that does not seek shelter below the storm is the eagle. It always soars above the storm clouds, out of reach of thunder and lightning. Even the birds hovering in the barn could not be always safe, because a tornado could demolish or blow the barn away.

All of us have storms in our lives. No one is exempt. They come in various ways – domestic, relationship, health, financial, sorrow, war, separation, loneliness, spiritual – all hurtful and damaging. We too seek shelter somewhere during our storms. Often there is someone to help, to come alongside. But, oh, wouldn't it be wonderful to be able to soar far above those storms and not be affected!

Well, we can do so! Jesus is the One to whom we can run and receive His shelter. He won't make the storm go away, but He will be alongside all the time. He will never abandon us. And with Him we can come out on the other side of the storm safely and often a better person. But we too can soar above our circumstances. In Isaiah we read that "They that wait upon the Lord shall renew their strength. They shall mount up with wings like the eagle." So, waiting patiently in God's presence, we can bear up above our circumstances. We will not faint nor grow weary.

When those storms hit us, of whatever nature, no matter it be mild or destructively severe, let's run at once to the Master over our storms, the Lord Jesus Christ.

Hast thou not known? Hast thou not heard, that the everlasting God, the Lord, the Creator of the ends of the earth, fainteth not, neither is weary? There is no searching of His understanding. He giveth power to the faint; and to them that have no might He increaseth strength. Even the youths shall faint and be weary, and the young men shall utterly fall: but they that wait upon the Lord shall renew their strength; they shall mount up with wings as eagles; they shall run, and not be weary; and they shall walk, and not faint. (Isaiah 40:28-31 KJV)

October 13   One of the Ten You Can't Break Alone

There are Ten Commandments God gave to Moses, etched in stone, which people were expected to keep. To keep them one would have to be holy. Since, no one within himself is holy, when a commandment was broken, the one breaking it was required to settle it by going to the priest and having him make a sacrifice to get atonement.

How grateful we are that there was a Perfect One who came and fulfilled every jot and tittle of the Ten Commandments and every other law required by God. That was Jesus. He did it in our stead, so that when we accept Him as Savior, we are forgiven forever.

In considering these Ten Commandments, a person can break nine of them without any other human being involved. A person can have other gods before God; a person can make a graven image all by himself and worship it; a person can take the name of the Lord in vain; that person can dishonor and do despite to the Sabbath. He can dishonor parents on his own; he can commit murder by himself; he can steal without anyone's help; he can bear false witness by himself and he can covet alone. But he cannot commit adultery all by himself. There has to be another involved. And when he commits adultery, he is causing another person to sin as well.

However, when someone sees one of us sin, no matter what the sin may be, it can cause harm to the one watching. They may go out and follow your lead and think if you do it, and they have such confidence in you, that they can do it also. Sin is sin, and it is bad stuff. We who have come to Jesus and received Him as Savior have our sins disposed of as far as our eternal life in heaven is concerned. But we have two natures: the inner and the outer. The inner is safe and secure. The outer is the fleshly one and it continues to sin, breaking God's laws. We are invited to come to Jesus, confess our sins, and He will forgive. But it is an every-day thing. And we must always be aware of others watching whom we might cause them to go the wrong way.

> But if we walk in the light, as He is in the light, we have fellowship one with another, and the blood of Jesus Christ His Son cleanseth us from all sin. If we say that we have no sin, we deceive ourselves, and the truth is not in us. If we confess our sins, He is faithful and just to forgive us our sins, and to cleanse us from all unrighteousness. (1 John 1:7-9 KJV)

> Give none offense, neither to the Jews, nor to the Gentiles, nor to the church of God: even as I please all men in all things, not seeking mine own profit, but the profit of many, that they may be saved. (1 Corinthians 10:32-33 KJV)

October 14   Redeem the Time Day by Day

Because God, the Giver of Life, alone knows the number of days He has allotted for each one of us, when we awake each new day, we ought to say "Thank You, Father, for this another day. Show me how You want me to use it." He has a purpose and plan for how we are to spend each day. Each of us has a sphere of endeavor to attend.

Someone said "Make out your To-Do List, writing with a pencil that has an eraser. Then, hand God the pencil, so He can erase and replace if necessary."

Another thing to remember is we can only live this day as the minutes pass. We cannot hold back a second nor go back and redo what has transpired.

There's a familiar saying which has been passed down for many decades, the person having written it is unknown. The words are "I shall pass through this world but once. Any good therefore that I can do, or any kindness that I can show to any human being, let me do it now. Let me not defer nor neglect it, for I shall not pass this way again." It crops up again and again in publications. It has been included in sermons and lectures.

It is a reminder to all of us that we do not live for ourselves alone, that we must do what we can to help others, to lighten a burden or soften a grief whenever the need arises that happens to come our way, in each of our own sphere. Whatever we encounter we need to trust God to lead and guide us that we might apply ourselves properly to bring about the desired effect He has purposed.

Just to think that the God of the universe, who can do all things without us, because He is omnipotent, delights in giving us another day and He allows us to serve Him in that day's realm. He watches and helps as we need Him, and we derive joy from it, and He gets the glory He deserves. Praise His wonderful Name!

To every thing there is a season, and a time to every purpose under the heaven. (Ecclesiastes 3:1 KJV)

As we have therefore opportunity, let us do good unto all men, especially unto them who are of the household of faith. (Galatians 6:10 KJV)

See then that you walk circumspectly, not as fools, but as wise, redeeming the time, because the days are evil. (Ephesians 5:15-16 KJV)

Walk in wisdom toward them that are without, redeeming the time. (Colossians 4:5 KJV)

October 15   **To Speak or Not to Speak**

My Dad was always known as "the quiet man." He never had a lot to say all of my life. But when he did speak, everybody listened. He did not waste words. When he gave his opinion on anything, he did not go into detail.

When I was just beginning to drive a car, Daddy would let me drive our family car on Sunday afternoons once in a while with some of my girlfriends. We would go to various places, mainly to see other young people driving. Sometimes we would meet and chat and other times just wave at each other as we drove.

One Sunday after church I told three of my girlfriends that we would go driving that afternoon. They were looking forward to it like I. After lunch, I went to the front porch where Daddy was reading the newspaper. I said, "Daddy, may I have the keys now so I can go pick up Laverne and Sue?" He did not answer. Just kept on reading the paper. I waited a while and asked him again, same question. No answer.

After the third time, he looked at me over the top of the newspaper and said, "No," and resumed reading the paper. No explanation. Nor did I ask why. End of dialogue. I got on our party-line telephone and told my girlfriends we wouldn't be going anywhere that afternoon.

One of our United States Presidents was known as a man of few words too: Calvin Coolidge. In fact, there is a story that when a dinner was held in Washington D.C. with all the Congressional dignitaries and their spouses, one wife of a senator said to another woman, "I'll bet I can get three words out of President Coolidge tonight." The other woman said, "I'll bet you can't."

After the dinner and the guests were chatting with each other, the woman who made the bet sidled up to President Coolidge. She said, "I made a bet with a friend here tonight that I'd get three words out of you."

He was quiet for a bit. Then he grinned and told her, "You lose." And he walked away.

There is time to speak and a time to be silent for all of us. Every person has probably made a statement that he wished he could take back. Once it is spoken, it cannot be retrieved.

The Bible has much to say about our words. One is "A soft answer turneth away wrath: but grievous words stir up anger. The tongue of the wise useth knowledge aright: but the mouth of fools poureth out foolishness." (Proverbs 15:1-2 KJV). Another scripture about speaking is "A time to rend, and a time to sew; a time to keep silence, and a time to speak," found in Ecclesiastes 3:7 (KJV).

So, when we have a thing to say, we should say it, but know how and when. A good rule is to say only what you would be willing to have on your lips if they should never speak again.

Let your speech be alway with grace, seasoned with salt, that ye may know how ye ought to answer every man. (Colossians 4:6 KJV)

October 16   Unharness Your Gear at Night

I grew up on a farm back in the 1940's and my Daddy plowed with a pair of mules for many years before he got his wonderful John Deere tractor. Every work day, the two mules, Sam and Shorty, allowed themselves to be harnessed and hooked to the cultivator or whatever other plow to be used that day. Sometimes, when the trailer was loaded with cotton, they towed it to the gin several miles away.

One thing that always fascinated me was to see how Sam and Shorty reacted when Daddy took the harnesses off them. Sometimes they would be sweaty and thirsty. But as soon as the harnesses were off, they got down in the dirt of the barnyard and, with their feet in the air, began tossing about on their backs in the dirt. Sometimes I would hear them snort (I figured it was a giggle). When they had finished romping around, they would head toward the drinking trough which I had just pumped full with cool water. After that they went to the barn for the food Daddy had put out for them. Then they were ready for a long night of rest, so they could be ready to be harnessed up again to do the field work next day.

We know the same goes for other animals, like the chickens who go to roost at twilight. And the cow moves to the barn from the meadow at night time.

Rest at end of day is important for man. God planned it so. He set aside one whole day in the week to just rest. He, who never grows weary, rested on the Seventh Day after creating all things.

Man is born into this world to carry a load; some carry heavier ones than others. But burdens are not so burdensome when they are unharnessed at night. We need to let go at end of day whatever we have been carrying, by merely placing it into the arms of Jesus. Then He and our Heavenly Father (both stay awake all night) will give us blessed rest for bodies and minds.

> The camel, at the close of day,
> Kneels down upon the sandy plain
> To have his burden lifted off
> And rest again.

I will both lay me down in peace, and sleep; for thou, Lord, only makest me dwell in safety. (Psalm 4:8 KJV)

Cast thy burden upon the Lord, and He shall sustain thee: He shall never suffer the righteous to be moved. (Psalm 55:22 KJV)

The sleep of a laboring man is sweet, whether he eat little or much: but the abundance of the rich will not suffer him to sleep. (Ecclesiastes 5:12 KJV)

October 17   Keep on Standing

During these times, it seems evil is growing by leaps and bounds in every area of human life. The ones who are targeted by evil ones are the innocent and especially the ones who take a stand for Jesus. In many places Christians are brutally punished and even killed. So, what are we who are Christians to do? We are to STAND! AND KEEP STANDING!

It takes courage to stand. To stand for the right and good sometimes a fellow may think himself alone. Of course, he is never really alone. Somebody said "One and God make a majority." So, stand, we must, with backbones straight, heads held high and our shoulders squared.

A mature, intelligent person will be able to discern right from wrong truth vs. falsehood, honesty vs. deceitfulness, genuine vs. counterfeit, and good vs. evil. That person has to make a choice of which action to pursue. Again, such a one knows the consequences will follow, for which he or she will assume full responsibility.

Perhaps the enemies of right and good do not realize that their unrelenting opposition only authenticates and adds more weight to the power of the virtues which they are resisting and fighting.

Remember, first the sneer, then the cheer. First the lash, then the laurel. First the curse, then the caress. First the cross, then the crown. Let the whole world know where you stand, and STAND!

Put on the whole armor of God, that ye may be able to stand against the wiles of the devil. (Ephesians 6:11 KJV)

October 18   **Blest Littles**

Of course, I'm thankful for the big things: shelter, clothing, food and
 good health
I'm grateful for loved ones and friends, my job and a portion of wealth.
But I'm especially mindful of small things that crinkle my face with a
 smile,
The ones over which I often stumble; those things that make life
 worthwhile.
I rejoice to see TRUST in a child's eyes, when he whispers a secret in
 my ear.
I feel loftiest pleasure for the HONOR when my poem being read aloud
 I hear.
Knowing the ANSWER to my prayer I am reminded God is a listener
 to me,
And to see His workings to grant my NEED proves He cares for me
 constantly.
When a deserved harsh scolding pounds me for unwise judgments on
 my part,
A friend's timely hug of KINDNESS comforts my stinging, dejected
 heart.
I am grateful for SUCCESS over a bad habit, the one hidden from my
 friend's view,

And I'm gladdened for the no-reason GIFT, with the card saying
   "thinking of you."
In spite of myself I'm even grateful for the INTOLERABLE man so
   hard to please,
Whose hideous annoyances keep me humble, and drive me often to my
   knees.
I appreciate the VOTE of confidence when I'm told my work is well
   done.
I'm encouraged to pursue with new vigor and make worthy marks under
   the sun.
I treasure INTIMATE hide-away places—Liturgies to draw me close
   to God.
These havens are my stanchion points scattered along charged paths I
   trod.
I delight in the addition of NEW things, ever looking for fresh finds
   around the bend.
I hold preciously each of my discoveries—a new word, a new skill, a
   new friend.
I am thankful for a measure of GROWTH in serenity, tolerance, and
   love for God's way.
For these blest littles I am grateful as I count my blessings every day!

> He that spared not His own Son, but delivered Him up for us
> all, how shall He not with Him also freely give us all things?
> (Romans 8:32 KJV)

October 19   Making Tracks

After dwelling in Arkansas for more than three-score years, I moved to
Tennessee where I will likely be a resident for the rest of my life. Being
an avid daily walker for years in Arkansas, immediately after my feet
alit on Tennessee soil, I mapped out a route in the neighborhood to
begin walking.

On my first day to walk I thought to myself "I'll begin making tracks
in Tennessee now, no longer rutted tracks of the past – all new tracks on

unfamiliar ground." My feet will take me into rooms of a different house, down the aisles of strange stores, up the stair-steps and down the halls of the building where I will be working, and to the welcoming doors, into the foyer, and to the pew of my newly selected house of worship. My steps will take me to new places and in front of new faces, wearing names I will have to learn.

As I began my two-mile walking route, I did not know what was around the bends. I did not know where the dips, holes and rough places were. I did not know that a dog barking from his back yard would startle me. Neither did I know that just over a certain ridge I would see the most glorious sunset, nor that I would thrill at seeing a stunning, pearly-white fence at another turn that would remind me of heaven's holy city walls described in the Book of Revelation. Passing one house, I could hear music, and at another, lilting laughter of children.

While walking one day, my thoughts focused on the fact that I have begun a brand-new year, and that in like manner as making tracks in a new geographical place, I will be taking new steps across the threshold of my new year journey. Likewise, I will not know what I will encounter around the bends. To be sure, there will be dips, such as disappointments, discouragements and set-backs, like sickness, misfortune, and, yes, perhaps even deaths of folks I love. My feet will stumble on rough places, and I might even fall down sometimes. On the other hand, now and then, I will turn a bend to discover a splendorous sight, and I will round another curve to find myself in the midst of beautiful music and lilting laughter.

As God has been with me for every track I made on rutted Arkansas soil, so will He be ever present with me as I make new tracks on Tennessee turf. Most importantly, as He has been with me on my more than three-score-year journey thus far, I know I can count on Him to walk beside me as I launch out from the starting gate, and, come what may, He will stay with me until I cross the finish line.

Fear thou not; for I am with thee: be not dismayed; for I am thy God: I will strengthen thee; yea, I will help thee; yea, I will uphold thee with the right hand of My righteousness. (Isaiah 41:10 KJV)

Many years ago, when our family went on vacation, among the places we visited in the area was a cave. The guide took a group down into the cave every hour. When our time cane to enter, there were about sixty or seventy of us. As we entered the cave, we saw lights along the walls. We followed the leader down, down, down to levels of descent. He would stop at each level and talk about historical matters about the cave. We listened with interest. We noticed as we walked down, the temperature inside became chillier. And it became damper.

Our daughter and her friend wanted to hold our hands as we continued the descent. Every now and then they would look behind toward the upward entrance. I kept thinking as we stepped deeper and deeper that, surely, we would soon hit bottom and then be able to return to the entrance.

Finally, we were there. I noticed also the noisiness of the crowd, which began with talking and laughing, had gotten quieter. By the time we reached bottom, it was intensely quiet. Not a single laugh could be heard. It seemed everyone was taking deep breaths. Then, to make the bad atmosphere worse, the leader used a gadget in his hand and turned out all the lights! Not a speck of light anywhere. It seemed people were holding their breaths and some, especially younger ones, began to whimper.

Not a minute had passed before a man yelled, "Turn on the lights!" And the lights came on. My daughter found herself being held by the hand by another woman, not me! I noticed people had moved close to each other.

We started back upward, step by step, and they were all hurried steps. Even the leader made haste toward the entrance door. What elation erupted from the crowd when we began to make our exit.

I realized that darkness is never, never good. God knew that when He began His creation of everything. On the first day, He said "Let there be light, and there was light." Before that darkness was upon the deep.

Nothing can exist without light. God created light before He brought forth plant life and animal life and His creation of the first man and woman.

Darkness is associated with sin and punishment for sin. Wicked deeds of all sorts are carried out in darkness. The Bible also says that those who reject Jesus as Savior will spend their eternity in darkness as well as in everlasting fire.

Even in our everyday lives, nobody likes intense darkness. It has a smothering effect and the heart begins to beat fast and it's hard to breathe evenly.

I never want to go to a cave again. And I like light. God knows all about that. In fact, because the whole sinful world was in darkness, God sent His Son, Jesus, to be the Savior of all who would receive Him personally. Jesus said, "I am the Light of the World." And He has told us, His followers, whom He has *lit*, that we are lights in the world.

And God said, Let there be light: and there was light. And God saw the light, that it was good: and God divided the light from the darkness. (Genesis 1:3-4 KJV)

Then spake Jesus again unto them, saying, I am the light of the world: he that followeth me shall not walk in darkness, but shall have the light of life. (John 8:12 KJV)

October 21   So Richly Blessed

I am glad I was born to my loving parents and into a family of doting kinfolks. I am glad my birth occurred in the United States of America, greatest nation in the world. Four beloved sisters joined me and we always kept close though geographically distanced after we grew up and got married and established our respective homes.

In every community I have lived, I've sat in pews of its steepled place of worship where I learned about the Giver of all good things. When I trusted Jesus as my Savior, He initiated me into the abundant life.

Getting twelve years of education and on-the-job training delighted me at every bend. I have held many various jobs and enjoyed my performance in them all. So indebted to God am I for giving me skills to achieve in those roles.

I am deeply thankful for the husband God gave me and our home together for thirty-six years, before God took him home. I thank Him so much for the precious daughter He entrusted to us, who continues to spread her sunshine in my life. I am glad for the husband God gave her and for their four children who grew up, married and have given me six great-grandchildren.

I am so appreciative of the hordes of friends who attached themselves to me along my journey and have stayed in touch decades and decades. I am thankful to have a voice in my nation's affairs, the main one being my voting privilege. Other things that make my heart sing are hearing human laughter, especially children's, birdsong, rain against my window, music of hymns and classics of masters, seeing colorful blooming things in their seasons, being able to read books written by wholesome-bent authors, especially God's Word, the Bible.

The list could go on and on of my blessings above measure, so I shout again with swelling acclamation, "Thank You, God of the Everywhere, for bestowing on me since my Beginning to my Now all of my Everythings!"

Unto thee, O God, do we give thanks, unto thee do we give thanks: for that thy name is near thy wondrous works declare. (Psalm 75:1 KJV)

The Lord hath done great things for us; whereof we are glad. (Psalm 126:3 KJV)

Great is the Lord, and greatly to be praised; and His greatness is unsearchable. (Psalm 145:3 KJV)

October 22   If Asked to Pray for Someone, Do It

Often during our interaction with fellow-Christians or family members or mere acquaintances, someone will sidle up to you and share a need and say "I want to ask that you pray for me." The natural response is to agree to do so, making it a promise.

But, every now and then, we forget that request. No prayer is offered for the one requesting it. Did you know when we neglect to pray for the person making the re quest we are sinning against the Lord? There is a situation in the Old Testament where the people of Israel asked Samuel to pray for them. They had gone against what God wanted them to do, and when they realized it, they begged Samuel to pray for them. Samuel did so, because he said "God forbid that I should sin against the Lord in ceasing to pray for you."

We have other accounts in the scriptures where people have sought the intercessory prayer of a brother in their behalf. Usually, the person requesting prayer tells why he or she is needing to be prayed for. Sometimes, the one praying for another does not know what to pray for in a situation, but, yet, the prayer should go up in that person's behalf. After all, God knows what the problem is and how to answer.

May we never take lightly when someone says "Pray for me," but we should honor that request, because the one asking sees your life and has confidence that your prayers get answered. And, often at a later time, the one asking for prayer will come to you and share how the problem for which he requested prayer had been answered. That is always a time for rejoicing and praising God.

> Moreover as for me, God forbid that I should sin against the Lord in ceasing to pray for you: but I will teach you the good and the right way. (1 Samuel 12:23 KJV)

> For this cause we also, since the day we heard it, do not cease to pray for you, and to desire that ye might be filled with the knowledge of His will in all wisdom and spiritual understanding. (Colossians 1:9 KJV)

October 23   Mud-Slinger's Target: The Clean

There have always been mud-slingers since the beginning of time. They were called mockers, scoffers, ridiculers, and other such deriding names. The ones who were so treated were not the already muddy ones, but the ones with integrity, dignity, courtesy, morally good: the ones with considerable cleanness.

Look back at the Lord's prophets in the Old Testament and His apostles in the New Testament. They were so ill-treated. The One most ill-treated was the Lord Jesus Himself during His thirty-three years of ministry on earth.

That type of slander and unmerited mistreatment has continued to this present time. The better a man or woman does, the harder the scoffers go about in search of even a speck of fault.

It is my observation that the ones slinging the mud are jealous or envious of the ones whom they are trying to bring to ruination. Deep inside themselves they long for that type of character and reputation. And, when they sling mud, they get their hands and clothes muddy as well, sometimes filthier than the one being hit with the mud.

Another observation, the one who is being hit by mud does not sling mud back, just takes it, and goes on his way. He has the good sense to know that if he slings mud back, he will just get even extra muddy. The poet James Russell Lowell penned: "Knowing what all experience serves to show, no mud can soil us but the mud we throw."

Dearly beloved, avenge not yourselves, but rather give place unto wrath: for it is written, Vengeance is mine; I will repay, saith the Lord. Therefore, if thine enemy hunger, feed him; if he thirst, give him drink: for in so doing thou shalt heap coals of fire on his head. Be not overcome of evil, but overcome evil with good. (Romans 12:19-21 KJV)

I planted an acorn; it was in my back yard.
I watered and cared for it; it was really hard.
The acorn soon sprouted; the sapling was strong.
I still cared for it all the year long.
When winter was over and spring was near,
I was pleased to see tiny buds appear.
Now many years later the oak tree does stand.
What once was an acorn is majestic and grand.
--Joshua Fee, my grandson

One of the many instructions I have kept in my creative writing education is, "You must use at least one word in your beginning paragraph also in your last paragraph of your story, article, feature, or other type writing."

Did you know, the Bible does the same? The first book in the Bible is Genesis and the last one is Revelation. Words found in the first three chapters of Genesis can be found in the last three chapters of Revelation. Look and see (all scriptures in KJV):

In the beginning God created the heavens and earth. (Genesis 1:1)
I saw a new heaven and a new earth. (Revelation 21:1)

The gathering together of waters He called the sea. (Genesis 1:10)
And the sea is no more. (Revelation 21:1)

The darkness He called night. (Genesis 1:5)
There shall be no night there. (Revelation 21:25)

God made the two great lights [the sun and moon]. (Genesis 1:16.)
The city has no need of the sun nor the moon. (Revelation 21:23)

In the day you eat thereof you shall surely die. (Genesis 2:17)
Death shall be no more. (Revelation 21:4)

I will greatly multiply your pain. (Genesis 3:16)
Neither shall there be any more pain. (Revelation 21:4)

Cursed is the ground for your sake. (Genesis 3:17)
There shall be no more curse. (Revelation 22:3)

Satan appears as deceiver of mankind. (Genesis 3:1, 4)
Satan disappears forever. (Revelation 20:10)

They were driven from the tree of life. (Genesis 3:22-24)
The tree of life reappears. (Revelation 22:2)

They were driven from God's presence. (Genesis 3:24)
They shall see His face. (Revelation 22:4)

Man's primeval home was by a river. (Genesis 2:10)
Man's eternal home will be beside a river. (Revelation 22:1).

October 25 — Notable Sayings About the Bible

George Washington: "It is impossible to rightly govern the world without God and the Bible."

Abraham Lincoln: "I believe the Bible is the best gift God has ever given to man. All the good from the Savior of the world is communicated to us through this Book."

Napoleon Bonaparte: "The Bible is no mere book, but a Living Creature, with a power that conquers all that oppose it."

Patrick Henry: "The Bible is worth all other books which have ever been printed."

Andrew Jackson: "That book, sir, is the rock on which our republic rests."

Robert E. Lee: "In all my perplexities and distresses, the Bible has never failed to give me light and strength."

Sir William Herschel: "All human discoveries seem to be made only for the purpose of confirming more and more strongly the truths contained in the Sacred Scriptures."

Henry Van Dyke: "Born in the East and clothed in Oriental form and imagery, the Bible walks the ways of all the world with familiar feet and enters land after land to find its own everywhere. It has learned to speak in hundreds of languages to the heart of man. Children listen to its stories with wonder and delight, and wise men ponder them as parables of life. The wicked and the proud tremble at its warnings, but to the wounded and penitent it has a mother's voice. It has woven itself into our dearest dreams, so that Love, Friendship, Sympathy, Devotion, Memory, Hope, put on the beautiful garments of its treasured speech. No man is poor or desolate who has this treasure for his own. When the landscape darkens, and the trembling pilgrim comes to the Valley of the Shadow, he is not afraid to enter. He takes the rod and staff of Scripture in his hand. He says to friend and comrade, 'Goodbye; we shall meet again," and, confronted by that support, he goes toward the lonely pass as one who walks through darkness into light."

Daniel Webster: "If there is anything in my thoughts or style to commend, the credit is due to my parents for instilling in me an early love of the Scriptures. If we abide by the principles taught in the Bible, our country will go on prospering and to prosper; but if we and our posterity neglect its instructions and authority, no man can tell how sudden a catastrophe may overwhelm us and bury all our glory in profound obscurity."

> Thy word have I hid in mine heart, that I might not sin against thee. … Thy word is a lamp unto my feet, and a light unto my path. (Psalm 119:11, 105 KJV)

> Heaven and earth shall pass away, but my words shall not pass away. (Mathew 24:35 KJV)

October 26   My Written Prayer Found in a Book

I have written prayers along during my lifetime and stuck them in random books or furniture drawers. I always find the things I prayed about had been answered by God. I found the following one recently and want to share it with you.

O God, My Heavenly Father, You are my Keeper, I can trust You. When I come into Your presence, I am sure of your ardent care.

You are now, and have been, all-sufficient in all my situations of every bent. You give me the succinct response for my every asked "Why?"

You delete all impossibilities that shudder and tremble me from all sides. You notice me. You listen to my every petition. You balm my hurting with peace.

The tender resonance of Your Voice calms my heart's restlessness. You stir my love for You, to sing with You, to laugh joyfully with You. I am awed at your Majesty! I worship You, O God!

In Jesus's Name,

Your Daughter Carlene

October 27   Being Wanted Better than Being Needed

Being needed by someone is such an honor. It makes the one being needed feel extra important. That one feels special to the one needing him. But sometimes when a person has been provided with everything needed, there is still an empty hole inside that one. Something or someone is missing.

An aged widow, over a decade past retirement age, continued to work at her job she had held for over thirty years. She continued to be as efficient as ever, in spite of Arthritis flare-ups. The fact that she could still perform the duties of her career gave her a special feeling of importance. She was so glad to be needed.

One day one of her supervisors, much younger than she, said to her, "Do you know it is a good thing to be wanted?"

She agreed that that was a good thing. Then he said "I just want you to know, you are wanted here in this place. When I see you at your post, no matter what difficulties I am dealing with, I get a whiff of peace. You are like the rainbow after a bad thunderstorm. Not just I, but others have said the same. Your presence seems to make the day go well."

She thought he was teasing, smiled, and said "Thank you." But he kept a solemn face, so she concluded he must have meant it. Then they both got down to the business of the day. But his words kept coming back to her throughout the day. She began to think of others who touched her life whom she *wanted* at times. She had no particular needs but at times she longed for someone to fill an empty hole. It always involved the personal presence of someone, a particular relative or a long-time friend. A phone call or getting a letter from that one might do, but the best thing would be face-to-face talking, in the same room, hearing each other's voice, or merely sitting quietly together.

I believe that is the way it is with Christians. The Lord as our Shepherd always provides every need of ours to the full. But afterward, there is that longing, yes, wanting more, to be close in His presence for fellowship, just to hang out together – I hope that is not irreverent. I believe Jesus had that *want* for His Father, because He frequently slipped away to spend time with Him in prayer. I believe Jesus also had this feeling toward His Apostles. He wanted them near Him those three years of His ministry, but especially during the last year. He wanted them with Him in the Garden of Gethsemane and all that followed afterward. After His Resurrection, He told the women who had come to the tomb to go and tell His disciples that He was risen and He would meet with them that day. I believe He enjoyed eating their leftover fish and honeycomb that evening when He came to them.

So, we need the Lord to provide our day-by-day needs, to be sure. But even after those needs are met, I believe we still have a deep *want* for Him. Indeed, it is good to be wanted by others, and to want others, and we should do what the supervisor did to the aged lady: tell that person "You are wanted. Being with you makes my day." But, oh, how much our *want* for Jesus's presence would be satisfied by spending time close to Him. And we should tell Him so!

> O God, thou art my God; early will I seek thee: my soul thirsteth for thee, my flesh longeth for thee in a dry and thirsty land, where no water is; to see thy power and thy glory, so as I have seen thee in the sanctuary. ... Because thou hast been my help, therefore in the shadow of thy wings will I rejoice. My soul followeth hard after thee: thy right hand upholdeth me. (Psalm 63:1-2, 7-8 KJV)

I am to have a caring heart – 1 Thessalonians 5:15.
I am to have a rejoicing heart – 1 Thessalonians 5:16.
I am to have a praying heart – 1 Thessalonians 5:17.
I am to have a thankful heart – 1 Thessalonians 5:18.
I am to have a pure heart, -- 1 Thessalonians 5:19-20.

(All scriptures below in KJV):

Thou shalt not suffer a witch to live. (Exodus 22:18)

A man also or woman that hath a familiar spirit, or that is a wizard, shall surely be put to death: they shall stone them with stones: their blood shall be upon them. (Leviticus 20:27)

There shall not be found among you any one that maketh his son or his daughter to pass through the fire, or that useth divination, or one that practices augury, or an enchanter, or a witch, or on observer of times, or an enchanter, or a witch, or a charmer, or a consulter with familiar spirits, or a wizard, or a necromancer. For all that do these things are an abomination unto the Lord... (Deuteronomy 18:10-12)

Therefore hearken not ye to your prophets, nor to your diviners, nor to your dreamers, nor to your enchanters, nor to your sorcerers, ... for they prophesy a lie unto you, to remove you far from your land; and that I should drive you out, and ye should perish. (Jeremiah 27:9, 10)

God will complete what He has begun in my life – Philippians 1:6.

The reason God has kept me here is because He still has a plan to work through me for His glory – Philippians 1:21-24.

God wants to use me to be a blessing and encouragement to my brothers and sisters in Christ – Philippians 2:1-4.

God does not want me to complain, but instead wants me to be blameless and harmless, because He says I am to be a light in a dark world of sin – Philippians 2:14-15.

God wants me to march always forward. My past years are history. My focus must remain on Jesus as I press on – Philippians 3:13-14.

I am in the world, but not of the world. My citizenship is in heaven where my Savior is. I can put up with this old carnal body I live in because someday God has promised me a glorious new body that will never get sick, grow old, nor die – Philippians 3:20-21.

I am to be content whatever my lot – Philippians 4:11.

I can accomplish nothing within my own self and strength, but I can do all things through Christ who gives me strength – Philippians 4:13.

God has promised to supply all my needs – not all my wants – by means of His riches in Christ Jesus – Philippians 4:19.

I am responsible to God, first and foremost:

1. Be a good steward of my physical body (Romans 12:1).
2. Be a good steward of my mind (Romans 12:2-3).
3. Fill my role(s) using the spiritual gift(s) God has entrusted to me in the church (Romans 12:4-8).

I am responsible to others:

1. Maintain and improve relations with fellow brother and sister Christians (Romans 12:9-21).

I am responsible to government:

1. Obey laws of the land and pay taxes (Romans 13:1-7).
2. Don't go in debt (Romans 13:8).
3. Practice Christian interaction with family, friends, neighbors (Romans 13:9-14).

I have responsibilities above and beyond the norm:

1. Help the struggling weak Christian (Romans 14:1).
2. Realize we need each other (Romans 14:7, 8).
3. I must not judge my brother nor put a stumbling block in his path (Romans 14:10-13, 21).
4. If I can be used to lift up or edify another Christian, I must seize that opportunity as an assignment from the Lord (Romans 5:1-5).
5. I must ever be mindful that all I am or do is to be for God's glory and honor (Romans 15:6, 7).

(I found names starting with all letters of the alphabet besides Q, U, and X)

Alpha, Almighty God
Bright and Morning Star, Bread of Life
Christ, Creator, Chief Cornerstone
Dayspring from On High
Everlasting Father
Faithful and True
God, Great I Am
High Priest
Immanuel
Jesus, Jehovah
King of Kings
Lord of Lords, Lamb of God, Lion of the Tribe of Judah
Messiah, Master
Nazarene
Omega, Only Begotten Son of God
Prince of Peace
Redeemer, Resurrection and Life, Rock
Savior, Shepherd
Truth
Vine
Wonderful, Way
Yahweh
Zion's King

I wrote the following lines when I was living in Arkansas. I was president of the local Writers Guild, and we had our own poetry column, Delta Voices, for many years. This was published in the local Blytheville

Courier News about two decades ago. It depicts all the many places in which a person belongs. Each one who reads can identify:

I am situated at a numbered address. In a house where my stuff is. This place sits on a named street, laid out on a plat of a section, of a documented and measured tract of land with meets and bounds numbers. The name given to my city is Blytheville. I am counted in its census.

My city fits inside Mississippi County and records of me can be traced to my beginning in the Recorder's Office of this county's court house. This county lies within the bounds of the State of Arkansas. My name can be found in records of this state's vital statistics files, my driver's license. I pay taxes to this state.

My state is snugly surrounded by sister states: Missouri, Tennessee, Louisiana, Mississippi, Oklahoma and Texas – you've got to cross the River to get to two of them – and they all join up with the others that make up one nation, the United States of America. My status as a native-born American daughter is documented in this nation.

With this endowment I am loaded down with privileges to claim in my own name. I pay tribute here every April. I pledge allegiance to this nation's flag.

My nation takes its place in the Norther Hemisphere of this globe's lands and waters. This hemisphere is located on the planet earth. I am an earthling. My earth holds its place in the Solar System in the area of the Milky Way. My Solar System is one of thousands of solar systems in the immeasurable universe.

My universe rests in the fathomless reaches of the Sovereign God Almighty, Creator and Sustainer of the whole. O! How marvelous that I should belong in God's universe and to Him.

> What is man, that thou art mindful of him? and the son of man
> that thou visitest him? For thou hast made him a little lower
> than the angels, and hast crowned him with glory and honor.
> (Psalm 8:4-5 KJV)

The Lord is my Staying Shepherd.
Today is alive; Tomorrow is unborn.
Ask, seek, knock; keep at it.
Don't journey hit or miss—Aim!
The family altar alters the family.
I'll row, Lord, but you steer.
Frontiers of undone things never disappear.
Confess the sin; then bury it.
Do someone a good turn anonymously
I am acquainted with my Shepherd.
My Staying Shepherd knows my name.

I am the good shepherd, and know my sheep, and am known of mine. (John 10:14 KJV)

Nevertheless the foundation of God standeth sure, having this seal, The Lord knoweth them that are His. And, Let every one that nameth the name of Christ depart from iniquity. (2 Timothy 2:19 KJV)

Each of us, except for a comparatively few, is endowed with two faithful servants that serve us well all our lives. These servants are our two hands.

It's when an infant takes hold of his parent's finger with his tiny, dimpled hand for the first time that he is bragged about as accomplishing his first big step. At the end of that life, as he lies in cold repose, is it any wonder that after viewing the person's face the one looking focuses on his folded hands? Between the first tug on his parent's hand and the last time for someone to look at his hands, what marvelous history those two servants will have written!

Those hands ministered to their master's needs: feeding, bathing, dressing him, fingering all the buttons and zippers and typing shoelaces.

Those servants took the lead with childhood chores like washing dishes, making the bed, sweeping and mopping the floor, raking leaves, shoveling snow.

Oh, what an achievement when those two-flesh-covered carpal, metacarpal and phalange bones were turned on to write his name the first time and to make arithmetic numbers, and to wield a yellow crayon to shape drawings of daisy petals on a tablet page! What a thrill that little one felt bubbling up inside when these servants held a book so he could re ad the words aloud for the first time.

Those two servants continued to master more skills, for his boy master's enjoyment, artfully unwinding and rewinding a kite string, dribbling a basketball, pitching a baseball, gripping a ball bat, making swimming strokes to stay afloat, reeling and casting a fishing rod. If these two servants belonged to a mistress, what joy they brought to her in dressing a Barbie or holding the rope for her to jump.

Whatever the hobby, these two servants meet the challenge, with delicate brushes for the artist at the easel, or with broad ones for the interior decorator. They befit with needles the knitting and embroidering enthusiasts. For the chef appropriate tools are taken up to scrape, flip, whip, peel and knead. They enjoy getting dirty, doing the sculptor's work with clay and chisel. No matter what musical instrument their master chooses, these two servants stand at attention to fulfill their tasks, applying just-right tuneful touches on the piano keys or the violin's strings.

These two servants convey emotions of their master. They tremble when he is afraid. They caress gently to express love. They whisk away tears when he is sad. They lend courage when they shake the hand of another. They wave a happy hello and a morose farewell. Their fingers interlace occasionally with another's. Their undersides sweat when their master is nervous. They fold reverently when he prays.

Oh, how intricately unique they are trained for their master's life work, whether he be a surgeon with life-and-death tools, a scientist in the lab maneuvering slides under a microscope, a bus driver at the wheel, a pilot with his flight instruments, a school teacher with a piece of chalk, an orchestra leader with his baton.

Oh, the magnificent servants, our two hands! Pause now to look at your own hands. Be they smooth, neatly manicured, bejeweled, warped, freckled or wrinkled, they are precious!

Now, go ahead and look toward heaven – yea, even raise your hands toward heaven – and thank God for giving you these two faithful servants. You may even want to give them a kiss!

And let the beauty of the Lord our God be upon us: and establish thou the work of our hands upon us; yea, the work of our hands establish thou it. (Psalm 90:17 KJV)

Whatsoever thy hand findeth to do, do it with thy might; for there is no work, nor device, nor knowledge, nor wisdom, in the grave, whither thou goest. (Ecclesiastes 9:10 KJV)

November 5   Calendar of Life

In January he is an infant, fresh and new. He arrives with joy to parents, siblings and other kin who at once begin bonding. He comes equipped by his Creator to perfect his purpose for being born. February finds him a young child, when he fumbles to master new things: sitting alone, pulling up, and then taking his first step, and feeding himself.

March is the running and climbing phase. He has learned where pitfalls and hurdles are. He recognizes the joy of pleasing his parents. He begins to learn about God, when he asks, "How did God make puppy's tail?" as he squats to watch. April is when he enrolls in kindergarten. He adds teachers and other boys and girls to his world, and learns the hard and sometimes lesson about sharing. He focuses on the alphabet, numbers past ten, music and one particular crayon he likes best.

The May of his life stretches long, from first grade until high school. He mines the intricate veins of math; explores the annals of history; masters the words in multi-genre books, and delves into the deep seas of science. June is his teen time, which really means "tween" time, as he moves past childhood toward young adulthood. His studies are more intense. He learns to drive a car. He begins to notice the opposite gender, and he might hold an after-school job.

July is his young adult era. It means a total change, whether he goes to college, or joins the military, or takes a job. Parents and mentors have moved back from the coaching sidelines to the cheering and applauding squad. Now he is accountable for each decision and its consequential outcome. Often, this is the point when he renews his closeness to his God, because he realizes He is the all-sufficient One for counsel and leadership.

By August he has established a career. Likely he has married and begun a family. He has established moral rules for his home. September is the mellowing season. The kids are educated and out on their own. He and his spouse spend "just-the-two-of-us" time together. October is the rewarding period, when he sees his children's prosperity and the handsome and beautiful grandchildren they have added to his lineage.

In November, he leaves his work place for good. He may travel, or resume an abandoned hobby, or opt to just live life at a slower pace. He especially enjoys spending time with fellow retirees with whom he can reminisce about the splendor of former years. Then comes December, when he knows his year is about to close. His bones creak, his shoulders slump, but he keeps on smiling because he knows his final celebration is about to happen. Just like the final holiday of the year, Christmas, when folks gather with friends and kinfolks, and enter into joyful gala, so the folks who have known him all his calendar year long will show up to celebrate with music and flowers and fond words: a tribute to his calendar of life well lived. The next calendar leaf will be January, and he will have moved to be with his God, where he will enjoy one never-ending calendar page.

> The days of our years are threescore years and ten; and if by reason of strength they be fourscore years, yet is their strength labor and sorrow; for it is soon cut off, and we fly away. (Psalm 90:10 KJV)

> And though after my skin worms destroy this body, yet in my flesh shall I see God: Whom I shall see for myself, and mine eyes shall behold, and not another; though my reins be consumed within me. (Job 19:26-27 KJV)

A long-ago friend, Tilda Kinnel, wrote a poem and gave it to me. It speaks to my heart every time I read it. She is now deceased. I can hear her voice as I read it:

PUT OUT TO SEA

Is your life like the old battleship
Upon the sea of life?
Has it been scarred by the things of this world?
Is it battered by worldly strife?
There is a harbor for safety
If you trust in the Savior above.
You can be used again by the Captain
And sail out to show others His love.

Also I heard the voice of the Lord, saying, Whom shall I send, and who will go for Us? Then said I, Here am I; send me. And He said, Go, and tell this people, Hear ye indeed, but understand not; and see ye indeed, but perceive not. … Then said I, Lord, how long? And He answered, Until the cities be wasted without inhabitant, and the houses without man, and the land be utterly desolate. (Isaiah 6:8-9, 11 KJV)

Now then we are ambassadors for Christ, as though God did beseech you by us: we pray you in Christ's stead, be ye reconciled to God. For He hath made Him to be sin for us, who knew no sin; that we might be made the righteousness of God in Him. (2 Corinthians 5:20-21 KJV)

Peggy felt she was not fulfilling her Christian duty in witnessing to lost people about their need of salvation. She was a widow and had health problems and was considered a shut-in for the most part. In the past she had been very active in teaching, visiting, and otherwise serving in her church.

So, she went to the Lord about it. "Lord, I want to be used by you to speak to someone today about You. Please send someone my way or reveal to me where I should go to find that person."

She then began to do her household chores – a tub of laundry, washing dishes in the sink, dusting the furniture. Then she needed to sit to rest awhile. She sat in her rocker and turned on the TV. Oops! Nothing! It would not come on. She then went to the desk drawer to get her manual that gave the proper telephone number to use to contact a repairer.

After many referrals, she finally was talking to a woman who told her whom to call, in her Tennessee home town, to get service immediately. Peggy was so grateful to get such speedy service. She told the woman she was a widow and had to rely on others to help her get things done. The woman asked, "Whom do you depend on to help you?"

Peggy at once told her, "I lean upon my Savior, the Lord Jesus Christ. I can trust Him. He leads me and guides me and gives me discernment. I could not get along at all without Him."

Then, the woman told her, "I am calling you from the Philippines on this cable repair call, and I have a few minutes to talk to you. Tell me about this Jesus whom you trust."

Peggy gave her personal testimony with such enthusiasm. The woman in far-off Philippines thanked her and said, "You've given me so much to think about. But now I must answer the other telephone."

Peggy called the number given to her, and the man said he would be out to repair her TV within the hour. She hung up the phone, and turned her heart to heaven. "Oh, Lord, you answered my prayer. You had to mess up my TV in order to do it. I was given the privilege to tell someone about you. I don't know her name, but you do, and I pray you will take the seed I planted and bring it to fruition. Oh, thank you, for using me for Your name sake today!

> Preach the word; be instant in season, out of season; reprove, rebuke, exhort with all longsuffering and doctrine. (2 Timothy 4:2 KJV)

> But sanctify the Lord God in your hearts: and be ready always to give an answer to every man that asketh you a reason of the hope that is in you with meekness and fear. (1 Peter 3:15 KJV)

November 8   Your Work, Not Finished

Shirley once sang solos at her church and taught Sunday School. As a widow she raised her one son, bringing him up in the nurture and admonition of the Lord. As an adult he continues to be active in the music department of his church. In her secular job, she was a type of counselor in financial and estate planning. Among hobbies, she enjoyed writing poetry, and had had some of them published. She excelled in all areas.

Then, she began having health problems, but she was able to persist at her job until retirement age. One physical ailment ended and another began. At length, she had to move into the home of her son. After many surgeries, she wound up using a walker, never being able to drive again. She continued to attend her church but began to feel she only filled a pew spot.

Then, one morning during her devotional time with the Lord, she asked, "Lord, I feel like I am useless for you. I cannot sufficiently fill any spot of service for you. But I love you and your kingdom work. If I am to stay here on this earth, show me how I can best serve you."

She felt a peace following that prayer. Another favorite of hers, on her days when she could manipulate the walker better, was to go out in the back yard and sit in her swing. While sitting there and enjoying the breeze and watching and listening to the birds, she saw an airplane sky-writing designs in the blue sky. Almost as if she heard God's voice, the word *write* came to her mind.

She began to laugh joyfully. Yes, Lord, I can write. That's one way I can serve you! When she went back indoors, and after the evening meal with her son, she took a tablet and pen and began to write. Words came fluently and rhythmically.

About a month later, she received a phone call from a former writer friend. She had not heard from her in several months. The friend said "Shirley, you have been on my mind lately. Are you all right? Are you well? I have just felt like I needed to talk to you."

Shirley assured her she was faring well except for some physical ailments. Then, their conversation took a completely different turn.

"Shirley, I've just been asked by a newspaper editor if we could come up with a poetry page again in his paper. I was wondering…"

Shirley interrupted with a burst of laughter. "Oh, Betty, that must have been God talking to you! Just lately, He urged me to begin writing poetry again, and I have done so. I've finished five. Oh, yes, yes! I will be so glad to have my poems in that column again!"

Elation and praise to their God, they both saw how God keeps His children here on this earth until they have finished His planned work for them!

> For we are His workmanship, created in Christ Jesus unto good works, which God hath before ordained that we should walk in them. (Ephesians 2:10 KJV)

November 9   I Am Resolved

Many of us make New Year Resolutions at the start of a year, with avid determination to keep them. Some we keep, and, yes, some we let fall. But, there are some resolutions we should take to heart, starting at any time, and they are listed in acrostic below. These should be our Rules and Regulations to keep with our whole heart.

R – Reverence God, Jesus, the Holy Spirit, and Myself

E – Esteem and Encourage fellow Christians

S – Serve faithfully at my post(s) in my church

O – Obey Jesus' Rules for upright living in His Sermon on the Mount

L – Love, in word and deed, my God, my family, my friends, and the unlovely

V – Voice my praises to God; Vote my convictions; Volunteer to do what the Holy Spirit impresses upon me to do

E – Enlist others to come along and go with me to the Glory Land

> Be kindly affectioned one to another with brotherly love; in honor preferring one another; not slothful in business; fervent in spirit; serving the Lord; rejoicing in hope; patient in tribulation; continuing instant in prayer; distributing to the necessity of saints; given to hospitality. (Romans 12:10-13 KJV)

November 10   God Provides Just Enough

When foreign missionaries were home on furlough and back in the United States, they were invited to churches as guests to tell in person of the results of their ministries. When they came to our church, always some family invited them to their home for lunch, and another family would invite them for dinner or an after-church get-together.

When a missionary family from Portugal visited our church, my husband and I were the ones who had planned to have them with us for lunch. Thinking it would be the missionary and his wife, I had planned a lunch for the two of them, my husband and me, and our teen-age daughter and her friend. Six people. Well, when they showed up at church that Sunday, there were six of the missionary family: he, his wife, and four teen-agers.

"Oh, my!" I whispered to my husband. "I don't know if I have prepared enough food for everybody." That thought stuck with me during the worship service, and I was praying for the Lord to take care of the situation. Back then, no grocery stores were open on Sunday so I could buy something to add. Then I remembered! Down in the bottom of my deep freeze were four packages of frozen brussel sprouts! Nobody liked them at our house except me, and I only fixed them for me when I was alone. That was the only item of food I had to add to the already fixed stuff. I had a sense of peace.

While everybody scattered to the living room and to daughter's room and some to the back yard, I finished getting the meal ready. I boiled all those sprouts and just added some butter, black pepper and salt to them. No cheese sauce nor anything else!

When the dishes and platters of food were set out on the counters, and the leaf-added dining table was set with another small table with chairs in the living room, all were invited to partake. The blessing was said, and afterward they lined up in buffet style with their plates and began filling them. All of a sudden, one of the missionary's teenage boys exclaimed, "Ah, look! Little bitty cabbages!" as he pointed to the sprouts. Another said, "Aha, we haven't eaten sprouts in a long time."

I looked at my surprised-face husband and we grinned at each other. Then, I lifted my heart heavenward and said, "Thank You, Lord, for filling the gap."

There was enough of everything for everybody. My experience was different from the one where Jesus took five loaves and two fishes and fed a multitude of over 5,000, because after they had all eaten, there were twelve baskets of scraps left over. Instead, I had empty bowls and platters and there was not a single sprout left! Praise the Lord! He provided just enough!

> And God is able to make all grace abound toward you; that ye, always having all sufficiency in all things, may abound to every good work. (2 Corinthians 9:8 KJV)

November 11   ## Ugly Covered by Beautiful

A seventy-year-old grandmother was dressing to go out to a dinner with other senior friends. Her eight-year-old granddaughter was watching as she draped a beautiful scarf around her neck and fastened it with a silver pin.

"Why do you wear that scarf on top of your pretty dress, Nana? Your dress is prettier without the scarf.

"Well, you see, it's like this, Honey. My old neck is so wrinkled and mole-spotted and dry and scaly, and that makes it so ugly," her grandmother replied. "I wear this scarf to cover my old ugly neck. Now you cannot see my neck, can you?"

"I don't think your neck is ugly, Nana, but if it makes you feel beautiful to wear the scarf, I guess you can just go ahead and wear it," the child concluded.

Such an incident has a good tug of inspiration to it. Every one of us human beings is ugly because of our sins, the one we inherited from our first parents when they sinned, and all the ones we commit ourselves and continually practice. We get dirty, scaly, wrinkled, and become marked with moles and freckles. There is no way within ourselves we can make ourselves pure, smooth, pleasant, clean or holy. We need to have our ugliness covered.

Someone has provided that covering for our ugliness. He is the Lord Jesus Christ, God's Only Begotten Son, whose whole purpose was to pay the price for our ugliness with His own pure, holy, clean, sinless blood, because He wanted us to be free of all ugliness. When an ugly sinner comes to Him and receives Him as Lord and Savior, He covers that ugliness with His blood. That person's ugliness disappears under that covering. The beauty of that covering adorns that person from that time forward. He is no longer ugly, but wonderfully beautiful!

And let the beauty of the Lord our God be upon us: and establish thou the work of our hands upon us; yea, the work of our hands establish thou it. (Psalm 90:17 KJV)

I will greatly rejoice in the Lord, my soul shall be joyful in my God; for He hath clothed me with the garments of salvation, He hath covered me with the robe of righteousness, as a bridegroom decketh himself with ornaments, and as a bride adorneth herself with her jewels. (Isaiah 61:10 KJV)

I was teacher of a class of junior high teens in my church. They numbered about fifteen. One Sunday, when it was starting time, I saw only ten were present. I began to wonder aloud, "Where is Susie today? Where is Rhonda? Where are Jerry and Kenny?" I suppose my face expression showed disappointment. Then something jolting incident occurred!

Leon, sitting on the back row, raised his hand.

"Yes, Leon," I responded.

Grinning, he said, "But I'm here."

That jarred me to my senses! My noticing those absent seemed to have made the attendance of others who had come of no importance. I suddenly felt tears rushing and about to spill.

"Oh, Leon, of course you are here! And so is Jimmy and Tammy and all of you here today. I want you to know, you are so important to me and especially to the Lord. You are faithful and loyal to your commitment to assemble at the Lord's house every Sunday. I am so glad all of you are here."

After class dismissal and all through the worship service following, I could not forget Leon's words. I realized that sometimes I took the faithful ones for granted and spent more time focusing on those who were absent. I asked the Lord to forgive me for my bad attitude, and I vowed to focus on those who were faithful in appreciation and fellowship and encouragement toward them. The Lord gave me a scripture to fit that situation. When the multitudes who had been following Jesus began group by group to leave Him, He asked His Twelve, "Will you also go away?" Peter assured Him they would never leave Him, and I know Jesus rejoiced.

Jesus expressed how much He loved His Apostles when He talked to them in the Upper Room after Passover and the Lord's Supper. They just numbered Eleven then, but He didn't ask, "Well, where are all the others who have promised to follow Me?" We know, even of the Eleven, often only three (Peter, James and John) were in His presence. Also, when He told the 500 who composed His church to wait in Jerusalem for the coming of the Holy Spirit to give them go-power for the Great Commission, only 120 were present. Even in our churches today, the whole crowd won't always show up, but, thanks be unto God, the faithful few will show up to give Him glory! In fact, Jesus said if only two or three gathered together in His name, He would join them!

> For where two or three are gathered together in my name, there am I in the midst of them. (Matthew 18:20 KJV)

November 13 — Why Not Glow Stunningly Bright?

On my drive to work in Nashville, Tennessee, I pass in front of the many-storied Marriott Hotel. Its exterior looks like all mirrors and steel. I approach it as the sun is coming up, and when the glorious rising sun is so brightly reflected in the exterior of that hotel, that I have to pull down my visor and hold my hand in front of my face because the glare is so strong. The sun beams beautifully in all its glory.

Jesus told His followers that they were the light of the world. And He told them to let their lights shine before the world so that others would see their good works and glorify God the Father. This is found in Matthew 5:14-16. Wouldn't it be wonderful if we so let our lights shine that those seeing us would have to put on shades to look at us?

Reckon we ought to be busy polishing our lamp globes so that we can reflect the glory of the "Sun of Righteousness?"

> But unto you that fear My Name shall the Sun of Righteousness arise with healing in His wings; and ye shall go forth, and grow up as calves of the stall. And ye shall tread down the wicked, for they shall be as ashes under the soles of your feet in the day that I shall do this, saith the Lord of hosts. (Malachi 4:2-3 KJV)

November 14 — Faint Not

I began writing a biography of my paternal grandfather a few years before his death. I would meet with him every Saturday where he lived since becoming a widower with his youngest daughter, Wilma, and her husband, John. He'd say, "Now, where did we leave off last Saturday?" I'd tell him and he would commence recollecting from that point, and I wrote down what he said. I didn't get finished before he had to go into a nursing facility, but, even then, we continued our Saturday sessions. He died before I finished, but by that time in his chronology, I had arrived on the scene and could use my own memories and those of others in the family.

I worked on the biography a little every day. Finally, shortly after his death in September, I had it published, and ready for dispensing in time for Christmas. It had taken me such a long time to get it done, and when I held the book with his picture on the front, what an unexplainable thrill for me to handle the book and turn its pages!

It was not an easy work. It had to be done line upon line, line upon line, here a little and there a little. How easy it would have been to quit many times. But the goal was worthy, and I yearned to reach it. And I did!

Have you begun something worthwhile and you are still working on it and wondering if you will ever achieve your goal? Keep at it, here a little and there a little. Don't faint or become discouraged. The seeming little you do each time is building toward the whole.

Have you prayed and prayed and prayed for a loved one to be saved and you almost faint at times because you can see no change in that person? Friend, keep at it. It will come to pass.

Are you trying to learn something new that you know the Lord wants you to learn to be more effective in His service, and your progress is slow? Could you be learning to overcome shyness so you can teach a class or do visitation? Are you learning a musical instrument or how to sing in the choir, or, as a new bride, how to be a good cook, and, so far, you have made flop after flop? Well, just keep at it!

Remember it takes time to accomplish anything good, and the pieces are put together little by little. That way we can appreciate the victory, or success, or achievement the more when it comes!

And let us not be weary in well-doing: for in due season we shall reap, if we faint not. (Galatians 6:9 KJV)

Is there someone who once was a close Christian friend and, because of an offense on your part, your fellowship is broken? You are no longer friends and may even consider yourselves enemies. You have gone to that person and apologized and expressed your desire that your friendship be restored. She has refused to hear you. She has consistently refused your invitation to your home. She has refused to be associated in any group where you are a participant. This has brought distress to you, and after a time your attitude has become, "Oh, well, it's a hopeless case. I've done everything I can. I'm going to just leave her alone."

But the Holy Spirit within you won't allow you to let it go. And you ask yourself, "Is there not just one more thing I might do in this matter?"

That one thing might be to pray, "Lord, melt her heart toward me. I want to be her friend again." Repeat that prayer so often that it will become a part of you. With your heart and mind both saturated with this thought, it will show in your face and actions when you are in the presence of that person.

Another thing you might try is to speak kindly and respectfully about that person. Point out her good qualities. Every person has at least one good virtue, and perhaps more. Focus on that.

Periodically invite that person (and spouse) to your home. If it is unlikely that they will come as one-couple guests, then include another couple who are common friends to both of you. This could be after church some evening or such other occasion.

If you both enjoy a common interest (ball game, school play, concert, flower show, fashion show, etc.) buy tickets and invite her to go with you.

Other casual friendly gestures you may continue as in years past, such as sending a Christmas card, or a postcard if you are away on a trip, or congratulations when due. Greet cordially, choose a seat near her when given the opportunity, strike up conversation with her.

These actions and attitudes on your part should topple any wall of offense between the two of you. If, however, she continues to refuse to respond favorably, some great good will come of it just the same. You will feel at peace in your heart toward her. Whether she ever recognizes it or not, she possesses something of tremendous value: a deeply caring Christian friend.

> Moreover if thy brother shall trespass against thee, go and tell him his fault between thee and him alone: if he shall hear thee, thou hast gained thy brother. (Matthew 18:15 KJV)

> Let all bitterness, and wrath, and anger, and clamor, and evil speaking, be put away from you, with all malice: and be ye kind one to another, tenderhearted, forgiving one another, even as God for Christ's sake, hath forgiven you. (Ephesians 4:31-32 KJV)

November 16   Ups and Downs

Our lives are made up of ups and downs. I recall one week in my life when there were more of each of these ups and downs than at any other time. My mother and I went to a National Baptist Meeting in Little Rock, Arkansas, an *up*. While there we learned a former pastor of my back-home church had died, a *down*. Mom and I went to hear my daughter's college choir perform at one of the meetings, after which we spent more time with her, an *up*. One day my car was towed off because I had unknowingly parked in an unauthorized place, a *down*.

After attending all the meetings and bidding goodbye to my daughter and other friends who also were there, I drove home safely, an *up*. My husband was glad to see me, another *up*. Looking through the pile-up of mail that had arrived while I was out of town, I found a letter from the IRS saying we owed more money than we had paid, a whopping *down*. But the Lord provided us with the funds, an *up*.

Also, among the mail were letters from a friend in Ohio and my sister in North Carolina, with all good news, providing me with two more *ups*.

A few days after being home, the brakes on our car went out, a *down*, but it happened in our driveway, and I was able to stop before running into the storage building, an *up*.

As these things kept happening, I looked forward to the next week, wondering if the many *downs* would have passed. I looked forward to attending church at scheduled times, teaching Sunday School class to junior teens, singing in the choir, attending our ladies missionary meeting, going to my secular job, writing assigned manuscripts for a publisher. All good things planned, but I knew there would come along some *downs*. Amazingly, counting up all the happenings, I have always discovered there were more *ups* than *downs*. And the good part about the downs: He is as constantly close to me during the down times as He is in the up times!

Man that is born of a woman is of few days, and full of trouble. (Job 14:1 KJV)

The Lord also will be a refuge for the oppressed, a refuge in times of trouble. (Psalm 9:9 KJV)

Beloved, think it not strange concerning the fiery trial which is to try you, as though some strange thing happened unto you: but rejoice, inasmuch as ye are partakers of Christ's sufferings; that, when His glory shall be revealed, ye may be glad also with exceeding joy. (1 Peter 4:12-13 KJV)

November 17   Obeying God Brings Riches

A friend told me "I had a choice to lie and receive $1,000, or I could tell the truth and remain poor. I just couldn't lie! Something inside me kept me from wanting to lie. So I am still poor!"

Her statement told me she was indwelt by the Holy Spirit who prompted her to remember the commandment of her Lord. Also, it proved there are yet people in the world who choose to do right just because it is right, no matter how severe the temptation to do the opposite.

Her statement that she remained poor by refusing to lie was true as far as the money was concerned, but it was not true in another light. By taking this stand she was far richer than if she had received $1,000. She became worth far more to me as her friend and to the others to whom she was talking.

But, most of all, she pleased the Lord and He is the One whose rewards are the most important.

Her courage is a great example for each of us. We should always listen to the Holy Spirit, our Guide, who lives within us. When we are tempted to sin, we should heed His direction for our own good, the good of others about us, and that our Master might be honored.

There hath no temptation taken you but such as is common to man: but God is faithful, who will not suffer you to be tempted above that ye are able; but will with the temptation also make a way to escape, that ye may be able to bear it. (1 Corinthians 10:13 KJV)

Submit yourselves therefore to God. Resist the devil, and he will flee from you. (James 4:7 KJV)

Be sober, be vigilant; because your adversary the devil, as a roaring lion, walketh about, seeking whom he may devour: whom resist steadfast in the faith, knowing that the same afflictions are accomplished in your brethren that are in the world. (1 Peter 5:8-9 KJV)

November 18   God's Design for the Male He Created

Groups of women are stealthily going about to elevate the woman out of her rightful boundaries which God has set and never has rescinded. Should they succeed, among other horrible things, they would:

1. Deface true nobility of manhood;
2. Rob the male of his God-designed order;
3. Bring rottenness to a man's bones;
4. Tear down his prestigious place in society;

5. Cause him undue health problems and bring him to an early grave;
6. Muddle and bewilder little boy children's opinion of themselves;
7. Reduce a two-pillar home to no more than a half of a trembling pillar;
8. Unsettle children in the home, adding fears and creating distrust;
9. Unarm the family against vices; and
10. Dishonor God's masterpiece of creation—the man—by putting him on a lower plane than God set for him.

The things these unsavory groups have set out to do would bring only havoc, if not banished from the earth. There are some things we can do that might help, but there is one definite thing each of us can do that will certainly defeat the debasement of the male, and that is pray! Also, we can be careful to honor and esteem manhood, by starting with our own husbands, sons, fathers, ministers, male government and business leaders. After all, God has commanded us to do so!

> For the man is not of the woman; but the woman of the man. Neither was the man created for the woman; but the woman for the man. (1 Corinthians 11:8-9 KJV)

> Wives, submit yourselves unto your own husbands, as unto the Lord. For the husband is the head of the wife, even as Christ the is head of the church: and He is the savior of the body. Therefore as the church is subject unto Christ, so let the wives be to their own husbands in every thing. (Ephesians 5:22-24 KJV)

November 19   Folly of Taking Things for Granted

I remember back in a 1960's winter when an ice storm hit our town, felling trees (four of our evergreens and one elm), downing power and telephone lines, affecting the natural gas pressure, and causing flooding in low areas. We performed the bare essential activities by flashlight or candlelight and did a lot of substituting and improvising. We were without electricity for four hours (we were some of the more fortunate), and when the power came back on, I felt like shouting for joy!

I realized again how much we take for granted our conveniences, going daily about life accepting the good things without really appreciating them. Until we are without them!

In reflecting on this experience, I realized there are so many other things I am prone to take for granted that I ought to thank God for.

Seeing those who are terminally ill should cause us to be grateful for our health as a gift indeed precious. Knowing of those who are grief-stricken because of death – one woman I knew lost her father one week and her husband the next – should cause us to breathe a "thank you" to God for having our loved ones still with us, and we should make time to spend with them in fellowship while they are yet among the living.

Knowing there are motherless children should cause us to be glad our children have parents. Reading and hearing about couples among us who have been denied becoming parents, who so yearn to have children, should cause us to praise the Lord anew He has blessed us with children.

Aware of many false-teaching cults spawned by Satan and his demons should cause us to be jubilant once more that we have a living God who sent His marvelous Son to earth for our benefit. Of His own mouth, He said "I am come that they might have life and that they might have it abundantly."

Oh, the abundant life we have in Christ! Let's not take it lightly! Ah, the folly of taking everything about Who He is and What He does for us day-by-day for granted!

> Bless the Lord, O my soul, and forget not all His benefits: who forgiveth all thine iniquities; who healeth all thy diseases; who redeemeth thy life from destruction; who crowneth thee with lovingkindness and tender mercies; who satisfieth thy mouth with good things; so that thy youth is renewed like the eagle's. (Psalm 103:2-5 KJV)

> The thief cometh not, but for to steal, and to kill, and to destroy: I am come that they might have life, and that they might have it

more abundantly. I am the good shepherd: the good shepherd giveth His life for the sheep. (John 10:10-11 KJV)

November 20   ## God Made No Two Things Alike

I saw recently a picture of a giraffe, and beneath the picture were the words, "Not one animal is like another. Each one is as unique as a human's fingerprints." That statement just shouts loudly that we have a Marvelous, Majestic Creator, the One and Only Almighty Sovereign God!

Don't you know God had such a good time creating an elephant with a wee tail on one end and the huge trumpet nose on the front? And painting the zebra in stripes, and the leopard with spots? And on fish and fowl day of creation, feathering birds differently in color and beak and tweet, and sea creatures in different colors, sizes, even manner of swirl. In nature, not a single tree has bark or leaves like another, nor are there two leaves on the same tree alike! Each snowflake is different from another in the same snowfall.

And, to think, He made all of those things for His masterpiece of creation – Mankind – to enjoy! This masterpiece, the human being, cannot be cloned. Each one is unique, exclusive, distinctive, without an exact match. Yes, each of us has an exclusive fingerprint, voice resonance, pigment, personhood. There's nobody like you! Even identical twins have differences.

Isn't that wonderful? I would hate to live in a world with everyone looking like me, and having a voice like mine, and performing all acts my way. Nor would I want to be like any other person! So, that's how God sees it and does it and designs it. All for His glory, because He indeed is Unique, Exclusive, Exceptional, Distinctive, Matchless, Irreplaceable, One and Only Sovereign!

For by Him were all things created, that are in heaven, and that are in earth, visible and invisible, whether they be thrones, or dominions, or principalities, or powers: all things were created by Him, and for Him: and He is before all things, and by Him all things consist. (Colossians 1:16-17 KJV)

O the depth of the riches both of the wisdom and knowledge of God! How unsearchable are His judgments, and His ways past finding out! ... For of Him, and through Him, and to Him, are all things: to whom be glory forever. Amen. (Romans 11:33, 36 KJV)

November 21   God Forewarns His Creatures of Events

We know God instructs ants to store up more when there is going to be less plenteous food, and they obey by making more tunnels in their hills. Geese know when to plan their V-formations for travel. Squirrels start earlier burying acorns when they are aware of a colder-than-normal winter, and even their fur grows heavier. I read an article in a paper one autumn that the wooly worms had thicker wool.

Also, have you noticed little critters are restless before a storm or other upheaval? Once before an earthquake tremor in my hometown, our little dog began to growl before it started, and then when it hit, she barked furiously.

Our Omniscient Forecaster is also displaying before our very eyes signs that indicate another event is just ahead: the return of the Lord Jesus. It will be a glorious time for those who have put a saving trust in Jesus Christ as Savior. It will be a catastrophe for those who have not trusted in Him.

Like animals and birds and worms and ants who become restless, have you also noticed how unsettled the individual Christian is today? The same is true with congregations, missionaries, and ministers. There is a lot of bustle and shifting in our midst these days, because we are seeing signs Jesus told us to watch for coming to pass. For sure, I believe we who are being made restless are saying in action, if not in word, "Even so, come, Lord Jesus."

But take ye heed: behold, I have foretold you all things. ... And then shall they see the Son of Man coming in the clouds with great power and glory. ... So ye in like manner, when ye shall see these things come to pass, know that it is nigh, even at the doors. ... Take ye heed, watch and pray: for you know not when the time is. ... And what I say unto you I say unto all, Watch. (Mark 13:23, 26, 29, 33, 37 KJV)

November 22   Missionary Vacation: First Stop, Texas

Although our family has always been interested in the mission program of our church, and we have supported missions financially and prayerfully, we had never visited a mission in person. One summer, my husband and I decided to travel to Western states and visit some of them. Our daughter, Lisa, was a young teen and she invited her good friend, Angela, to go along. The four of us got all things together and set out.

We left Northeast Arkansas and drove across state into Oklahoma, spending a couple of nights on the road. Our first missions contact was in Lubbock, Texas at the Casa Bautista Misionera de Publicaciones, the Spanish Publishing Agency of the BMAA, where we enjoyed visiting with the ones publishing Sunday School and other literature for our Spanish-speaking missions around the world. My husband being a printer, he really became fascinated with seeing what Enlarged Literature Ministry was accomplishing.

Next door was the Mision Bautista Calvario. The pastor gave us a tour of the building. I sat in a pew and picked up a hymnal, but after thumbing through it, I put it back, as it was written in Spanish. At the time a revival was in progress, and the evangelist was from Fort Worth, Texas. Before leaving, we met the evangelist and his wife and their two sons and enjoyed visiting with them.

It was a blessing to us to have made our stop there, and our prayers thereafter for them are more meaningful, since viewing the work close up.

And He said unto them, Go ye into all the world, and preach the gospel to every creature. (Mark 16:15 KJV)

A friend and I were talking about the daughter of a mutual friend getting married soon. Both she and I had gone to the shower for the bride-to-be. It was several weeks later when we were talking. She asked "Have you gotten a thank you from her for your gift?" I replied that I had not.

Then she confided that one of the traditions of practice in their home was that when given a gift, it was not worn, nor taken a bite of, nor read, nor listened to, nor otherwise enjoyed until the one receiving the gift had sat down with pen and note card and a note of thanks was written, enveloped, stamped and put in place to be immediately mailed.

Afterward I thought about all the gifts God gives me daily. He loads me with benefits. Do I sometimes neglect to stop and say an audible "thank you, Lord" to Him. In fact, it would be all right to say to Him, before I open His gifts, "Thank You, Lord, for all the gifts I am sure to receive from You this day." Then I will delight myself as each time I open one.

> In every thing give thanks: for this is the will of God in Christ Jesus concerning you. (1Thessalonians 5:18 KJV)

Our second mission stop was in Albuquerque, New Mexico. We found the missionary's home without trying and without calling them first. We found them working in the yard. We visited with them that evening. Next morning, we three girls stayed at our motel, but my husband returned to the missionary's home and they two went out to look at property the mission wanted to buy and build a church. That evening we accepted their invitation for dinner (delicious homemade chili and stew). Leaving the girls (our two and the missionary's two) with the dishwashing, the missionary and his wife and my husband and I drove through Old Albuquerque, where we saw among other things, the Indians or Mexicans continuing their old ways of selling their wares on the sidewalks.

Another trip took us to the convention center where the National BMAA Annual meeting would be held in 1978. We were happy to find the security guard there and he gave us a splendid tour. The place was fabulous, spacious, elegant, comfortable, convenient, and I could go on and on with adjectives. I especially liked the plush red theater seats.

Our four girls went bowling and we visited more in their home. Also, in their home was their son, but also visiting with them was a little boy from the Texas Baptist Home for Children, whose name was Randy.

Sunday, we attended their church services. We were blessed and learned to love them even more. We felt God had great things in store for them and Albuquerque.

Ye have not chosen me, but I have chosen you, and ordained you, that ye should go and bring forth fruit, and that your fruit should remain: that whatsoever ye shall ask of the Father in my name, He may give it you. (John 15:16 KJV)

November 25   Missionary Vacation: Arizona

Next stop for a longer stay was Phoenix, Arizona. We were fascinated by the palm trees and the "another world" sensation. We looked up my husband's relatives first, as they were expecting us, and spent the evening with them: a man and wife, two teenage boys, and two aunts. Our two girls and the teenage boys got acquainted and played some yard games.

Next day we went to visit a missionary and wife and three children. They took us out to the Desert Cove Church where he had worked and which then had its own pastor. Then they drove us to the place they were next doing mission work. They were enthused about the prospects. We had a marvelous time of fellowship with them.

The missionary's wife remarked that what they really missed most was fellowship with sister churches. The Arizona churches were at great distances from each other. The pioneer work is a lonely work. I realized that perhaps we who have churches close to each other take that fact too much for granted. Her remark caused me to begin praying more for them in their longing for fellowship with other Christians.

We had to leave their home before we had finished visiting, but we had to go because my husband's two aunts had lunch waiting for us in another section of Phoenix. When we arrived, they served us "Mountains of Java," which is an interesting dish of unlikely type foods layered upon each other.

While visiting with these two aunts in their condominiums, their pastor came by and we enjoyed fellowshipping with him.

Leaving there, we visited my Uncle Edward and Aunt Mary where we ate dinner. Before leaving that late evening, we all gathered around the organ and sang hymns, with Aunt Mary playing.

Next morning early, we called the missionary once more to say farewell and to wish him Godspeed.

Then we headed northward. While still in Arizona, we toured Montezumba Castle and drove through picturesque Oak Creek Canyon, as well as breathtaking Grand Canyon. Everything was beautiful, even the barren deserts of the Navajo Reservation. We stopped there and the girls bought beads from the little Indian children. At one such stop we saw an Indian mother with her little Papoose. I asked her if I could hold the baby. She smiled and said yes. My husband took a picture with me holding the baby, but everything has its price. When I returned the infant to her, she said "One dollar." We gave her a Five Dollar bill.

One stop was in Provo, Utah, the hometown of the Osmond family. The girls, being fans of theirs, took pictures of their cars and home, but did not see the stars. Just north of there was Salt Lake City, and during the time we were there, we learned Ronald Reagan was there, too. Unfortunately, we did not run into him.

We turned eastward into Wyoming. There we saw *the deer and the antelope play* on the ranges. Back in Utah, we had seen *sheep in the meadow* and *cows in everyplace.*

While riding along I thought about God's fascinating world and to what great length He had gone to make the earth a place of grandeur for His beloved mankind. Great to be sure, it in no way compares to the immeasurable extent He went to provide the Plan and Sacrifice for His beloved man's redemption, and the incomprehensible degree of His love for sinful people. Praise be to His Wonderful Name!

That Christ may dwell in your hearts by faith; that ye, being rooted and grounded in love, may be able to comprehend with all saints what is the breadth, and length, and depth, and height; and to know the love of Christ, which passeth knowledge, that ye might be filled with all the fulness of God. (Ephesians 3:17-19 KJV)

November 26   Missionary Vacation: Colorado

We stopped in Fort Collins, Colorado on a Saturday night. Immediately upon arrival, we called the missionary in Denver. He gave us good directions for getting to his mission. Sunday morning, we left the inn in plenty of time to get there for services. It wasn't long before we began to doubt that we would make it on time, if at all. For one thing, we came upon an accident, an overturned motor home, and my husband joined others to assist. Then, in our hurry to make up for lost time, we missed seeing the turn-off and had to go many miles out of the way. We stopped twice more for directions and were even escorted part of the way by a policeman.

We did get there, however. The missionary and his wife were just winding up singing a beautiful duet, "Jesus, I Come," when we entered. Also visiting the mission were a pastor and his wife from Oklahoma, and that pastor brought the morning message on "Don't Muzzle the Ox." Little did we surmise that someday in our future, that particular pastor would be come to our town and be the pastor of a sister church!

Before we had arrived at the church that morning, my husband told us to hurry to the car immediately after services; that we would try to beat the heavy traffic out of Denver, and we would try to eat lunch somewhere out of town, because we had reservations for the night in far-off Salina, Kansas.

Well, after services we were talking with the friendly folks of the mission there, and, to top it off, the missionary's wife said to me matter-of-factly, "We have prepared lunch for you. So, come on over to the house," which happened to be next door. What happened was, we four, together with the visiting pastor and wife, accepted the invitation and went to their home for lunch. We had a marvelous time in Christian fellowship. Our daughter and her friend enjoyed visiting with the missionary's daughter. We were made to appreciate them and their work even more after being with them.

The missionary's wife remarked that she missed the fellowship of sisters in Christ in the work there. She spoke almost the same words as the other missionaries had expressed. It seemed they wanted to keep extending the visit. I sensed there was a kind of lonesomeness on their faces when we would leave.

We left after two o'clock and got into Salina after eleven, tired indeed, but I would not take anything for the time we spent in Denver with those wonderful Christian friends.

Another interesting coincidence of being in the same place at the same time of a celebrity occurred when we were in Denver. The few hours we were there was the same time Princess Grace of Monaco came to that city. Unfortunately, as with Ronald Reagan in Salt Lake City when we were there, and we did not see him, neither did we run into Princess Grace in Denver. But, of course, we flitted through!

After Salina, through Missouri, stopping only to see the Truman Library, we arrived at last in good ole Arkansas, settling down for two days in Harrison. Then on home, bone weary, but with a memory brimming with wonderful missionary visiting and fellowshipping experiences!

That which we have seen and heard declare we unto you, that ye also may have fellowship with us: and truly our fellowship is with the Father, and with His Son Jesus Christ. (1 John 1:3 KJV)

November 27　　　　　　　　　　## A Delight to Get an Allowance

As a kid, did you get an allowance in money for you to spend however you wished? I did during high school, way back in the 1940's and 1950's, and it was one dollar per week. That was before the days of free lunches, so I used part of that for lunch in the school cafeteria. Lunches were a quarter a day, so that meant I could eat at least two and maybe three lunches during the week and have another quarter to spread out over the other two days.

I liked Monday's spaghetti lunch and Friday's vegetable soup and half a peanut butter sandwich and half a grilled cheese sandwich. We always had milk with our meals. If I spent all but one quarter for lunches, I went next door to the little store where I bought foods like chips and candy bars one day at a nickel apiece. With my last dime I'd go to the grocery store on the corner from the school and buy an apple.

Did you know the Lord doles out allowances for His children? On one occasion He moved a compassionate king to release one of God's people from prison and gave him a daily allowance. The man's name was Jehoiachin. He wasn't given a great supply of goods to last him for months, but was given his allotment day by day. (See the scripture below.)

This is fitting for each one of God's children. A daily portion is really all we need. We do not need tomorrow's or next week's or next month's supply, for those times have not yet dawned and the needs for those days unborn. Each day's supply is all we can enjoy. Jehoiachin's story is our story, for we too have a guaranteed supply given to us by our King. It is a perpetual and generous portion, just enough. In Jesus everything you will ever need has been stored up for you. So, let's enjoy our day by day allowance, and don't fret a bit about our tomorrows.

> And [the King of Babylon] spake kindly to [Jehoiachin], and set his throne above the throne of the kings that were with him in Babylon; and changed his prison garments: and he did eat bread continually before him all the days of his life. And his allowance was a continual allowance given him of the king, a daily rate for every day, all the days of his life. (2 Kings 25:29-30 KJV)

> Give us day by day our daily bread. (Luke 11:3 KJV)

> But my God shall supply all your need according to His riches in glory by Christ Jesus. (Philippians 4:19 KJV)

Do you know, God is looking for persons to stand in the gap or between hedges? In other words, He needs someone to fill an empty spot or to block a hole between hedges at times.

There is a woman, whose name is Sally, whom I have identified as a *gap or hedge filler.* She is a retired widow. Her children and grandchildren live far away in other parts of the country, and she does not get to spend time with them as she would like. But she looks out for other women's children, other widows, those she is acquainted with, and even with strangers.

She is especially available for filling spots made empty in her church. When someone who normally folds the Sunday bulletins is unavailable, she steps in and does the bulletin folding. In Sunday School class, when she hears of someone who has a doctor appointment and does not have a ride, she at once says she will do it. Even though she is not an avid garden club person, one day the leader of the local garden club did not know the place in another city where the meeting was to be held. Sally quickly said she would find the place and drive her to that meeting. To do so, she learned the address, and a few days before the meeting drove alone to the site, marking the various roads to take.

Once Sally heard of a shut-in who was having difficulty making her own meals. She learned that person liked a beef pot roast. Sally hurried to the grocery store, bought the fixings for a pot roast and took it to her the next day at noon. The shut-in was so happily surprised. It being enough for several servings, she lauded Sally exuberantly with "Not only was it good for lunch and dinner, but the next day I ate some of it for breakfast."

Yes, Sally goes about filling empty places, placing herself in gaps, all for her Lord. Although she leaves those she serves wonderfully blessed, she gets more delight than anyone, because she looks for ways to exalt and serve her Lord.

The people of the land have used oppression, and exercised robbery, and have vexed the poor and needy: yea, they have oppressed the stranger wrongfully. And I sought for a man among them, that should make up the hedge, and stand in the gap before me for the land, that I should not destroy it: but I found none. (Ezekiel 22:29-30 KJV)

And whatsoever ye do in word or deed, do all in the name of the Lord Jesus, giving thanks to God and the Father by Him. (Colossians 3:17 KJV)

November 29   I Suffer No Lack

Our Heavenly Father owns everything, and He wants to bestow good things on His children. He supplies material things, as food, shelter and clothing. He decorates the earth with color and fragrance and music from all directions for our hearing and seeing with enjoyment.

He equips our minds with knowledge, so we can discern how to go about living and prospering on this earth. Best of all, He gives us a hunger and thirst for Himself in our inner being. By studying His word and spending time with Him in prayer and meditation, we come to know the fruits of the spirit: love, joy, peace, longsuffering, gentleness, goodness, faith, meekness, and temperance.

He delights in each one of us. First and foremost, He wants you and me to have the relationship of Father and child, and this is accomplished by repenting of sin and accepting God's Beloved Son Jesus Christ as personal Lord and Savior. Then, that one is a born-again Christian, a member of God's family.

From that point forward, God begins to bless His child with all manner of good things, and enables him or her to enjoy the abundant life. As we travel our Christian journey the rest of our lives, we can look around and see not one of us suffers any lack!

And God is able to make all grace abound toward you; that ye, always having all sufficiency in all things, may abound to every good work. (2 Corinthians 9:8 KJV)

Whom do I love? Let me count them …

Earliest loves were my parents, the two I saw first every morning and last at end of day, from infancy through toddlerhood. It was a *trusting love*. When each of my four siblings came into our home, with whom I had to learn to share space and parental attention, I felt a *bonding love*. By the time we had grown up, I loved each one for her own unique self.

When I selected my life's mate, he took an enormous portion of my love. I thought I loved him the most possible on our wedding day, but as passing anniversaries grew in number, wherein we shared the delights and rigors of all seasons of our marriage, I found I loved him more and more. Ours was a *melding love*.

Oh, what affection I knew when I looked into the precious face of our baby the first time! I was awestruck that God would entrust such a fragile little person into her Daddy's and my custody to care for and bring up. That was a *doting love*.

When our daughter grew up, married, and gave us four grandchildren, I was so thankfully thrilled to be present on the day of each one's birth. I felt an *all-encompassing love* for each, as I watched them grow up and excel in their endeavors and achievements.

Other loves I have known – old houses I called home, from childhood to the present. Old school houses I attended have fond places in my heart. These I consider *sentimental loves*.

I hold fast a *patriotic love* for my country, so grateful to God who allowed me to be a native-born person of this great America, and for endowing me with countless liberties. I love the three churches I have belonged to, the first being during my growing up years, the second one where my husband, child and I worshiped together, and the present one, where, since my move to another state after becoming a widow, I now worship. This love is two-fold: *devotion to Jesus love* and *fellowship with others love*.

I treasure the assortment of friends and kinfolks who have merged into my life along the way, whose interactions have honed off some, but not all, of my rough edges. From them I am the beneficiary of *encouraging and supporting love*.

And for God, the most important One, I feel a *deep-in-my-heart adoration*, which grows more wonderful the longer I live. I thank Him, the Source of all love, for granting me all the loves of my life. If I have learned anything at all during my life's journey, it is that the one ingredient that makes the whole of life worth living is *love*.

As the Father hath loved Me, so have I loved you: continue ye in my love. ... This is my commandment, That ye love one another, as I have loved you. (John 15:9, 12 KJV)

Love worketh no ill to his neighbor: therefore love is the fulfilling of the law. (Romans 13:10 KJV)

Beloved, let us love one another: for love is of God; and every one that loveth is born of God, and knoweth God. ... Beloved, if God so loved us, we ought also to love one another. (1 John 4:7, 11 KJV)

December 1   Wholeheartedly Thankful

Some said one time that the favorite and most-quoted Psalm is the "Shepherd Psalm," being the twenty-third. And running a close second is Psalm 100. It is extra special at Thanksgiving. I love both of those psalms, and thought I knew them through and through.

Then I listened to a speaker from North Carolina expound Psalm 100. Being a free-lance writer, and knowing the importance of *who, what, when, where, why* and *how* in writing, I was awe-struck when she spoke using those "Five W's and One H." I took notes and found out I had not searched out the many gold nuggets she brought to my attention. Turn in your Bible to Psalm 100, and discover these nuggets of gold.

It is totally a Psalm of Praise. It contains seven active verbs.

The *who* is The Lord who is mentioned four times in this Psalm. He is the One who deserves our thanks for all things as He is the giver of all our blessings.

The *what* is to praise His Name.

The *when* is now. The Psalm is written in the present tense.

The *where* is inside His gates, referring to His house of worship, and in His Courts, which means everywhere outside.

The *how* is where the active verbs come into significance:

"Make" a joyful noise (using lips and voice; no silence allowed).

"Serve" with gladness (no trace of sadness).

"Come" before His presence with singing (tuneful or not).

"Know" for a fact who God is and what He has done, is doing, and will do (using the brain and just thinking about it all).

"Enter" means to get up, walk, move forward and show by action (no sitting down on the job).

"Be thankful" personally for all His benefits (He loads us with benefits).

"Bless His Name" for He alone is worthy. Adore Him (expressing your love for Him, for He delights to hear you say it).

The *why* is found in the last verse. For the Lord is good. His mercy is everlasting; His truth endures to all generations (especially in the now in which you and I live).

December 2   Five Senses Significant to Faith

The human body has five senses: seeing, hearing, smelling, tasting, and touching. In God's Word we find the use of those senses pertaining to our faith. All scriptures below are KJV.

The sense of hearing ranks first, because we read in Romans 10:17: "So then faith cometh by hearing, and hearing by the Word of God." Also, in Isaiah 55:3, God says, "Incline your ear, and come unto Me: hear, and your soul shall live..." One has to hear the Word before he can act on it.

The next sense would be the seeing. That person would have to see by thinking through what he has heard. He would realize to whom he needed to look for salvation. In Isaiah 45:22, we read, "Look unto Me, and be ye saved, all the ends of the earth: for I am God, and there is none else."

After coming to an understanding of what he has observed by faith, and he receives Jesus as Savior, his sense of smell comes into being.

The one having placed faith in Jesus realizes the preciousness of his position. His dirty, sinful, filthy, stinking past has been replaced by having been cleansed and he is in a new environment. He has come into the family of the Rose of Sharon and the Lily of the Valley, both of which emit a pleasant fragrance. David expresses this in Psalm 45:8: "All thy garments smell of myrrh, and aloes, and cassia, out of the ivory palaces, whereby they have made thee glad." Enjoying such peace and gladness with this sense, the person then seeks ways to taste the sense of faith.

Being in the closeness of Jesus, the person can say "O taste and see that the Lord is good: blessed is the man that trusteth in Him," Psalm 34:8. He seeks to know more about his Lord, by studying His scriptures. Like David he will be able to say "How sweet are thy words unto my taste! Yea, sweeter than honey to my mouth!" Psalm 119:103.

The touch of faith comes from the Holy Spirit. When a sinner hears the gospel message, the Holy Spirit accompanies the message and touches the heart of the hearer. He touches urgingly for that one to trust Christ as Savior. When that person says yes, then the Holy Spirit comes to indwell that person from that point on. He makes His touch known all during that person's life, guiding, steering, enlightening, disciplining, and in other ways, all for the good and joy of that person as he serves the Lord.

December 3   Spread Joy to Joyless

During all of our years as a married couple, my husband and I spent only one Christmas alone, and that was our first one. Funds were skimpy and family members were distanced. I gave him a pocket knife (which he kept all his life), and he gave me a chenille robe (which I wore many years thereafter). Our special food was torn up angel food cake with boiled custard from the grocery store poured over it. We had a happy time that first year.

But all years thereafter, we were mixing and mingling with many members of both our families. We were at their houses or some were coming to ours. We always looked forward to our Christmases. First of all, it was because our Savior was born and His birth brought hope and joy to our living.

As years passed, my husband noticed some folks were left alone and neglected during this wonderful season. Among them were two in his extended family. The man lived alone and all his siblings and even his own children were thousands of miles away and never invited him to be with them nor did they visit him at any time. Another was a widow, who had no children, nor any close relative, nor apparently any close friend. We did not know why they had been abandoned. We did not want to know.

So, he laid his plan out before me, and I thought it a wonderful idea. On one of the nights when we would have family members together for a meal during Christmas week, we would invite both of these loners. Hesitatingly, and perhaps surprised, they did accept, and showed up. They joined in the hustle and bustle and noise of the crowd, and we saw radiance replace their drooping countenances. After the meal, with tables spread out all over the house, we gave gifts. They brought no gifts but were given gifts. Again, I saw the eyes of both to shine. I think the woman's eyes had blurred with tears.

I am so glad my husband came up with this idea. That became our tradition every year thereafter. I always felt a special peace and joy in being a participant in those events.

The joy we know we ought to spread to others who lack that joy. We are commissioned by Jesus to be salt and light to others who seem to have no hope. Most of all, we are to share the good news of our Savior, how He cares for everyone, no matter the situation a person has fallen into. Amazingly, the joy we saw on the faces of these two brought double joy to us!

> And the Lord said unto the servant, Go out into the highways and hedges, and compel them to come in, that my house may be filled. (Luke 14:23 KJV)

> Put on therefore, as the elect of God, holy and beloved, bowels of mercies, kindness, humbleness of mind, meekness, longsuffering; ... (Colossians 3:12 KJV)

A lot of folks have the idea that vacation time from work and retirement from work are the only times of fun. Well, if only at those times would one find joy, what an awful kind of life. Finally, when having thought it through, those with ideas like that, they will find the idle, non-productive life becomes boring. They come to the conclusion," I must find a work to do! I must accomplish! I must produce!"

That's a sensible conclusion! Even God, the Creator, continues to work. The first instruction to Adam was that he was to work, to tend to the garden and animals God had created. Only after Adam and Eve sinned did God allow the hindrances to make their work harder.

There is a world of joy in life once we know where to find it, and it involves work, labor, employment, industry, toil, sweat, grind, but the end is accomplishment, goal reaching, promotion, growth, and so much more.

It has been proven that working people are healthier people, stronger and most successful. The idea of working is not to deny ourselves happiness, but to bring help and happiness to others, and consequently to ourselves.

Even things of nature radiate joy and emit that joy to people. Birds sing, flowers bloom, trees leaf, the moon shines in its cycle. Everything does its work.

Work is an outward expression of one's ambition, energy, and desire for accomplishment. It is the path over which one's desires travel. Accomplishment invariably leads to the threshold of joy. That is why the diligent worker sings or whistles at his task, for he is expressing that which is in his heart. The better he works, the louder he sings; the more joy he finds in his work, the finer his labors.

And the Lord God took the man, and put him into the garden of Eden, to dress it and to keep it. (Genesis 2:15 KJV)

So built we the wall; and all the wall was joined together unto the half thereof: for the people had a mind to work. (Nehemiah 4:6 KJV)

I must work the works of Him that sent Me, while it is day: the night cometh, when no man can work. (John 9:4 KJV)

In reading after some of the historical facts pertaining to our American leaders, I always find delight in reading the comments, and even prayers, of some of them. Trusting God always brings success during the tenure of such leaders. Here are words of some of them:

"Direct my thought, words and work, wash away my sins in the immaculate blood of the Lamb, and purge my heart by Thy Holy Spirit. ... Daily frame me more and more into the likeness of Jesus Christ." George Washington, first U.S. President.

"There are a good many problems before the American people today, and before me as President, but I expect to find the solution to those problems just in the proportion that I am faithful in the study of the word of God." Woodrow Wilson, twenty-eighth U.S. President.

"We all can pray. We all should pray. We should ask the fulfillment of God's will. We should ask for courage, wisdom, for the quietness of soul which comes alone to them who place their lives in His hands." Harry S. Truman, thirty-third U.S. President.

"America was founded by people who believed that God was their rock of safety. I recognize we must be cautious in claiming that God is on our side, but I think it's all right to keep asking if we're on His side." Ronald Reagan, fortieth U.S. President.

"The Lord our God be with us, as He was with our fathers; may He not leave us or forsake us; so that He may incline our hearts to Him, to walk in all His ways . . . that all people of the earth may know that the Lord is God; there is no other." George Bush, forty-first U.S. President.

Moreover thou shalt provide out of all the people able men, such as fear God, men of truth, hating covetousness; and place such over them, to be rulers of thousands, and rulers of hundreds, rulers of fifties, and rulers of tens. (Exodus 18:21 KJV)

A kid needs a dad who loves the kid's mother and shows it in the presence of the kid, so that the kid will be spared the harsh, deserted feelings that come should a dad and mom part. A kid needs a dad to hold him or her in his lap and give a tight hug, so close the kid can feel his unshaven whiskers. Then that kid will feel steadfastly secure.

A kid needs a dad who brags on him when winning, as well as hugs and grins if there is a no-win. That way the kid can see dad's love is unconditional. A kid needs a dad who lays down his newspaper or turns off the TV to give full-faced audience when his kid wants to talk. So, then that kid will know he is important.

A kid needs a dad who allows his kid to grow up and make independent decisions, and then that same kid needs a dad who stays as loyal comrade when consequences come in.

A kid needs a dad who believes in and worships God and takes his place as head of the home, and a kid needs to hear dad saying his kid's name when he prays, so the kid will want to do right.

A kid needs a dad who shows he enjoys his kid's company, who likes to talk to his kid, and play with his kid, spending time alone with his kid, so that that kid will know deep down inside that the he is special.

A kid needs a dad who salutes his nation's flag, obeys his nation's laws, and votes in every election, to promote and secure the good of his home, his community, his country, and especially his kid.

> And ye shall teach them your children, speaking of them when thou sittest in thine house, and when thou walkest by the way, when thou liest down, and when you risest up. And thou shalt write them upon the door posts of thine house, and upon thy gates. (Deuteronomy 11:19-20 KJV)

> And, ye fathers, provoke not your children to wrath: but bring them up in the nurture and admonition of the Lord. (Ephesians 6:4 KJV)

Strangers, we met at a writers' conference. We kept jostling into each other there in the crowd of authors and publishers. Finding ourselves sitting at the same table for the third time that day, we chuckled at our coincidences. We set a time to meet for dinner that evening.

That began an acquaintance that blossomed. We learned we each had a daughter, her Kate and my Lisa. We both liked to write poetry. Comparing our respective maidenhood suitors, we admitted we each had married the man we loved. Her Brick was already deceased; my Bill was still living, to whom I introduced her later, at the Awards Banquet of that event. A special bonding commenced.

Living a far distance from each other, we saw each other only every two or three years, always at another writers' convention. But we kept in touch by random note or phone call. When she had a problem, she called me. When I needed someone to jolly me along, her sunny voice and words did just that.

When my beloved Bill died, I called her. I felt her deep-caring hug over the phone line as she sobbed with me.

The last time we were together in person at another writers' meeting, she told me she had developed a vision malady, and was not able to see except peripherally. So, she arranged that I be seated to her left, her best visual position.

Then, one day her Kate called me to say her mother had become ill suddenly. All too soon, she called again to say my writer friend had died. What a weighty ache I felt!

Although her death had been a decade past, one day I felt an aching lonesomeness for my friend. Oh, how I wished she were here to jolly me along! Then, I remembered a book she had given me containing some of her poems. Scampering to the book shelf, I took it down, opened it and began to read her penned words. I could hear her voice again. My throbbing lonesomeness took flight! Yes, her words jollied me along. I closed the book, and joyfully thanked God for providing this wonderful friend, who at that time, based on her profession, was in the presence of God Himself.

The great man of God, Charles H. Spurgeon, said: "Friendship is one of the sweetest joys of life. Many might have failed beneath the bitterness of their trial had they not found a friend."

A friend loveth at all times, and a brother is born for adversity. (Proverbs 17:17 KJV)

Open rebuke is better than secret love. Faithful are the wounds of a friend; but the kisses of an enemy are deceitful. (Proverbs 27:5-6 KJV)

December 8   Esteem for Buildings

We know we are not to reverence or put godly awe on anything or anyone other than God, but certain architecture erected for godly purpose always finds a high respect in those who see or enter them. In the Bible, Solomon's Temple was so honored. In fact, God was the architect who selected what materials were to be used. That building had a special place in the hearts of all Hebrews.

In many countries there is at least one special building of renown that the citizens are proud of and want to speak of in heart-felt boasting, such as the Notre Dame in Paris. Many are centuries old.

The White House, the home of Presidents of the United States, is commonly believed to be the oldest building in Washington. Construction began in 1792, while George Washington was still President, and it was first occupied in 1800 by John Adams, the second President, and his family while still unfinished. Every President since Adams has lived there for at least a portion of his term of office. The building was designed by an Irishman, and erected on a site recommended by a Frenchman. Later, during the War of 1812, it was partially destroyed by fire ignited by the British. The edifice was first painted white after the War of 1812 to conceal the smoke stains left by the fire. It was freshly painted every four years, just prior to the inauguration of a new President.

Although it had been unofficially called "The White House" long before the time of Theodore Roosevelt, it was he who suggested to Congress that that appellation become the official designation for the

President's home. It has always stood on its present tree-shaded grounds on Pennsylvania Avenue. The White House holds a special patriotic place in every American's heart. Also, the Capitol Buildings of all fifty states of our country are impressively designed by great architects and are built with the best of materials. One couple I knew visited every state's capitol building except the ones in Hawaii and Alaska during their summer vacations after they had reached retirement age. They were always delighted to tell anyone who would listen of the magnificence of the buildings, and were ready to show photos of those places.

But you and I know, the finest, most elaborately designed building is only temporary. All of us like such wonderful things to last on and on. Praise God, we can look forward to buildings in our future that will last forever, never need refurbishing, never suffer erosion. God has promised His children those wonderful buildings in which we will live and enjoy their beauty eternally. Jesus said He was going away to prepare mansions for His followers. He has been doing that now for over two millenniums. Ever wonder what our manses will look like? Whatever mine shall be, it will be just right! How about you?

> In My Father's house are many mansions: if it were not so, I would have told you. I go to prepare a place for you. And if I go and prepare a place for you, I will come again, and receive you unto Myself; that where I am, there ye may be also. (John 14:2-3 KJV)

December 9   Lavished with God's Jewels

I believe every human being likes jewels, the wealthy who can afford them, and the poor who can only wish for them. An infant, when sitting on the lap of someone who has rings or a bracelet, will begin to finger the colorful, shining things.

Although we were not a wealthy family when I was growing up, we always had our ample needs provided and we adorned ourselves with some luxuries. However, I remember when I was a child, Daddy surprised Mama by handing her a little box that held her birthstone.

She was so excited, she suddenly hugged Daddy and kissed him right there in front of us kids.

Jewels have to do with wealth, to be sure, but also with royalty, prominence, and celebrity. Jewelry is associated with weddings. I've read that a Hebrew bride is given the jewels of her bridegroom's father which she adorns herself with on her wedding day.

And Who is it that set all the many jewels in the clay of this earth? Our Wonderful Almighty God, who created everything that exists, that's who! He left it to mankind to unearth them, and polish them, and mount them in all places. He wants His children to enjoy them.

While we enjoy gems in all their beauty on this earth, someday we will be able to delight in them in all their wondrous array in eternity. We read in Revelation that the twelve gates of the Holy City will be of pearl. The twelve foundations will be of gems. Because Jesus is the Bridegroom of His Bride, the Church, there will be a wedding to take place, and don't you reckon those composing that Bride will be decked out in fine array with jewels?

> I will greatly rejoice in the Lord, my soul shall be joyful in my God; for He hath clothed me with the garments of salvation, He hath covered me with the robe of righteousness, as a bridegroom decketh himself with ornaments, and as a bride adorneth herself with her jewels. (Isaiah 61:10 KJV)

> And the wall of the city had twelve foundations, and in them the names of the twelve apostles of the Lamb. ... And the foundations of the wall of the city were garnished with all manner of precious stones. The first foundations was jasper; the second, sapphire; the third, a chalcedony; the fourth, an emerald; the fifth, sardonyx; the sixty, sardius; the seventh, chrysolite; the eighth, beryl; the ninth, a topaz; the tenth, a chrysoprasus; the eleventh, a jacinth; the twelfth, an amethyst. (Revelation 21:14, 19-21KJV)

The Bible has account after account of impossible happenings. It proves over and over that where mankind, science and even common sense says "No Way!" God has caused an impossibility to become a possibility.

Some examples include:

+   The Red Sea split so people could walk through on dry ground. (Exodus 14:21-22)
+   A donkey talked. (Numbers 22:21-39)
+   The sun and the moon stood still about a whole day. (Joshua 10:13-14)
+   Three men were thrown into fiery pit, heated seven times hotter than just hot, and they did not burn nor did their clothes even get singed. (Daniel 3:19-27)
+   A man thrown into a den of human-eating lions, but untouched. (Daniel 6:16-23)
+   A fish swallowed a man and then vomited him out. (Book of Jonah)
+   The most important one: A virgin had a Baby. (Luke 1-2)

In the New Testament Jesus performed miracles that were supernatural, which those who saw them take place thought "this is just not possible." He fed over 5,000 with five loaves and two fishes; He gave sight to a man born blind; He raised a man from the grave who had been dead four days, and so many, many more. And He continues to do the impossible today. He heals the person to whom the doctor says "There's nothing else that can be done for you. You will die."

Ah Lord God! behold, thou hast made the heaven and the earth by thy great power and stretched out arm, and there is nothing too hard for thee. (Jeremiah 32:17 KJV)

But Jesus beheld them, and said unto them, With men this is impossible; but with God all things are possible. (Matthew 19:26 KJV)

Now unto Him that is able to do exceeding abundantly above all that we ask or think, according to the power that worketh in us, unto Him be glory in the church by Christ Jesus throughout all ages, world without end. Amen. (Ephesians 3:20-21 KJV)

December 11   Exalted Above the Heavens

We've heard the expression "The sky is the limit," as though there is nothing above the sky. And we are awestruck when we see a brilliant display in our sky, such as "the northern lights," otherwise known as the aurora borealis. The splendor of that sight is beyond description.

The heavens above have always amazed man's perception. Stars, planets, clouds, meteors, lightning bolts, and the rainbow have staggered man's comprehension. The Bible has numerous expressions of the splendor of the heavens, especially the Psalmist David. Even the stars we chance to see as we look up into our piece of night sky are only a teeny part of the whole. Only God knows how many trillions of stars He created, and He has named each star. Indeed, the Psalmist speaks of all things in the heavens as glorious.

But, the Psalmist goes farther than that – he describes in majestic words the One who created the heavens – The Almighty God! All the splendor and excellence and grandeur of the heavens pale significantly when compared to the glory and honor and magnificence of God who created everything. He says God is exalted above the heavens. Everything contained in the heavens is but a dim shadow of the Creator's majestic Being. His glory surpasses everything in His creation!

What a wonderful God! Although so glorious, He so cares for all persons He has created, and He wants to share all of creation, especially someday in the heavens with us. He has made a way we can have that privilege. He sent His Son Jesus Christ to pay our sin debt, and by receiving Him into our hearts as Lord and Savior, He will someday bring us to heaven to behold all the wonders He wants to share with us. Praise His Holy Name!

Be thou exalted, O God, above the heavens: let thy glory be above all the earth. (Psalm 57:11 KJV)

The Lord is high above all nations, and His glory above the heavens. (Psalm 113:4 KJV)

Let them praise the name of the Lord: for His name alone is excellent; His glory is above the earth and heaven. (Psalm 148:13 KJV)

December 12   God's Gifts to His Children

Someone who was visiting me recently looked around the room and said, "You have so many interesting things." I told her nearly everything around the room were gifts from kin and friends – vases, pictures on the wall, books in shelves, coasters, framed photos, throws and afghans, music box, and so many more things. Each one is a treasure with a sentimental scenario attached.

After she left, I thought about my many gifts that I treasure. Which one would I consider my best? I could not prefer one over the other.

Then, I begin to focus on the gifts God has given me. I realized I was enveloped with His gifts, day by day. In searching for a scripture to fit, there are so many scattered from cover to cover of the Bible. I finally settled on one: Joshua 1. Here are just a few of God's wonderful gifts to me, and to you, His child, that we need day by day.

> Purpose to Pursue (Joshua 1:2)
> Protection to Prevail (Joshua 1:5)
> Principles to Practice (Joshua 1:7)
> Prosperity Potential (Joshua 1:8)
> Peace to Placate (Joshua 1:9)
> Presence of God permanently (Joshua 1:9)

Every good gift and every perfect gift is from above, and cometh down from the Father of lights, with whom is no variableness, neither shadow of turning. (James 1:17 KJV)

December 13   You Cannot Steal My Joy

You can curse at me, but you cannot curse me: I belong to the King of Kings. You can push me down and trample me, but you cannot break my spirit: I belong to the King of Kings.

You can rob me of my possessions, but you cannot touch my inheritance: I belong to the King of Kings. You can burn my house and all its furnishings, but you'll fall in defeat against my future heavenly mansion: I belong to the King of Kings.

You can mutilate my body and cause pain above measure, but you cannot stand against my promised immortal resurrected body: I belong to the King of Kings.

You can harm my beloved family, but you cannot separate us. We'll be reunited in heaven: We belong to the King of Kings.

That the trial of your faith, being much more precious than of gold that perisheth, though it be tried with fire, might be found unto praise and honor and glory at the appearing of Jesus Christ: whom having not seen, ye love; in whom, though now ye see Him not, yet believing, ye rejoice with joy unspeakable and full of glory. (1 Peter 1:7-8 KJV)

But ye are a chosen generation, a royal priesthood, an holy nation, a peculiar people; that ye should shew forth the praises of Him who hath called you out of darkness into His marvelous light. (1 Peter 2:9 KJV)

I live in Mid-Tennessee, and I have discovered there is not a level piece of ground nor a road without a bend or curve in it. I cannot see far as I drive the avenues, boulevards, lanes, roads and streets. I must always drive with caution for I don't know what I will encounter over the ridge I approach or around that curve ahead. I must stay focused.

Reflecting on this fact one day, I compared it to this earthly journey we Christians are on. When we set out to perform our assigned duties, we have no idea of what we will be thrown across our lanes of travel. The Lord said we would have all manner of obstacles to cope with, but He promised that He would never leave us nor forsake us. He meant that for whatever melee we run into.

Every now and then we might happen upon a smooth road, but it usually turns out to be too short. Someday, we'll enjoy streets of gold that God has promised us: no bumps, ridges or scary curves. So, until then, let's just trust Him as we make our journey here below.

Trust in the Lord with all thine heart; and lean not unto thine own understanding. In all thy ways acknowledge Him, and He shall direct thy paths. (Proverbs 3:5-6 KJV)

As we begin to focus on Christmas at this time of year, sometimes it brings on a great deal of stress. Besides buying gifts and traveling distances, sometime, there are other things that make some folks glad when the season has passed. They fret about all manner of insecurities – their careers, kids going to college, ill health – to name a few. Their weighty stresses cause absence of peace in their lives, mentally, physically, intellectually, and especially spiritually.

Absence of this peace is a paradox to what the angel said to the shepherds concerning the birth of the Christ Child. "And the angel said unto them, Fear not: for, behold, I bring you good tidings of great joy, which shall be to all people. For unto you is born this day in the city of

David a Savior, which is Christ the Lord. ... And suddenly there was with the angel a multitude of the heavenly host praising God, and saying, Glory to God in the highest and on earth peace, good will toward men. (Luke 2:10-11, 13-14 KJV). His purpose in coming was to bring peace.

When Jesus was speaking to His apostles about going away, He told them He would give them peace. After His resurrection, when He appeared to them, He again said "Peace be unto you." (John 20:21 KJV)

As children of God, peace should be our normal state. We need to do what King David wrote: "Seek peace and pursue it," and the stresses will lessen and even vanish. We need to begin each day pursuing peace, and all during the day as stressful situations crop up in our lives. Also, it would be good to refer to Psalm 23 and adhere to the words "He maketh me to lie down in green pastures: He leadeth me beside the still waters."

The Apostle Paul knew the importance of peace. He began many of his epistles with the words "Peace be unto you." He ended many of them with "Grace, mercy and peace be yours." Peace is the alpha and omega of the Christian's well-being.

Depart from evil, and do good; seek peace, and pursue it. (Psalm 34:14 KJV)

Thou wilt keep him in perfect peace, whose mind is stayed on thee: because he trusteth in thee. (Isaiah 26:3 KJV)

December 16   A Regal Beginning and Resplendent Future

God's Word gives definite answers to life's questions, answers that give us hope.

+ *Where did I come from?* I came from the heart and mind of the Omnipotent and Omniscient God, who made me in His image.
+ *Who am I?* I am a child of God, heir of God, and co-heir with Jesus Christ His Son.

- *What is my purpose or reason for being on this earth?* I am here to serve and glorify the God who created me, and to delight in pleasing Him.
- *How am I supposed to live, or what is my conduct supposed to be?* I should live according to the commandments which God has given me in His Word, which are set down for my best and for my maturity. I am to so conduct myself both in word and deed that will cause others who do not know Jesus as Savior to want to become as I am, a child of God, with all the magnificent amenities!
- *Where do I go when I leave this earth?* I will go to Heaven where God is and will enjoy all that He has prepared for me – the finest habitat, royal clothing, and so much more!
- *How long will I live with God in Heaven?* Forever. Eternally. Never ending. I will live as long as God lives, and He is from everlasting to everlasting.

For since the beginning of the world men have not heard, nor perceived by the ear, neither hath the eye seen, O God, beside thee, what He hath prepared for him that waiteth for him. (Isaiah 64:4 KJV)

But as it is written, Eye hath not seen, nor ear heard, neither have entered into the heart of man, the things which God hath prepared for them that love Him. (1 Corinthians 2:9 KJV)

December 17　　　　　　　## What Gold Means to a Poor Child

Always we learn of the needy of our communities needing various items, and the ones who have means to provide for them come to the forefront, because of deep compassion for them. Recently, when such a need was made known, especially for school children, someone asked "What do the children delight in receiving the most?" To the amazement of the ones asking, the reply was "Socks."

Apparently, many of the children had shoes but they wore them without socks because they had none. At once, folks went out and bought socks, all sizes for children, all designs, all colors, and they were provided for them. Of course, the children liked shirts and pants and underwear and mittens and pajamas, but their eyes shown when they were each given three or four pairs of new socks! One mother said tearfully, "My kids are so pleased with the clothes they get, but each one of them really loves to get these socks. They are as precious to them as gold." Just think how much joy we can bring to a needy child in our giving! Gift of gold!

If there be among you a poor man of one of thy brethren within any of thy gates within thy land which the Lord thy God giveth thee, thou shalt not harden thine heart, nor shut thine hand from thy poor brother: but thou shalt open thine hand wide unto him, and shalt surely lend him sufficient for his need, in that which he wanteth. (Deuteronomy 15:7-8 KJV)

December 18   Waiting Expectantly

One of my favorite pictures on my wall is *Two Sisters (On the Terrace)* by Renoir. I have had it since my early years of marriage. It is a picture of a woman and little girl sitting and seemingly biding their time. Our daughter was about five years old when we got the picture, and she looked at it and said, "That's me and Mommy waiting for Daddy." We spent a lot of time waiting for him while he shopped for fishing and hunting items, and we sat waiting in the car.

Have you ever thought about how much waiting you do in your lifetime? As kids, we waited for the school bus; as a bride-to-be we waited for the wedding date to come; when a baby was on the way, the mother waited for the nine months to come to fruition. There are other waiting times, like a family waiting for the soldier to return from an overseas battleground; the high school senior getting his diploma; a gardener or farmer waiting for the seed planted to shoot out of the ground with green vitality, and so many more.

All waiting has a hopeful expectation. When that expectation is fulfilled, there is always rejoicing in the heart of the one who has waited.

There is one special event all of God's children are waiting for with great, joyful expectation. That is the return of the Lord Jesus Christ. He said He would go away after His death, burial, resurrection and ascension, back to heaven with His Father, and there He would prepare a place of all His followers. After that was all completed, He said He would return again and receive all who have accepted Him as Savior and Lord, and He would take all back to heaven with Him.

The Christians who have died will rise with new, immortal bodies. The ones living when He returns will have changed, immortal bodies, and we will all go up together. After that event, all who are with Him will begin to experience all manner of wonderful delights, which our finite minds now cannot even fathom. He has promised this, and we hopefully wait for that wonderful event! Even the Apostle John, who wrote the last book in the Bible, Revelation, closed his writings with "Even so, come Lord Jesus."

> For the Lord Himself shall descend from heaven with a shout, with the voice of the archangel, and with the trump of God: and the dead in Christ shall rise first: then we which are alive and remain shall be caught up together with them in the clouds, to meet the Lord in the air: and so shall we ever be with the Lord.
> (1 Thessalonians 4:16-17 KJV)

December 19   Ambassador for Christ

Our nation chooses ambassadors to interact with other countries. Each one goes with a specific message. It makes for workable solutions against problems between nations. They definitely manifest themselves positively when keeping peace between nations.

Did you know every Christian is an ambassador for Christ? Each one is chosen and charged to go out with a message to those in that person's sphere of influence.

Dr. Wilfred Grenfell, long-time missionary in Labrador, was being entertained at a luncheon, and the woman seated next to him remarked, "I understand you are a missionary."

"Yes, I am," he replied, "and so are you, too."

"Oh, no," she disputed. "You have been misinformed. I have never been out of this small community."

"I know that," he continued, "but just the same you are a missionary, for everyone who has been reconciled to God is a missionary."

Our Lord's parting words, "You shall be witnesses unto me," was not so much a command as it was a statement of fact. Believers are witnesses because they are believers. And we have a message, the Good News that Jesus is the Savior who wants every lost sinner to know Him in the free pardon of sin. He uses His ambassadors to accomplish that purpose.

Now then we are ambassadors for Christ, as though God did beseech you by us: we pray you in Christ's stead, be ye reconciled to God. (2 Corinthians 5:20 KJV)

She
held Him
in her arms
and watched Him sleep.
Gently she lifted
His tiny, dimpled hand
and kissed His precious fingers.
She caressed in adoration
His perfect-shaped, velvety-soft feet.
Tears dripped and wettened His swaddling blanket.

December 20   Sights and Sounds of Christmas

Red and gold baubles dangle from a green tree;
Silver stars wink against a jet sky.
The log in the fireplace spits yellow flames;
The ground becomes white as snowflakes fly.
Carolers' voices pierce the cold night air;
In the mall Como and Crosby croon;
Bells and chimes rumble from church steeples,
And the postman whistles a merry tune.

The evergreen scatters whiffs of cedar;
The fruit cake emits an orangey scent.
The tapered candle sends out bayberry;
Apple cider wafts its peppermint.
A festive green wreath hangs on the front door;
Candles in windows cast a warm glow.
Garlands of bright tinsel drape the mantel.
The lamp post flaunts its red bow.

Mother repeats her choicest recipes;
Dad waits in long lines at the store;
Children crowd close to the reader's chair
To hear Luke chapter t wo read once more.
Colors and music would be meaningless;
Fragrances and décor of no worth,
Unless love governs all acts of Christmas
Which began the night of Jesus' birth.

--Carlene Poff Baker

For unto us a child is born, unto us a Son is given: and the government shall be upon His shoulder: and His name shall be called Wonderful, Counsellor, The mighty God, The everlasting Father, The Prince of Peace. (Isaiah 9:6 KJV)

For unto you is born this day in the City of David a Savior, which is Christ the Lord. (Luke 2:11 KJV)

December 21   Something Missing

I phoned a friend one spring day just to chat and get an update on happenings. When she answered, I heard a background of music, and it sounded like "O Holy Night." I asked her about it. She laughed and told me "Yes, it's Christmas music. It's something I started after Christmas last year."

She explained that after all her many guests had left last Christmas, the house was exceedingly quiet for herself and her husband. She felt a restlessness and an emptiness. She was missing the people with whom she had spent Christmas week. She could not readily come up with the reason for her melancholy. After all, it was the celebration of Jesus's birthday.

As she put away her gifts and thought about what she had given to each one of her visitors, she realized why she was feeling so despondent: she had not really focused on whose birthday she was celebrating! She had been in such a constant bustle, with all the ado of making everybody joyful, that she had placed Jesus in a corner and left Him there, out of her way.

She began to cry and asked Him to forgive her. At once, she felt His peace. Then, she made Him a promise. "You are so precious, Lord Jesus, I will celebrate your birthday all during the year, not just in December." And she fulfilled that promise. She kept out the Christmas tapes and discs and randomly played them at least once a week.

She caused me to realize I too could get so caught up with the many doings of that winter season that I would move Jesus out of the way. Yes, we need, like my friend, to reflect all during the year on the wonderful birth of our Lord, because without His having been born, and accomplishing for us His provision of salvation, we would be hopelessly empty and despondent, without hope.

> Giving thanks unto the Father, which hath made us meet to be partakers of the inheritance of the saints in light: Who hath delivered us from the power of darkness, and hath translated us into the kingdom of His dear Son: in whom we have redemption through His blood, even the forgiveness of sins: Who is the image of the invisible God, the firstborn of every creature. (Colossians 1:12-15 KJV)

December 22   It Began That First Christmas

Why is there a plaintive yearning to go home at Christmas? Might it be because the Nazareth couple made their way home to Bethlehem?

Why do we light up everything – eaves, roofs, trees, lamp posts – with candles, and bulbs? Perhaps it is because the glory of the Lord lit up the sky over the shepherds.

Why do we surround ourselves with angels and sing carols about them? Maybe it is because an angel told Mary she would give birth to Jesus, and an angel spoke to the shepherds. Why does a weather-worn barn take on an aura at this season? Could it be because Jesus was born in such a place where donkeys and sheep bedded down, and cows ate hay from mangers?

Why do we give stars so much attention now? Could it be they shine their brightest now to remind us of the special star the wise men followed that led them to the Christ Child? Why do we give gifts at this time more than at any other time? It must be because the wise men set the precedent when they presented their treasures to the newborn King.

> And Joseph also went up from Galilee, out of the city of Nazareth, into Judaea, unto the city of David, which is called Bethlehem; (because he was of the house and lineage of David:) to be taxed with Mary his espoused wife, being great with child. And so it was, that, while they were there, the days were accomplished that she should be delivered. And she brought forth her firstborn son, and wrapped him in swaddling clothes, and laid him in a manger; because there was no room for them in the inn. (Luke 2:4-7 KJV)

> And when they were come into the house, they saw the young Child with Mary His mother, and fell down, and worshiped Him: and when they had opened their treasures, they presented unto Him gifts; gold, and frankincense, and myrrh. (Matthew 2:11 KJV)

December 23   Angels All Around

An angel first visited Mary as she readied for her wedding day.
He said she'd give birth to Jesus who would come to take sin away.

Mary submitted to the Holy Spirit and conceived God's sinless Son.
When she told Joseph about it, from the marriage he wanted to run.

As Joseph lay in the darkness thinking of his bethrothed so dear,
To this broken-hearted bridegroom an angel of the Lord did appear,
Who told him the truth about it, that Mary had not betrayed his love,
And the baby she was carrying had been conceived by God above.

Right on schedule the birth happened just as prophets had foretold.
An angel shouted the news to shepherds, saying, "Fear not, for behold
I bring you good tidings of joy, a Savior is born this day."
Multitudes of angels joined him. Shepherds heard the grand host say:

"Glory to God in the Highest; on earth peace, goodwill to men."
The shepherds hurried to find Him, in a stable out back of an inn.
Wise men came laden with treasures seeking the Babe of royal birth.
They found Him and adored Him, bending their faces to the earth.

Hateful Herod wanted Him banished and demanded the wise men
    return
To tell him all their findings, so the place Jesus lived he would learn.
Again. An angel came with a message to the wise men that night as
    they lay.
He told them to go home another route, and King Herod's order to
    disobey.

When Herod's scheme was thwarted, he issued a bloody decree
That little boys under t wo be murdered to get rid of Jesus he would see.
While Joseph, Mary and Jesus lay sleeping unaware of their plight,
In a dream an angel spoke to Joseph: "Take the child and leave for Egypt
    tonight."

He obeyed and escaped Herod's anger; toddler Jesus played in Egyptian
    sand.
Then one night the angel informed Joseph: "It's safe to go home again."

No wonder we think of angels at Christmas, considering all the work
they have done.
Ah! How faithful these heavenly beings when God sent into the world
His Son!

And the angel said unto her, Fear not, Mary: for thou hast
found favor with God. And, behold, thou shalt conceive in thy
womb, and bring forth a Son, and shalt call His name JESUS.
(Luke 1:30-31 KJV)

But while he thought on these things, behold, the angel of the
Lord appeared unto him in a dream, saying, Joseph, thou son
of David, fear not to take unto thee Mary thy wife: for that
which is conceived in her is of the Holy Ghost. And she shall
bring forth a son, and thou shalt call His name JESUS: for He
shall save His people from their sins. (Matthew 1:20-21 KJV)

December 24   **Best Gifts**

The finest gifts of Christmas are not measured
by big spending so one can boast.
It is the gift that does not cost a cent
which is often treasured most.

The gift of *cheer* bestowed to the lonely
needs no bright ribbon to flair.
A hug or a handshake, using both hands
are ways you can show you care.

You could never wrap *hospitality*,
so just leave your door ajar.
Welcome to your hearth homing wanderers,
be they close by or from afar.

What box could enclose the *remembering*
of all the Christmases past?
Fond recollections of happy times shared
rehearsed once more make them last.

To *instill* your family's traditions
handed down from year to year,
you entrust as a gift to the young ones,
so they too will hold them dear.

You jostle against all kinds of shoppers
whose faces say "I just can't cope."
Your full-attention *smile* could be just right
to ignite a spark of hope.

A piece of your *time* is of such value;
it will leave an afterglow.
Bestow it on a child, or a teen, or
one with hair white as snow.

You don't have to buy a tape or song book
when you give a *music* gift.
Sing a carol, or hum or whistle—
It'll give your hearers a lift.

Appreciation words said or written
mean more than rare gems or gold.
They lift the collar bone, bloom out the cheeks,
and make drooping spirits bold.

On a clear night, *share the sky* with kids.
Let them find the brightest star.
Tell them of the star the Wise Men followed,
the story so thrilling, nothing can mar!

The finest gifts call for no money;
These simple things anyone can do.
In so doing, you'll feel you've really given,
because you will have given a piece of you.

> Every man according as he purposeth in his heart, so let him
> give; not grudgingly, or of necessity: for God loveth a cheerful
> giver. (2 Corinthians 9:7 KJV)

December 25   ## If Christmas Were Not

If Christmas came to an end, families would be missing
all the joys of reunions with hugs and reminiscing.
If Christmas should ever die, a shut-in would never know
the thrill of being sung to by youngsters with cheeks aglow.

If Christmas became extinct, some hungry would say unfed,
for at this season only even misers share their bread.
If Christmas ceased to be, there would be no chance to send
bright, festive greeting cards, friend would lose touch with friend.

If Christmas should be no more, some people would never hear
The story of the Christ Child told more often this time of year.
At Christmas time, frowners smile and tight-wads loosen their grip.
Travelers don't mind gas prices as they make their homeward trip.

At Christmas-time, tensions ease, and grudges somehow get lost.
Folks at odds try extra hard to make peace at any cost.
I'm so glad we have a Christmas with all its wonderful ways.
The good that comes with Christmas we ought to keep all other days.

> He that spared not His own Son, but delivered Him up for us
> all, how shall He not with Him also freely give us all things?
> (Romans 8:32 KJV)

And above all these things put on charity, which is the bond of perfectness. And let the peace of God rule in your hearts, to the which also ye are called in one body; and be ye thankful. Let the word of Christ dwell in you richly in all wisdom; teaching and admonishing one another in psalms and hymns and spiritual songs, singing with grace in your hearts to the Lord. (Colossians 3:14-16 KJV)

December 26   Dialogue of the First Christmas

(Paraphrased by the author:)

Angel:	Fear not, Mary, for you are highly favored. You have been chosen to be the mother of Jesus.
Mary:	How can this be, since I know not a man?
Angel:	You will conceive by the Holy Spirit of God. This Child will be the Messiah, the Savior of the world.
Mary:	So be it, my soul magnifies the Lord.
Joseph:	I will not marry Mary, since she is with child. I will put her away in a quiet manner.
Angel:	Fear not to take Mary to be your wife, for the Child she is carrying was conceived of the Holy Ghost.
Augustus:	Write this law: Every person in my kingdom shall be taxed. Each one will go back to his native town to enroll.
Joseph:	Mary, we have to go to Bethlehem to be taxed.
Mary:	I will get ready. I will pack some swaddling clothes because I feel sure my baby will be born while we are there.
Inn Keeper:	I'm sorry, but there is no more room in my inn. I have not seen so many travelers in my whole life. There is a stable out back. Will it do?
Shepherd:	There is a strange stillness out here on the hills.
Shepherd:	Yes, even the sheep are more hushed.
Angel:	Fear not, for behold I bring you good tidings of great joy. For to you is born this day in Bethlehem a Savior

	which is Christ the Lord. You'll find the Babe wrapped in swaddling clothes and lying I n a manger.
Shepherd:	O, Lord, that's an angel!
Shepherd:	Look! There are hundreds . . . or . . . thousands more of them!
Angel Host:	Glory to God in the Highest, and on earth, peace, goodwill toward men.
Shepherd:	Reckon it's so?
Shepherd:	It must be. Those were angels! Let's go see!
Wise Man:	Look! This is a spectacular star!
Wise Man:	Yes, it means a new king is born.
Wise Man:	And He is the King of the Jews
Wise Man:	Come, let's get ready to travel.
Wise Man:	I'll pack our gifts.
Wise Man:	Another thing about that star: it's a leading star.
Wise Man:	Where is He that is born King of the Jews?
Herod:	I don't know what you're talking about. But I'll find out. You, there, call for the scribes, and ask about the birth of a king in Israel.
Scribe:	O King Herod, it is prophesied that in Bethlehem such a One should be born.
Herod:	Go, travelers, and find such a king and return to tell me where He is so I can pay homage to Him too.
Wise Man:	We saw His star in the East and have come to worship Him. He is a special King. Here are our gifts to honor Him: gold frankincense and myrrh. Now we must go, as we have a long way to go back home.
Angel:	Do not go back to Jerusalem. Go back home another route. The king intends to do harm to the Christ Child, so you are not to go back home by way of Jerusalem to tell the king where He is.
Herod:	Have every Jewish male child in Bethlehem slain under the age of two years. That way I'll be sure to kill the newborn King of the Jews.
Angel:	Get up, Joseph, this very night, and take Mary and the Babe into Egypt. King Herod has decreed to harm to the Child.

Jesus:	Are we leaving Egypt, Mother?
Mary:	Yes, Son, we're going back home. Cruel King Herod is dead.
Jesus:	Where are we now, Mother?
Mary:	This is Nazareth, our old home town. Joseph says this is where we will live. Oh, Jesus, this is where the wonderful miracle of You began. The angel came to me here and told me that I was to be the one God would use to bring His Only Begotten Son into the world. You, my precious Jesus, are the One.

December 27   Reflection

So now, a year has passed, it's time to pause in deep reflection.
I see the goals I set have measured short of their perfection.
I've watched my fondest dreams erased to naught without revival.
Although these came my way, I learned survival.
I wept when good friends left feeling bereft of their warm presence.
I laughed with loved ones near whose close embrace was sweetest essence.
I felt stark, coinless days when I would wish I'd been a miser.
Oh, yes, I made it through. Now I'm the wiser.
My old year has closed; here is the new.
The new abounds with good to do.
I've set new goals; I've aimed them high
To do before the year goes by,
And at the end, I hope I'll see a grand reflection

December 28   One Today at a Time

The old year, like the sun at day's end, has slipped behind its turquoise drape, but it keeps shimmering the twilight with reflecting glories of the year spent, one yesterday at a time.

Strokes of red and fuchsia and mauve speak of good health I enjoyed the whole year. Dabs of opulent gold aptly describe special persons who crossed my path for the first time and fastened themselves to my heart.

Boldest colors dye the fabric threads of my life, the joys of interacting with the closest loves of my life – beloved daughter, precious grandchildren, and the youngest four who answer to me as great-grandchildren, four sterling princes.

The new year comes up in splendorous rosiness, ever brightening with its climb across the scroll-like sky, bumping up anticipation for my tomorrows, one today at a time.

I shall again anticipate glad times and low times. I will devotedly involve myself in lives of loved ones, nurture old friendships, and cultivate new ones. I will become more acquainted with my God who will, like all past years, order my steps, one today at a time.

> Resolved--
> I will forget
> disappointments and fears
> that sought to hold me fast under
> last year.

> Resolved—
> I will clutch close
> joys and accomplishments
> to cast pleasant shadows across
> me now.

> Resolved—
> I will pursue
> opportunities laid
> across my path as I tramp through
> next year.

The New Year will give me 366 golden days to spend as I choose. I can spend them wisely and reap worthy fruits, or I can waste them and harvest regret and loss. To help me achieve my goals, in making the world a more lovely place, the New Year has readied me with at least four special things to help me achieve my goals.

The first item handed me is a blank sheet of paper. "Fill the Page" New Year says. So, I must write down happenings of special note – celebrations of times together with loved ones, conversation with someone whose endearing and encouraging words are held close to be remembered often; new names added to the decades-long list of friends.

The second piece of gear is an unlit candle. I am to take into a dark room and light it to chase away fears of all sorts sure to loom up along the way. With its flickering glow, I can reach out to the lonely and make him know someone cares; to the grieving to help her hope again.

The third tool from the New Year is a door knob not yet turned. The knob will open a door to a room over which I am to keep the watch. What I see and feel are mine to cope with, to make a difference for the good all around. Perhaps the room will have someone who merely wants to be listened to or to be smiled at when she feels ugly. Or, perhaps in that room somebody is seeking peace with God, and I have been chosen to show him the way.

The fourth thing set before me is a path untracked where I have the opportunity to place my feet into the unknown, being careful to set up clear landmarks, leading to truth, honestly and integrity, all based on Bible principles.

At the end of the year's 366 days, if I have filled my sheet of paper with evidence of having lived with purpose, and if my candle has been lit so many times it is smutty and waxed down, I will have been a good steward of New Year's assignment.

I will not have wasted my time by turning the door knob and dealt with what I found there if just one to whom I listened or watched or smiled at or showed the way to God will have responded joyfully.

My having marked the way down an untracked path will have been worthwhile if just one who sees my tracks determines to find his own untracked path and leaves his own comfort zone, to set out to make good tracks himself for others to follow.

Oh, that I will launch out to reap worthy fruits and not waste a single day that will bring regrets. I know I can achieve only as I trust in the Lord with all my heart and lean not unto my own understanding. I can do all things through Christ who gives me strength.

> And whatsoever ye do in word or deed, do all in the name of the Lord Jesus, giving thanks to God and the Father by Him. (Colossians 3:17 KJV)

December 30 Prayer of Jabez: Good Model for New Year

Jabez had been given a bad name which meant *pain* because his mother gave birth to him in sorrow. The sorrow is not revealed. Anyway, Jabez was branded with that sad name all his life. It did not keep him down, however. Circumstances did not dominate him. He was not satisfied with the status quo. So, he came before the Right Source, the God of all Sufficiency. The things he asked of God in his prayer is a model for what each of us should ask of God as we begin a New Year.

> "And Jabez called on the God of Israel, saying, Oh that thou wouldest bless me indeed, and enlarge my coast, and that thine hand might be with me, and that thou wouldest keep me from evil, that it may not grieve me! And God granted him that which he requested." (1 Chronicles 4:10 KJV)

First, he wanted God's blessings upon him. Oh, that everything we endeavor to do, say or be would receive God's blessing!

Next, he asked that his borders be expanded or enlarged. He wasn't wanting to be more prosperous, but he was asking for opportunities to bless others, to move on out further for the Lord. That should be our goal as well. Reach out farther to other areas of ministry than in previous years.

He wanted the Lord's involvement in all areas of his life. He felt inadequate to accomplish anything alone without God's presence. Isn't that what you and I want? Yes, we desire that He be pleased with our every decision and activity.

Fourth, Jabez wanted to steer clear of any evil, because he knew it would cause pain to himself, to God, and to those whom he loved and who loved him. We all have come to realize, when one does wrong, it has long-range effects. No wrong can be done without hurting someone else. None of us deep down want to cause anyone we love to feel pain because of our wrong doings, so we must be on guard all the time to keep ourselves from doing so.

A good prayer, akin to what Jabez prayed, would be: "Lord, bless me a lot today so I can make a difference for good for you and for the good of others, and enlarge my realm of endeavor while You are at it to move beyond the usual. I want You to stay alongside me all through the day. Make me alert to lures of evil so I won't get caught up in anything that will bring reproach upon You, debase myself, or break the hearts of the people I love best."

Starting each day of the New Year with this type of prayer, and practicing it, will surely bring to each one of us the joy of living the abundant life Jesus has promised.

December 31   One Year Line Crossed: Look Ahead

You have finished your course for this year. God has blessed you abundantly. Now, all that has happened will be memories. You have experienced all manner of happenings, but each one was arranged and organized by the One who has given you life to have made it thus far.

Now, tomorrow you will begin a new year. It is like a book with 365 pages. Each day will be a new leaf in the book for you to dip your quill in indelible ink and imprint your activities, dreams, goals achieved, something new learned, a new friend's name, and how you spent your time with God.

It remains your choice to make of your year what you will. If you write with determined faith-in-God strokes, the pages will be a joy for you to look back upon when that year moves out of the way for the next one.

Your book opens its pages blank before you. Once each day is spent, it can never be called back. It's up to you, with your indelible inked quill, what you will imprint in your book. Endeavor at the start to fill your pages with the best of the best.

Prayer of the Author (And, Hopefully, the Reader)

Heavenly Father, thank you for this out-going year You have given me. It has been filled with an abundance of good happenings. Amidst some of the good times have come trials and disappointments and even sadness. But, through it all, knowing You were alongside at all times, keenly aware of the details of each occurrence, I have made it through with joy in my heart. I know you will be and do the same for the curtained-off year ahead of me, so I just want to say, I need you and will trust you, come what may. May I learn to love you more and be a blessing to others who cross my path. Get glory out of my life each day of the New Year.

In Jesus's Name, Amen.

CPSIA information can be obtained
at www.ICGtesting.com
Printed in the USA
LVHW040008091219
639857LV00018B/943/P

9 781973 671640